MARKETING TO THE CHANGING HOUSEHOLD

MARKETING TO THE CHANGING HOUSEHOLD

Management and Research Perspectives

Edited by
Mary Lou Roberts and Lawrence H. Wortzel

BALLINGER PUBLISHING COMPANY
Cambridge, Massachusetts
A Subsidiary of Harper & Row, Publishers, Inc.

International Standard Book Number: 0-88410-986-0

Library of Congress Catalog Card Number: 84-12288

Printed in the United States of America

Library of Congress Cataloging in Publication Data
Main entry under title:

Marketing to the changing household.

Bibliography: p.
Includes index.
1. Households—United States—Addresses, essays, lectures. 2. Marketing research—Addresses, essays, lectures. 3. Marketing—Management—Addresses, essays, lectures. I. Roberts, Mary Lou. II. Wortzel, Lawrence H.
HF5415.3.M278   1984   658.8   84-12288
ISBN 0-88410-986-0

CONTENTS

v

LIST OF FIGURES

LIST OF TABLES

FOREWORD

The American household has held the attention of demographers, sociologists, psychologists, journalists, novelists, playwrights, filmmakers, and others for much of the post–World War II era. There have been many changes in the composition and characteristics of American households—smaller households on average because of fewer children, more single-person households, more mixed-children households when divorced parents re-marry, greater acceptance and visibility (as well as numbers) of unmarried live-together households.

Despite speculations about the decline, even demise, of the traditional family household, the fundamental values of family structure have proven to be remarkably robust. Both the changes and basic continuities have been well observed and reported in the popular press and the academic literature. The interesting question for marketers—both practitioners and academic researchers—is the extent to which changes in the characteristics of households have produced equivalent changes in the nature of household behavior as a consumption unit. It was with this in mind that Professors Mary Lou Roberts and Lawrence H. Wortzel, with the sponsorship of the American Marketing Association and the Marketing Science Institute, organized a workshop to examine a number of factors relating to consumer behavior within the household unit. The papers included in these proceedings were presented at this workshop, which was structured around four issues:

1. household composition and life cycle concepts;
2. household roles;
3. household consumption choices; and
4. decisionmaking units and processes.

Papers reflected a variety of disciplines and individual perspectives and presented concepts, theory, and empirical data. As always, the research reported offers some answers but raises additional questions. The workshop proceedings provide insights into household consumption in the early 1980s and also point to a direction for future research on important aspects of household purchase behavior.

—Alden G. Clayton
President and Managing Director
Marketing Science Institute

INTRODUCTION

Mary Lou Roberts and Lawrence H. Wortzel

Marketers accept that for many purchases of consumer products and services the decisionmaking unit (DMU) in a multiperson household is the household, not an individual in the household. Even where the decisionmaker is apparently an individual, others in the household exert significant explicit or implicit influence on the decision.

Many marketers who recognize the relevance of the household as the appropriate DMU, however, use outdated or incomplete models of the household in their research and their practices. Two key marketing tasks are to identify correct targets and to position appropriately against them, and in accomplishing these tasks marketers tend to use as a model the traditional American family of a husband, wife, and 2.7 children. They also tend to assume that each individual within the family performs according to traditional role expectations. The past few years, however, have brought about massive changes in the composition of households, such that the traditional American family household is now a minority. Moreover, roles have changed significantly, even within the traditional family. Because of changes in household composition, in consumption choices, and in decision processes, assumptions about targeting and positioning require reexamination.

The papers in this volume explore and interpret aspects of the changing household. This introduction highlights the breadth and depth of topics covered in the papers and then discusses the marketing management and research implications of the changing household.

CHANGING HOUSEHOLD COMPOSITION AND A NEW HOUSEHOLD LIFE CYCLE

The number of U.S. households increased by 25 percent during the 1970s while population increased by only 9 percent. This increase was fueled by rising divorce rates and by a greatly increased propensity for the large baby boom generation to set up single-person households. It has resulted in a decrease in the proportion of husband-and-wife households from 70.5 percent in 1970 to 59.8 percent of all households in 1981. The traditional household of husband, wife, and one or more children now represents just 43 percent of total households; thus, the proportion of childless husband-and-wife households has increased also.

These changes have many complex causes that are difficult to sort out. One obvious reason for change has been the need for many women to grow beyond traditional roles of wife and mother. Some of these women seek the same fulfillment from jobs and careers that men have sought in the past; others have been forced into the work force by economic pressures and often have to do relatively unsatisfying work.

As more women discovered that they were able to earn a living (and some even discovered that they enjoyed it), marriage and childbearing became an option to be chosen or rejected rather than a requirement. As women's economic power grew, divorce became a more possible, and soon a more acceptable, option for those who were in marriages they considered undesirable. Both men and women began a heightened search for self-fulfillment that contributed significantly to the divorce rate and perhaps even more to the increasing proportion of young adults who were single.

These changes and many others are still very much in process and indicate that there will be further shifts in the number and composition of households. However, there is disagreement as to the future extent and direction of these shifts. Yankelovich (1981), for example, proposed that the search for individual self-fulfillment will gradually give way to an ethic of commitment. If this occurs, one result is likely to be more and longer-term relationships. Cherlin and Furstenberg (1982:6), analyzing the results of many studies on the future of the family, came to a somewhat different conclusion. They predicted that the diversity of household form will continue to grow and that it will be common for children born in the 1980s to:

> live with both parents for several years, live with their mothers after their parents divorce, then live with their mothers and stepfathers, live alone for a time when in their early twenties, live with someone of the opposite sex without marrying, get married, get divorced, live alone again, get remarried, and end up living alone once more following the death of their spouse.

MANAGERIAL IMPLICATIONS

The changing American household presents many challenges and opportunities for marketers of consumer products and services. How does the individual manager or firm identify and capitalize on them?

Before confronting specific marketing situations, managers should examine their own models of the marketplace. Cultural values and established managerial thought processes often consider the traditional household to be the norm even though this is clearly not the case. The challenge is to replace an outmoded model with one that reflects the complexity and dynamism of the American household in the 1980s and beyond. Failure to do so will result in marketing mistakes and lost opportunities.

Some significant opportunities may not be apparent from the usual household composition data. For example, a store manager in a large grocery chain recently identified as an extremely lucrative market segment one nontraditional household unit—homosexual males. He observed that homosexual male partnerships result in households that tend to be social, affluent, and therefore good customers for upscale food products. Whether this is a market segment that can be reached selectively is open to question. On the other hand, marketers who recognize the existence of such a segment and who can identify its special needs may be able to devise strategies for attracting segment members and making them feel comfortable with the product or store without alienating other segments.

Even when we consider more easily identifiable examples of household units, a traditional view may blind marketers to emerging opportunities. We all know that the U.S. population is aging. But many marketers still see older segments (whether single-person or multiple-person households) as poor, infirm, and willing to be relegated to the backwaters of a youth-oriented culture.

An intriguing study of age perception (Underhill and Cadwell 1983) found that "ages 30 to 39 last forever psychologically" and that we must "talk appropriately to the younger person inside the older consumer." Since older consumers in the empty-nest stage of the family life cycle have a disproportionate amount of discretionary income, it is critical that marketers carefully examine their needs and preferences. It is safe to say that the consumption patterns of this often-neglected market segment extend well beyond Geritol and denture adhesives. Sexagenarians (and older) still play tennis, work, and even buy home computers. Such phenomena will become increasingly common as a greater proportion of the population enters its later years having led physically active and technologically sophisticated lives.

Moreover, the empty-nest stage may arrive later and later. In many large cities, women having their first child at age thirty-five are not uncommon; similarly, some men in their early fifties now start second families with second wives but without second thoughts. Thus, the full-nest stage now can extend into the early fifties for women and late sixties for men. We have not yet begun to explore the effects that smaller families and older parents have on children's roles. There is, for example, some evidence that children of older parents have more exposure to adults and adult activities earlier in their lives: Young parents may participate in children's games with their children, while older parents may be more likely to take their children to adult restaurants.

The role of children in marketing decisions is still not fully understood, especially in light of factors such as single-parent households and two-parent households in which both parents work. There is mounting evidence, for example, that children from households in which both parents work are more peer oriented. But what does this mean, if anything, to marketers? Should advertising aimed at children use children as authority figures? What do children learn from each other about being consumers?

On the other hand, interest in parenting has increased, and norms may be developing that encourage parents to become more involved with their children, even if only for one minute at a time. Does this heightened interest herald an increasing concern with guiding children's purchase behavior? Is the Christmas 1983 phenomenon of the Cabbage Patch doll a response to children's desires for a particular toy or a manifestation of parents' desire to provide them with it? What does this say about the marketing of toys?

The press reports increasing parental concern about children's intellectual development and a growing tendency to think of children as small adults—to share with them what some have called the "secrets" of adulthood. What might be the implications of these changes for both parents and children?

Even as we make these points, we recognize that, like our mental models, many published models fail to reflect fully the current reality of the changing household. Murphy's discussion in this volume of "Family and Household Changes: Developments and Implications" does an examplary job of updating the model of the family or, better yet, household life cycle. But few other conceptual models take into account changing household forms and broadened or changed participation in household decision-making. Our own paper on "A Dynamic Model of Role Allocation in the Household: Marketing Management and Research Implications" suggests the care that should be taken in developing conceptual models that can guide marketers in their search for relevant information. But these works are only starting points for the kinds of inquiry that marketers must undertake if they are to identify marketing opportunities.

Good research is an increasingly important input to marketing decisions. It is crucial to have suitable models and to ask the right questions in order to obtain the right information through research, but more is necessary. Just as managers frequently operate on the basis of incomplete models, they frequently fail to challenge market researchers to confront the many difficult issues inherent in obtaining valid information from the changing household.

Both the cost and difficulty of doing marketing research are increased by the problem of studying households (rather than individuals) as decision-making units. The research problem is to identify multiple-decision influences (both partners and often children) and then to reconcile the inevitably divergent answers from multiple respondents within the same household. Rather than examine the complex processes by which shopping, product, and brand decisions are made, it is much easier for marketers to focus either on decision outcomes (e.g., which products and which brands are selected) or on the equally complex patterns of consumption within the household unit. It could be argued, of course, that an understanding of influence patterns and decisionmaking processes is necessary to provide the insight into consumption-related activities of the household that managers need.

Knowing only what is selected and by whom is not very useful in making marketing decisions. Knowing only outcomes is of limited use even in selecting targets: It cannot be assumed that the buyer is also the decider, and it is even more tenuous to assume that the benefits sought in a particular purchase can be identified on the basis of knowing only the outcome of that purchase. Managers and researchers must improve the quality of strategies that aim at attracting and influencing the household and its individual members. Creative approaches to research are needed, not mindless repetition of routine approaches.

SEARCHING FOR NEW PRODUCTS AND NEW POSITIONS

We have discussed why marketers should revise how they currently deal with marketing problems related to the household unit. If marketers are concerned with new product ideas, perhaps they should do more than simply revise current approaches.

One way to open up new ways of thinking about the household is to contrast traditional and newly emerging household tasks and the benefits, both old and new, that are derived from them (Table 1). (It must be remembered that tasks can be new to the individual performing them or new to the household.)

Table 1.   Household Tasks and Benefits

Task	Benefit
Cooking meals	Serving healthful, attractive meals
Cleaning house	Performing necessary tasks efficiently to allow for personal leisure time
Day Care	Custodial care for the child
Managing and using home computer system	Retrieval system for information difficult to access

An existing task, such as preparing meals, may retain the old benefit of fulfilling the household's nutritional needs either in pragmatic manner (as sustenance) or with a heavy component of nurturance (food prepared and served with loving care). An emerging concern may be to serve food that is interesting. Another existing task, such as cleaning house, may be performed quickly but competently in order to leave time for more enjoyable leisure-time pursuits.

What about new tasks such as shopping for, choosing, and then regularly delivering a child to day care? Day care may simply provide an old benefit, custodial care, in a new way. But parents may also look for new benefits, such as early education, when selecting a day care provider.

Household tasks, whether old or new, are increasingly susceptible to technological solutions or at least to assistance by technology. In some task areas, such as cooking, technology has penetrated significantly by providing new benefits through products such as food processors and microwave ovens; these products help users serve foods that were formerly too difficult or time consuming to prepare. The VCR is another example of a "new benefits through technology" product that offers the benefit of watching existing programming at the user's choice of time rather than the network's. It also opened up a home market for X-rated movies.

In other task areas, however, the development of genuinely new benefits seems to be a major stumbling block for the expensive new household technologies. The presence of a home computer system, for example, may allow household members to perform tasks that were formerly so difficult or time consuming that they were simply left undone; hence, the possibility of new benefits. A personal automated retrieval system for important facts or sources of information based on a keyword process *could* be managed with index cards, but individuals who were never able to maintain an index card system now gleefully maintain all sorts of fact files on their personal computers. Will they continue to do it when the 'new' wears off their personal computer? The answers to such questions may decide the long-run future of the mass market for home computers.

While Table 1 shows a useful way of looking at general developments in the household unit, it is not precise enough to solve specific problems. An ideal approach would focus on specific product classes. Table 2 is an example of an approach that might stimulate the thinking of a food products manufacturer for both product development and positioning purposes.

The old methods of task performance, whether they provide new or old benefits, are not difficult to assess, nor are old benefits with new methods. The new task with new benefit cell is a difficult one to develop, but it is the area in which the most exciting new opportunities may exist. Individual firms and managers may wish to pursue this approach in much greater depth. For instance, the "Old" and "New" headings for methods of task performance could be replaced with specific headings, such as "Scratch Cooking," "Preprocessed Ingredients," "Prepared Foods," "Microwave Cooking," and any other methods of meal preparation that seem appropriate. This type of brainstorming should produce useful insights.

Whatever marketers choose as their creative approach to the changing household, the objective is clear. Marketers cannot expect households to always be able to tell them what new products and benefits they desire to meet their changing lifestyles or how they might make use of new technologies. Marketers must gain an understanding of how households operate in order to develop new products and reposition old ones in accordance with the needs of today's and tomorrow's households. Marketing research will play an important role in this search for

Table 2. The Task/Benefit Matrix

	Old Benefit	New Benefit
Old task		
Cooking from scratch	Performing useful tasks for the household Nurturing	
Using prepared foods		Cooking ethnic foods without specialized knowledge
New task		
Microwave cooking	Convenience Speed	
Using exotic new products		Displaying sophistication to friends

understanding, but it first must deal with issues that frequently limit its ability to produce managerially useful information about the household.

RESEARCH IMPLICATIONS

Research must deal with the household as the unit of analysis. The papers in this volume emphasize that as the marketplace of individual consumers is becoming increasingly fragmented, so is the marketplace of households. But rarely are households segmented on variables other than demographics. While McCall, in "The Workwife: A Powerful Change Agent of This Century," highlights the usefulness of new types of demographic segmentation, it is likely that segmentation beyond demographics will add to our understanding of the household just as it has done with individuals. "Sharing of Household Maintenance Tasks in Married-Couple House- holds," by Douglas-Tate, Peyton, and Bowen, presents a behavioral segmentation that illustrates the potential richness of approaches that go beyond demographics. If developments in household segmentation do indeed parallel those in segmentation of individual consumers, attitudinal and lifestyle segmentation may have useful applications.

Examining the behavior of households seems to be a straightforward approach to market research. That we have not already used this approach implies that we have progressed farther in our understanding of the individual consumer than in our grasp of the psychosocial aspects of household unit. Increasing our understanding of the behavioral aspects of the household presents a difficult problem for researchers. We lack even simple techniques for posing a single question to a group of individuals (household members) and for then combining their multiple and usually divergent responses in some way that allows comparison of responses across households. Either the response of one household member is used as a surrogate for the responses of the entire household, or the responses of different household members are examined separately (e.g., husbands versus wives). Even if the results gleaned from such methods are not actually incorrect, they ignore potentially rich and highly useful data.

Hendrix and Qualls present a useful approach to solving this problem. In "Operationalizing Family-Level Constructs: Problems and Prospects" they propose classifying households according to the similarity, or lack thereof, of husband and wife responses. One problem with this approach, however, is that it could become cumbersome with the addition of other household members. It also would require very large samples in order to insure adequate representation of the many cells that could result from such an analysis. Advances in multivariate techniques that allow either aggregate or disaggregate group responses would be extremely useful in working with the resultant data.

Both data collection and analytical considerations have encouraged a focus on decision outcomes rather than on decisionmaking processes. But until we understand the manner in which households process information and make decisions, we cannot hope to affect decision outcomes except by accident.

The pattern analysis algorithm described by Bonfield, Kaufman, and Hernandez in "Household Decisionmaking: Units of Analysis and Decision Processes" is a promising methodology that focuses on process. Initially this algorithm was applied to the information search process, but it appears potentially applicable to other research areas, such as information processing and patterns of influence. Furthermore, it may suggest the broad direction in which the development of analytical techniques is moving. Instead of focusing on statistically significant variables or factors, marketers may find that a more promising approach is to look for patterns within large data sets that are composed to a great extent of imprecisely measured variables.

Another result of the focus on outcome rather than process is reliance on cross-sectional studies to the almost complete exclusion of longitudinal studies. In "Families under Pressure: Meeting Their Demands for Services" Lein underscores the richness of understanding that can be gained from an in-depth study of even a small sample over an extended period of time. Consider her findings in the light of "The Value Structure Map: A New Analytic Framework for Family Decisionmaking," Gutman, Reynolds, and Fiedler's methodologically quite different work stressing the importance of values and effects of changing sex roles. In reading these papers, the need for more in-depth longitudinal research becomes painfully apparent. Since this type of research deals with basic household processes and practices, it is an ideal multiclient undertaking for multiple clients that are separate divisions within a firm, for separate but noncompeting business entities, or perhaps for trade-association-sponsored projects. The insight to be gained is well worth the investment, despite possible difficulties of coordination.

Another way to focus on process instead of outcome is to look more closely at the *results* of consumption and use, not just at which products are consumed or used. In "Households and Technology: The Case of Home Computers—Some Conceptual and Theoretical Issues," Venkatesh and Vitalari present data that suggest the insights obtainable from from such a study. New technologies may well change both the content and the quantity of interaction between household members. The societal implications of such changes are great. In addition, of course, consumption-process information is a key to understanding sustained adoption and repurchase of a category or brand.

This issue does not affect only the new technologies, however. Old household tasks may take on new meanings as the task performer changes. Although no published evidence confirms this argument, no evidence of this type has yet been sought on a systematic basis. Recent commercially focused groups composed of husbands who both shop for groceries and prepare meals have supported the hypothesis that males who perform traditionally female tasks approach them differently than females do. If this is generally true, marketers are overlooking rich sources of data that can indicate changes in product use and performance expectations.

Another path to improving the quality of both basic and applied research on the household is to rely more heavily on relevant research in the behavioral sciences. The bibliography to this volume indicates that much useful research is currently being done outside the discipline of marketing. Much of this research can guide our thinking about consumption-related research by providing using empirical data and provocative theoretical concepts.

There are pitfalls to avoid in using this research, however. Most research in the behavioral sciences deals with societal rather than consumption-related issues. We should resist assuming, for example, that because men increasingly recognize competence in women they will be willing to turn over household financial decisions to their wives. The standard warning about not inferring behavior from attitudes applies here. Several papers in this volume allude to research findings that indicate that many men agree that household tasks should be shared equitably and that many men state that they are performing many household tasks: Data, however—especially time budgets—do not indicate that overall task performance by males has increased greatly.

In addition, a largely unrecognized methodological issue relates to the application of behavioral science research to the study of consumer behavior. Marketing researchers have been known to borrow measuring instruments developed by behavioral scientists with little concern for their appropriateness. Bem's androgyny scale and various other measures of sex-role orientation are good examples of this tendency. Again, the issue is one of context. These instruments have been developed for applications that relate only peripherally, if at all, to consumption behavior. They may not measure those aspects of attitudes and behavior that are most strongly related to consumption behavior. Our recommendation, then, is for marketing researchers to carefully follow research developments in the behavioral sciences and glean from them insights that advance understanding of household processes, while at the same time being wary of borrowing concepts and methodologies that do not indicate a parallel intent.

The problems confronting marketing and consumer behavior researchers are many. Two sets of such issues surface in this volume:

(1) The terminologies used by researchers are often inconsistent: They are confusing to researchers themselves and frequently incomprehensible

to managers. For example, in this book alone, three different terms are used to describe what seems to be the same phenomenon. Bristol and Qualls talk about "interrupts," Leigh and Martin base their paradigm on "transitions," and Roberts and Wortzel talk about "critical life events." The differences in these concepts, if any, probably have no practical significance, yet researchers actually appear to prefer to invent their own terminologies, viewing them as a "contribution." This tendency should be viewed with alarm by the research community since it is a major stumbling block in communicating with managers.

(2) The second issue was mentioned at the beginning of this introduction: the lack of a complete, dynamic, and easily operationalized model of household decisionmaking. Without one we are limited to fragmentary, ad hoc models whose use adds to the confusion among terms and concepts. The search for a workable model is primarily a task for researchers, but it is a task that could benefit from the input of practicing researchers who wrestle with the need for actionable information on a day-to-day basis. Let us hope that the papers in this volume will stimulate the further work that needs to be done.

HOUSEHOLD COMPOSITION AND LIFE CYCLE CONCEPTS

1 FAMILY AND HOUSEHOLD CHANGES
Developments and Implications

Patrick E. Murphy

In the last several years the changing family and household in the United States has been analyzed from various perspectives. Consumer and marketing researchers, family sociologists, demographers, and others have frequently noted the significant societal changes affecting family makeup. Specifically, the growth in households, divorce rates, and declining family size have resulted in a changed social structure.

This paper identifies the most significant trends within family and household formation, development, and dissolution. The family life cycle (FLC) serves as the primary benchmark for analyzing these recent developments. The paper's major categories of analysis are stages identified in the "modernized" version (Murphy and Staples 1979), including young single, married with and without children, divorced with and without children, and older married and unmarried, but it incorporates other conceptualizations (Gilly and Enis 1982; Stampfl 1978) and some of their stages (i.e. cohabitating couples and mature singles). Finally, lifestyle, consumer decisionmaking, marketing management, and academic research implications are drawn for these emerging family and household trends.

Number of households increased 25 percent in the 1970s while the population grew only 9 percent (Hu 1980), and this pattern is expected to continue in the 1980s. Specifically, husband-and-wife families have decreased as a percentage of total households from 78 percent in 1950 to 61 percent in 1980 (Hu 1980). Rising divorce rates and increasing numbers of singles account for most of this change. Furthermore, the size of family households is on the decline. The average household is now 2.81 persons compared to an average in 1970 of 3.14 and in 1940 of 4.0. In fact, 53 percent of all households now number only one or two members (Norton and Glick 1979).

The current status of households in the United States is shown in Figure 2–1. Increases in nontraditional stages of life cycle caused dramatic changes in household composition during the 1970s. Since marriage remains the preferred state for most Americans, the family life cycle still seems the appropriate standard for analysis. However, the strength of these emerging trends must be recognized.

SINGLE STAGE

Young Single

Although the young single stage has been examined extensively in the context of the traditional FLC (Wells and Gubar 1966; Wortzel 1977a), it is discussed here because of the phenomenal growth in the number of individuals in this stage. In 1979, the number of never-marrieds rose 20 million from the 1960 level (Melko and Cargan 1981). The number of singles living alone increased from 2.8 million in 1970 to 5.4 million in 1979, primarily due to baby boom members setting up their own households (Russell 1981). About one-third of young adults now live apart from their parents or other relatives, a substantial increase since 1960 when only one-fifth of young singles lived alone (Wilkie 1981).

The number of individuals in the young single stage has grown, and so has the number of years that males or females remain single. The average age at the time of first marriage rose from 20.3 in 1960 to 22.1 in 1979 (U.S. Bureau of the Census 1980). Eleven percent of women and 19 percent of men between the ages of 25 and 29 had never been married in 1970, while the percentages rose to 22 and 34 percent respectively in 1981 (Weed 1982: 17). Reasons for extending this stage include reduced social pressure for early marriage, increases in education, especially by women (Bomball, Primeaux, and Pursell 1975; Van Dusen and Sheldon 1976), and expanded opportunities for young people to explore career and lifestyle options. These developments have significant implications that are explored later in the paper.

Mature Single

Several writers (Gilly and Enis 1982; Kobrin 1976; Stampfl 1978, 1979) have proposed that individuals who remain single throughout their lives be

Figure 1–1. Traditional Family on the Wane.

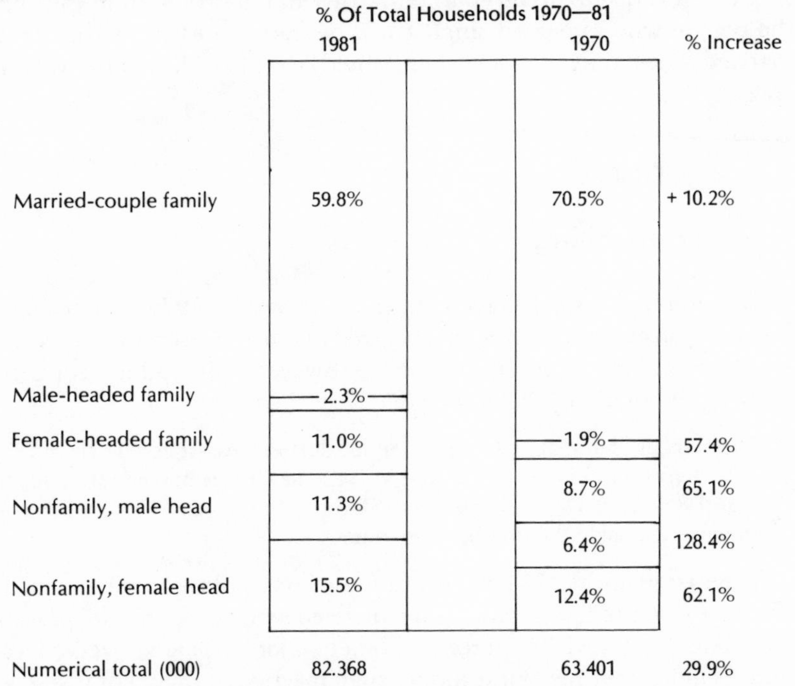

| | % Of Total Households 1970—81 | | |
	1981	1970	% Increase
Married-couple family	59.8%	70.5%	+ 10.2%
Male-headed family	2.3%		
Female-headed family	11.0%	1.9%	57.4%
Nonfamily, male head	11.3%	8.7%	65.1%
		6.4%	128.4%
Nonfamily, female head	15.5%	12.4%	62.1%
Numerical total (000)	82.368	63.401	29.9%

Source: *Sales and Marketing Management,* July 26, 1982, A–22.
Details may not add to 100% due to rounding.
Note: Previously, the male was always considered the family head, and households were broadly divided into families and unrelated individuals. The terminology shown in this table was adopted by the Bureau of the Census to fit in with changing family concepts and the increased presence of nonfamily households.

included in life cycle analyses, under labels such as bachelor I, II, III; mature singlehood; and primary individual. The number of individuals in this 35 to 64 age group is small, however, considering that about 90 percent of all men and women marry at some point in their lives. Mature singles are characterized by financial and decisionmaking independence with moderate or high incomes.

Model Based on Individuals

A recent methodological article (Espenshade and Brown 1982) suggests that due to the impermanence of families and households, the individual is a more appropriate unit of analysis for life cycle changes. The techniques of multistage demography could be applied to individuals as they move from single to married to divorced to remarried and to widowed. In this model, the person who remained single could be traced as easily as the one who married. The family life cycle, then, would be replaced by the individual life cycle.

COUPLES

Cohabiting

This writer and his colleague (Murphy and Staples 1979) did not include cohabitation as a stage in the modernized FLC because it represented such a small percentage of the population. However, this option seems to be growing in popularity (Spanier 1982:17):

> The number of unmarried couples tripled during the past decade, from 523,000 in 1970 to 1.6 million in 1980. And in 1981 the Census Bureau estimated there were 1.8 million. Of all couples in the United States today, about 4 percent are unmarried, double the number five years ago.

The vast majority (72 percent) of these households contain no children. They are also predominantly never-married who are young (67 percent of men under 35 and 76 percent women under 35) and well-educated. Furthermore, they make less money than married couples. For instance, 53 percent of cohabiting men earned less than $10,000 in 1980, compared to less than 13 percent of married men (Spanier 1982:19). Other cohabiters are individuals previously married who do not desire to remarry. Finally, the number of cohabiting couples is heavily concentrated among whites, but the rate of cohabitation among blacks is three times that of whites (Glick and Spanier 1980).

Several reasons can be advanced for this dramatic growth in cohabitation. First, liberalization of social pressures to marry at a young age probably makes cohabitation an attractive temporary life style for some (Glick 1978). Second, increased sexual freedom among adolescents and young adults (Spanier 1979) means that couples can live together without fear of having unwanted children. Third, the postponing of marriage may be related to the trend toward cohabitation. Fourth, the novelty of this experience may attract some cohabiters.

Young Married without Children

This FLC stage has historically been one of short duration and is sometimes referred to as the honeymoon stage. The most significant development in this stage is the trend toward delayed parenthood, caused in part by the widespread availability and use of contraceptives. In 1960–64, first children were born about fourteen months after marriage, while in 1975–78 the interval increased to twenty-four months (U.S. Bureau of the Census 1979a). By 1978, almost one-third of first births were to women age 25 years and older (U.S. National Center for Health Statistics 1980). Another contributing factor to this trend toward delayed parenthood is that more women seek educational and career opportunities in their first years of marriage. Many college-educated women choose to use their education in the working world because of the large investments in time and money spent in attaining that education. In fact, the better-educated women account for most of the delay in childbearing (Wilkie 1981). First births are delayed most often for economic motives, such as saving to buy a house (Young 1977). Although this trend toward postponing parenthood has been concentrated mainly in the better-educated segment of the population, it may spill over to other sectors of the population as well.

Childless

The modernized version of the FLC recognizes the option for couples to remain childless. The childless group has traditionally been small, but there are indications that it is growing. It was reported recently that 11 percent of women ages 18 to 34 claim that they do not intend to have children. This changing attitude can be attributed to growing acceptance of contraception, availability of abortion, rising economic expectations, changing attitudes of women toward marriage and family, and two-career households. The proportion of married American women under age 30 who have never had a child doubled between 1965 and 1979 (Pebley and Bloom 1982).

Couples may remain childless because of medical problems, economic hardship, uncertainty, and voluntary choice. The final category is growing most rapidly, and its characteristics can be described as follows (Pebley and Bloom 1982: 20):

> Typically, the voluntarily childless woman is white, lives in an urban area, and is highly educated, employed, not devoutly religious, and more likely than other women to be separated or divorced. Couples with higher incomes also are more likely to remain childless. These are the characteristics of a group whose members are likely to be economically successful and to have many options in life.

There is some debate as to whether the number of childless couples will increase in the future, but the decisions of childless couples to postpone or abstain from childbearing are closely monitored by demographers. Blake's (1976,1979) research found that women desire fewer children but that the percentage wanting to remain childless is still very small. Pebley and Bloom (1982) indicate that their figure of 11 percent is understated.

Married with Children

The most typical stages in the traditional family cycle are those where children are present. These are often labeled full nest with infant, young (age 4 to 12), or adolescent children. The lifestyle adjustments and financial commitment to children are well documented. During the decade of the 1970s, the fertility rate dropped for several years, which raised concern about a continuing decline.

The traditional stage warrants discussion here because of several recent developments. First, the birth rate has climbed to 17.1 babies per 1,000 population in 1981 from a low of 14.5 in 1976 (Reed 1982:54). The total of 3.5 million births in 1980 was the highest since 1971 (Lindsey 1980). This increase has been labeled the "baby bloom" by *Time*, a mini-baby boom by other recent periodicals, and probably most accurately a baby "boomlet" by *American Demographics* (Robey 1982). The causes for this fertility rate reversal are spelled out by Lindsey (1980:1):

> As possible causes for the rate increase, they cite factors that range from increased concern over the safety of oral contraceptives to the growing immigration of Hispanic aliens, to a return to "traditional" values after two decades of social experimentation and to a "now or never" attitude regarding motherhood.

The current debate is on whether the recent upswing in fertility rates will continue (Easterlin, Wachter, and Wachter 1979; Westoff 1979).

A second reason to closely monitor this stage is the absolute number of women of childbearing age. Citing Census Bureau statistics, Lindsey (1980) stated that in 1980 there were 18.2 million women between the ages of 25 and 35, up from 12.7 million in 1970. These women are part of the post–World War II baby boom. Another writer (Robey 1982) defined the baby boom generation somewhat differently and stated that people age 16 to 24 in 1980 were 53 percent of the generation. However this group is delineated, many women are currently of childbearing age. These numbers should be kept in perspective because, as Figure 1–2 shows, women are having substantially fewer babies in this era.

Third, the aforementioned delayed marriage and birth of first child by educated women has accounted for part of the fertility increase. "Although three-quarters of all babies continue to be borne by women in the 18-to-30 age group, there has been an astonishing 15.2 percent rise in the birth rate

Figure 1–2. Birth and Childbearers, 1950–80.

In the 1950's only 35 million women in the childbearing ages produced more than 4 million babies a year. In 1980, 53 million women produced less than 4 million babies.

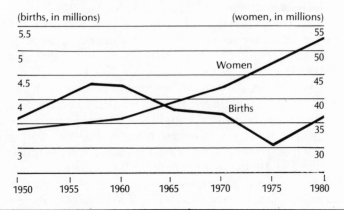

Source: Robey 1982: 19.

of women who were once thought to be slightly beyond their childbearing years: the 30-to-44 year olds" (Reed 1982:52). Further evidence that children are being postponed rather than foregone is that even though childlessness among women age 20 to 24 has been rising, at age 35 and older it has not increased beyond the level of 1960 (U.S. Bureau of the Census 1980). One implication of this later childbearing is that the empty-nest stage, which has been lengthening in the last several years (Glick 1977), will probably be shortened for these couples.

DIVORCED

Changes in the traditional or nuclear family have been the most dramatic in the last two decades. One recent article (Carlson 1980) stated that instability in the nuclear family was most marked after 1960. He attributes this instability to three major factors: the demographic bulge, the second sexual revolution, and the collapse of the nuclear family norm. The demographic bulge is the vast number of baby boom adolescents in the 1960s. Many families have not been able to cope with confused, questioning, and sometimes rebellious youth (Carlson 1980:74). The second sexual revolution refers to the diminished importance of marriage and children as necessary concomitants to sex. Third, many influential societal groups, including family counselors, social workers, and sociologists, no longer strongly support the nuclear family norm (Carlson 1980: 77).

The most obvious byproduct of the instability in traditional families is the growing incidence of divorce in the United States. For instance, twenty years ago eight to nine divorces were granted per thousand married women. The rate increased slightly to 11.2 in 1967, but by 1979 it stood at 22.8 (Weed 1982). The rate leveled off in the late 1970s and early 1980s. This means that at today's divorce rate, 39 percent of marriages reaching the fifth anniversary and 27 percent reaching the tenth will eventually end in divorce (Weed 1982:14).

1980 Census figures show that 7.2 percent of women and 5.4 percent of men were divorced at that time ("Married Is Still the Favorite State" 1982: A-33). Even though the divorce rate is high, a relatively small percentage of divorced people is in the divorced category because most remarry. Approximately seven out of ten divorced women remarry within five years of their divorce, and divorced men are more likely to remarry than women. "In 1979, for example, an estimated 44 percent of all marriages were remarriages, up from 30 percent in 1969" (Weed 1982: 13). Projections are that divorces will likely remain high (Weed 1982:17):

> The large numbers of divorces are themselves a force that could keep the divorce rate high. With marriages so often ending in divorce, many previously married people are joining the pool of available marriage partners. Since the large majority of divorced people remarry, and remarriages have a higher overall risk of divorce, the general divorce rate is likely to rise as a result.

Divorced without Children

Some marriages end in divorce before children are present. Recent research offers a profile of those most likely to divorce. Women who married at a young age are more likely to be divorced than those who marry later, and there is an inverse relationship between age at first marriage and a women's education (Norton 1980; Spanier and Glick 1980b). This finding is corroborated by Locksley (1982), who states that "for both males and females the incidence of divorced decrease precipitously as educational attainment increases" (Locksley 1982:437). These data imply that the trends toward delayed marriage and postponed childbearing on the part of better-educated women will eventually affect the divorce rate.

Whether the young divorced individual has the same attitudes, lifestyle, and behavior as the young never-married is unclear. Since most divorced people do remarry, it can be assumed that they again actively participate in courtship. Specifically, women who were divorced before age 30 were three times more likely to remarry within five years than older women (Spanier and Glick 1980a). Financial and psychological adjustments can be difficult for some divorced women, but not enough is known about this group to draw definitive conclusions.

Divorced with Children

Children are present in about two-thirds of all divorces (Glick and Norton 1977).[1] The number of one-parent families increased 49 percent in the 1960s and 76 percent between 1970 and 1978, while two-parent families increased 8 percent and decreased 3 percent during the same periods. Of the 30.4 million families with children under age 18 in 1978, almost 20 percent had one parent (Bane and Weiss 1980). Ninety percent of the time this parent was a woman. Over 70 percent of these mother-headed households resulted from divorce or separation.

These single-parent families are characterized by moving of the household, lower income, and lower levels of happiness. Although the husband almost always moves out during a divorce, about 75 percent of the mothers and children move at least once within four years after marital breakup (Bane and Weiss 1980). Naturally, the household income is lower with at most one employed adult. The size of the difference is large: Husband-and-wife families earned $20,651 in 1977, but female-headed families made only $8,340 (Bane and Weiss 1980: 12). Not suprisingly, mothers who are no longer married are not as happy as married mothers. Furthermore, children of these families experience more emotional and behavioral problems than children of two-parent homes (Bane and Weiss 1980:15). These results largely confirm the physical, financial, emotional, and behavioral hardships experienced by divorced mothers with children.

OLDER

The older segment of the FLC usually includes individuals at or beyond retirement age. In recent years this group has attracted more attention, and some writers have expanded the older category to include those age 50 and over (Bartos 1979; Cohen 1981). Figures from the 1980 Census indicate the growth in this expanded older category (Robey 1981: 14):

> The 1980 census counted 9.3 million more people age 50 and older than did the 1970 census. Every age group from 50 on up increased in size. On census day, 59 million Americans were age 50 or older—more than 26 percent of the total population. The 65-and-over age group grew by a healthy 5.6 million people between 1970 and 1980. The census counted 25.5 million people in this group, 11.3 percent of the total population.

Married

Older couples near or at retirement age are a significant group: Twelve million individuals live in husband-and-wife households (Allan 1981a). It is expected that improved health care will continue to extend life expectancy of older individuals in this stage. Stereotypes abound regarding older married couples and their lifestyle patterns. They are neither as rich as the retirees in Florida, Arizona, and California are portrayed nor as poor as the indigent couples on Social Security are thought to be. They have significant purchasing power and spend approximately 28 percent of all discretionary money in the marketplace (Allan 1981a).

As stated in the modernized FLC, it is possible for widows or widowers to remarry after the death of a spouse, although statistics show that this is a relatively small group. For women married ten years or more before widowhood, "the large majority (84 percent of whites and 90 percent of blacks) had not remarried" (Spanier and Glick 1980a: 294). Although the percentage of remarriage is presumed to be larger for men (U.S. Bureau of the Census 1970), the life expectancy of women is several years longer than men. Therefore, the absolute number of males who remarry in the older stages is likely to be rather small.

Unmarried

This stage in the FLC is commonly known as the solitary survivor. For the reasons mentioned above, this individual is more likely to be a woman. One factor contributing to the growth in the number of households in the United States is the greater tendency in recent years for widows to live alone rather than with family members. One-third of women age 65 or over were living alone or with nonrelatives as heads of separate households in 1970. This figure stood at 13 percent in 1940 (Kobrin 1976). The emotional, physical, and financial hardships that this stage places on an older individual are not well understood. Although more widows are now living alone and can afford it financially, it is unclear if this is their preferred lifestyle.

This portion of the paper has concentrated on specific stages within the FLC that recently have grown in importance. Although some of the stages (young single, divorced without children, older unmarried) do not technically fit within the family label, the FLC represents the common framework used in most sociological and demographic analysis. Other writers have suggested that women (Bartos 1982) and consumers (Stampfl

1978) rather than families could be used as the benchmark to analyze life cycle. These alternative conceptualizations are integrated into the next section on implications of the FLC.

IMPLICATIONS

Projected Growth

Table 1-1 shows the projected growth of the previously discussed stages, including the well-known decline in the number of young adults. According to population projections (U.S. Bureau of the Census 1979b: 2), husband-and-wife households are expected to decline from 2 to 10 percent by 1995 from the current level of 62 percent of the population. Therefore, the mature single, cohabiting couples, and divorced without children are expected to increase in numbers. Of course, these groups are currently rather small, ranging from 0.1 percent to 4 percent of the population (Gilly and Enis 1982; Murphy and Staples 1979). The largest increase is anticipated in the older category, which as mentioned previously is becoming a significant segment of the overall population. The maturing of the baby boom generation into the middle-age stages of the FLC represents the largest segment in absolute size. Since a certain percentage of them will remain single, childless, or divorced, these developments will also cause these groups to increase in number.

Lifestyle

At the risk of being too simplistic, a one-word description is used to explain the lifestyle of each of the FLC stages shown in Table 1-1. Within the single stage, the young are characterized as being in a transitional lifestyle. As Wortzel (1977b:327) points out in the following quote (and in the statistics noted on delayed age at first marriage), the length of their transition has increased in recent years and changed in focus:

> This life cycle is evolving from one in which the principal activities seemed to be searching for a mate and preparing for marriage to one in which the principal concerns are personal growth, the establishment of a personal identity and credentials, and the accumulation of a variety of personal experiences. Thus, singlehood is now becoming a life cycle stage to be enjoyed in its own right, rather than one to pass through as quickly as possible.

According to Stampfl (1979: 25) mature singlehood "begins when single people make serious commitments to single lifestyles and careers." It would

Table 1–1. Implications of Family Life Cycle Stages.

| | Family Life Cycle Stages | | | | | | | | | |
| | Single | | Cohabiting | Couples | | | Divorced | | Older | |
Implications	Young	Mature		Married without children	Childless	Married with children	Without Children	With Children	Married	Unmarried
Growth	Decrease until 1995	Increase	Increase slightly	Stable	Increase	Decrease slightly	Increase	Stable	Increase	Increase
Lifestyle	Transitional	Patterned	Impermanent	Hedonistic	Carefree	Child-centered	Self-centered	Constrained	Active if healthy and not poor	Sedentary
Consumer Decision-making	Individual	Individual	Independent	Joint	Joint	Complementary	Individual	Joint	Complementary	Individual/family
Marketing Products										
Durable	Basic furniture, automobile	Condominiums, high-quality home furnishings	Low-cost furniture	Sensible furniture, insurance	Smaller homes, sports cars	Toys, larger homes	Fashionable furniture, apartments or condominiums	Inexpensive furniture, low-cost housing	Retirement homes, jewelry	Apartment
Non-durables	Records fashion-oriented clothing	Individual-size servings, home maintenance		Career clothing	Small packages, convenience foods	Family-size packages, functional clothing	Small packages, small appliances	Inexpensive clothing, discount foods, toys	Cosmetics, sports equipment	Salt-free products
Services	Travel, restaurants	Better restaurants, financial planning investments	Lower budget travel, individual financial services	Movies, travel, restaurants	Theater tickets, house cleaning service, luxury travel	Family or fast-food restaurants, discount entertainment	Dating service, travel, clubs	Fast-food restaurants	Travel, brokerage services	Cruises, home delivery services, mass transportation
Promotion										
Message	Special interest me-oriented	Quality appeals	Buy-now appeal	Appeal to both spouses	Quality, luxury	Family oriented	Me-oriented appeals	Low-price appeals	Owe yourself appeals	Enjoyment and comfort appeals
Media	Magazines, radio	Personal selling	Mass media	Mass media	Special interest	Women's magazines, mass media	Mood magazines	Mass media especially TV	TV & newspapers	TV

Source: Adapted partially from Wells and Gubar (1966), Pebley and Bloom (1982), Stampfl (1978, 1979), Allan (1981a), Murphy and Staples (1979), and Gilly and Enis (1982).

seem, then, that these individuals have settled into a pattern or routine that they find comfortable.

In the couples stages, the lifestyle options depend on the outlook of the couples occupying a particular stage. Cohabiting couples usually pursue this lifestyle for a relatively short time before they marry or separate. Therefore, their lifestyle can be characterized as impermanent. Glick and Norton (1977) reported that 63 percent of unmarried couples share the same house or apartment for less than two years. Although the duration of this stage is short, the following quotes (Glick and Spanier 1980:30; Spanier 1982: 42) indicate that society finds it an acceptable lifestyle:

> Increased freedom in adult behavior, less pressure to marry at traditionally normative young ages, and greater acceptance of unmarried cohabitation as a lifestyle are evidently providing a context in which this way of living is becoming increasing accepted as an alternative to marriage or as a temporary arrangement preceding or following marriage.

> Indeed, should the increase in unmarried people living together continue through this decade at the same pace as the past decade, we will have to begin viewing this living arrangement less as an alternative lifestyle and more as a fact of life.

Young married couples without children pursue what is labeled in Table 1–1 a hedonistic lifestyle. Wives in these young families increasingly look at their work as a career, and many plan to stay in the labor force permanently (Bartos 1982). Some of the most successful of the young professionals analyzed by *Fortune* (Kinkead 1980) expect an immediate, relatively high standard of living. Although many young couples are not well off financially, postponed parenthood and two incomes mean that they are relatively better off than their parents or others of a similar socioeconomic background have been historically.

Married couples who remain childless are described as being carefree (Murphy and Staples 1979), and recent research reports that childless couples tend to have higher incomes (Pebley and Bloom 1982) (see quote earlier in paper). Attitudes toward childlessness also seem to be changing. A study conducted by Young and Rubicam found that more than 80 percent of all women in 1980 said that children were not essential for a full and happy marriage (Walsh 1982a:28). The childless lifestyle may tend to grow in importance in the future.

The addition of children to any family causes dramatic changes, and married couples with children usually follow a child-centered lifestyle (Table 1–1). The needs of the children are almost always met before those of parents are fulfilled. With more two-income and career-oriented families, child-centeredness may decline from its peak during the era of the nonworking mother. However, sociologists are finding that couples who have smaller families spend large amounts on the children and are deeply concerned about the quality of care their children are receiving (Reed 1982).

Divorced individuals with and without children do not live the same kinds of lives. The divorced person without children often pursues a self-centered lifestyle to remove the memories of an unhappy marriage or because "I owe it to myself to have fun." Divorced families, on the other hand, are usually constrained in their lifestyle options (Table 1-1). As mentioned previously, certain physical and emotional adjustments and adaptations must occur as former spouses move and start a new life. The financial status of both the husband and wife is usually worse because the husband must provide child support, the wife must continue or begin working, and they both must bear the cost of maintaining separate households.

The lifestyles of older married couples or individuals are varied. As Table 1-1 indicates, healthy older couples that saved for retirement often experience an active lifestyle including travel and other postponed purchases. Declining health and low income can cause this stage to be an unhappy and unfulfilled one. The solitary survivor is likely to live a more sedentary lifestyle because of advancing age and other factors.

Finally, little mention has been made in the lifestyle implications about the income level of individuals or couples in these stages; however, dealing directly with subcategories within each stage would entail expanding this analysis to an unwieldy length. Naturally, race, education, family size, and employment status are closely related to socioeconomic status. Lower income and lower social class cause families, couples, and individuals to experience more lifestyle hardships than generally noted above.

Consumer Decisionmaking

The manner in which decisions are made by individuals or couples within these stages has important implications for marketing managers and researchers. Consumer decisionmaking (Table 1-1) can be characterized as primarily individual, joint, complementary, or independent. Stampfl (1978, 1979) discussed the adolescent decisionmaking process as part of the consumer life cycle, but a discussion of that area is beyond the scope of this paper.

In households with only one person—young and mature single, divorced without children, or older unmarried—individual-dominated decisions are made. However, the table does not distinguish some important nuances of this individual decisionmaking: The mature single is likely to be more sophisticated and knowledgeable than his or her younger counterpart; experience within the previous marriage probably influences decisionmaking by the divorced individual; and the older solitary survivor may depend on family members or institutions at some point to make decisions for him or her.

Cohabiting couples tend to represent a classic example of independent decisionmaking: The individual makes decisions independently of the partner. Since these couples do not know whether their relationship will become permanent, important decisions about durable goods are especially likely to be independent. For example, one partner may buy an automobile that he or she needs, and the other may buy a piece of furniture that he or she wants; if they later marry, this pattern of decisionmaking may or may not change.

Young married couples practice joint consumer decisionmaking. Part of the process of getting to know one another is to become jointly involved in most major decisions.

According to Table 1-1, divorced individuals with children are also listed as primary joint decisionmakers. If the oldest children are adolescent, the mother may consult them on important decisions. Other nuclear (or extended) family members or even friends may play the surrogate spouse role in decisionmaking.

Complementary decisionmaking is likely to be practiced by married couples with children and by older couples. The presence of children limits the time that spouses can spend making joint decisions and a division of labor usually evolves. This does not mean that no decisions are made jointly. Certainly, a decision to move the family residence or redecorate the entire house is likely to be a joint one. For older couples who have had children, it may be difficult to return to joint decisionmaking. Once again, empirical research is needed to evaluate how older couples make consumption decisions.

Marketing

The marketing implications of the traditional (Wells and Gubar 1966), modernized (Murphy and Staples 1979), recycled (Gilly and Enis 1982), and modified (Schlachter, Rozzouk, and Mills 1979) FLC have been discussed previously. Furthermore, family influence on marketing has received treatment for well over a decade (Reynolds and Myers 1966; Rich and Jain 1968). Table 1-1 includes products, services, and promotional strategies that are appropriate for the stages examined here.

Another important aspect of marketing strategy not shown in Table 1-1 is that firms should not assume that each of these FLC stages are homogeneous groups. The products and services demanded by parents with small children are different than those needed by families with teenage children: These distinctions are generally apparent to marketers. However, some divergences are not as well understood. For instance, Linden (1979) listed five separate segments for the young single stage (under age 35).

Probably one of the most stereotyped and least segmented markets is the older category (Allan 1981a, 1981b; Bartos 1979). Bartos has delineated four important segments for individuals over age 49: (1) active affluents (workers peaking in earning and professional accomplishments) (40%); (2) active retireds (those over age 65 in good health) (15%); (3) housewives (homemakers above the poverty level) (22%); (4) disadvantaged (individuals or couples living below the poverty level (17%); (5) other (6%). These groups represent vastly different marketing opportunities.

The list of products and services shown in Table 1-1 suggests various approaches to these marketing opportunities. For example, better restaurants could appeal to the mature single, young married couple, childless couple, or active affluent older group. Furniture manufacturers and marketers could develop separate product lines for the young single, married with children, or divorced without children. Alternately, the furniture firm may choose to target its products to only one or two of the most profitable FLC stages. Within services, travel agencies can offer vastly different packages to childless couples, older unmarrieds (probably active retireds), and young singles. The insurance industry has targeted four female segments that cut across several stages: career women, homemakers, working women, and single parents (Walsh 1982a).

The promotional implications that can be drawn from Table 1-1 are tied closely to the FLC stages. Promotional messages should be tailored to the lifestyle chosen by the group: for mature singles and childless couples, a quality-oriented appeal; for young marrieds without children, an appeal to both spouses because of the tendency toward joint decisionmaking. Although television, radio, and newspapers are the dominant promotional vehicles, magazines such as *Smithsonian* for childless couples (because of their presumed interest in culture) and *Parents* or *Good Housekeeping* for marrieds with children (for children's products) would pay greater dividends to the advertiser. Personal selling seems to be important for the mature singles category, since these individuals probably are more discerning consumers.

Other significant marketing implications of the various FLC stages that are not shown in Table 1-1 should be reviewed briefly. The importance of the singles to many marketers can not be overlooked. For example, in a recent year 17 percent of all home buyers and 25 percent of all new car buyers were single and those age 18 to 40 took three times as many vacation trips as the rest of the adult population (Schlachter, Rozzouk, and Mills 1979: 41).

The population groups that are largest in absolute numbers are the couples stages. This is pertinent because the baby boom generation is moving into these stages and because the significance of two-income families makes them especially noteworthy for marketers (Michman 1980). These professional-managerial couples have been labeled the superclass (Jones 1981a). Couples fitting this description have postponed childbearing and might "spend up to $2,500 on clothing, furniture and equipment by the time the baby comes home from the hospital" (Reed 1982: 54). Firms that are too closely identified with the youth culture of the baby boom generation may have trouble adjusting to this new marketplace where the median age is higher (Jones 1981b), but projections for family income should make marketers aware of the need for diversifying their offerings (Linden 1980: 55):

> During the Eighties, according to estimates, the total real income accruing to nuclear families with families with annual earnings of under $20,000 will actually decline, while the buying power of the secondary households in that same bracket will grow by more than two-fifths. This is a development to be watched closely by the mass merchandise and discount businesses.

Marketers are beginning to understand the divorced categories better. From a strategy standpoint, it may not be meaningful to separate young divorced from young single. Scarpa (1982) contends that divorced parents spend more time on their children and that this has favorable implications for firms like Binney and Smith (Crayola crayons manufacturer), Hasbro (toy manufacturer), and Eastman Kodak. Although marketers may have an ethical responsibility not to exploit divorced women with families, Bane and Weiss's (1980) financial and psychological profile of this category indicates that marketers selling other than discount merchandise will find that this is not an attractive segment.

Implications of the aging of the population need close study. By the year 2000, one person in eight will be at least age 65, a 40 percent rise from today's level (Taeuber 1979). The changing consumption patterns that this trend will bring have been analyzed (W.A. Cox 1981). Espenshade (1981) urges companies to gradually shift to products for the retired and elderly, rather than the young, consumer. Some of the specific examples recounted by Allan (1981b)—such as Elizabeth Arden introducing Millenium cosmetics line for the mature woman and Vic Tanny's appeal to this segment— indicate that certain firms are beginning to make this transition toward the mature market.

Academic Research

In the past few years, academic researchers have subjected the FLC to several methodological and applications investigations. Teachman (1982) advocated the use of the proportional hazards model, which uses the number, timing, and sequence of life-course transitions (marriage, divorce, birth of child, etc.) to study families. Spanier, Sauer, and Larzellre (1979) evaluated the FLC and concluded that other developmental stratification schemes, such as age cohort, should be used to develop a more accurate model for researchers. Nock (1979) argued that the length of marriage and presence of children are the key dimensions in using the FLC as a research tool. Derrick and Lehfeld (1980) felt that the variables used to come up with FLC stages could be used efficiently for research purposes if studied independently. These researchers working independently have attempted to refine the FLC, but joint and interdisciplinary perspectives are needed.

The FLC continues to be used for application purposes in research. Schram (1979) critically reviewed marital satisfaction's relationship to the FLC and recommended more sophisticated methodologies to understand the complexities of family stages. McAuley and Nutty (1982) analyzed residential preferences in the face of escalating housing and energy prices over FLC stages. Residential mobility commonly experienced during the stages may not be possible in the future. Fritzsche (1981) examined energy consumption across the FLC stages and found the modernized (compared to the traditional) FLC to be a meaningful construct in his analysis. Applications-oriented research will continue in the future, and perhaps researchers will compare different FLC conceptualizations, as Fritzsche did, in their applications.

Table 1–2 lists some possible avenues for research into each of the FLC stages. For the young single, research is needed on attitudes of the young single toward consumption. For example, are most singles interested in accumulating durable goods, or do they want simply to get by until moving to a later stage? The relative influence of peers versus family in decisionmaking needs examination: As more singles move away from the family home, what happens to the strength of parental influence? In addition, does the influence of peers, which is so strong during adolescent and college years, continue in the young single stage?

Mature singles comprise a small but growing group, and their decision-making processes (extended, limited, or habitual) are of interest. Since they probably have more time for comparison shopping than families do, does this pattern dominate their decisionmaking? As a consumer, the mature single may be future-oriented and looking forward to retirement, or he or she may be more present-oriented and have a "live for today" philosophy.

Since cohabiting couples often separate after a short time, their attitudes toward purchasing durable products warrant study. In other words, is the partner consulted on purchases, or does the individual make a strictly personal decision to buy a stereo or piece of furniture? Furthermore, are individuals who follow the nontraditional lifestyle innovators in buying consumer products?

Table 1-2. Academic Research Implications.

Single			Couples			Divorced		Older	
Young	Mature	Cohabiting	Married Without Children	Childless	Married With Children	Without Children	With Children	Married	Unmarried
Attitudes toward consumption	Decision-making process	Attitudes toward purchase	Percentage of joint decisions	Expenditures allocation (budgeting)	Family decision-making	Reference group influence	Family roles	Personal versus family orientation	Amount of personal decision-making
Influence of reference groups versus family	Future orientation	Innovativeness	Relative influence of partners	Amount of searching	Influence of children	Attitudes toward consumption	Step-family influence	Spending priorities	Attitudes toward products and services

The decisions of young married couples without children need to be studied. Although it is well known that they tend to have the highest percentage of joint decisionmaking, how high is it? This questions seems especially pertinent in an era of delayed marriage where the partners may have established strong product and search preferences prior to marriage. When both spouses work, does power in family decisionmaking fall to the greater resource contributor or to the more interested partner (Engel and Blackwell 1982)? It is conceivable that though the wife may earn less than the husband, she may be comfortable with her income level and therefore in the power position because of the least-interested-partner theory.

Childless couples generally are more affluent than families. How do childless couples allocate money for consumption expenditures? Do they engage in less budgeting than the traditional family and less or more searching for products or services? Since they generally have more money, are they impulsive shoppers, or because they also tend to have more time, do they enjoy spending it to search for and evaluate products and services together? Alternately, do they have what is called a roommate marriage, where each partner independently pursues his or her career and spends money on himself or herself?[2]

Family decisionmaking in the married with children stages needs to be monitored. The excellent work of Davis and Rigaux (1974) should be expanded and replicated with a broader audience, particularly their investigation of the postpurchase stage of the decisionmaking process and the marital roles. The influence of children in an era of smaller families should be analyzed: Do they exert more or less influence on parents?

Divorced individuals' consumer behavior is not well understood. One possible research topic is to investigate the influence of reference groups on divorced person's decisionmaking. After marriage, are they more or less susceptible to influence by others? Furthermore, after divorce do they become active consumers in order to compensate for lack of marital success? How do decisionmaking and attitudes differ for those who have been divorced less than two years compare with those divorced longer than five years?

Divorced parents with children represent a challenge for researchers and marketers. Family roles should be analyzed in this type of family: Are older children joint decisionmakers in this family? Do children assume more of the purchaser role for the working mothers? Who is the "gatekeeper" in this type of family, or is the role not operable? The decisionmaking of various family types should be compared; the preliminary conclusions drawn by Kourilsky and Murray (1981) regarding traditional and single parents need further study.

More divorced parents are remarrying, and more than six million persons under age 18—10 percent of all U.S. children—lived with a stepparent in 1976. This percentage was double the 1960 level. Researchers and marketers need to become more aware of decisionmaking products for this type of family (Klein 1982: 1):

> "Even Hallmark is against us," says Emily Visher, a psychologist who with her husband, psychiatrist John Visher, in 1980 formed the Stepfamily Association of America in Palo Alto, California, to provide information and other help. She explains: "Go into a card store and you'll find greetings for moms and dads, sons and daughters, grandparents, in-laws, aunts and uncles, nephews and nieces, and friends. Everything but stepparents and stepkids.

Although marketers are paying more attention to older consumers, researchers should study their attitudes, perceptions, and intentions more fully. For example, do older couples who are parents and grandparents have a personal view toward consumption, or are they concerned with buying products and bequeathing money to their offspring? What are their spending priorities? Do they view extended vacations as necessities or luxuries? Are they willing to continue to contribute to nonprofit organizations? Does spending for food and shelter leave them little choice for discretionary spending?

The older unmarrieds should also receive research attention. Are they free to make personal decisions, or do family members play the decider as well as influencer role? Further, their attitudes towards products and services are not well known. Are they still active participants in the consumer game, or have they lost interest in brands and products?

CONCLUSION

This paper has broadly reviewed the study of families and households. The growth of smaller households warrants continued study, as do the new FLC stages—by sociologists and consumer marketing researchers as they already have been analyzed by demographers. This discussion of consumer lifestyles, consumer decisionmaking, marketing, and academic research should not be viewed as more than the first step in a long road toward a better understanding of families and households.

NOTES

1. Those who are most likely to divorce are women who drop out of school and bear children at a young age (Spanier and Glick 1980b).
2. This phrase and idea is credited to Wortzel, Lawrence H. (1980).

2 THE HOUSEHOLD LIFE CYCLE
Implications For Family Decisionmaking

Julia M. Bristor and William J. Qualls

The concept of the family life cycle (FLC) has its roots in the sociological literature of the 1930's (C.P. Loomis 1936). It refers to a variable employed by sociologists to describe the development of the family unit as it evolves over time from its formation to its dissolution. By definition, only family households in which the husband and wife were legally married were incorporated into the FLC. Several stages were developed, based primarily on three factors: (1) husband's age, (2) marital status, and (3) age and presence (or absence) of children. These variables were the foundation for the development of numerous conceptualizations of the composition and number of FLC stages (C.P. Loomis 1936; Glick 1977; Rodgers 1967; Duvall 1971).

Consumer behavior research has assumed that an individual's position in the FLC is more important than age, income, or other household variables in explaining and predicting family decision and consumption behavior. The FLC as an independent variable for explaining consumer behavior has received considerable support and use from consumer researchers and marketing practitioners since the mid-1950s. Howover, the FLC as developed by sociologists suffers from several conceptual problems that impair its usefulness in marketing research. This paper considers the FLC in light of current social and demographic trends and changes in the household and re-examines its usefulness as a tool for marketers. It introduces a marketing alternative to the FLC—the household life cycle

(HLC)—that provides a starting point for redirecting research focus and marketing effort to the study of household decision behavior.

ORIGINS OF THE FAMILY LIFE CYCLE

The developmental approach is commonly used to study the family as a unit. Originating in the sociology literature, the FLC concept seeks to describe and understand developmental changes occurring within a family over time (Rodgers 1967). By designating stages of development that coincide with important events such as the birth of the first child and the launching of the last, the developmental approach provides a conceptual framework within which researchers can engage in the longitudinal study of families.

Since its initial introduction into the sociological literature (C.P. Loomis 1936), many modifications of the FLC have appeared. However, the majority of FLC variations have been associated not with conceptual issues but with the degree of detail within stages or the number of stages in the FLC. One such variation in the FLC concept its illustrated by Duvall's (1971:121) eight-stage FLC. Her stages consist of:

1. married couples (without children);
2. childbearing families (oldest child under age 30 months);
3. families with preschool children (oldest child age 2½ to 6 years);
4. families with school-age children (oldest child age 6 to 13);
5. families with teenagers (oldest child age 13 to 20);
6. families as launching centers;
7. middle-aged parents (empty nest to retirement); and
8. aging families (retirement to the death of both spouses).

Duvall's (1971) FLC is similar to that of others (C.P. Loomis 1936; Glick 1977; Rodgers 1967) in that the three factors employed as the basis for discriminating between stages include: (1) age of household head (husband), (2) marital status, and (3) age and presence of children. All these cases consider the first stage of the FLC to be the establishment of the family unit by marriage and the dissolution to be the death of at least one spouse.

Several researchers (Glick 1977; Nock 1979; and Spanier, Sauer, and Larzellre 1979) have suggested the need to reexamine the FLC and update it to reflect today's social and demographic trends. All three studies acknowledge the need for alternative classification schemes for FLC stages in the continued study of the formation, maintenance, change, and dissolution of the family unit.

USE OF THE FAMILY LIFE CYCLE IN MARKETING

The family life cycle is one of the primary independent variables employed in marketing research to predict family decision and consumption behavior. Lansing and Morgan (1955) successfully related stages in the FLC to specific decision practices within the household. They found that the amount of the income, durable good purchases, asset and debt accumulation, and perceptions regarding financial position differed for families at different stages of the FLC. In a follow-up study, Lansing and Kish (1957) found similar findings and demonstrated that FLC was more accurate than age in predicting household consumption and purchase behavior.

Wells and Gubar (1966) provide the most comprehensive review of the early use of the FLC concept in marketing and reaffirm that FLC is the best variable available for discriminating and predicting household purchase behavior. Their cross-classification scheme combines FLC stages and household consumption behavior and forms the basis for most current theories of family decisionmaking and household consumption behavior. Several studies (Rich and Jain 1968; Hisich and Peters 1974; E.P. Cox 1975; Reynolds and Wells 1977) suggest that FLC is superior to such variables as age, income, length of marriage, and social class in explaining and predicting family consumer behavior.

In borrowing the FLC concept from sociology, marketers have failed to question its validity and applicability to consumer research issues. This paper argues that the usefulness of the traditional FLC has diminished substantially over the past several years because of changes in the household caused by shifts in social norms, volatile economic conditions, and structural demographic changes. These changes cannot be accurately captured and portrayed by the existing FLC stages or by variables used to delineate such stages, and consequently, the explanatory and predictive power of the FLC concept as it relates to family decision practices has been significantly reduced.

More recent studies have attempted to adapt the traditional FLC to changing conditions within the household. Among the first in marketing to propose a modernized family life cycle were Murphy and Staples (1979), who expanded the stages in the FLC to include both divorced-parent households and married couples without children. Similarly, Gilly and Enis (1982) included more stages by incorporating single adult households into the above framework.

Although Murphy and Staples (1979) and Gilly and Enis (1982) have taken steps toward reconceptualizing the FLC, both studies fall short in several ways. While the FLC seems to be the appropriate framework for studying household decision behavior, it is inadequate for use in marketing. Marketers have never questioned the basic purpose for which the family life cycle concept was developed. While sociologists typically employ the FLC to study the development of the traditional family unit over time, marketers are more interested in examining its usefulness for explaining and predicting household purchase and consumption behavior at specific points in time. Such differences in research objectives suggest that marketers may have inadequately investigated the validity of the structural variables that delineate FLC stages. Most generalizations about the FLC and specific decision and consumption behavior are based on a concept that has never been tailored to the needs of consumer behavior research.

Current marketing conceptualizations of the FLC present three major problems: (1) The lack of a single classification scheme delineating FLC stages that is accepted by today's researchers interferes with comparisons of various FLC studies and models of family decisionmaking; (2) inadequacy of current FLC stages to reflect today's traditional and nontraditional household types leads marketers to unnecessarily restrict their scope by equating the household with the traditional family unit; and (3) the structural variables used to delineate FLC stages fail to capture marketers' interest in household purchase and consumption behavior. These criticisms and others found in the literature (Derrick and Lehfeld 1980) are symptomatic of marketers' myopic view of the family and their failure to question the appropriateness of a concept developed for different research objectives within another discipline. After being borrowed from sociology, the FLC has never adequately been tailored to the needs of marketing and consumer research.

Marketers need flexible, operational tools to study household consumption behaviors. To begin, the household can be designated as the unit of analysis without having restrictions placed on its composition. It provides a framework within which the consumption processes and purchase behavior of both traditional and nontraditional family units can be studied. Finally, it allows researchers to approach the study of household behavior from an evolutionary perspective in order to capture the dynamic nature of the household decisionmaking process.

THE HOUSEHOLD LIFE CYCLE

Similar to the original FLC, the proposed household life cycle (HLC) takes a developmental perspective. It should be emphasized at the onset that the HLC is not another revision of the FLC but a reconceptualized model that is a process linked to consumption behavior rather than a description of social phenomena: It views the household as a decisionmaking unit that evolves and matures over the course of its existence. It extends the study of decisionmaking processes over time from the traditional family unit to the broader study unit of the household. Granbois (1971a) and Davis (1976) have long argued that the appropriate unit of analysis for consumer research is the household. Understanding the processes by which household purchase and consumption decisions are made will increase our understanding of consumer behavior in general and our ability to explain family decision practices specifically.

Three variables form the basis for the various points in the HLC. The first two relate to the composition of the household (household type and presence/absence of dependents), while the third refers to a household's development (age of the household).

There are no clear-cut stages that all households are expected to pass through at predetermined points in time. Instead, a household may experience various interrupts during the course of its development that can alter decisionmaking roles and practices and position in the life cycle. "Interrupts" are defined as events that significantly alter one or more aspects of a household's decision behavior. Interrupts may alter the composition of the household or change the household type, but more important they may act as catalysts in shifting a household's position in the life cycle. Examples of interrupts can be suggested but not specified because any event causing these kinds of changes is considered an interrupt. For example, the birth of a child, a wife's entering the work force, the addition of dependents, and the launching of dependents would affect and possibly alter the decision environment. Relevant interrupts are partially determined by the research problem. A discussion of the three variables that delineate HLC position follows.

Household Type

The proposed HLC encompasses many types of households and allows for the inclusion of others that may evolve over time. Although categories might be developed for various reasons, the distinctions made between the present categories were not arbitrarily chosen but were developed based on their adaptability and applicability to most problems studied in consumer marketing. Four households types are proposed: (1) single-person, (2) family, (3) cohabitation, and (4) cooperative. Briefly, single-person households are units in which only one adult is present. Included here are individuals who are divorced, widowed, or have never been married. Family households consist of legally married couples with or without dependents.

A cohabiting household consists of two members of the opposite sex living together without legal marriage, while cooperative households consist of two or more adults who share household responsibilities.

One factor used to distinguish between households is level of commitment. Each category falls somewhere on a continuum that runs from no formal commitment to formal commitment. The level of commitment that exists within a household may indicate the expected duration of the household's existence and its probable decision practices.

Dependents

A second factor that determines a household's position in the HLC is the presence or absence of dependents. Dependents are defined as additional household members who do not, will not, or cannot live alone for reasons of age, health, economics, or preference. While often referring to children, dependents may include in-laws residing with children, adult children remaining at home, or other relatives. The dependent classification of a household can shift back and forth between household types due to interrupts.

Household Age

Previous FLC models placed a family in a specific life cycle stage according to the age of the household head. A more relevant criterion is how long the household has been in existence. Support for such a position is found in Rodgers' (1967:77) suggestion that units of time should "be able to capture differences which occur in processual time." Households are distinguished by variations in the structure of decision roles and responsibilities at two comparative points in time. According to the proposed HLC model, units of time are bounded by interrupts and depend on the household's age.

In addition, the HLC finds that household behaviors are affected more by the age of the household than by the age of the individual members. Although the age of individual members may help marketers to draw generalizations about product usage, it does not necessarily contribute to our understanding of how individuals, as a household, learn to interact and make decisions. Past family research suggests that over the course of marriage husband-and-wife decisionmaking increases in efficiency as the partners learn to assimilate the preferences and opinions of individual household members (Wolgast 1958; Blood and Wolfe 1960; Kenkel 1961; E.P. Cox 1975). While patterns are likely to differ for various household types, they will be better observed by extending the concept of length of marriage to age of household.

Examining the biological evolutionary life cycle provides some excellent clues for devising a framework appropriate for classifying the age of households. The development of a household is a dynamic and evolutionary process: Stages in the HLC are indeterminate in length, and each stage is capable of preceding or following the other, as determined by interrupts. The following typology captures the nature of the household as it progresses through the HLC from formation to dissolution:

Newly formed households have members who are no longer dependent on others for maintenance and operationalization of household responsibilities. Household decision tasks and responsibilities are not clearly defined: This is the stage where household decision roles are clarified (e.g., a newly married couple).

Adaptive households are characterized by changes in composition, development of defined decision responsibilities, and/or changes in household types. The individual holds clear perceptions of household repsonsibilities but must adapt these to household needs (e.g., a divorced spouse deciding to cohabit).

Mature households have stabilized over time with changes in household composition or changes in decision task environments (e.g., a family household no longer having dependents).

Combining the age of the household with the underlying forces of the HLC (household type and presence or absence of dependents) suggests that positions in the life cycle are not predetermined but are evolutionary.

POSITIONS IN THE HOUSEHOLD LIFE CYCLE

The usefulness of household life cycle extends beyond providing marketers with a conceptual model of the household. The HLC as depicted in Figure 2–1 is intentionally general to allow both flexibility and also adaptability to any study of household decisionmaking. It is based on the three variables discussed earlier (household type, presence or absence of dependents, and household age). Implicit in Figure 2–1 is the household age variable, which cannot be preclassified. The figure shows the four major categories of household types that were discussed in the section on household type. Although these categories have been adapted to reflect the intent of this

Figure 2–1. Household Life Cycle.

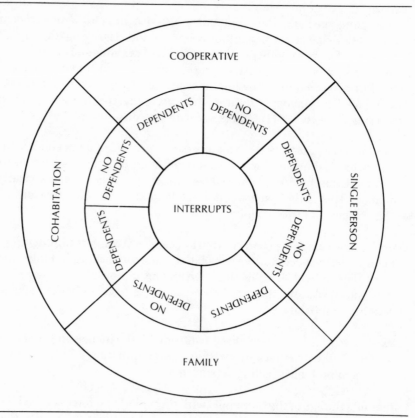

paper, Wortzel (1977a) applied a similar structure and classification scheme to explain the life styles of young adults. Three of his life cycle divisions (single, married, and cohabitation) are similar to their equivalents in the HLC, but Wortzel retained the use of the critical FLC determinant—age as the primary descriptor variable. In Figure 2-1, households are either single-person, family, cohabitation, or cooperatives. The discussion of each household type that follows suggests possible behaviors and trends.

Single-Person Households

A large part of the increase in nonfamily households comes from a 75 percent increase in the number of adults living alone with and without dependents. Of the 22.1 million nonfamily households in 1981, 18.9 million were headed by single adults. Kobrin (1976) has concluded that single-person households are the fastest-growing category of new household formations. Delayed marriages, increases in the rate of divorce, and changing social standards are thought to have contributed to these trends. Wortzel (1977b) contends that the single stage of the life cycle has changed its focus from mate-searching and marriage preparation to personal growth and enriching personal experience. Such shifts in the usual starting point for household formation have changed traditional patterns of purchase and consumption of household goods.

Formerly passed off as a phenomena only among young adults, the single-person household has now become a life style desired by all ages. Only a few studies explore the consumer behavior and decisionmaking practices of single-person households. Wortzel (1977a) provides the most comprehensive review of this area and focuses on the young-adult market. The lack of research in this area is directly attributable to the myopic viewpoint of those who research the traditional family unit.

As illustrated in the HLC, the single-person household is only one component in the cycle of household development. At any one point in time, an interrupt can occur that changes the composition or type of household (marriage, birth of child, change in habitation state, etc.). These interrupts also change the decision environment and decision practice of the single-person households. Researchers must address questions such as which decisions are made jointly that were once autonomous. Wortzel (1977a) has argued for several years that investigation of single-person households' purchase and consumption behavior should be an integrated part of any household study. The HLC is one step toward addressing this concern.

Family Households

The family household is by far the most representative of the traditional family life cycle. Our knowledge regarding household decision behavior is based entirely on this framework. Even with the dramatic increase among single-person households, traditional husband-and-wife households (with or without dependents) declined only slightly (2.4 percent) between 1970 and 1981. Approximately 60 percent of all households in 1981 were maintained by persons who were legally married and still living with their husband or wife.

Although the number of traditional married couples has changed very little, the decision practices within the households may have changed drastically. The increased number of working wives, the equal rights movement, and smaller families are thought to account for most of these changes. Research suggests that an increase in autonomy among household members (especially wives and children) has shifted the decisionmaking practices and role behaviors within the family unit (Haas 1980).

Evidence also suggests that the traditional family household based on the institution of marriage will continue to be strong in the future but that household family members will change more often and better express their personal needs. Other changes in the traditional family unit are an increased number of young adults who remain at home with their parents, fewer young adults who start new households (U.S. Bureau of the Census 1981c), and more parents who move in with their children. The net result of these structural changes in the household unit affects our conceptualizations of how families make purchase and consumption decisions.

Cohabitation Households

Cohabitation is a nontraditional family household that is not well documented. It is unknown whether cohabiters are reluctant to report their living status or whether researchers have not been able to adequately classify this group. Although cohabitation is typically believed to be a lifestyle practiced by young adults, cohabitation by all ages is increasing. Newcomb (1979) notes that cohabitation among older couples is increasing but reports a paucity of empirical research on the topic. While the reasons for the trend may be economic, its implications for household purchase and consumption behavior are dramatic.

It is believed that decisionmaking patterns of cohabiters are somewhat different from those of traditional family couples. Research suggests that cohabiters purchase very few household items and individually purchase and own personal care items. One reason for these differences may be the degree of commitment that exists or is perceived to exist between household members. One study by Danziger and Greenwald (1977:232) views commitment as being either: (1) casual, (2) transitory, (3) stable relationship, (4) trial marriage, or (5) permanent alternative to marriage. The Danziger and Greenwald classification scheme can be used as a starting point for understanding and explaining a cohabiting couple's purchase and comsumption behavior, and Wortzel (1977a) suggests that further study employ this framework. The decisionmaking practices of cohabitation households are worth studying not only because of their behavior as independent, unique household types, but also because the decision experiences of cohabiters will likely affect their decision behavior in any future household type.

Cooperative Households

One nontraditional form of household that has received little attention from researchers has been that of the cooperative. Cooperatives are households that contain at least two adult members with or without dependents. Although cooperative households are linked to young adults, especially college students, there is a trend toward shared living arrangements among older adults. Cooperative households are known to exist, but no attempts have been made to document their behavior as a viable unit of household analysis. From all indications, cooperatives exhibit consumer behavior as a unit, and their decision behavior is different from other household types.

As with cohabitation households, variations in cooperative arrangements are so numerous that discussion of the various types cannot adequately be covered in this paper. Cooperative households are believed to exist because of a commitment to the development and maintenance of a household for any number of reasons (economic, security, etc.). Danziger and Greenwald's (1977) classification makes three distinctions in an individual's commitment:

Convenience: Household members share common facilities but are behaviorally and economically independent. They remain members of the household as long as the situation is convenient for them.

Temporal: Household members share common facilities and decision-making tasks and may or may not be behaviorally and economically independent. They view the existence of the household as lasting for a specific time period.

Stable: Household members share facilities for a specific period of time as determined by a formal agreement. Decision behavior and economic responsibility is shared and defined by the formal agreement. Household members may change, but the existence of the household unit is viewed as lasting indefinitely.

The existence of the cooperative household and its degree of commitment is relevant only when examined in light of the household purchase and consumption decision process. Not one published study investigates this phenomena. One starting point for research could be a framework similar to the one that Wortzel (1977a) proposed relating type of ownership and decisionmaking to cooperative household type. Figure 2-2 illustrates how classifying cooperative household type by type of decisionmaking can lead to

Figure 2–2. Type of Ownership and Decisionmaking.

Cooperative Household Commitment	Autonomous		Dominant		Syncratic	
	Alternating	Parallel	Male	Female	Consensus	Concession
Convenience						
Temporal						
Stable						

Source: Wortzel (1977a).

new research questions and issues. Future research could describe the purchase and consumption behavior that applies to each square in the figure.

The household life cycle Figure (2–1) is dynamic and changes constantly due to interrupts that occur over the span of the HLC. Unlike the family life cycle, the HLC allows individuals to enter the life cycle at any stage under any of four household types. For example, a young adult may leave the parents' household and start his or her own by forming a single-person household or by moving into a cooperative situation. Subsequent moves through the life cycle may be ignited by significant interrupts in the system (i.e., marriage, graduation from college, birth of child, etc.). The ultimate dissolution of single-person household ends in death or a change in status to dependence in another household.

FUTURE RESEARCH DIRECTIONS

This discussion of household types has dramatized the need for researchers to examine family decisionmaking from the broad perspective of all households. The lack of information about nontraditional households has created a gap in knowledge about consumer decision practices. This section suggests possible directions for future research and the implications this research will have on understanding household decisionmaking.

Expanding the life cycle to include both traditional and nontraditional households automatically broadens the sample base. As many as 34 percent of respondent households in some FLC studies were not classified into one of the traditional stages. In contrast, the HLC accounts for the majority of household types and can be adapted to account for new forms.

The HLC's dynamic view of the traditional and nontraditional family encourages a longitudinal research perspective. It allows an individual to be traced through the HLC from birth as a dependent to the formation of his or her own household and its ultimate dissolution. This kind of study would allow investigation of the impact of generational effects on household decision practices. Evidence drawn by Stafford, Backman, and Dibona's (1977) study of the traditional family suggests that parental modeling has a strong impact on later household task division of labor.

Internal changes can affect household consumption processes, but changes external to the household can also have significant effects. For example, changing social norms regarding women's economic role have influenced the development of new household types and affected household decisionmaking processes. There is clear evidence of increasingly egalitarian sex role attitudes among today's households (Thornton and Freedman 1979; Cherlin and Walters 1981). The impact of these changes is not yet fully understood, but several studies (Scanzoni and Szinovacz 1980; Qualls 1982) suggest that shifting sex-role perceptions have resulted in a restructuring of household decision roles and responsibilities. We need to examine how these external changes influence the evolution of household decisionmaking patterns. As mentioned earlier, research indicates that over the FLC husband-and-wife decisionmaking shifts from jointly shared decisionmaking to more autonomous decisionmaking; our knowledge must be expanded to include nontraditional households.

Increases in the number of divorces and in the number of single-parent homes should renew researcher's interest in the influence of children in household decisionmaking. Very little is known about this type of decisionmaking behavior in the household, but it is believed that children learn decisionmaking skills from the socialization that occurs in the household. Research should be done on how the influences and interactions that a child encounters affect the decision influences and decisionmaking interactions that they develop within their own households.

Given the diversity of household types, research is clearly needed to assess how different household compositions differ in their decisionmaking processes and outcomes. Since many individuals are members of several households during their life spans, it would be useful to determine how consumers develop and learn to adapt their decisionmaking behaviors to a variety of household compositions.

Similarly, more information is needed on how interrupts alter HLC position, determine decisionmaking environments, and influence role adaptation among household members. For example, when a family household is interrupted by divorce, it re-forms into two households: Each individual takes different decision skills into different household types, and other individuals either adapt their own roles or require the original family household members to change theirs. By focusing on interrupts, we can study their causal effects on the decisionmaking structure of the household.

We have proposed three variables to distinguish between HLC stages, but further research is needed to validate and standardize a set of structural variables that researchers can use to form HLC stages. Since much consumption and many purchases occur at the household level, the household, not the individual, is the relevant unit of analysis. Marketers seek to explain and predict what products and services consumers will buy and what decision processes a particular type of household will employ. To meet this need, researchers must test the link between HLC and decision behavior.

Although researchers have extensively examined the role behavior of husbands and wives in the traditional family unit, one aspect that needs further attention is the role behavior of nontraditional household members. At this point, only assumptions or generalizations can be drawn regarding the likely household role behaviors. Marketers who focus only on traditional household units miss a substantial potential market and ignore the opportunity to facilitate the decisionmaking and socialization that occurs during the evolutionary life cycle of a household.

The research issues presented here only partially identify questions that must be answered by future research. It is hoped that they can provide an agenda for researchers to follow in focusing on household decision behavior.

CONCLUSIONS

This paper has critically examined the concept of the family life cycle and questioned both its use in marketing and the implicit assumption that the FLC is the appropriate conceptual tool for the study of household decision behavior. It introduces the household life cycle in order to provide marketers with an alternative model that encourages a developmental approach to the study of household decisionmaking.

The proposed model utilizes three dimensions to classify life cycle positions: age of household, household type, and the presence or absence of dependents. These variables allow households to be studied from their inception to their dissolution. Changes in life cycle positions occur in response to interrupts that exist in the system.

There are three primary differences between the FLC and HLC: (1) The FLC is a deterministic model whose fixed stages follow each other in a predetermined manner, while the HLC is dynamic and evolutionary in its development with positions in the cycle not predetermined but defined by household type, household's age, and presence or absence of dependents; (2) the FLC focuses only on the behavior of the traditional family unit, while the HLC encompasses both traditional and nontraditional family types; and (3) while the FLC was originally conceptualized to reflect developmental changes in the family unit, the HLC has been developed to reflect the purchase and consumption decision behavior of today's households.

Future research will test the assumption that the household life cycle is better than the FLC in explaining the relationship between household purchase and consumption behavior and life cycle position. This will involve studying how the decision processes of different household types in different life cycle positions evolve over time in response to various interrupts. The present paper has set the research agenda by illustrating changing household trends that do not fit into the concept of the family life cycle.

3 THE ROLE OF CHILDREN IN HOUSEHOLD DECISIONMAKING
Application of a New Taxonomy of Family Role Structure

Richard W. Olshavsky and Maryon F. King

Many researchers have urged that studies of consumer behavior focus less on the single individual and more on the family. They argue that most consumer purchases are made by families and that major changes are taking place in the internal structure of families.

Progress in the area of family decisionmaking has been hampered by several factors. Not only is research on family decisionmaking considerably more difficult and demanding than research on individuals, but researchers have lacked a comprehensive theory of family decisionmaking. Burns and Granbois (1980:221) discribed extant research in this area as:

> a preponderance of empirical studies and a paucity of recent theoretical or conceptual publications. . . . With notable exceptions, the theoretical underpinnings of the research studies are generated from subjective observation and a considerable amount of intuitive reasoning. Inductive logic and low levels of abstraction prevail.

Operationalizing and formalizing a comprehensive theory are complicated by the complex multi-individual, multi-interaction character of households.[1] Moreover, the researcher has been handicapped by imprecise terms and definitions. The concept of role structure has been the foundation for study of family choice processes, and it will be particularly problematic in further research.

This chapter refines the familiar and highly researched concept of role structure. It reviews a new taxonomy of family role structure, introduced by

41

Olshavsky and King (1982), and discusses the implications of this new taxonomy. Finally, in an application of this new taxonomy, the chapter sets forth some specific hypotheses about how the role of children changes across type of product, stage of the decision process, age of children, and number of children.

THE ROLE STRUCTURE CONCEPT

Much research on family choice processes focuses on identifying who in the family (husband or wife or both) is responsible for making the choice. This allocation of choice responsibility has been labeled "role structure," a concept borrowed from sociology. Davis and Riguax (1974) and others have identified husband-and-wife role structures that involve dominance by one spouse or the other. Davis and Rigaux (1974), Green and Cunningham (1975), and others also have identified the two choice processes that involve joint participation: (1) The "autonomic" involves a single dominant spouse who varies with circumstances; husband and wife perform the task equally often; (2) "syncratic" choice process involves *both* husband and wife. Filiatrault and Ritchie (1980), Davis (1970), Davis and Rigaux (1974), and others identify a modified type of shared choice processes in which one spouse has more influence than the other, and Filiatrault and Ritchie have found some influence exerted by the children.

While identification and description of these basic types of relationships have significantly advanced understanding of family decisionmaking, these four categories fail to describe all of the important structural arrangements that families involving two or more persons can adopt. In particular, "husband dominant," "wife dominant," and "autonomic" all refer to a structural arrangement in which only one individual is involved. Only the syncratic category allows for interaction between two individuals or more. In addition, the manner in which these individuals are organized structurally is completely ignored.

There also has been a paucity of research describing the specific nature of the influence that children and other extended family members exert on the family choice process, especially how children influence the type of choice-process structure adopted. Extant studies dealing with the family role structures avoid the fact that the family functions as a small group (Granbois 1963; E.P. Cox 1975 in which children and other family members may substantially influence the family choice process (Davis 1976; Filiatrault and Ritchie 1980; Turk and Bell 1972). Previous research, which deals primarily with dyadic relationships, has not recognized that family decision structures approximate the structure adopted by small groups. As Davis (1976) notes, the "family" in most studies of household decisionmaking is in reality just the husband and wife. The few attempts to incorporate children into the decisionmaking structure have taken the dyadic form as well (e.g. wife and child, parents and children (Bernhardt 1975)).

ROLE STRUCTURE VERSUS ROLE ADOPTION

It is important to distinguish between role structure (the interrelationship between roles that is adopted by the family for a particular decision process or stage thereof) and role adoption (the adoption of particular roles by individual members of the family within the selected configuration). The emphasis in this chapter is on role structure—that is how members of a family arrange themselves within the decisionmaking process—and not on the specific roles that various individuals within the family adopt within any selected structure. Extant research on the role structure concept fails to distinguish between the purely structural aspects of a family unit (i.e., role structure or configuration) and the functions performed by the various members of the family unit (role adoption).

A number of research findings have indicated that individuals within the decisionmaking unit are unable to determine or recognize which role they actually adopted within the particular decisionmaking process (Davis 1970; Granbois and Willett 1970; Park 1982). This confusion regarding role adoption may have two separate causes. First, individual members of the household may adopt multiple roles during the various stages of a particular decision process and may be unable to recognize this multiplicity of roles. Second, individual members of the decisionmaking unit may not understand the types of role interrelationships that may be adopted during a decision process and the flexibility of role adoption over the stages of the decision process; therefore, members of a household may be unable to articulate their various and changing relationships with other members of the decisionmaking unit over the course of a decision process. The new taxonomy discussed in this chapter can help researchers as well as respondents to more accurately recognize and classify the roles and the relationships adopted by members of a household over the course of a decision process.[2]

A New Taxonomy of Family Role Structure

The concept of a family role structure suffers from a number of limitations. In an attempt to overcome these limitations, Olshavsky and King (1982) developed a new taxonomy of family role structure based on the distributed processing system now used in designing computer systems. Distributed processing is a system in which networks of computers linked by telecommunications perform information processing tasks. Its two basic classes are: (1) homogeneous systems, in which similar computers are linked together in order to share processing tasks, and (2) heterogeneous systems, in which specialized computers each perform a specific function or process different types of information (J. Martin 1981). The network's design depends on the nature of the task: Computers may be programmed to perform specific functions independently or to "cooperate with one another to solve a common set of problems." (J. Martin 1981: 96). In cooperative processing, a task may be initiated by one computer and completed by another or simultaneously processed by several computers before it is completed. Basic alternative configurations described by systems designers are the hierarchical form, the ring form, the two star forms, and the parallel form (described below and illustrated in Figure 3–1). While these configurations represent the basic forms used in distributed processing systems, Olshavsky and King (1982) note that an almost endless array of hybrid configurations may be formed from two or more of the basic forms.

Hierarchical Form

The hierarchical form is established by arranging a number of computers in a "line" that contains computers with differing levels of processing ability and therefore differing ranks (i.e., either more functional capacity or more stored information). The information or problem is generally introduced to the lowest-level computer, which proceeds to process the information. In the event this computer cannot fully process the information due to inadequate (limited) hardware or software, the partially processed problem is passed up the line to the next level, a more sophisticated computer, where the information is further processed. This procedure continues until the problem is completely solved and output is made available. In addition, information can be introduced at any level to any computer in the line. Each computer has input and output capability, that enables it to accept information and output results. Thus, all computers can work on problems simultaneously, and nested hierarchies may exist.

Ring Form

The ring form consists of several computers in a "circle," which allows any computer to communicate (directly or indirectly) with any other computer

Figure 3–1. Alternative Structures within a Multi-Individual Consumer Unit.

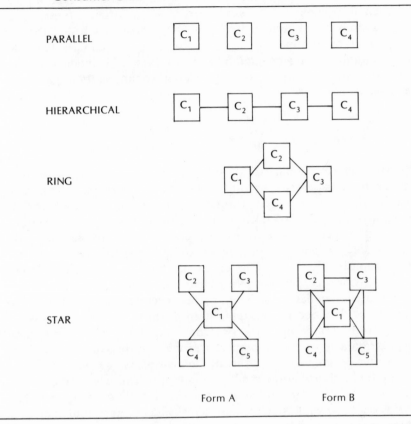

in the ring. Each computer has input and output capability, enabling it to accept information to be processed. Each computer in the ring is designed to process different information; generally the software packages are diverse, while the hardware is similar. There is no rank or hierarchical ordering with respect to the intelligence or ability of each individual computer; they mainly differ with respect to the type of information they can process and thus are accorded peer status.

Star Form

There are two types of star configurations. Both employ a central computer and several satellite computers, with the central computer acting as a coordinating and information storage unit. Information to be processed may be introduced to any of the satellites or fed into the central computer and then distributed to the satellite computers. After processing, all information is stored in the central unit. Output may flow from either the central unit or any of the satellite computers. Version B allows for communication among the satellites as well as between individual satellites and the central computer; only the latter communication pattern is available in version A.

Parallel Form

The parallel form is unlike any of the other three: It lacks formal linkages between the computers operating within its configuration. The parallel form consists of two or more computers working on the same problem simultaneously but independently and occurs in basically two situations. First, this replication of efforts may occur in order to "fail safe" the problem-solving process. Since each computer is independently and simultaneously solving the same problem, a built-in double check system exists that insures consensus on the problem solution. This type of system is typically used in military installations where decisionmaking of a high-risk nature takes place. Second, this replication of efforts may occur as a result of lack of communication. Two or more computers within the same organization may work on a particular problem at the same time without the systems personnel being aware of the multiple assignment; inefficiencies and replication of effort result. Parallel form is included in the present discussion of alternative configurations primarily to illustrate how so-called distributed processing systems can actually degenerate into individual processors under particular circumstances.

It should be noted that while four basic distributed processing configurations have been described, an almost endless array of hybrid configurations may be formed from two or more of the basic forms. For example, the star form (either version) may be combined with the hierarchical form to result in a star configuration in which the central computer is of higher rank order than the satellite computers.

IMPLICATIONS OF THE NEW CONCEPT

Several advantages characterize this new distributed processing concept of role structure. First, it is relatively easy to use this new concept to organize past research based on role structures. Old role structures can be mapped onto the new configurations defined in distributed processing systems. Role structures that involve dominance suggest the hierarchical form. In this configuration, the entire decisionmaking process may be made by the dominant spouse, or the nondominant spouse (lower rank order) may initiate the decision process while the spouse of higher rank order takes this partially processed information and makes the ultimate choice. Nested hierarchies may be conceptualized as children dominated by one parent, who in turn is dominated by the other parent.

Role structures that involve the autonomic category are also reflected in the hierarchical form. As with the dominance category, the entire decisionmaking process may be made by one spouse, or the nondominant spouse may initiate the decision process while the other spouse takes this information and completes the processing task. The distinguishing feature of the autonomic category is simply that on different occasions *either* spouse plays the dominant role.

The syncratic role structure category recognizes that two or more individuals may be involved in the decision process. The precise structure adopted is left unspecified, yet several possibilities include the hierarchical, the ring, the star (forms A and B), and the parallel. It is important to identify which particular structure is adopted because of the differences in information processing capabilities that characterize these structures. For example, the ring structure is superior to the parallel structure in terms of information processing capacity and efficiency.

The above illustrations of the use of the new concept are by no means exhaustive. Any previously published study in the area of family choice processes and role structure can readily be incorporated within this framework by using one of the basic configurations or some hybrid configuration. Indeed, this model should encourage researchers to identify more precise types of role structures that have been studied in the past. Further, this framework is extremely flexible because several of these structures may be collapsed to handle dyads and all may be expanded to include more family members.

Certain configurations resemble a single individual engaging in choice processes. For example, if in the hierarchical form one individual can accomplish the entire task alone, then there is no difference between individual or family choice processes. Similarly, the parallel form illustrates the juncture of family and individual choice processing. The original role structure concept can adequately capture the situation in which family decisionmaking does not differ from individual decisionmaking, but by convention such structures are viewed as family choice processes. This refined concept of role structure has the potential to bridge the gap between existing theories of individual choice processes and family choice processes. While it is beyond the scope of this paper to present a new theory of family choice processes, we believe that a viable theory can be achieved by an appropriate extension of the information-processing theories of Bettman (1979) and Newell and Simon (1972).

This new concept offers a degree of precision and richness that escaped researchers who used the simpler concept of role structure. While role structure involves only a few specific types of intrafamily relationships (i.e., dominance, autonomic, syncratic), the distributed-processing concept encompasses the entire range of configurations possible within a family or household. The syncratic structure in particular is replaced with a preciser and richer set of structural configurations.

In addition, the new concept can help describe more precisely the dynamic and subtle changes that occur in role structure. Several studies have identified changes in role structure across products (Davis 1970), across stages of the decision process (Davis and Rigaux 1974), and across stages of the family life cycle (Ferber and Lee 1974). The new concept may guide the discovery of more and different types of transition phases (e.g., from star form A to form B)

APPLICATION OF THE NEW TAXONOMY

Olshavsky and King (1982) indicate that children can influence in either or both of two ways. The child can influence the goal formulation process by simply being an integral member of the family with wants and needs that must be satisfied, or the child (depending upon his or her abilities) can play an active role in the choice process as an additional information-processing individual. Extant studies are unclear about which of these two influence processes is involved; here the focus is only on the role that children play in the choice process.

In general, children participate in family decisionmaking in any one of the five structures identified by Olshavsky and King. For example, children can participate as equal partners in the ring structure or as less capable participants in the hierarchical structure. The various structures adopted within particular households deserve attention. It is hypothesized that the particular structure adopted will be determined by variables such as the type of product or service involved, the stage of the decisionmaking process, and the age and number of children.[3]

Type of Product

Previous research (Davis 1970; Ferber and Nicosia 1972) has found that role structure changes across types of products and services. It is expected that when children are involved, the structure will also change. In general, we expect that as the expense and importance (risk) of a product increases, the star structure or hierarchical structure will be adopted. For less important purchases the ring structure will be adopted, and for certain types of personal goods (e.g., clothing) the parallel structure will be adopted.

Stage of Decision Process

Previous research has found that family role structure varies across stages of the decisionmaking process (Davis and Rigaux 1974). It is expected that when children are involved similar changes will occur. In general, we expect that the information-acquisition stage will be characterized by the ring or parallel structure, that the evaluation stage will involve the hierarchical or star structure, and that, depending on the nature of the product, children may be excluded from the evaluation stage completely.

Age of Children

Age is used here as a proxy for stage of general cognitive development and degree of socialization (Flavell 1963). Accordingly it is expected that as children grow older they will play a progressively greater role in family decisionmaking. Specifically we expect the structure to vary as follows:

Infancy (age 0 to 2). It is expected that during infancy children will play a minor or inconsequential role in decisionmaking directly; in effect, the infant is excluded from the structure. Indirectly, however, the infant can change or influence the structure adopted by other members of the household whenever the care of the infant demands time from one or more of the members. A ring formation may shift to a hierarchical structure with the arrival of a newborn. It must be recognized that certain other effects may result from the presence of an infant. For example, if the mother stops working temporarily in order to care for the newborn, then the mother may have more time than in the past and the structure may shift from, say, a hierarchical to a ring form.

Preadolescence (age 3 to 12). During preadolescence we may expect that children will participate but in a limited fashion. Hence, the star form and the hierarchical forms are expected. For certain products (e.g., toys) or stages (e.g., information search) even very young children may share an equal role, and the ring and parallel forms may appear.

Adolescence (age 13 to 18). At this stage, the child approaches adult cognitive capacity (Flavell 1963), and we expect that for many products and services the child will play an equal role. This means the parallel or ring structures are most likely to be adopted. Certain adolescent and parent relationships may be so strained, however, that certain types of structures may not occur. Personality problems that so frequently occur among teenagers may preclude certain structures and result in the parallel structure.

Number of Children

As the number of children increases from one to several we expect that certain systematic changes in structure will result. Before examining these changes, however, it should be noted that the number of children affects the structure in ways that cannot be completely separated from the ways that the ages of the children affect the structure. The interaction of these effects is, at least in part, responsible for the structure adopted. In addition, the presence of one or more children within the household may cause either an increase or a decrease in the responsibility assumed by other family members.

One Child. Two different situations must be considered in determining the structural changes that may be attributed to the entrance of a single child into a household. First is the situation in which the child enters a household that consists of only one adult. In this case, the adult has adopted an autocratic approach to decisionmaking, and the influence exhibited by the child (again, depending upon the child's age) can be almost limitless. In this situation, any of the structures described for dual households may be adopted, depending on the nature of the decision to be made and the stage of the decision process. The second situation involves the entrance of a single child into a household consisting of two (or more) adults. In this case, the child may participate in an existing ring or hierarchical structure or may cause the structure to shift so that rather than adopting a hierarchical structure, the household adopts a star form or perhaps shifts an existing star formation, to a more equalized ring formation. As previously noted, the presence of a child may result in an increase *or* decrease in the degree of participation of other family members in the decisionmaking process. This scenario is significant, especially in light of the rapidly increasing number of single-parent households, and warrants extensive future research.

Two Children. An interesting phenomenon may occur when a household contains two children. Rather than acting independently, the two children may elect to pool their influence, resulting in the adoption of a ring formation consisting of three units (mother, father, and the two children acting as one unit) in lieu of the more likely star or hierarchical form. This phenomenon would most likely occur when the children are preadolescent (age 3 to 12) and when the pending decision is important to them.

Three or More Children.   With three or more children in a household, it is unlikely that (except for very young children) a strict hierarchical form will be adopted. A ring formation probably would not be feasible because of the large number of interacting members would cause the decision process to become unwieldy and disorganized. It is expected that one of the star forms (A when the children are in early preadolescence and B when they are in later preadolescence) would most likely be adopted. As the children progress through adolescence, the parallel structure would be adopted more and more frequently.

CONCLUSIONS

This paper has applied a new and more comprehensive taxonomy of family role structure to situations in which children are included in the household and thus directly or indirectly influence the household decisionmaking process. While the hypotheses advanced here require empirical validation, they far extend extant theoretical development, which deals primarily with dyadic relationships. This paper not only indicates important areas of future empirical research but offers a framework for classifying and interpreting such empirical endeavors:

1. This taxonomy incorporates both direct and indirect influence of children.
2. This taxonomy accounts for varying types and degrees of influence exhibited by virtually any number or age of children.
3. This taxonomy offers greater precision than was previously possible in defining the interaction of two or more individuals engaged in the decisionmaking process.
4. This taxonomy can easily handle changes that occur during the family life cycle and can model household relationships despite rapidly changing composition of family life cycle stages.
5. This taxonomy can be implemented and measured as easily as the old taxonomy (but as illustrated, with far more precise results) and can be used to classify any of the extant empirical studies on family decisionmaking.
6. This taxonomy can be integrated with existing consumer information-processing models (e.g., Bettman 1979; Newell and Simon 1972).

NOTES

1. For a more complete discussion regarding operationalization of family decisionmaking theory, see Hendrix and Qualls (this volume) on operationalizing family-level constructs.
2. The taxonomy of role structures discussed in this paper can easily be interfaced with the model of household role allocation offered by Roberts and Wortzel (this volume).
3. For a more extensive discussion of the effects of the household life cycle on family decisionmaking, see Bristor and Qualls (this volume).

4 OPERATIONALIZING FAMILY-LEVEL CONSTRUCTS
Problems and Prospects
Philip E. Hendrix and William J. Qualls

Much of the marketing research literature describes and explains variations in patterns of consumer behavior. The unit of analysis is typically the individual consumer, despite the obvious importance of the family as a decisionmaking and consumption unit. Davis (1976) notes several factors that emphasize the appropriateness of the family as the unit of analysis: (1) A significant number of products and services are "jointly consumed," such as entertainment, housing, food, and others; (2) even for products and services consumed by individuals (e.g., cosmetics, clothing), other family members represent one of the most important sources of feedback and influence (Ostlund 1973); and (3) stages in the consumption process (such as initiating, deciding, purchasing, etc.) may be divided among family members, and in such cases "a sole focus on the individual could be quite misleading" (Wind 1978:657).

The prevailing focus on the individual as the unit of analysis ignores group-level constructs fundamental to our understanding of consumer behavior. As various researchers have observed, the lack of such measures impedes the development of theory and practical applications (Roscoe, LeClaire, and Schiffman 1977). In the area of market segmentation, for example, consumption measures often reflect household buying behavior, while measures for many independent variables correspond to a single household member. Frank, Massy, and Wind (1972) conclude that this inconsistency impedes explanations of variation in consumption across households. In addition, the limited success that researchers have had in explaining consumer behavior with personality variables may be attributed to the exclusion of other more pertinent measures, such as preferences of family members (Kassarjian 1971). Frank, Massy, and Wind (1972) suggest that a widely discussed analysis of the relationship between personality and brand ownership (Evans 1959) may have yielded quite different results had the personality characteristics of both husband and wife, as opposed to husband alone, been included. Undoubtedly in many other instances the choice of some multiperson unit of analysis, such as husband and wife or family, would be more appropriate than that of the individual (Michman 1980).

Problems are associated with the adoption of a multiperson unit of analysis in consumer behavior, however, Wind (1978:657) noted that researchers tend to ignore the multiperson issue for the following reasons:

1. conceptual difficulties involving the development of multiperson variables and hypotheses;
2. methodological difficulties involving the analysis of the multiperson data;
3. operational difficulties involving added time and monetary costs for collection and analysis of multiperson data.

This paper proposes to demonstrate that the difficulties associated with conceptualizing and operationalizing multiperson constructs are not insurmountable. After a brief review of the literature of measures useful in describing and analyzing multiperson consumer behavior, the paper presents measures used to operationalize selected constructs. The data are drawn from a national study conducted by the Institute for Social Research in 1976 in which both spouses provided a wide array of information about their lifestyles. Since data from children were not available, our analyses focus on the husband-and-wife dyad. Hypotheses are also presented to further suggest the potential usefulness of the measures. This study is an exploratory effort designed to stimulate interest in a largely unexplored area. As such, its results should be regarded as preliminary and subject to refinement and extension.

RESEARCH ON FAMILY CONSTRUCTS

Research on family constructs appears in four somewhat different contexts. The first set of measures is concerned primarily with household socioeconomic and demographic characteristic (Ellis 1975; Lansing and Morgan 1955; Murphy and Staples 1979; Wells and Gubar 1966). The second set of measures in consumer behavior literature examines the decisionmaking processes that precede the choice and acquisition of various goods and services (Davis 1976). This research, which comprises the majority of work done related to the family in the consumer behavior literature, has characterized households in terms of authority and power, responsibility for various tasks, conflict, and other relevant dimensions.

The third set of measures, developed and used primarily in family sociology, includes a large number of social and psychological constructs (Bagarozzi and Wodarski 1977; Booth and Welch 1978; Clark, Van Nye, and Gecas 1978; Haas 1980; Jaco and Shepard 1975; Jorgensen 1979; Walker 1973). The fourth and most useful set of measures relevant to the household is drawn from the organizational literature. In one of the few papers addressing the topic, Wind (1978) argues that concepts related to organizational buying behavior may be extended to household consumer behavior. Although his arguments are compelling, few attempts have been made to operationalize the concepts he proposed or to test the related propositions empirically.

Two other references to the marketing literature are noteworthy. Some time ago, Alderson (1957) suggested that households vary along two dimensions that affect their consumption behavior: (1) compatibility of members' attitudes and preferences and (2) coordination of goal-directed activities. Alderson speculated that the uncoordinated, incompatible family is likely to be an unpredictable purchasing unit. Such families may also be less likely to engage in consumption that requires pooling of resources or extended commitments (e.g., they may rent instead of purchase a home). In one of the few empirical studies related to the topic, E.P. Cox (1975) examined the consequences of what he called the process of adjustment within families—that is, the convergence in lifestyles and preferences, the degree of role specialization, and so forth—that occurs over the life of the family. The results, though limited in scope, were generally supportive of the hypothesized process.

An ample number of sources, therefore, provide potentially useful household-level constructs. In light of their demonstrated applicability to organizational buyer behavior, Wind's (1978) concepts appear to be especially appropriate candidates for further development. Those measures cover a wide range of variables and provide an effective vehicle for operationalizing family-level constructs. The next section presents operationalizations for several concepts, most of which are discussed in Wind (1978). Although the measures presented are drawn from existing data, it is hoped that alternative, superior measures will be developed.

FAMILY CONSTRUCTS: OPERATIONALIZATIONS

Demographics

As noted above, demographic and socioeconomic characteristics of households have been more widely studied than other measures, but only a small subset from the potential array has been extensively examined. This section focuses on measures that have received less attention in the literature but nonetheless appear promising.

Some demographics may be applied interchangeably to either individuals or households (e.g., region, community, housing status), although the resulting distributions will differ according to the unit of analysis. Other variables, such as income, hours worked, and so forth, may be extended to the household level by aggregating across individuals. Households may not, however, view such aggregates as homogeneous: For example, the wife's income may be viewed differently from that of the husband. Equivalence should not be assumed, and composite measures should be evaluated critically.

Other individual variables may also be aggregated to the household level, although alternative representations may be more useful. The total age of husband and wife would seem to be less useful, for example, than their mean or median age or perhaps the difference between their ages. A joint distribution, as shown in Table 4-1, may provide even more insights, particularly with finer categorizations. Such a representation may reveal, for instance, a decreasing age differential between spouses, which implies a corresponding decrease in the projected number of future households comprised of widows. A similar cross-tabulation on employment status (Table 4-2) clearly identifies the significant proportion of households in which both the spouses are employed outside the home, a phenomenon of considerable importance in marketing (Bartos 1978a; Ferber and Birnbaum 1980; Reilly 1982; Strober and Weinberg 1980). Another joint distribution (not presented here) shows a high degree of similarity between spouses'

Table 4–1.   Husband's Age versus Wife's Age.

| Wife's Age | Husband's Age | | | |
	18 to 32	33 to 50	51 to 97	Subtotal
18 to 32	29.0%	5.8%	0.0%	34.8%
33 to 50	1.5%	29.3%	5.8%	36.6%
51 to 97	0.0%	0.8%	27.8%	28.5%
Subtotal	30.6%	35.9%	33.6%	N = 792

Table 4–2. Husband's Employment Status versus Wife's Employment Status.

Wife's Status	Husband's Status			
	Unemployed	Employed part-time	Employed full-time	Subtotal
Unemployed	14.3%	1.3%	40.1%	55.7%
Employed part-time	0.6%	0.2%	5.9%	6.8%
Employed full-time	5.1%	0.1%	32.3%	37.5%
Subtotal	20.0%	1.5%	78.3%	

Table 4–3. Number of Years Married.

1 to 5 Years	6 to 15 Years	16 to 25 Years	More than 25 Years
15.9%	27.0%	29.9%	36.2%
n = 123	n = 209	n = 162	n = 280

education: The correspondence may affect the division of power within the household and task allocation.

In contrast to the measures examined above, other household demographics have no counterpart at the individual level. Table 4–3 shows, for instance, the number of years that couples have been married; such a measure may indicate family stability or, as used by E.P. Cox (1975), congruence between spouses. Still other measures have counterparts at the individual level, but nonetheless are difficult to assign uniquely to household members—for example, assets and liabilities as evidenced by divorce proceedings.

These types of household demographics, then, may be profitably operationalized. While some measures from this group, such as family life cycle, have been used extensively, there remains considerable potential for further research and development.

Roles

The concept of role is multifaceted (Nye and Gecas 1976). Role norms prescribe certain responsibilites, while role enactment pertains to actual behavior. Role identification refers to the intrinsic satisfaction or dissatisfaction individuals derive from performing activities associated with the role. Role conflict may arise because an individual's roles are incompatible, because one's role norms differ from norms held by others, or because one lacks appropriate role behavior (Goode 1960; Marks 1977). Each of these may be measured at the household level.

Role norms held by various household members, for example, are likely to be important determinants of various facets of household production (Becker and Michael 1973; Etgar 1978), including who does what, when, how, and according to whose standards. These facets of household production must be taken into account in developing and implementing marketing strategies. Evidence of such role norms can be provided by responses to the statement, "There is some work which is for men and some work which is for women." Sixty percent of the men and 40 percent of the women who responded agreed with this statement. Furthermore, 28 percent of the women wished their husbands would help more with household chores, which may be attributable to spouses' differing role norms.

Role identification is another important construct. Table 4–4 shows the joint distribution of spouses' enjoyment of three household tasks: cooking, household repairs, and grocery shopping. Interestingly, both spouses

Table 4–4. Husband's versus Wife's Enjoyment of Three Household Activities.

	Husband		
Wife	Does not enjoy	Enjoys	Subtotal
Does not enjoy	18.6%[a]	12.4%	31.0%
	25.6%[b]	43.5%	69.1%
	50.9%[c]	15.5%	66.4%
Enjoys	40.3%	28.7%	69.0%
	11.1%	19.8%	30.9%
	22.9%	10.7%	33.6%
Subtotal	58.9%	41.1%	N = 499
	36.7%	63.3%	
	73.8%	26.2%	

a. Cooking.
b. Home repairs.
c. Grocery shopping.

reportedly enjoy cooking in nearly 30 percent of the households. Neither spouse enjoys grocery shopping in slightly over one-half of the households. Such joint role identities may contribute to very different patterns of household role behavior. For example, households in which neither spouse enjoys a task such as cooking may delegate the task to the market by using convenience foods or eating out instead of preparing meals in the home. Households in which only one spouse enjoys the activity may be characterized by a higher degree of role specialization, while households in which both spouses enjoy the activity may exhibit role overlap. It would be particularly interesting to examine how responsibility is determined for a task which neither spouse enjoys.

Role enactment and resulting division of responsibilities among household members have received significant attention in recent years (Berheide, Berk, and Berk 1976; Berk and Berk 1978). Accurately measuring role behavior is not as straightforward as it may seem, however, as recent studies have shown (Berk and Shih 1980; Hendrix and Qualls 1978). Although men are supposedly increasing their share of household chores, Table 4-5 shows that the reported division of responsibility differs depending upon the sex of the respondent. Additional evidence suggests that males tend to overstate their participation in housework, perhaps in order to appear more consistent with emerging norms.

Role conflict in the household may arise because the husband or wife occupies a role that is inconsistent with the spouse's preferences. In households in which both spouses are employed, for instance, 44 percent of the husbands would prefer that their wife not work outside the home. In contrast, only 14 percent of the husbands whose wives are not employed would prefer that their spouse work outside of the home. Conflict may also arise because household members lack the time to adequately satisfy the various roles they occupy. Table 4-6 shows the joint distribution of spouses' responses to the question, "How often are you rushed to do the things you have to do?" Both spouses in one out of ten households are always rushed, while both spouses in nearly two-thirds of the households are at least sometimes rushed. These figures indicate the varying degrees of role conflict within households. The sources and consequences of such conflict warrant closer examination.

Household Technology

Very different mixes of goods and services are owned and consumed by households. For instance, Table 4-7 shows the number of time-saving appliances owned by households; Table 4-8 shows the number of "productive goods"; and Table 4-9, the number of leisure goods. The

Table 4–5. Subjective Report of Responsibility for Household Tasks by Sex of Respondent.

		Household Task					
		Cooking		Household Cleaning		Grocery Shopping	
		Male	Female	Male	Female	Male	Female
Response to Question "Who usually does the (task)?"	Wife	76.8%	93.6%	68.7%	89.7%	48.4%	75.4%
	Husband and Wife	13.7%	4.6%	19.0%	8.8%	35.3%	20.5%
	Husband	9.5%	1.9%	12.3%	1.5%	16.3%	4.1%
	N	285	373	268	340	312	391
	x^2	39.09		48.17		61.41	
	Probability	0		0		0	

Table 4–6. Husband's versus Wife's Feeling of Being Rushed.

Wife	Husband			
	Always	Sometimes	Almost Never	Subtotal
Always	10.6%	10.6%	3.5%	24.8%
Sometimes	14.7%	28.3%	7.0%	49.9%
Almost Never	4.7%	11.9%	8.7%	25.3%
Subtotal	30.0%	50.8%	19.2%	N = 573

Table 4–7. Number of Time-Saving Appliances Owned by Households.

0	1	2	3	4	5 or more	
14.8%	14.0%	18.9%	20.7%	15.5%	16.1%	N = 1500

Table 4–8. Number of Productive Goods Owned by Households[a].

0	1	2	3	4 to 5	
14.9%	26.7%	19.6%	23.4%	15.4%	N = 1120

a. Sewing machine, power drill, garden tractor, power garden tools, power saw.

various role dimensions discussed earlier significantly affect the technology present in households: Identifying these and other factors affecting the household's stock of technology is important for consumer behavior research (Strober and Weinberg 1980; McFall 1969). An equally important concern is the influence that technology exerts on household behavior (Stafford and Duncan 1979). Do households that possess numerous productive goods spend most of their leisure time in activities related to the home, such as gardening or woodworking? How does subscribing to cable television affect viewing behavior? As more information becomes available via cable, subscribers (25 percent of households in our sample) may shop

Table 4–9. Number of Leisure Goods Owned by Households.

0 to 4	5 to 6	7 or more	
29.0%	42.4%	28.6%	N = 1147

differently (Rosenberg and Hirschman 1980). Measures of household technology, as presented above, stimulate these and similar questions.

Authority Structure

Households exhibit very different patterns of authority, ranging from democratic to autocratic. The consumer behavior literature has paid considerable attention to how decisions are reached and who exerts how much influence, particularly during the various stages of acqusition (Burns and Granbois 1980; Davis and Rigaux 1974). Table 4–10 presents the responses of both husband and wife about who has more say in each of six decisions: whether the wife works; with whom the couple socializes; which relatives are visited; when the couple goes out; which television programs are watched; and how much money is spent for various major items. The marginal responses provided by husbands and wives are similar, with a few exceptions: For example, wives claim more influence on "couples seen" than husbands attribute to them, and wives attribute considerably more influence to their husbands on "TV programs watched" than husbands claim.

Within households the extent of disagreement is considerable: The degree to which spouses' perceptions differ is dramatic. For example, 42 percent disagree as to who has more say regarding the wife's working. Responses in one out of four households are direct opposites. Similar patterns typify each of the other dimensions examined. Such intra-household disparities may limit the usefulness of responses obtained from one or the other spouse (Granbois and Willet 1970). On the other hand, the extent, causes, and consequences of such differences are topics worth examining (Berk and Shih 1980).

Preferences

The joint preferences of individuals within households are rarely examined despite their relevance in analyses of activities in which household members participate (e.g., eating out, attending movies, or attending

Table 4–10.   Who Has More Say in Six Decisions.

Wife's Response	Husband's Response			
	Husband	Equal	Wife	Subtotal
Husband	11.8%[a]	3.6%	10.5%	25.9%
	16.5%[b]	8.1%	8.5%	33.1%
	8.8%[c]	9.4%	6.4%	24.6%
	24.5%[d]	10.3%	9.2%	43.9%
	32.2%[e]	13.3%	10.5%	56.0%
	25.7%[f]	9.6%	10.2%	45.4%
Equal	2.5%	2.2%	4.9%	9.6%
	5.8%	12.2%	7.2%	25.2%
	5.5%	18.2%	12.1%	35.7%
	7.2%	9.6%	7.4%	24.2%
	4.6%	11.6%	5.5%	21.7%
	7.0%	14.0%	5.7%	26.8%
Wife	14.1%	6.5%	44.0%	64.5%
	9.9%	13.2%	18.6%	41.7%
	6.8%	14.5%	18.4%	39.7%
	9.0%	10.3%	12.7%	31.9%
	5.5%	5.0%	11.8%	22.3%
	8.3%	7.9%	11.7%	27.8%
Subtotal	28.3%	12.3%	59.4%	N = 448
	32.2%	33.5%	34.3%	N = 484
	21.1%	42.1%	36.8%	N = 456
	40.6%	30.1%	29.3%	N = 458
	42.2%	30.0%	27.8%	N = 457
	41.0%	31.4%	27.6%	N = 471

a. Wife working.
b. Couples seen.
c. Relatives seen.
d. When couples go out.
e. Television programs watched.
f. Amount spent on high-cost items.

Table 4–11. Husband's and Wife's Preferences for Home versus Market-Supplied Services.

Wife	Husband		
	Home	Market	Subtotal
	35.1%[a]	7.8%	42.9%
Home	48.7%[b]	18.7%	67.4%
	39.3%[c]	14.9%	54.2%
	39.7%	17.3%	57.0%
Market	17.9%	14.7%	32.6%
	22.0%	23.8%	45.8%
	74.8%	25.1%	N = 473
	65.7%	34.3%	N = 472
	61.3%	38.7%	N = 463

a. Meals (home-cooked versus restaurant).
b. Movies.
c. Music.

concerts). Table 4–11 shows the joint preferences of spouses for these three activities. Again, such a representation is revealing: For example, both spouses prefer viewing a movie in the theatre instead of at home in only 14.7 percent of the households, in contrast to the nearly 50 percent of the households in which both spouses prefer viewing movies at home. Table 4–11 also reveals that husbands are more apt to prefer home-cooked meals than eating out, both absolutely and relative to the preferences of their wives. In fact, there exists a substantial proportion of households (40%) in which the wife would prefer to eat out while the husband would prefer a home-cooked meal (perhaps because the wife is generally responsible for preparing the meals). As Kassarjian (1971) has noted, such information regarding joint preferences and attitudes may help explain consumer behavior more effectively than the individual-level measures alone.

Domain Consensus

The phenomena above may be due in part to the varying degrees of domain consensus between spouses. One out of eight wives feels that her husband does not understand her very well.

Interaction

The lack of domain consensus may in turn result from infrequent interaction or communication. Evidence from the time use study reveals that the degree of communication between spouses varies significantly across households. Furthermore, spouses' perceptions of the frequency of talking with one another differ considerably.

Satisfaction

All of the constructs examined above are likely to affect spouses' satisfaction. Despite differences in perceptions and infrequent communication, spouses reportedly enjoy spending time together, have relatively few problems getting along, and describe their marriage as relatively happy. The satisfaction corresponding to specific role behaviors of spouses (e.g., housework) may vary more widely, however.

Social Orientation

Additional analyses reveal that households tend to have stronger ties to friends than to relatives. Visits with friends are much more frequent than visits with relatives. The wife's relatives are visited slightly more often than the husband's.

CONCLUSION

The measures presented above are designed to suggest how family-level constructs may be operationalized and to stimulate discussion regarding their potential usefulness. Such measures have been examined in a number of different contexts, although discussions in the consumer behavior literature have remained largely conceptual in nature, for reasons noted above. The empirical evidence presented suggests that operationalizing family-level constructs (actually husband-and-wife measures here) can reveal unique and potentially useful insights that cannot be derived from analyses of individual consumer behavior.

Additional conceptual and empirical work in this area is needed, and work that extends Wind's discussion (1978) would be particularly useful. Empirical research that examines the validity and explanatory power of such measures is also needed. Despite seminal articles (Davis 1976) encouraging comsumer researchers to devote more of their attention to family consumption, the potential of this area is yet to be realized.

II HOUSEHOLD ROLES

5 RECENT ADVANCES IN RESEARCH ON THE INFLUENCE OF SEX ROLES ON FAMILY DECISION PROCESSES

W. Christian Buss and Charles M. Schaninger

Since we prepared our research framework (Buss and Schaninger 1982), new findings and methodological improvements have been made in the area of family behavior research. This paper reviews recent research findings, examines recent methodological improvements, and develops a list of research topics and alternative theory formulations that are likely to become increasingly important to understanding family decision behavior.

MIDDLE-RANGE THEORIES OF FAMILY BEHAVIORS

Engel, Blackwell, and Kollat (1978) suggested that consumer behavior and by extension family behavior can benefit from the development of middle-range theories. Family researchers have investigated several midrange theoretical constructions.

Exchange Theory

Social-exchange theory as it relates to families is examined in depth by Nye (1979), who developed the concept as a basis for evaluating marital interactions. The theory states that individuals compare alternatives to maximize benefits and minimize costs by choosing among exchange

69

opportunities. Nye developed 121 hypotheses based on exchange-choice theory and gave a summary of the theoretical and empirical evidence for each. These hypotheses differ from many of the concepts examined in Figure 5-1. For example, Nye hypothesized that the optimal level of communication for husbands is lower than for wives, which leads to a potential source of problems in marital interaction. He also suggested that smaller women are more likely to marry and remain married because men view smaller women as more feminine and smaller women are less able to perform strength-type tasks.

Economic Model

An economic model of marriage and divorce has been developed by Becker and his associates (Becker 1974; Becker, Landes, and Michael 1977). In the 1974 article, Becker suggested that families have a production function, act so that output from that production function is maximized, and thus enhance total family and individual welfare. The Becker, Landes, and Michael study used this framework to analyze factors that affect the U.S. divorce rate, such as age, age at marriage, education, and earnings. These factors are considered assets that each spouse brings to the marriage; the greater the value of these assets, the greater the spouse's opportunities in the marriage market—and thus the greater the probability of marital dissolution. Huber and Spitze (1980) used Becker's formulation to examine the causes of marital instability. They examine the factors that increase thoughts of divorce in the wife (work experience, youngest child age 6 to 11, egalitarian housework norms) and in the husband (wife's work experience, wife's egalitarian housework norms, children under age 6). A wide variety of other family economic issues are developed in a book of readings by Schultz (1974).

Systems Theory

Spreye (1979) summarized recent work on the application of systems theory to marriage. Married couples exhibit many characteristics of general systems (i.e., they have boundaries, process inputs, and manage sub-systems), and the viability of the family can be enhanced when principles of general system survival are met. Thus, if the family system is open to outside input, manages conflict and tension in the system, opens more communication channels between members, and so on, the probability of its surviving marital stress increases. Propositions of systems theory can be used to study family behavior, but little if any empirical research has been

Figure 5–1. A Schematic of a General Family Decision Process.

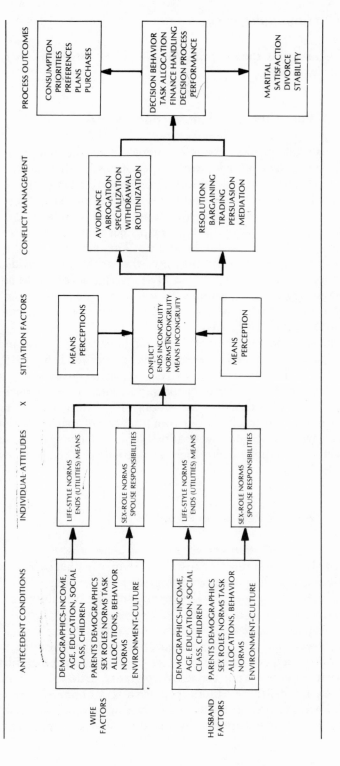

71

based on systems theory, primarily due to the difficulties in generating testable hypotheses.

Role Theory and Interaction Process

Individuals adopt role sets that interact with the role sets of other individuals; individuals adopt role expectations for their own role sets as well as for their alters' role sets. Burr, Leigh, Day, and Constantine (1979) developed an extensive overview of role theory in marriage. They examined factors such as role enactment, role strain, number of roles, and ease of role transition. They also developed several propositions about role assumption and role performance—for example, "The perceived quality of role enactment in a relationship influences the satisfaction individuals in the relationship have" (1979: 69) and "The amount of consensus on relevant role expectations in a relationship influences the satisfaction with the relationship" (1979: 73). The special case of sex-role norms will be examined in more detail later.

A related model by Spanier, Lewis, and associates (Lewis and Spanier 1979: Spanier, Sauer, and Larzelere 1979; Spanier and Lewis 1979) adapted an exchange orientation to the analysis of marital quality and satisfaction. They identified four classes of factors: attractions in the marriage, tensions in the marriage, alternative attractions, and external pressures. These factors interact to result in four combinations of marital outcomes: low quality/low satisfaction; low quality/high satisfaction; high quality/low satisfaction; and high quality/high satisfaction. This model is reviewed in more detail later.

Models Related to Figure 5–1

The editors of *Contemporary Theories about the Family*, volume 2, presented a model similar in form to our framework but conceptually more complete, although ignoring consumption behavior (Burr, Hill, Nye, and Reiss 1979:13). In their model, environmental variables (complexity, uncertainty, and constraints) yield exogenous input variables to the family (goals, resources, affiliations, etc.) that force internal organization variables (rules, power allocation, support structures, etc.). The family then develops levels of certain performance variables (marrying, adjusting, child rearing, etc.) that produce output variables (solidarity, satisfaction, status attainment, etc.). Finally, the editors specified a set of important residuals like family learning, intergenerational variables, and so on. The variables in this general model are not specifically linked, so research hypotheses are more difficult to develop from their model than from our framework. In an article in that book, Burr, Leigh, Day, and Constantine (1979) expanded the model into a model of family-interaction processes that provides both explicit and implicit hypotheses about the linkages between family-interaction variables, especially marital satisfaction, role enactment, antecedents of role strain, and role-transitions theory (1979: 72–89).

ANTECEDENT CONDITIONS

Figure 5-1, reproduced from Buss and Schaninger (1982), develops three sets of antecedent conditions that affect both husband and wife: demographic variables, parental variables, and environmental/subcultural variables. Some additional work has been performed on each of these variables. Demographic variables are discussed last, since most of the recent work on demographics has tested linkages between demographics and other variables.

Parental Variables

Zaltman and Wallendorf (1983) stated that the dearth of research on the intergenerational transfer of values and consumption behavior is a deficiency in the social-class literature. Recent research examines two of these issues in more depth: value transfer and role transfer.

Hoge, Petrillo, and Smith (1982) examined the transmission of religious and social values from parents to teenages. They found that topics for which parent-and-child agreement is strongest are those that are (1) visible, (2) concrete, and (3) of lasting concern to parents, and (4) are those about which parents' hold homogamous values. Values without these character-istics are only weakly transmitted between generations (Hoge, Petrillo, and Smith 1982:571). Parent-and-child value congruence was studied using 1976 data from tenth-graders and their parents in Roman Catholic, Southern Baptist, and United Methodist churches. In general, with 254 complete triads, parent-and-child correlations on thirty-three measures of values were weak, with only three affecting religious value transmission: (1) younger age of parents, (2) parental congruence on religion, and (3) good parent-and-child relationships. The effects varied by specific value across sons and daughters. Denomination membership predicted children's religious values more accurately than parental values.

Another parental factor that affects the marital processes in offspring couples is how the mother's employment affects the children. The first issue is the transfer to children of the sex-role norm of whether or not a mother should work. One study by Powell and Steelman (1982) using 1977 data from 1,511 adults across the United States examined the effect of maternal demographics on children's attitudes toward a wife's working. They summed equally weighted scores on four, four-point scales that measured attitudes on maternal employment and got a dependent variable with values ranging from 4 to 16. With ordinary-least squares, they found maternal characteristics did not affect attitudes of female respondents; for males, maternal education and maternal employment during preschool years related to positive attitudes toward female employment.

Acock, Barker, and Bengston (1982) used ANOVA and multiple-classification analysis to examine the effect of several parental attributes on derived factor scores for religious beliefs, sexual beliefs, family orientation, and commitment to the work ethic. Using 647 triads of parents and postadolescent children, they related postadolescent responses to attitude items with parents' attitudes, mother's employment and occupation status, and associational and affective measures of parent-and-child solidarity. Maternal employment had little effect on parental or combined-spouse influence on offspring attitudes. The most significant effects were between mother's occupational status and offspring attitudes. Offspring of mothers in high-status positions held more modern views on the four factors, except for family orientation.

We examined the relationship between perceptions of parental task allocation and the task allocation in offspring families by using data from the University of Illinois Panel (Schaninger, Buss, and Grover 1983). Using canonical correlation, we found that intergenerational task-allocation transmittal was generally stronger for husbands than for wives; wives tend to shift toward more egalitarian task-allocation patterns than husbands. No evidence was found for the hypothesis that transfer to the next generation was more likely when parents exhibited congruent patterns than when parent patterns differed.

Environmental Influences

Most of the recent work on environmental influences examines different issues in different cultures and subcultures. Haas (1981) received responses from 128 Swedish couples and found that Swedish sex-role ideology was radically more modern than in the United States but this did not affect actual task allocation. Craddock (1980) used forty-two engaged couples who married in Sydney, Australia, and found that homogeneous value systems reduced the time taken to resolve conflict and that centralization of authority reduced time to resolve conflict only when homogeneous value systems were extant. There was some evidence that when husbands used centralized authority they increased the number of ameliorative acts toward their wives. While not demonstrating cultural differences, the study did use a non-American sample.

Two recent articles examine two types of behavior in Chicano couples. Ybarra (1982) conducted one hundred interviews with married Chicano couples in central California. Using cross-tabulations she found that the strongest impact on sex-role attitudes came from whether or not the wife worked outside the home; more egalitarian sex-role attitudes resulted from the wife's working. Based on her review of the literature, she also concludes that Chicano families tend to have more egalitarian role structures than other American families. Finally, Cooney, Rogler, Hurrell, and Ortiz (1982) collected data from 111 intergenerationally linked couples in New York to examine decisionmaking power allocation. They found that parents born and raised in Puerto Rico were more traditional than their offspring born and raised in the United States. In both sets of couples, half of the decisions in the inventory were shared, and the higher the wife's education the more decisionmaking was shared.

Demographics

Little evidence has emerged to contradict our earlier conclusion based on a literature review in Buss and Schaninger (1982) that modern sex-role norms are found in couples who are younger, have higher social status, and have more education. However, two demographic factors that were not examined earlier also influence family behavior: wife's employment and wife's career success. In addition, several recent studies have examined the link between demographics, sex-role norms and other variables.

A woman's working affects the family's finances and attitudes. Marianne Ferber (1982) examined the factors that have increased the entry of women into the work place. She said that the old factors (rural-urban migration, reduction in the work week, decreasing cost of household labor saving devices, and the expansion of female occupations) have peaked and other causal factors are emerging. Using data from the University of Illinois Panel, she identified one new factor (attitude change) and suggested four others: (1) changing attitudes toward wives, (2) increased education for women, (3) increased labor opportunities, and (4) increased demand for purchased commodities. The primary factors that affect the woman's work behavior have been shown to be husband's attitudes (Spitze and Waiter 1981; Spitze and Huber 1982) and husband's and wife's resources (Rank 1982). The two articles by Spitze and her associates used two large nationwide probability samples to demonstrate several points about women who work. In white couples, the primary determinant of the wife's work behavior is her husband's attitudes, with the husband's attitudes being revised in response to his wife's beliefs in early marriage. In black couples, the husband's attitudes do not appear to shift, and the wife's attitudes are generally more favorable toward a woman with young children who works. In the study by Spitze and Waiter (1981) six percent more black women than white women worked. Rank (1982) used data from 378 couples in Seattle to examine the effects of husband's and wife's resources on the influence of each on decisionmaking each exercised about the wife's employment. As the wife's resources (education, income) increase, her influence on her employment decision increases; as the husband's resources increase, his influence decreases because (1) the wife becomes less economically dependent on the husband and (2) the husband is socialized into more egalitarian sex-role norms, or (3) both of these events occur.

A related issue is the effect of the wife's career success on marital behavior and work behavior. Hiller and Philliber (1982) review the literature on the wife's career success in the marriage and conclude that the effect on the marriage depends on the sex-role norms of both spouses. If both spouses are androgynous(our term is "sex-role modern" or "egalitarian"), then the couple is more likely to adjust successfully when the wife's career success exceeds her husband's. If either is masculine or feminine (our "sex-role traditional"), family pressure are likely to result in either the wife's switching to a lower status or a "female" job or in marital dissolution. Housekneckt and Macke (1981) examined 663 women with graduate professional degrees from Ohio State between 1964 and 1974. Although they hypothesized that marital adjustment would be higher for working women compared to nonworking women, they found that marital adjustment did not depend on employment status but on the extent to which the husband and family circumstances were supportive of the woman's career whether at work or at home.

The last area we examine tests the linkages between demographics and other variables. We have previously summarized the literature linking demographics to task allocation (Schaninger and Buss 1982a) and found several weaknesses. Various studies have related sex-role norms and demographics, but few used multiple demographic items, examined data from both spouses, utilized multidimensional measures of sex-role norms, or applied multivariate tests. Moreover, generalizations of sex-role norms and measures of demographics were applied. In that study we examined canonical correlations of demographics to sex-role norms, sex-role norms to task allocation behavior, and demographics to task-allocation behavior. We found that the canonical correlation coefficients and redundancies (after adjusting for the number of variables in each set) were larger between demographics and sex-role norms, as well as between sex-role norms and task allocation, than between demographics and task allocation. This is the expected result if the causal linkages are from demographics to sex-role norms to task allocation. That paper also reviewed and critiqued previous research on demographics as they relate to sex-role norms and task allocation. We were unable to use LISREL IV because of data limitations.

INDIVIDUAL ATTITUDES

Most recent research relevant to this paper deals with attitudes and behaviors classified as sex-roles. We will not review sex-role research here because an excellent review was done by Scanzoni and Fox (1980). Most post-1980 sex-role papers have been tests of linkages with other variables, and they are reviewed elsewhere in this paper.

One major problem underlying the constructs contained under the rubric of sex-role attitudes is the plethora of terms that are used to describe similar attitude patterns. We are primarily concerned with sex roles. Sex roles are a set of constructs that are determined by gender. Terms that have been applied to gender-determined variables are "sex roles," "sex-role norms," "sex-role attitudes," "sex-role orientation" (also used to define degree of masculinity and femininity), and "task allocation behavior."

The most recent and widely accepted approach views sex-role norms as multidimensional and as wider in scope than many earlier approaches. Scanzoni and Fox (1980) recommended the term "sex-role preferences" to examine what have variously been referred to as "gender norms," sex-role "attitudes," and sex-role "ideologies." These preferences represent evaluations of and reactions to the sexual stratification system and gender linked division of labor as well as "preferences regarding how rewards and costs should be distributed between sexes both in households and in the larger society." Modern sex-role preferences are tied to "egalitarianism between the sexes, in terms of both household and external behaviors."

Most studies of the latter type have employed Likert-scaled batteries tapping several dimensions to arrive at one overall sum score (Brogan and Kutner 1976); to measure a priori defined dimensions (Osmond 1975) to identify underlying dimensions or in conjunction with factor or principal components analyses (Brown, Perry, and Harburg 1977; Scanzoni 1975). Although no one scale has emerged as a widely accepted standard, these studies have produced three common attitudinal dimensions:

1. sex-based division of labor (wife's work and husband's work);
2. traditional wife orientation (home, husband, and children); and
3. wife's versus husband's career importance.

Scanzoni (1975) generated separate factor analyses with varimax rotations on husbands' and wives' responses to two sets of items identified a priori as tapping wife wife and husband sex roles. Comparable factors emerged for both husbands and wives for both sets of variables; however, the items classified a priori as husband or wife could have been performed by either spouse, and varimax rotation forced correlated underlying factors to be orthogonal. Combining all items and running factor analyses separately on both spouses with oblique rotation would have been more appropriate. Tomeh (1978) related demographics for samples of men and women to simple sum scores created on the basis of a modified version of Scanzoni's factors. Brown, Perry, and Harburg (1977) used principal components analysis to identify three factors emerging from eighteen Likert items. These studies and Brogan and Kutner's (1976) scale employed a number of similar items. Both the Scanzoni (1975) and Brown, Perry, and Harburg (1977) studies concluded that each sex-role factor should be examined separately when relating sex roles to other variables.

Cherlin and Walter's (1981) major finding is of direct relevance to sex-role research. Their anecdotal evidence indicates that a significant shift in sex-role norms has come about over the last fifteen years. Using large annual surveys of approximately 1,500 respondents over the period 1972 to 1978, they found a significant shift from traditional modern norms with almost all of the shift occurring from 1972 to 1975 and with sex-role norms holding almost constant from 1975 to 1978. This result occurred for both white men and women, while blacks of both sexes exhibited little shift in sex-role norms from 1972 to 1978.

Significant methodological changes have also been made: Many studies now employ multivariate statistics, using both spouses where the couple is the unit of analysis, gathering information from large national samples, and testing linkages between several sets of family-behavior variables. For example, Acock and Edwards (1982) used data gathered by Scanzoni (1979) to analyze the causal determinants of wife's income in 1971 and 1974 using LISREL. Women's education and age at marriage determined 1971 income, and 1974 income was mediated by sex-role attitudes. The Cherlin and Walters (1981) study and the work by Spitze and her associates (Spitze and Waiter 1981; Spitze and Huber 1982) are further examples of the improvements in current family-behavior research.

CONFLICT RESOLUTION AND MANAGEMENT

Sex-role norms and other attributes of marital behavior interact to create potential conflict situations. Couples resolve this conflict through a variety of strategies and tactics, which we identified in our earlier paper. That paper, however, did not summarize several areas pertinent to conflict management, particularly the methodological procedures applied to the analysis of conflict management. We now review the application of content analysis to the resolution of conflict, the effects of marital distress on conflict resolution behavior, and two conflict management devices—power and bargaining.

Methodological Advances

Gottman and his associates have developed an observational coding system that measures couple interaction in conflict-resolution and problem-solving situations in a laboratory (Gottman, Notarius, Markman, Bank, Yoppi, and Rubin 1976; Gottman, Markman, and Notarius 1977). Gottman's thesis is that marital-satisfaction outcomes (and, we believe, other marital behaviors) derive from communication processes that result from the interaction of persons within the family. His communication structure is three-part: (1) positiveness (being positive and encouraging, with its converse, negativeness), (2) reciprocity (A returning a behavior pattern given to him or her by B), and (3) dominance (A's behavior is more predictable from B's past behavior than vice versa). Gottman's book (1979) presents hypotheses about marital interaction and its relationship to marital distress and develops a content analysis approach that examines three types of clues: (1) content (what is said), (2) affect (nonverbal behavior of the speaker), and (3) context (nonverbal behavior of the listener in response to the speaker's actions). Using this system, which he entitled *Couple Interaction Scoring System*, he found many differences between distressed and nondistressed couples. For example, nondistressed couples were characterized by higher agreement-to-disagreement ratios, were less sarcastic, were more likely to reciprocate a positive act, and were less likely to reciprocate a negative act. This work has also been extended to develop marital therapies that alleviate communication and interaction problems among distressed couples.

This type of approach is time consuming and costly but valuable. Analyzing individual acts of communication reduces the probability that valuable information will be lost by averaging interaction processes through Likert or some other amalgamating but more efficient research techniques. Furthermore, Gottman's research shows unequivocably that the coding of nonverbal behavior significantly enhances the predictability of results at least between distressed and nondistressed couples. This type of approach should also improve our understanding of family decisionmaking.

Other methodological approaches to laboratory research have been used to study conflict and resolution in the marital dyad. Billings (1979) used the Interpersonal Behavior Rating System, which rates each behavior act on scales of friendliness or hostility and dominance or submissiveness. Gray-

Little (1982) estimated relative power between spouses by using relative talking time, the relative number of interruptions, and self observation. Sprenkle and Olsen (1978) used SIMFAM to score influence attempts as power positive when accepted, power zero when ignored but not overtly rejected, and power negative when rejected. Relative scores are developed from ratios of the frequencies of events in each category for both spouses.

Review Articles

Two recent review articles are relevant to the conflict-management process. Scanzoni and Polonko (1980) review the research and theory of marital negotiation and find that current negotiations are affected by past negotiations and form the basis for future interactions. MacDonald (1980) reviews the literature on marital power from 1970 to 1979 and develops a reasonably complete conceptualization of the power variable, its sources, and its results.

PROCESS OUTCOMES

Our earlier paper identified three general classes of outcomes as resulting from marital interactions: (1) decision behavior, (2) family consumption, and (3) marital outcomes. We now examine recent research relating to all but family consumption, since recent family consumption research has dealt with decision influence.

Decision Behavior

Cooney, Rogler, Hurrell, and Ortiz (1982) used one hundred intergenerationally linked Puerto Rican couples to examine the factors that affect six family decisions: husband's job, insurance, wife's employment, home improvements, vacations, and residence. Each item was measured on a three-point scale: usually husband, usually shared, usually wife. Results varied by generation, but significant factors on husband's influence (to shared influence) included parent husband's education (-), offspring husband's education (+), wife's education (-) for both generations, and wife's employment status (0) in offspring couples.

Using the University of Illinois Panel, we examined the relationship between sex-role attitudes and family finance handling and decisionmaking (Schaninger, Buss, and Grover 1982). We reduced twenty-four Likert-scale items into four sex-role attitude factors and tested the effects of the sex-role factors on sixteen finance-handling and decisionmaking items related to both finance management and expenditures for a variety of products. Four questions about the last large durable purchase were also analyzed. Three-point scales were used for each finance item, and purchase-influence items were recoded to three points. We found that for those items usually under the purview of the wife (food, appliances, clothing, etc.) sex-role modern couples showed less wife influence and more joint or husband influence. A similar, but opposite shift occurred on items traditionally controlled by the husband (transportation, savings plan, etc.). In general sex-role modern couples showed more wife or joint influence, and the sex-role attitudes of the wife had a stronger effect than the husband's sex-role attitudes.

In a separate paper, we (Schaninger and Buss 1982b) examined the relationships between the same sex-role factors and task allocation in the family using MANOVA. While that study found that wives still perform the bulk of traditional household tasks, it also indicated a small detectable shift toward more task sharing in sex-role modern couples. This result did vary for some sex-role factors. Again, the wife's sex-role attitudes had more effect than her husband's. We also applied canonical correlation to the same data set: The first significant canonical correlation analysis verified the above findings; the second two significant canonical variates, however, evidenced substantial incongruity between the two spouses' sex-role attitudes and perceptions of task allocation. This we interpret as evidence that some families were in a state of sex-role attitude and task allocation transition from traditional to modern.

Marital Satisfaction

One recurrent theme in the marriage and family relations literature has been the conceptualization and measurement of marital satisfaction. Hicks and Platt (1970) argued that a uniform set of concepts and reliable, validated scales needed to be developed. Both Hicks and Platt (1970) and Spanier and Lewis (1980) have reviewed the various concepts used as surrogates of marital satisfaction: "happiness," "success," "adjustment," "satisfaction," "stability," "functionality," "integration," "consensus," "role tension," "quality," and "love." Since 1970, marital satisfaction research has made considerable conceptual and measurement strides. Spanier and Lewis (1980) provide the most up-to-date and cogent review of developments in this area. Perhaps the oldest commonly used scale is the Locke-Wallace Marital Adjustment Scale. Researchers in the field seem to be evenly divided between using a sum score or single-item measure (e.g., Rhyne 1981; Chadwick, Albrecht, and Kunz 1976) and using multidimensional scales (e.g., Snyder 1979; Spanier 1976). Spanier's (1976) Dyadic Adjustment Scale has more recently become a widely accepted multidimensional measure with demonstrated reliability and validity.

Demographic variables positively associated with marital satisfaction are: parental socioeconomic status, husband's and family income, husband's occupational status, husband's and wife's education, and age at marriage for both spouses (up to mid-twenties). Wife's occupational status, employment, and income, as well as presence of dependent children, have variously been shown to be negatively correlated or uncorrelated with marital satisfaction. Family life cycle has generally been shown to demonstrate a curvelinear U-shaped relationship to marital satisfaction. Other research has demonstrated homogamy (similarity) in values, personality, religion, role perceptions and expectations, sex-role norms, age, social class, and educational background (parental and current dyad) to be positively related to marital satisfaction.

Spanier and Lewis (1980) identify a number of significant trends as typifying research in the marital quality literature between 1970 and 1980, among them:

1. increasing use of husbands and wives rather than only wives;
2. greater attention to measurement methodology, reliability, validity, and so forth;
3. larger and more representative sample sizes;
4. growing interest in cohabiting couples;
5. recent increasing use of multivariate statistics;
6. recognition of the problems of cross-sectional designs;
7. increasing attempts to build theories that relate marital quality to other literatures; and
8. development and use of observational data collection techniques.

Family Decisionmaking and Marital Outcomes

Locke (1951) compared happily married couples to divorced couples in a large national probability sample. The former were characterized by shared rather than husband-dominated finance handling, by joint or shared decisionmaking, and by discussion and mutual compromise. Divorced couples were characterized by more domination (mostly husband but also wife) in family finance handling and decisionmaking, by more conflict, and by one partner's yielding most often. Happily married husbands and wives also described their mates more favorably than divorced couples did on directorial abilities (assumes responsibility), on leadership, and on ability to make decisions quickly. The other spouses were also less likely to be either dominant or easily influenced.

Blood (1960) suggested that marital conflict can be avoided by role specialization in family decisionmaking and finance handling, with one partner (usually the husband) maintaining final authority. He also suggested that conflict may be avoided by increasing facilities for family living (homeownership, two phones, two bathrooms, two televisions); by assigning priorities for the use of money (budgets) and limited resources; by enlarging areas of autonomy in decisionmaking, financial management, and individual activities; by tension-relieving safety valves such as vacations and autonomous individual escape activities; and by counseling or by talking with others. Perhaps existence of these characteristics among surviving families reflects their effectiveness at helping families to resolve or avoid conflict (Campbell 1970; Centers, Raven, and Rodrigues 1971; Orthner 1975).

Blood and Wolfe (1960) found highest marital satisfaction among families practicing syncratic (joint) decisionmaking, followed by autonomic decisionmaking, and then by husband and wife domination, respectively. Centers, Raven, and Rodrigues (1971) found wife dominance in family decisionmaking to be negatively correlated with marital satisfaction and that highest marital satisfaction occurred among families characterized as syncratic. Kolb and Strauss (1974) derived observational measures of husband-to-wife power in laboratory problemsolving sessions: They found high husband power to be associated with marital happiness and very low wife power or high wife power to be associated with marital unhappiness. They suggested that marital unhappiness arose either from husband incompetence at performing his role set and the resulting sex-role confusion or from the wife's assumption of power, which thus violates widely accepted cultural norms. The current validity of these conclusions may be questioned, given recent shifts toward modern sex-role norms.

Osmond (1977) found that intact marriages among low-income black and white welfare applicants and recipients were characterized by joint decisionmaking and democratic and mutual compromise as modes of conflict resolution. Gray-Little (1982) also examined both self-report and derived behavioral measures of decisionmaking power. Her data were obtained by interviewing black couples in their homes having them discuss assigned topics relating to marital problems, and having them play a problemsolving game. That study found marital satisfaction to be highest among couples classified as husband dominant by self-report measures of decisionmaking dominance and of concessions made to the other spouse. It also found that husband-led families, as measured by talking time and number of interruptions, were highest in marital satisfaction and that egalitarian couples were lowest. Large absolute differences in husband-and-wife decisionmaking influence and concessions were linked to low marital quality. Marital quality also was positive when the husband rated the wife as having more power than she rated herself as having.

Most of the studies in this area have been cross-sectional or ex-post-facto designs: They compare intact to divorced couples or correlate marital satisfaction to one but seldom both spouses' perceptions of marital decisionmaking influence. Ex-post-facto studies, however, measure family decisionmaking or power after the marriage has been disrupted. The other studies exclude divorced couples from the sampling and thus restrict range. Moreover, most studies have used overall measures or a composite of decisionmaking power and have not examined decision influence or finance handling across a number of products or areas. Longitudinal panel studies, starting with a proability sample of newly married couples, should avoid the methodological weaknesses of earlier studies. Data should be collected from both spouses, and an attempt should be made to measure decision influence or finance handling across a number of different products or areas.

Consumption and Marital Outcomes

Economic Security.   The importance of economic security is reflected in findings that early age at marriage and lower educational, occupational, and income status increase the probability of divorce. Levinger (1966) found that financial problems were a major complaint of wives, particularly lower-class wives, in families seeking divorce. Although this was not a major complaint among lower-class husbands, it was for middle-class husbands seeking divorce. Kittson and Sussman (1982) also found finance handling, decisionmaking, and finances to be major complaints among couples who seek divorce. Although most earlier (up to the mid-1970s) studies found low income to be associated with divorce and low marital satisfaction, more recent studies have questioned this relationship. Jorgensen (1979) found that wives' perceptions of their husbands as competent providers and satisfaction with spouse's income were positively correlated with marital satisfaction, while income was not. Price-Bonham and Balswick (1980) regard income adequacy and wife's attitudes toward family income as more important determinants of divorce. Mott and Moor (1979), in a longitudinal panel study, found marital separation to be more strongly related to debt accumulation and lack of improvement of financial situation than to income. Cherlin (1977) found that couples with savings of $1,000 or more were less likely to become divorced.

Ownership of Goods.   Locke (1951) found home ownership, value of house, and ownership of telephones, refrigerators, washers, and radios to be higher among happily married than divorced couples. These variables may represent economic security and income adequacy dimensions or they may reflect Blood's (1960) view that increased facilities for family living decrease family conflict. Unfortunately, no recent empirical studies relate consumption and goods ownership to divorce or marital satisfaction.

Becker's (1974) economic theory of marriage and Becker, Landes, and Michael's (1977:1152) economic theory of marital instability suggest that couples invest in "marital specific capitial" ("including houses, children, market and non-market skills, and information"). While he regards investments in household appliances and automobiles as valuable if the marriage dissolved," he argues that the accumulation of marital-specific capital raises the expected gain of staying in a marriage and therefore discourages dissolution (1977:1152). Levinger (1966), employing a social-exchange viewpoint somewhat similar to Nye's (1979), argues that the receipt of "goods, services, or money" in a marriage increases the attraction of the marriage and that their potential loss acts as a barrier to keep spouses within a marriage. He also suggests that home ownership and other couple property that represents truly joint investments stabilize the marriage tie and provide additional security. Furthermore, he states that the "desire not to break up family financial assets becomes significant restraint against marital dissolution when those assets are sufficiently large." Thus, while we have some recent theoretical contributions relating consumption and asset accumulation to marital happiness and divorce, the only empirical work to date remains Locke's (1951) ex-post-facto study.

Product and Leisure Consumption Activities. Alcohol consumption has been clearly linked to propensity for divorce and marital dissatisfaction (Levinger 1965, 1966; Renne 1970; Orford, Oppenheimer, Egert, and Hensman 1977; Nye, Carlson, and Garrett 1970), although researchers disagree about whether it is a cause or effect of marital problems. Locke (1951) found indifference on the part of both husband and wife to drinking, gambling, and playing cards to be related to marital stability. Indulgence on the part of both partners in such activities, however, was much less likely to lead to divorce than indulgence on the part of one partner and disapproval by the other.

Several research studies have demonstrated that shared or joint leisure activities are positively associated with marital stability (Locke 1951; Levinger 1965, 1966), particularly social activities and contact with others (Renne 1970; Locke 1951). Orthner (1975) found that joint activities (e.g., dining out, visiting friends, affectionate or sexual interaction) were positively correlated but that individual activities were negatively correlated, with marital satisfaction during early and later marital career periods. Parallel activities (e.g., watching television, visiting a museum) were positively related to marital satisfaction during early (0 to 5 years of marriage) and later (18 to 23 years of marriage) marital career periods for husbands and during later marital career periods for wives. No significant correlations between individual, joint, or parallel activities were found for couples in the two middle (6 to 11 and 12 to 17 years of marriage) periods. Taking vacations as joint activities has been shown to result in greater marital satisfaction and to serve a stress-relieving, stabilizing effect on relations during critical periods (Orthner 1975).

IMPLICATIONS FOR CONSUMER BEHAVIOR RESEARCH

In identifying and examining conclusions about the behavioral processes in families, we have examined many areas that relate to the consumption behavior of families. Many of the conclusions derived by family researchers may have a significant impact on consumption behavior, and we will summarize them here:

1. Some evidence exists that shifts in sex-role norms have reached a relative stable plateau (Cherlin and Walters 1981), which probably will eventually stabilize the effect of sex-role norms on consumption behavior. Since extensive evidence shows that actual behavior adjustment lags significantly behind sex-role changes (Haas 1981; many others), changes in consumption behavior related to sex-role norms will likely occur for a significant length of time and be gradual.
2. Substantial evidence exists that norm-conflict and sex-role norm adjustment is still occurring in families, although norms may have stabilized (Schaninger and Buss 1982a, 1982b; Spitze and Waiter 1981; Haas 1981; others).
3. There is some related evidence that (a) the sex-role norm dimensions of husbands and wives are the same (Schaninger and Buss 1982a) and (b) wives hold more complex and conflicting patterns on those sex-role dimensions (Schaninger, Buss, and Grover 1982).
4. Women's sex-role norms appear to affect task-allocation behavior, finance handling, and decision influence more than men's sex-role norms (Schaninger, Buss, and Grover 1982; Schaninger and Buss 1982a).
5. Little evidence has been found concerning parents' ability to pass their values or task-allocation patterns on to their children, although some factors were shown to affect the effectiveness of integration transfer (Hoge, Petrillo, and Smith 1982).
6. Different cultural environments have different effects on sex-role norm adoption. Puerto Rican couples are relatively modern. Swedish couples are radically more modern in attitude if not behavior (Haas

1981). Black couples frequently show different sex-role norms and behavior patterns than white couples (Spitze and Waiter (1981).

7. Some evidence has been developed linking demographics, sex-role attitudes, and task-allocation behavior (Schaninger and Buss 1982a).

SUGGESTIONS FOR FUTURE RESEARCH

Since the late 1970s, advances in methodology have been applied to family behavior processes. The five methodological weaknesses we identified earlier (Buss and Schaninger 1982) have been also recognized repeatedly by others (e.g., Price-Bonham and Balswick 1980; Schram 1979; Spanier and Lewis 1980). In addition, much recent research overcomes many of these problems:

1. Many studies gather data from both husbands and wives; from husbands, wives and children; or from parental husbands and wives with offspring husbands and wives.
2. Multidimensional sex-role norms from alternative sources have been used, although the standard approach is still for each researcher to customize their own sex-role scales; an accepted uniform method for measuring sex-roles would be a significant advance.
3. Most studies reviewed in this paper examined at least two and sometimes more of the linkages posited in family behavior processes.
4. Several longitudinal studies have examined sex-role changes.
5. Many recent sudies have used national samples, and almost all use tests of multivariate relationships, although one dependent variable is still typical; bivariate tests are now the exception rather than the rule.

Further improvements are still possible:

1. Family researchers need to become familiar with techniques that analyze dynamic processes. Applying appropriate calculus procedures to catastrophe theory and to much of the theory of evolutionary processes should yield substantive returns in developing a theory of change in family behavior. Catastrophe theory evolved from the mathmatical science of topography and explains rapid shifts from one relatively stable state to another (i.e., from married to divorced); evolutionary theory was derived by biologists to explain changes in animal species over time.
2. Content analysis in family decisionmaking processes similar to the work of Gottman and his associates (Gottman, Notarius, Markham, Bank, Yoppi, and Rubin 1976; Gottman, Markham, and Notarius

1977) should increase our ability to understand and predict decision-process outcomes.
3. Other individuals (i.e., extended-family members) need to be incorporated into the research methodology.

Emerging Issues in Family Behavior Research

The family is undergoing significant structural changes. The crude divorce rate in the United States increased from 2.5 to 5.3 per 1,000 population from 1965 to 1979 (Price-Bonham and Balswick 1980). Sex-role attitudes of men and women became more modern from 1972 until 1978 (Cherlin and Walters 1981). Anecdotal evidence shows that people live longer, more couples cohabit, and individuals retire earlier. Thus, many of our empirical findings about the family are probably obsolete and need to be reconstructed. We particularly need to reevaluate our conclusions about family decisionmaking and consumption.

Older couples will be an increasingly important market segment. Streib and Beck (1980) reviewed the trends in older couples that were observed in the 1970s. They examined the effects of increasing age on marital satisfaction (generally U-shaped with lowest levels occurring in the middle years when stress occurs from career demands and children), economic effects (effects of Social Security primarily), residential functions, and legal and cultural effects. Borland (1982) develops a theory of the effects of children's leaving the home (primarily mother's depression, called the "empty-nest syndrome") for three ethnic groups. She hypothesizes that the empty-nest syndrome is more likely to occur in white women than in black or Mexican-American women due to unique social circumstances and unique family and sex-role norms. Both the increasing numbers of elderly and the empty-nest syndrome are likely to have profound effects on the consumption behavior of these groups.

The family-life-cycle concept is in critical need of reevaluation. For example, Spanier, Sauer, and Larzellre (1979) used census data and found that age of husband and wife and length of time married are equally as effective at predicting attributes of family-development stages as family life-cycle stage. They conclude, and we concur, that current conceptualizations of the family life cycle no longer reflect the emerging family. Factors such as divorce (Norton 1980) and working wives (Waite 1980) significantly affect both the specific family life-cycle stages and the attributes that a family exhibits at each stage. An evolution-based model that explains behavior change over time is probably required to better understand changes in family life.

The increasing presence of what Price-Bonham and Balswick (1980) call the noninstitutions needs to be explored more fully. They identify divorce, desertion, and remarriage as noninstitutions, and we suggest the addition of cohabiting couples and possibly those who remain single. How do these noninstitutions, which serve as family substitutes, differ from the traditional family dyad? Are their behavior and decisionmaking patterns different? Research is needed here.

With the emergence of several methodological improvements in family research, many topics can now be studied more fruitfully. Research on husband-and-wife influence and power can benefit from both the application of content analysis, which Gottman (1979) did for marital satisfaction, and the application of ideal-point mapping, which compares actual choice with the ideal-point profiles of each spouse to determine relative behavior shifts. If the field also can develop researchers with the necessary quantitative background, they can make significant advances in the area of behavior change over time and over other relevant variables. This type of research presumably will yield more accurate predictions and more realistic theories of the family decision process.

We have reviewed much of what has been done to date in the area of family behavior. We look forward to advances in the field that will further the understanding of families.

6 THE WORKWIFE
A Powerful Change
Agent of This Century

Suzanne H. McCall

Women have entered the labor force at an accelerated rate over the past decade. According to the U.S. Department of Labor (1975), approximately fourteen million women entered the work force during this period (60 percent of the increase in the work force), while ten million men entered the work force (40 percent of the increase). The characteristics of these women have altered even more dramatically than their numbers.

Since World War II, the number of working mothers has increased tenfold, and the number of working women tripled. In 1980, 55 percent of all mothers with children under age 18 and 45 percent of all mothers of preschool children were working outside the home. To identify the working married woman with children still in the home, the author introduced the term "workwife" (McCall 1977). The 1977 work identified the differential in consumer behavior and the resulting marketing effect of working versus nonworking women. The term "housewife" presently identifies only a small minority of our female population. The U.S. Department of Labor (1975) estimates that well over 84 percent of the women between ages 16 and 64 are either in the labor force, divorced, widowed, or separated.

In addition to increased numbers of households that have a workwife, a number of other household types show a rapid increase in numbers over the past decade. Singles represent a 40 percent growth, and elderly (age 65 and over) show a 25 percent increase. Most acceleration in household type, however, has occurred in number of unmarried couples living together, which has tripled, and in number of divorced persons, which has doubled. Unlike these households, the significance of the workwife is in how she changes and affects an entire family unit. For that reason, a change in her life style, attitude, consumer behavior, and value structure acts as a powerful change agent for a large segment of the population.

THE WORKWIFE STUDY

The original workwife study, (McCall 1977) conducted in 1973, investigated how the consumption of the working woman differed from that of the nonworking woman. Differences and similarities were analyzed to determine how they affected the performance of marketing institutions and functions.

The study revealed that working and nonworking women perceived differently how a working woman's income is spent. The nonworking woman perceives the income of her working counterpart to be used to provide luxuries in both products and services, while, in fact, 68 percent of working women stated that it was used for support purposes, including raising their families' standard of living, maintaining it during inflation, or providing the sole support of their family. This reinforces the hypothesis that these groups of women do not identify with each other due to different lifestyles and interests.

Working women were found to be much more independent in their shopping behavior than the nonworking women. More than twice as many nonworking women needed approval from the spouse before purchasing a car, furniture, or appliances as did the workwives. This suggests that the working women should be treated as an independent market force. Many institutions that sell expensive items disregard the woman purchaser who is unaccompanied by a man or hesitate to issue credit to a woman without the co-signature or endorsement of her spouse. Herein lies an untouched market that may well prove very productive.

Price consciousness does not increase when women work. The activities associated with being an astute shopper include reading newspaper advertising, visiting many stores, comparing prices, shopping sales, and related time-consuming acts. Since time is a precious commodity to the working woman, she does not usually engage in these activities. Most important for the working women is convenience, which includes one-stop shopping, ample checkout facilities, familiarity with store arrangement, wide assortment of stock, and appropriate location. This may well suggest two different markets: The nonworking woman is less loyal to a single store but is more easily attracted by price promotion, whereas the working

Table 6–1. Relationship of Work Status of Females
to Consumer Behavior (percentage).

	All Women	Not Working	Working
Food			
Shops several times a week	45.4	51.27	38.06
Shops once a week or less	52.54	46.81	59.70
Shops evenings	18.36	6.41	36.84
Shops Monday through Thursday	52.43	62.18	38.35
Shops Saturday	20.0	11.54	33.08
Spends $26 to $50 per week	54.57	61.39	40.60
Spends $11 to $25 per week	27.96	16.46	45.86
Is major food shopper	90.35	94.30	84.33
Found newspaper advertising helpful	62.22	73.42	53.73
Clothing			
Prefers self service	42.74	38.22	47.01
Shops evenings	12.50	3.85	21.64
Uses newspaper to select store	11.76	15.28	7.94
Shops same store	24.41	19.44	32.54
Considers price	17.53	23.65	11.72
Considers flattering fit	57.49	60.81	47.66
Services			
Uses maid once a week	22.47	28.48	16.03
Never uses maid	70.68	65.19	80.15
Uses mail-order catalog (phone)	52.05	57.05	40.74
Uses two or more vending machines	28.22	19.35	40.60
Uses discount coupon in newspaper	14.53	18.71	6.98
Eats out once a week or more	51.36	46.80	56.30
Use of Media			
Reads paper once daily	82.66	95.90	76.30
Watches television (3 hours)	55.38	46.84	61.48
Opinion of Media			
Finds advertising helpful	72.38	80.77	65.16
Sees women portrayed as housewives	39.89	42.76	35.11
Sees women portrayed as sex symbols	34.83	32.89	38.93
Miscellaneous			
Needs spouse for car purchase	67.90	83.54	49.63
Needs spouse for furniture purchase	54.28	71.52	37.04
Applies for credit	44.04	39.24	53.13

woman may be more profitable to the market (with her lesser concern for value) and less easily wooed by competing institutions.

Work affects the consumer behavior of females not solely because of the act of work itself but rather because of the time consumed by work. In this study, the part-time worker was more closely allied to the nonworking woman than the full-fime worker in her consumer behavior.

Working and nonworking women were found to be similar in the following consumer categories:

Frequency and site of vacation. More than 50 percent took at least one vacation per year. Sightseeing and exploring new places were chosen by over half of the women; visiting relatives, by one-fourth.

Type of restaurant service preferred. More than 70 percent of both groups preferred a full-service accommodation.

Method used to introduce a new product. Fifty-nine percent of the respondents preferred a free sample mailed to the home over coupons and in-store samples.

Door-to-door salespersons. This retail institution received a negative acceptance by both groups of women. More than 70 percent would not allow the salesperson into the home and would make an effort to turn the person away.

Attitude toward self-service. Both groups of women accepted this as part of the new lifestyle but showed considerable resistance in areas formerly associated with full-service (e.g., gasoline stations, restaurants, car repair, and discount houses).

Of the demographic factors observed, age, education, and income, respectively, were found to be of considerable importance in predicting consumer behavior:

Age. The most astute and informed shoppers were over age 55, read more newspaper advertising, shopped more stores, and clipped more newspaper coupons. Those under age 34 were the least likely to read the newspapers and placed the lowest value on advertising.

Education. Women with a high-school degree or less used more newspaper advertising, shopped once a week, visited more stores, and preferred national brands and evening openings. The more educated were suspect of advertising, compared prices on brands of goods, and used their leisure time for reading instead of shopping.

Income. This variable was significant in predicting the quantity and variety of services and credit cards used, which were based not on the need of the individual but on the amount of combined family income. Higher income did not indicate that the consumer was necessarily a more astute or value-oriented shopper, but it did reveal higher mobility, which exposed the shopper to a greater number of stores and types of products. Higher-income women were most negative in their reactions to advertising messages.

PROJECTED TRENDS FOR THE MARKET PLACE

Change in Lifestyles Produces Shift in Values and Attitudes

1.   Lifestyle appears to be more important than social class as an indicator of consumer behavior. Work status crosses all boundaries in social class. In 1974, women were more often found in white-collar jobs (62 percent) than in blue-collar jobs (16 percent) and service jobs (21 percent). Men's employment was distributed quite differently, with 41 percent in white-collar jobs, 46 percent in blue-collar jobs, 8 percent in service jobs, and 5 percent in farm jobs. Since more than one-third of all working women (34.5 percent) are clerical workers, it is not uncommon for the workwife of a blue-collar worker (plumber, mechanic, etc.) to be employed as a secretary to an executive. It is suggested that she identifies more with the values of her work place than those of her husband, as claimed in the traditional social class assumption. This makes the work status of the wife an important correlate in determining the consumer behavior of a family.

Also significant to the family's consumer behavior is the mobility of our present population: Twenty percent of all families move every year. This produces new neighborhood associations with constantly changing reference groups. The consumer behavior patterns of families that move will reflect more of a desire to maintain established lifestyles than to adapt to their new neighbors' habits.

2.   Working women may well be assuming a reverse role in the marketplace—that of trendsetters. Society's cultural acceptance of the working woman has made her image more attractive. The increasing numbers of women in managerial and professional positions will encourage this trend. Several phenomena support the trend. The Bureau of Advertising (1972) conducted a study to determine how working and nonworking women view their roles in terms of satisfaction, achievement, and stature. While women in both groups viewed themselves more positively than their counterparts, working women fared better in ratings by both groups. The classic Haire study (1950) of two identical shopping lists, with the exception of instant coffee on one list and brewed coffee on the other, was replicated by Webster and von Pechman (1970). In the original study, the instant-coffee shopper was associated with the negative adjectives "lazy"

and "non-family" oriented; the updated study produced no appreciable differences in opinion.

Today's working woman projects new values to her daughters, particularly the postponement of marriage until adequate educational or vocational goals have been achieved. Later marriage suggests that there will be greater acceptance of working for the upcoming generation of women. In addition, the attitudes of husbands are changing. Twenty years ago, a man apologized if his wife worked because it was generally assumed that such an activity implied that he was unsuccessful in supporting his family. Today, the husband of the nonworking woman often explains that his wife is not in the work force because she is busy with the children's activities, club work, volunteer work, PTA, and so forth. This shows an obvious desire to justify her nonworking status. Many women are completing their formal education during middle age, and it is probable that these women will seek employment, further increasing the status of the working woman.

3.   Women in general—and working women in particular—are seeking a more clearly defined personal identity. With a new-found freedom of role selection, they are becoming more introspective and asking, "Who am I?". They no longer identify with the masses. This may indicate the demise of mass advertising and a need for market segmentation that reaches specific groups of women. The search for personal identity already has surfaced in the rejection of the pattern of being "fashion sheep." In this study, only 2.3 percent of the respondents listed high fashion as the major criterion for clothing selection. Most women were concerned with how flattering the garment appeared on them. Less than 4 percent needed advice from spouses or other family members when buying personal clothing. Creativity manifests itself in a wide variety of other ways: a nostalgic return to the past, creative hobby stores, and home sewing.

"Keeping up with the Joneses" may become a cliché of the past. Women are less interested in keeping up with neighbors, whom they may not even know, and more concerned with developing a lifestyle that satisfies their personal needs. Security and economic independence are found by joining the work force and are reflected in individual lifestyles and behavior patterns. We are seeing the beginning of new status symbols: In the past, a family might buy a new car each year, but now they are substituting a new pool, a camper, a boat, or travel for this expenditure. The marketplace can no longer prepare one predictable advertisement for the masses. Consumer research is more important than ever before and must locate specific markets for individual products.

4.   Working women accept leisure time for pleasure and are less likely to be plagued with the guilt associated with the traditional work ethic. The respondents in this study were forthcoming about how they used their leisure time. Seventy-five percent admitted using leisure time for watching television. Nearly one-half listed talking with relatives and friends as a

leisure time activity, and one-fourth noted sleeping as preoccupying their spare time. This seems to indicate that industry can promote a wide variety of leisure-time activities and expenditures because they no longer are considered unacceptable nor imply a non–work-oriented individual. Women in the work force place a higher value on their free time than their nonworking counterparts do and tend to seek out time-saving products. Ready-made clothing, convenience foods, disposable products and containers, and rental agencies for goods and services are among the many items that benefit from this trend. The additional household income provided by the working woman makes the market for these categories even more significant.

5.   Increased educational opportunities for women have had a multi-faceted effect: an increase in consumerism, a rejection of distasteful, unrealistic advertising messages, and a rise in the level of taste as well as fashion consciousness. Since education is the prime motivator for women who enter the work force, working women may form the most important nucleus of potential purchasers of new, exciting, fashion products.

The present rise in consumer activism may well be attributed to the working woman's outspoken criticisms of the marketplace. Her newfound security, vis-à-vis education, indicates a spiraling effect that increases demand for government to take a more active role in monitoring consumer activities. Management needs to carefully monitor its own business activities or the right to do so may be relinquished to federal agencies.

6.   The new lifestyle of the workwife may make her less important as the family purchasing agent since she shares this role with her spouse or other family members. Twelve percent of the women in this study had already adopted this pattern in shopping for food, which was once thought to be the sole dominion of women. This suggests that advertisers should promote their products to a dual-sex audience and upgrade the image associated with the shopping role to attract the male shopper. Socialization of the new lifestyle, in which the husband participates more actively in household duties, will be greatly assisted by the image it projects in the market place. Interestingly, when a woman enters the work force, the husband is the least rewarded socially. While the monetary and psychological rewards increase for the woman, the negative rewards of housework and allied duties increase for the man. It is projected that the socialization of this role will originate in the marketplace, which could effectively upgrade the role in response to attracting a new customer—the male shopper.

7.   The cultural emphasis is on youth, which is reflected in a myriad of lifestyle changes. Women are pursuing younger lovers and husbands. There is an alarming increase in the reported number of runaway wives. Yesterday's movie idol never grows old on today's screen, as plastic surgeons upgrade their facelifting techniques.

All this has great significance to marketing. Promotion of products and services must accent youthful ideas. The cosmetic industry, which now addresses men as well as women, must increase its generic market. The allied industries of wigs and toupees, figure-molding paraphernalia, and hairstyle salons are also participating in this new market. The search for the young, natural look affects even labeling (i.e., herbal fragrances, lemon accents, gay colors).

The flow of fashion trends, formerly called the trickle-down theory, is showing a swing to a trickle-across theory. Direction no longer comes exclusively from the wealthy or the aged: It may originate at any social class level or age group and move simultaneously throughout society. Marketing must detect trends from a wide variety of sources.

Institutional Changes

1.   Advertising and promotion must make considerable changes in order to accommodate the new lifestyles of working women. The emphasis that these women place on convenience will generate new kinds of messages: The service derived from the product appears to be more important than the product itself. For example, with wash-and-wear garments, the consumer is not as concerned with the garment's style or function as he or she is with how it must be cared for. The appeal for this kind of product is based not on emotion and sex, product differential, or price, but on service derived from the products' use.

2.   Role portrayal of women shown in advertising must be assessed more realistically in terms of relating particular products to particular lifestyles. This study found that most women interpreted ads as portraying women as housewives or sex symbols and that nearly half of today's women do not identify with this symbolism. Women think of thmselves as economically independent, rational persons whose scope reaches far beyond the kitchen and the bedroom. In addition, men will be purchasing more goods for the household: Very few men are attracted to an advertisement that portrays an apron-clad woman in ecstasy over a wash so bright that she dons sunglasses to view it.

3.   Truth in advertising is becoming more critical than ever before. Ample evidence is required to support claims for product performance and for tests proving superiority of one product over a competitor's.

4.   Diversity of lifestyles and the search for personal identity makes market segmentation much more complex. This increases the amount and cost of research for advertisers, increases the number of promotional markets, and greatly reduces the effectiveness of the traditional mass-marketing approach to advertising.

5.   Today's shopper's emphasis on convenience suggests that retailing

must adapt. The large one-stop shopping center becomes more important. The large store in a free-standing location isolated from shopping centers should aim for large assortment and good service; price appears to be of secondary importance to the consumer.

6.   The demise of the downtown area as a major shopping center has meant that department store branches have become more important to the consumer. This creates a need for increased inventory selections at the outlying locations. In the past, the best selections were found in the downtown (parent) store, and limited quantities were distributed to the branches. Increased suburban population not only reinforces this trend but also isolates the consumers who prefer to shop close to home. This may require construction of multiple branch units that will serve the clientele living in widely dispersed areas, in contrast to a central downtown unit that served this function in the past.

7.   The high cost of labor tends to encourage firms to institute more self-service operations. The challenge here is to search for and find lost sales, a task formerly performed by salesclerks. The computer does not take note of the shopper who does not find the wanted item and leaves the store dissatisfied.

8.   The low percentage of working women in this study who used the newspaper for shopping purposes suggests a need for new types of promotion. One recommendation is that organizations begin a series of advertised sales that begin at 6:00 P.M. This would provide a real incentive for the working woman who traditionally has been unable to benefit from sales beginning early in the morning. Another alternative is to use door-to-door handbills to announce merchandise offerings, which would perhaps reach women who do not read a newspaper regularly.

9.   To compete with large stores, the small store must capitalize on superior sales service and a high degree of merchandise specialization.

10.   The demand for night openings of retail stores will continue to increase in geometric proportions. The new lifestyle produces a fragmented work day, impulsive planning of activities, mobility in transportation, and less emphasis on the productivity of sleep. In addition, families today use the shopping center as an entertainment center and tour large, exciting stores in the evening.

11.   One major institutional change that may develop is night repair service. The family with a working wife increases the number of mechanical, time-saving products it owns as a result of need and affordable income. Thus, the families who are most likely to require repair services are the ones least likely to be at home during the daytime to admit a repairman. This is a prime example of an inverse relationship of demand and supply. The same syndrome applies to delivery services, which operate exclusively during daylight hours. Institutions that market products of high unit value

and/or bulk may find that a night delivery service is productive and competitive.

Product Changes

1.   Because time is becoming more valuable, management must concentrate on developing and promoting products that require a minimum of time for care and use. Disposable products will probably greatly increase in demand.

2.   Packaging of products must undergo change. The consumer today wants to save time and quickly get product information. The advent of self-service requires more informative packaging and more physical appeal in order to attract the hurried customer.

3.   The life cycle of a product will probably be reduced: Not only is technology constantly making present products obsolete, but the new consumer is more receptive to trying new products than ever before, since he or she is looking for better ways to cope with a new lifestyle. This kind of trend greatly reduces the time normally allotted for the introductory and growth stages of a new product and results in a shorter time in which management can recoup its initial investment. Since the cost of investment has historically been passed on to the consumer, this trend will raise prices at the consumer level. In high-cost products, the used or second-hand market will gain prominence.

4.   The commonly expressed comment, "I'll wait to buy when the price comes down," will become passé. Today's product is generally replaced by a new product (traditionally introduced at a high price) long before the maturity or decline stage of its cycle has been reached or fulfilled.

5.   The size or quantity offered in the product package will change. Smaller families (including the one-person household) and diminished use of leftovers by working women indicate a need for smaller-quantity packaging. In all product categories, the ease of use or preparation and the "instant gratification" philosophy of today's population suggest a proliferation of the new type of goods.

THE WORKWIFE'S HUSBAND STUDY

In 1978, the author made a study of the workwife's husband (McCall 1978) in order to determine how he perceives the changes taking place in his family as a result of his wife's working. The study's most significant finding was to identify the prime factor that determined a husband's satisfaction with his working wife. Satisfaction was directly related to the percentage of the total family income the wife contributed: He was more satisfied and less disturbed by lifestyle change when the wife's contribution was high and considerably less satisfied when it was low. The major findings and analysis of this study follow.

Major Findings and Analysis

Husbands are basically happy when their wives work. Fifty-one percent of all men in the sample indicated satisfaction. Their happiness is directly related to the percentage of income contributed by their wives. If she contributes 40 percent or more of the family income, 70 percent of the husbands are happy; if she contributes 10 percent or less, only 39 percent of the men are happy. The wife's education is also a factor. Men with wives who are college graduates were happiest, with 89 percent indicating so, whereas only 46 percent of husbands whose wives were only high school graduates were happy about her working. This finding of cultural dissimilarities has far-reaching implications for business and society. Presumably a wife whose income is substantial spends more time at the workplace and less time in the home. This normally would be considered more disruptive to family life. The findings of the study show that this simply is not so. It also can be inferred that husbands with workwives are concerned less about the family and more about finances. Wives in the future may well become more career oriented and less job oriented, since their families' happiness apparently rests with their income contribution.

Table 6–2.   Factors Affecting Workwife's Husband's Happiness.

	Percentage Happy
Wife's contribution to family's income	
40%	70
10%	39
Wife's education	
College graduate	89
High school graduate	46
Perceive wife as happy working	
All men	71
Wife controls 40% or more of income	86
No children at home	90

Most men (71 percent) believe that their wives are happy when working. This percentage escalates to 86 percent if the wives contribute 40 percent or more of the family income and 90 percent if they have no children in the home. Husbands apparently have accepted the new lifestyle of the working wife, since 55 percent of the men with daughters indicated that they anticipated that their daughters would become workwives.

For centuries, society has assumed that a wife's shopping behavior is closely aligned to the social class of her husband. In this study, we asked husbands if their wives received ideas on where to shop and what to buy from their employers or friends at the work place. Sixty-five percent of the men answered affirmatively. This percentage escalated to 90 percent if the wife was a college graduate and/or she contributed 40 percent or more of the family income. This finding indicates that the occupation of the workwife is more important than the social class of her husband in determining the pattern of her consumer behavior. Since 46 percent of all men are blue-collar workers and only 16 percent of all women workers are blue-collar, many women work in a white-collar environment that promotes different values from these held by their blue-collar husbands.

Husbands indicated that they helped their wives with shopping duties, and 40 percent indicated that they were the major shoppers for food for the household. This has major implications for advertisers who presently direct all advertising appeals to the female. The husbands' enthusiasm for other role-sharing duties was considerably less. For example, only 27 percent helped with the housework, 22 percent took on child care responsibilities,

Table 6–3.   Husband's Attitudes Towards the Workwife.

Attitudes	Percentage of Total
Anticipate daughter will be workwife	55
Wife gets ideas for shopping at work place	65
Helps wife with shopping duties	
Major food shopper	40
Helps with housework	27
Helps with child care	22
Rearranges work schedule	37
Why wives work	
Like income	58
Economic need	29

and 37 percent rearranged their work schedule in order to perform household tasks. The husbands also believed that they were responsible for major household purchases. When asked if they believed that their wives would make a major purchase such as a car or major appliance without their assistance, only 21 percent responded affirmatively. Wives' independence apparently increases with income contribution, however, since 43 percent of the husbands with wives contributing 40 percent or more of the family income indicated that their wives would feel free to make such a purchase independently.

When asked why they believed that their wives worked, the men gave different replies than the women did. For example, 58 percent of the men believe that their wives work because they "like" the income or were happier working. Only 29 percent of the men indicated that their wives worked because of economic need. When working women are asked this question, some 85 percent respond that they need the money. Perhaps today's inflationary economy requires a new definition of the term "need." The term also is defined differently by persons of various lifestyles. For example, does a person "need" a Cadillac or a Volkswagen? What may be a need for some may well be a high standard of living for others. Moreover, traditional values may be surfacing with this question. Society has been more receptive to women who work because they claim that they "have to" for economic purposes than it has to men who claim that they put their wives to work because she "needed" the income. Men may find solace in listing happiness as the reason that their wife works.

Among the most significant findings regarding consumer behavior is that the family eats out in restaurants more often as a result of the wife's working: Forty-three percent of all men claimed that their families did so. Only 23 percent of the families entertain more often, however, suggesting that eating out is a family affair and a way to save time for evening

Table 6–4. Consumer Behavior Factors Affected by Wife's Working.

	Percentage of Total
Eat out (restaurants) more often	43
Entertain more often	23
Shop in evening	51
Make more luxury purchases	40
Use more credit cards	31
Take longer or more vacations	29

shopping. Fifty-one percent of the men responded that their families shop for food, clothing, and household items in the evening.

Forty percent of the husbands claimed that their families made more luxury purchases as a result of their wives' working. The most significant purchase was an automobile. Fifty-six percent had more cars per family as a result of their wife's working, and 66 percent of the families purchased a "new" as opposed to "used" car. Only 13 percent of the men indicated that their families were planning to purchase another home within the next six months. Of interest here is the fact that 37 percent of the men indicated that their savings were growing because their wives worked and that these savings might be used to make future purchases.

The ownership and use of credit cards is directly correlated to the presence of a workwife. Thirty-one percent of all husbands indicated that their families owned and used more credit cards as a result of their wives' working. Their increased use was especially apparent in families with increases ranging from $7,000 to $10,000, where 62 percent of the husbands claimed increased use of credit cards.

Nearly one-third (29 percent) of the men indicated that their families were taking longer or more vacations since their wives began working. Not all of the families were primarily concerned with purchasing goods new in stores. Fifty-seven percent of all the men responded affirmatively when asked if they or their families frequented garage sales or bought used goods. In this case goods outweigh services, since only 11 percent indicated that their family used either full- or part-time household maids. Many families, however, value time and convenience over low prices. More than one-third (35 percent) of the men indicated that their wives were more concerned with saving time at the store than shopping for the best prices. In families with an annual income of more than $25,000, 71 percent of the men indicated that convenience and time saving were primary considerations.

Continuing education programs benefit from the fact that wives work. The men were asked if they anticipated that either they or their wives would return to school for more education or to update their skills. Twenty-five percent responded affirmatively. The percentage escalated to 67 percent if the wife and/or husband already had a college degree, suggesting that graduate education was rated as a premium. This question provoked strong reactions from the respondents. Many men indicated through unsolicited comments that they indeed felt liberated by their wives' income and that they would feel free to return to school, change jobs, or pursue a new career because the family was not solely dependent upon their income for survival.

The workwife's husband listed sports activity (38 percent) and television (30 percent) as his major leisure-time activity. Thirty-one percent of the men indicated that they and their wives jointly participated in a sport such as bowling, tennis, golf, or jogging. A third (34 percent) of the wives engaged in one or more hobbies, and only 13 percent of the wives had given up club membership or activity as a result of their working. The overall mood of the husbands was one of harmony. Most seemed resigned to the fact their wives worked and accepted their lifestyle as "a way of life." Only 24 percent indicated that they were having more trouble controlling or disciplining their children as a result of their wives' working; however, 33 percent indicated that they gave more money and/or gifts to their children as a result of their wives' income.

Although the husbands interviewed for this survey apparently accepted the changed lifestyles that resulted from their wives' working, they were aware of potential problems. When asked if they personally believed that the recent rise in the divorce rate in this country had anything to do with the fact that women were working, 46 percent of the men responded affirmatively. This opinion closely parallels the response received from working women who were asked this question; 55 percent shared this belief.

In summary, this survey indicated that most men are happy that their wives work and have adapted to the lifestyle that has accompanied this development. They are optimistic about the future and believe that their daughters will follow in their wives' footsteps and become workwives. They are realistic and speak openly about the problems but apparently believe that the advantages outweigh the disadvantages. Above all, the survey shows that yesterday's value system can no longer be used to cope with today's new world.

THE EARN-ALIKE COUPLE STUDY

In 1981, the author identified a new trend involving the workwife: the working woman whose annual income is consistently greater than her spouse's (McCall 1981). The U.S. Department of Labor (1975) estimates that 20 percent of all working women are paid as much or more than their spouses. The 1980 study interviewed both husbands and wives and was labeled "The Earn-Alike Couple." A summary of the major findings of this study follows.

The wife in the earn-alike couple perceives herself as different from other working women. She is more verbal, assertive, confident, better organized, goal-oriented, more supportive of other women, has different reasons for working, is countercultural in her perception of defined marital roles, and appears confident that marriage and family life can be combined successfully with a permanent job or career. She and her family tend to live in culturally mixed or nontradition-bound neighborhoods that reflect her personality of trend setter. She is family-oriented, appears less concerned with socializing or "keeping up with the Joneses," and concentrates on building a unique lifestyle of which her family is supportive. The responses from these women indicate that they are happy and successful in doing what they have set out to do.

Most of these women appear confident and happy in their work and would not stay home even if they could receive the same income for doing so. Their work is not perceived as threatening to the spouse or family members, nor do they possess guilt feelings about it. For example, they feel free to discuss their disproportionate contribution to the family income with friends and relatives. Their spouses are more free to change jobs or career patterns, and their families enjoy higher standards of living than would be possible without their efforts. They place a high value on education and job preparation for women. One of the greatest concerns of these women was a dissatisfaction with an educational system and culture that poorly prepared them with skills and information about the work world. Many of them believe that stereotyped roles dominate childrearing, and they are determined that stereotyping will not be inflicted on their children. Women with daughters expected that they would become workwives in the future.

These women have not found their careers to be easy, and most worked their way up to their present positions. Although they believe that they relate well to other women and do not object to having a woman boss, they have perceived considerable discrimination from men in their work places. They are mobile and would readily move for job advancement and thus provide a target market for industries that are dependent on frequent employee transfers.

The earn-alike couple reflects a new trend that reinforces the effectiveness of women in the work force. Income differential, traditionally acceptable only when the husband earns more than the wife, can and is being reversed for many married couples. This may mark the beginning of a new era where options to adopt different lifestyles, even though counter-cultural, will be explored.

Self Appraisal

Most (57.6 percent) of the women believed that they are the person most responsible for their success, which reinforces other evidence of their self-confidence. They related well to other women (93.5 percent responding affirmatively). More than half (56.4 percent) interviewed believed that other women were not jealous of them. Their parents (83.1 percent) were very supportive of their careers, and 76 percent credited parents with contributing to their daughters' work attitudes and career preparation. This, however, was not sufficient job preparation, as noted in the response of the women to the question regarding changing one major event in their past. Some 43.6 percent would have opted for more or better job training and direction. Presently, 18.2 percent of the women aspire to enter another job field, presumably because of misplacement or inadequate preparation.

Attitudes toward Their Work

The earn-alike couples were overwhelmingly happy about the wife's working, according to 97 percent of the husbands and wives. Some 68.6 percent of the women indicated that they would not stay home even if they could earn the same amount of money for doing so. Seventy-five percent of the women perceived no guilt feelings about working. They are achievement-oriented: Forty-nine percent had higher career aspirations, while 83 percent indicated that they were assertive both on the job and in the home. Sixty-one percent were discriminated against by the men with whom they worked. In contrast, they were supportive of women associates, with 87 percent indicating they do not suffer from the "queen bee syndrome" (i.e., not wanting competition from other women at the top) and 88 percent indicating that they would not react negatively to a woman boss. Most of the women either were promoted into their present work positions (54.3 percent) or applied (20.8 percent) for those positions.

A major consumer behavior finding is that when asked what their family would do if a job-advancement opportunity involved a move out of town, 70.7 percent indicated that they would move and 59.3 percent would move for either spouse. Earn-alike couples are a target market for employment by companies that seek mobile families.

Perception of Other Working Women

The data indicated a clear need for better jobs and better career preparation for women. Some 43.6 percent of the women believed that parents and schools should provide better career preparation, and 48.3 percent believed that schools should stop stereotyping by sex. They also believed (47 percent) that cultural stereotyping is the main reason that most working women earn less than their husbands.

Eighty-seven percent of the women predict that working women in the future will have fewer, if any, children. They also appear confident that workwives represent a permanent lifestyle, since 76 percent of the women with daughters believe that they too will become workwives.

108 HOUSEHOLD ROLES

The women of the survey appeared unaware of the changing social conditions that have resulted from the large number of women who work outside the home. When asked why so many successful women were single or divorced, 17.4 percent of the respondents were either unaware of the condition or did not have an answer. Of those who answered the question, 39.4 percent believed that the husband felt threatened, and 11 percent believed that women became independent with their own income. To the question of how best to handle volunteer jobs in schools, clubs, and charitable organizations, 66.5 percent did not know or did not answer. The earn-alike wives saw other women's reasons for working as different from their own or even those of their husbands. The earn-alike women apparently perceived that other women worked because of need but that they and their husbands worked because they were happy in their work.

Attitudes toward Married Life

Satisfaction with lifestyle is very apparent in the respondents' answers in this category. The women appear generally confident that marriage can be successfully combined with a job or career for the wife.

Family members are supportive of the earn-alike wife's work. Of the 52.5 percent of the sample who had children, most (55%) indicated that their children were proud of their mother's work, and 33 percent indicated that their children were indifferent and accepted it as normal. Eight-three percent of the parents stated that they experienced no difficulty in

Table 6–5. Workwife's Perceptions of Why She Works (percentage).

	Why You Work	Husband's Perception	Why Other Women Work
Needs money	41.5	22.5	80.1
Likes money for higher standard of living and luxuries	5.9	35.2	5.1
Is happier working	35.6	39.4	7.6
Uses training or educational preparation	16.1	N/A	5.1
No answer	0.9	2.9	2.1
	100.0	100.0	100.0

disciplining their offspring. The earn-alike mother is not perceived as "different" by her children (59%) or by her husband, since 55 percent indicated they did not earn more respect in the home for contributing a considerable portion of the family income. This indicates good adjustment by the children to their lifestyles, regardless of how unconventional they might be. Of the women who need child care, 35 percent use a day care center, 21 percent use a private home, 20 percent use a relative, and 24 percent let child stay alone (presumably with older children) after school.

The earn-alike women strongly (82.6%) believed that their husbands were freer to change jobs, careers, or return to school. When queried about future educational plans for their families, 66.5 percent wanted college for their children, 50.8 percent wanted to return to college themselves, and 32.5 percent reported that their husbands wanted to return to or enter college. This data supported a previous finding that indicated that the women desired better job training for themselves and their families.

Sixty-three percent of the women believed that they better organized household activities than nonworking women did. Role sharing of household duties by family members presented further evidence of a family support system. Women in the study indicated that their husbands were either mostly responsible for or shared equally in each of the following categories:

Housework	39.0%
Food shopping	43.6
Child care	57.2
Cooking	41.5
Chauffering children	51.0

The respondents were openly opposed to structured or conventional role playing. In fact, they seemed to enjoy a support system that enables each spouse to assume any necessary role.

When asked how their married life had changed as a result of an elevated salary, only 3.4 percent of the women said "worse"; one-third indicated "no change," and 50.8 percent said that they "enjoyed more freedom and/or a higher standard of living." They are apparently conscious of cost factors, since 43.2 percent listed "curb inflation" as the number-one national priority.

Leisure-Time Activities

The women were highly family oriented, as was evident in their preferred leisure-time attitudes and activities. Some 73.7 percent spend leisure time with their families, only 16.9 percent preferred to spend it alone, and 9.3 percent chose the company of others. In order of listed preference, the leisure-time activities were:

Reading	58.1%
Hobbies	56.8
Television	51.3
Visiting relatives or friends	36.9
Gardening	31.8
Participating in sports	28.4
Attending sports event	27.1

(These figures add up to more than 100 percent, since most of the women listed more than one activity.) The activity shared by most respondents, reading, was well supported by the women's stated use of the media.

Media Use and Appraisal

Most (74.2 percent) of the respondents read a newspaper once a day, 57.6 percent read newspapers for advertising specials, and 57.2 percent read classified advertising for the purchase of used goods when needed. This indicates that the newspaper is an excellent medium for reaching the earn-alike couple. Some 63.4 percent of the women watched less than three hours of television per day; only 11.9 percent watch more than three hours per day; and 24.6 percent rarely or never watched it. Because of the long hours that these women spend at the work place, they are likely targets for specific timing for positioning television advertising. Another excellent medium for reaching these women appears to be the radio. Sixty-eight percent listen less than three hours per day; 16.1 percent listen more than three hours; and only 14.8 percent rarely or never listen to the radio. The earn-alike wife reads regularly, with 84.3 percent reading at least one magazine per month, 49.6 percent reading two to five periodicals per month, and 28.8 percent reading more than five magazines per month.

The women in the survey felt that women are depicted in the media in a range of sexist roles. Twenty-eight percent thought that women are treated as sex symbols in advertising, 27.5 percent as housewives, 11.9 percent as dependent on men. Less than one-third (30.5%) thought that women are portrayed as a workwife or otherwise favorably regarding their societal roles, and 2.1 percent had no opinion. When asked how business could improve its image, only 8.5 percent of the women complained about advertising, indicating relative satisfaction with the content of the advertising even if not with its symbolism.

Mail-order catalogs were not used heavily by the earn-alike wife: 56.8 percent reported that they rarely, if ever, used them. Seventy-two percent stated that they rarely, if ever, placed an order for products by telephone. Nevertheless, both mail-order and telephone sales are appropriate media to reach working women who place a high value on convenience in shopping.

Entertainment

Most (52.1%) of the women entertained in their home, and 21.6% go to events with their family. Restaurants were highly favored; 68.7 percent ate at least one meal per week (other than lunches) at a restaurant, and more than one-third (35.6%) ate two to three meals a week at a restaurant. Vacations are also important to this group; 70.4 percent of the families took at least one vacation out of town each year, and 40.3 percent took two or more vacations per year.

Consumer Behavior

Fifty percent of the respondents were more interested in saving time and in convenience than in price when shopping for products or services. This suggests that retailers and service businesses should accommodate themselves to the workwife's limited number of hours for shopping. The time may have come for night and weekend repair and delivery services.

Nearly two-thirds (64%) of the women got ideas on where to shop and what to buy from persons at their workplace, and most (60.6%) said that these ideas agreed with those of their husbands. This means that business should segment the market by the workwife's occupational category, since work provides the major source of information for her shopping behavior. The family's social class is no longer a corollary of the husband's occupation.

Although the work place is a significant source of ideas, the earn-alike wife still relies on her husband for help in decisionmaking with regard to large or luxury purchases. Some 77.5 percent of working women still do not feel free to purchase this type of item without consulting their husbands. This egalitarian role-sharing in decisionmaking is equally apparent in the responses to questions about how each spouse's income is handled in the household. Some 85.2 percent of the couples pool their funds.

Credit cards are an integral part of these families' consumer behavior. Bank cards (Visa, Mastercharge, etc.) are used by 72 percent of the couples, gasoline credit cards by 60.2 percent, department store charge cards by 59.3 percent, and American Express cards by 25.4 percent. Only 5.1 percent of the couples listed "less use of credit" as a way to fight inflation. Some 54.2 percent of the wives indicated that they pay the bills; the national average is 75 percent. Savings institutions should be encouraged to find that 78.8 percent of the earn-alike couples contribute regularly to a savings account.

The women were not critical of business in general. Their major complaint (46.6%) was the poor quality of sales service or the lack of any sales service at all. Second in importance was inadequate repair service (28.8%), followed by insecurity in knowing how or where to file a complaint (18.2%). Only 17.8 percent of the respondents listed being overcharged as a problem, and 14.8 percent were concerned with old or stale merchandise. The women were even less informed regarding suggestions about how business might improve its image; 38.6 percent of the women "did not know" or did not answer the question. About one-third (34.7%) wanted sales help to be better trained both in product information and general attitude toward the customer.

In response to the question regarding the efforts of their families to fight inflation, which they listed as the number-one national priority, 44.5 percent indicated that they were doing more bargain shopping. This correlates with the large percentage (57.2%) of respondents who indicated that they bought second-hand merchandise at garage sales and flea markets and the 57.6 percent who read newspapers for advertisements of special sales.

The earn-alike couple's food shopping profile is: once a week (45.8%), evenings (45.8%), Saturdays (37.7%), at one store (58.9%), with 55.1 percent of the women being the major shopper for the household's food. Some 12.7 percent of the women reported that the husband was the major food shopper, and an additional 30.9 percent share this responsibility with their spouses. Merchandisers should target their advertising appeals to the male, who is assuming much of the shopping responsibility.

Among the nonstore retailers (door-to-door salespersons, vending machines, and mail-order catalogs), vending machines faired the best, with only 46.2 percent of the women abstaining from their use. In contrast, 96.6 percent of the respondents rarely, if ever, used the door-to-door salesperson method, and 56.8 percent rarely, if ever, used a mail-order catalog.

One-sixth of the respondents (16.5%) recommended other earn-alike couples to be considered for this survey.

More than two-thirds (66.5%) of the respondents feel free to discuss the differential between their incomes and their spouses' incomes with family, friends, relatives or peers. More than three-fourths (77.1%) would be willing to share the details of their lifestyles with the local and national press. This seems to confirm that the earn-alike couple is confident and secure in its choice of lifestyle.

CONCLUSION

Thirty-five trends have been identified that should have measurable effects on individual lifestyles, institutions, and the marketing of products and services in the next decade. Research into these categories would provide a plethora of data for future analysis.

Present Trends	*Future Effects*
1. Trading down	smaller families less beef consumption less apparel, with trend to discounting smaller living quarters smaller cars and fewer new ones; less gasoline consumption less heating and cooling of homes; less energy consumption less saving
2. Twenty-four hour shopping	repair services, delivery services, entertainment
3. Disposable products	convenience and high cost of repair
4. Entitlements	wants converted to rights
5. Instant gratification	credit versus cash (85 million credit cards with over $0.70 of each dollar) convenience products and services automated all-night banking self-service for instant delivery of goods
6. Theology of pleasure	living in present, not future elderly not saving to leave inheritance for children since children make more than they do, thus spend now planned leisure time and more of it; growth of hobbies, creative projects, travel, sports participation

7.	New services	dentists and doctors in retail stores (Sears) financial services in malls valet parking service renting of products and services
8.	Life simplification	no cooking, ironing no repair for disposables labor-saving appliances cars with power steering, brakes, windows
9.	Morality revolution	fastest growing household is the unwed couple use of sex for all types of advertising women taking an equal role in initiating dates, paying their share
10.	Emphasis on youth	
11.	Institutional reliance	people used to rely on themselves, now on institutions (hospitals, job benefits, government, welfare, unions, laws) before 1950, 26 percent of the population was self-employed; today, less than 7 percent is self-employed ironically, less confidence in institutions (wide separation of management from ownership, high labor turnover, consumerism, work rights)
12.	New types of jobs	widens generation gap
13.	New eating habits	eating habits adapt to sedentary jobs
14.	Crisis immunity	television desensitizes
15.	Less "keeping up with the Joneses"	more interest in a satisfying family lifestyle, since neighbors are strangers
16.	Reverse spending patterns	more functional gifts, since wife is working

17.	Use of unused resources	churches, office buildings at night nursing homes for elderly next to orphans' homes, rehabilitation of convicts while incarcerated
18.	Electronic funds transfer	
19.	Computerized home	education, purchasing, functioning, household
20.	Mail order	15 percent of retail business by 1985 correspondence schools
21.	Discount for cash	
22.	Component financing of homes	
23.	Graying of America	those over age 65 will comprise 30 percent of the population by 1995
24.	Nation of night owls	currently night workers comprise 20 percent of the work force
25.	Hispanic market	60 percent of growth in past decade (18 million persons)
26.	More government legislation	
27.	Decentralization of trends	five bellweather states (California, Colorado, Connecticut, Florida, and Washington)
28.	Growth of singles	now comprise 40 percent of population; half are age 35
29.	Employment	flextime one-third working couples with child under age 14 30 percent work in underground economies (cash and flea markets)
30.	Competition	transfer from price to nonprice (credit, services, return policy, warranties, prestige, etc.)

31. Department stores   management seminars for women
                                    versus fashion shows
                                 mobile on wheels

32. Advertising   by professionals
                                 geared more to men as shoppers
                                 cult figures

33. Charity   working women inactive
                                 garage sales (sell it don't give it)

34. Women prepare for   education, $311 per week; social work
     low-paying jobs $286; secretary $229; versus
                                    engineer, $547 per week; physician
                                    $512; plumber $404

                                 do not play computer games
                                 taught to hide intelligence, which does
                                    not transfer into management roles
                                 no role models

35. Changing composition   binuclear families of friendly divorced
     of households   couples
                                 singles of all ages
                                 elderly
                                 unmarried couples living together

Research on the workwife from an economic, sociological, and psychological perspective should be ongoing. The U.S. Bureau of Census (1980) estimates that by 1995 participation in the labor force will increase by 34 percent for women and 14 percent for men. Society has accepted women of all ages in the work force. Business disciplines in general, and marketing in particular, will be well rewarded for constant surveillance of this significant trend.

7 FAMILIES UNDER PRESSURE Meeting Their Demands for Services

Laura Lein

One subtle revolution in family life in the United States has been the increasing participation of women in the labor force. Not only are more and more women in paid jobs, but they are working more years of their life. In fact, the most rapid increase in women's employment is now among mothers of young children. In 1955, only 17 percent of mothers of young children were employed full- and part-time. By 1980, that figure had increased to almost half (Luech, Orr, and O'Connell 1982:1).

This change in the demography of women's employment has had far-reaching implications for family life in the United States and for the goods and services that family members need. The traditional American family, once typified as a wage-earning father, a mother at home, and a couple of children, has changed significantly; now only 12 percent of American families fit that model of family life (Johnson and Hayghe 1977: Table 4). Furthermore, husbands and wives are employed in about half of all married couples; only one spouse is employed in 25 percent of the couples; and neither is employed in the remaining 25 percent (Hayghe 1982: Table 4). The dual-earner family is becoming part of the mainstream of American life.

The analysis of family life reported in this paper is based primarily on data collected by the Working Family Project between 1973 and 1977 from twenty-three white, middle-income, dual-earner families.[1] Family income ranged between $6,000 and $20,000 at a time when the median family income in the United States was approximately $13,000 according to

117

information from the U.S. Bureau of the Census and the U.S. Department of Labor Statistics. Research staff interviewed husband and wife separately and together. Observations were performed in the home with the husband alone with children, the wife alone with children, and the couple together with children.

Intensive, qualitative research on families helps explain how changing patterns of family life affect the choices and decisions made by mothers and fathers. Changing family demography often leads to the adoption of different practices and patterns by individual families. Through the detailed interviews and observations undertaken in more qualitative studies, it is possible to trace how families conceptualize the circumstances that face them and the internal family dynamics underlying family responses to these changing social and economic conditions. Through such research, it is possible to better understand how families make decisions and how a changing society influences the kinds of decisions they must make.

Thus, qualitative research encourages the development of new and innovative hypotheses about family decisionmaking. Once developed and refined, these hypotheses can suggest new directions for large-scale data collection and surveys of American families. A combination of intensive methodologies and large-scale surveys can then result in the development of particularly illuminating profiles of American family life.

MOTHERS' EMPLOYMENT AND FAMILY LIFE

For several reasons, this paper concentrates on research on two-parent, two-earner families with children (Lein 1984; Dougherty 1981; Howrigan 1977; H. Weiss 1977). First, such families are a large and growing proportion of American families. Second, although there has been a pronounced increase in the number of single-parent families, most families with children still are made up of two parents for at least part of their family life history. Third, the period of family life when parents are both employed and also have responsibility for children is a time of considerable stress (Peters 1976).

Parents in dual-earner families bring values and critieria specific to their family model and life cycle stage to the decisions they make about procuring services and goods. They represent a large market that faces significant pressures on time and energy. These parents are eager for assistance and support in a number of different areas of responsibility. Through a detailed understanding of how daily pressures affect family life and how families respond to these pressures, it is possible to draw conclusions about family needs that extend beyond the issues of convenience and efficiency.

White two-earner families in the United States have characteristics distinctly different from those of black and other ethnic families and from those families in many other societies. One particularly marked difference is that adolescent children lack responsibility and carry a limited workload in the home (Peters 1976). Most changes and negotiations in workload among the families described in this paper occurred between husband and wife because these parents expected few changes in the workload and responsibility assumed by their adolescent or younger children.

Two phenomena have a strong effect on how parents in dual-earner families with young children select and evaluate many of the goods and services they eventually purchase. First, particularly in considering those goods or services that substitute for the parents' lack of time with the family, parents try to purchase those goods and services that reflect their personal values and expectations of what family life should be. The obvious variables of convenience, cost, and endorsement by professional experts explain only part of the decisions that parents make. Instead, they are likely to think about their purchases in terms of investment in the future in general and in their children in particular. Dual-earner families, particularly two-career families, are likely to be considered an exciting new market and a market susceptible to purchases based on whims—that is, purchases expressive of relatively transient feelings and needs. However, families, even dual-earner families, with young children retain an instrumental mode of purchasing, even though they may have significant resources at their disposal. They continue to invest in the long-term future, particularly the future represented by their children.

Second, fathers are becoming increasingly active participants in family life, and they are playing a new and more active role in the selection and purchase of family goods and services. However, in most families the involvement of fathers in daily family life has not yet reached the proportions of characteristic change, and the changes that are occurring are not always easy. Almost universally, communication between spouses is considered something to be fostered and encouraged, but communication as husband and wife meet the combined stresses of two paid jobs and family responsibilities, can be time-consuming, repetitive, and, at least in the short term, less than rewarding to both participants. Talking about who has to do what and when can become the main—sometimes the only—topic of conversation.

PARENTS AND PURCHASES

Parents with young children feel that many of their selections reflect their parental ability and commitment. They expect to spend time, thought, and energy in getting what will be best for their children and families and what best suits their values as parents. As parents spend less time with their children, they often become increasingly concerned with the purchases that they make of care services, of food, of toys, even of clothing—all of which must protect and nourish their children even during periods when the parents themselves cannot be present.

Parents do not feel that they must merely select quality goods and services for their children. Many parents feel that they can best exercise their responsibilities as parents when they select needed goods and services for child rearing and maintaining family life from a reasonable array of choices. Forced decisions among limited options restrict their decision-making possibilities as parents and leave parents feeling that they have been denied the opportunity that they require to exercise their parental responsibilities.

Parents' sense of their responsibility toward their children and the creation of a warm and secure family life is evident in the way they discuss a number of decisions: decisions about where to live, what kind of house to buy, educational programs and even toys, and services such as child care, housekeeping services, and entertainment. The significance of these concerns in parents' lives distinguishes parents from adults without responsibilities for children. They are likely to think of major purchases and service contracts as an expression of their serious responsibility for children and the quality of family life, rather than as a reflection of personal whims. The energy and caring that parents devote to decisions affecting family life reflect their commitment to their families and the high value that they place on family life.

Furthermore, decisions about family services and goods often reflect the joint decisions of husbands and wives. The fundamental changes in family life caused by rapidly increasing mothers' employment have drawn fathers into somewhat more active participation in family life and homemaking. Just as employed wives are more likely to be active in assessing the advantages and disadvantages of such family issues as a geographic move or the assumption of a new job with increased stress and demands, so are husbands of employed women more likely to be actively involved in the selection of goods and services for the home. The patterns of decision-making in dual-earner families, however, are not necessarily clear-cut.

FAMILY MODELS

Observers have tended to conceptualize families with both parents employed as moving along a continuum from a traditional model of family life to an egalitarian model. The traditional model is typified by sex-stereotyped expectations of the work to be performed by men and women in families. In the egalitarian family, both women and men are expected to contribute equally. Therefore, according to theory, as the expectations of men and women change, so too does the work actually accomplished by men and women in households. Also, according to this theory, the pressures on dual-earner families should push them toward a more egalitarian system for undertaking responsibility for the work of the home.

However, families do not change in a simple progression from traditional to egalitarian. Family ideology and family practice do not necessarily change together. In fact, shifts in family practice often occur without any significant change in family ideology. Thus, mothers and fathers in traditional families with an ideology of sex-segregated labor in the home may maintain their ideology while adapting their practices to changing circumstances by helping each other. Husbands and wives in ideologically traditional dual-earner families often decide that when mothers go to work, it is too hard for them to undertake all of the labor in the home. These women are, in fact, helping with the man's traditional task of breadwinning. Therefore, the husband should help out with some of the work of the home.

This is certainly not universally true among traditional dual-earner families. Some ideologically traditional dual-earner families persist in assigning the wife's income to the purchase of relative nonessentials so that it is not considered as contributing to the family's living. Wives in these families are likely to persist as the primary, indeed the sole, homemaker. Such families are unlikely to change until it becomes clear that the wife's income is buying more than nonessentials.

Mothers and fathers aspiring to an egalitarian marriage may discover that the costs of negotiating a full partnership system are too high. It takes considerable time and energy, as well as commitment, to move away from the family models they experienced as children and to develop new family models for which there are few available examples. As the pressures on them increase, they feel the need to fall back on the more familiar sex-segregated division of tasks. Parents tend to draw strength from their own backgrounds and experience and comfort from doing things as their parents did.

Not all egalitarian families revert to this compromise solution. Some adopt rigid patterns of alternation of tasks between parents in order to maintain equal contributions to homemaking. However, when the time devoted to actual negotiations over who will do what task becomes burdensome or the rigidity of the system for sharing responsibility too strenuous, such families are likely to fall back on a somewhat more sex-segregated pattern of work in the home simply because it is easier to manage.

Husbands and wives in egalitarian families frequently find themselves involved in intense negotiations over who will do what work around the house, in part because the activities of homemaking are so numerous and so complex. Adults seem to agree that household tasks with greater flexibility, visibility, and opportunity to socialize are more desirable and enjoyable to the performer. In fact, as husbands and wives renegotiate tasks, the first tasks that move from the women's to the men's domain are those that rate high on each of these qualities. Husbands, therefore, are more likely to take on chores that allow considerable socializing with their children (outings, bedtime, supervision of play periods), cooking of special meals and desserts for company or for special family occasions, and chores, such as floor washing and vacuuming, that enjoy a good deal more flexibility in terms of scheduling than dishwashing, cooking routine meals, and preparing children for school. (H. Weiss 1977).

In order to arrive at a genuinely egalitarian sharing of responsibilities, men and women are apt to find themselves immersed in lengthy negotiations. When such discussions do not occur, wives tend to find themselves left the less rewarding tasks at the same time that husbands may feel unappreciated, even though they have assumed responsibility for many tasks in addition to those traditionally performed by men. Having arrived at this dead-end position, both men and women are likely to ask themselves if achieving an egalitarian arrangement in housework will ever work for them. They discover that homemaking is not a homogeneous job that can easily be split. It is a large number of tasks with different rewards and costs that must be shared in egalitarian families.

Difficult family negotiations can be impaired by the lack of support that many men receive from male friends and colleagues. Men who are part of social networks in which they and their friends refrain from speaking about their family responsibilities or their feelings for their families receive relatively little reinforcement outside the family for taking an active role in daily family life. Furthermore, many men's social networks discourage their more active participation. Not only do men in social networks offer each other little praise for the assumption of significant family responsibilities, but they may actually see such family involvement as unmanly and illustrative of a looser commitment to jobs, colleagues, and men in general (Lein 1979b).

Even though family pressures suggest that both husband and wife should contribute to earning a living and to homemaking, many families today still feel that family life requires a mother to maintain her primary orientation to the home and a father to maintain his primary orientation to the work place. Other families are able to sustain a completely egalitarian model of family life in spite of the fact that negotiations over who should do what are time-consuming and occasionally difficult. The issues of family ideology and practice are not abstract ones for the mothers and fathers involved. These parents respond in terms of their beliefs about what is best for the family. In spite of ambivalence, however, parents perceive an overall change in American families from traditional to egalitarian, and time-use studies over the past twenty years support the perception that amounts of time devoted to housework by men and women have changed (Lopata and Pleck 1983).

Families do not simply become egalitarian under the pressures of life in a dual-earner family. There is no one clear progression from traditional to egalitarian; ideology or practice may be altered. Family members negotiate their responsibilities and adapt ideology and practice to reflect their own experiences, the social context within which their family lives, and the stresses they face in the family, on the job, and in the larger social community.

AN EXAMPLE OF THE SELECTION OF A FAMILY SERVICE: CHILD CARE

The selection of child care by families with two employed parents illustrates the complexity of the process by which parents mediate between their ideologies of family life and the pressures of daily existence. It illustrates the increasing involvement and concern of fathers. It demonstrates the continuing commitment of parents to exercising control over the environments in which their children are cared for.

In spite of recent changes in family life, most child-care work and responsibility is taken on by the mother in the large majority of American families (Howrigan 1977). When the mother is employed, an alternative for caring for her children must be found. The range of selected options is large, and the reasons for parental choice of any given option are complex.

What kinds of child care do employed American parents select? In fact, the use of day-care centers, probably the most debated child care option, is a relatively infrequent choice. Of American preschoolers of full-time employed mothers, only 14.6 percent are cared for in day-care centers; for children under age 3, that percentage is even smaller, 9.1 percent (Luech, Orr, and O'Connell 1982:6). Children of full-time employed mothers are cared for in the following ways (1982:6): care in their own home, 28.6 percent; care in someone else's home, 47.4 percent; and day-care center, 14.6 percent.

How do American parents decide what kind of child care to use for their children? Cost, convenience, and the hours of service provided certainly play a part in parents' decisions. But parents also expect that the services they acquire for their children will be consistent with family values and that the selection of a service will allow parents to maintain their decision-making and control over the environment in which their children will be raised.

Parents care about the same qualities in child care that they are concerned about in their own parenting: the emotional warmth of the caretaker, his—or more usually her—consistency with children, values and disciplinary measures that are similar to those espoused by the parents, and the physical safety and protection of their children (Lein 1979a:12). Compatibility with family values is an increasing concern for families that must substitute purchased or exchanged services for those traditionally undertaken in the family by the mother. Parents, however, differ considerably not only in the values they hold but also in their assessment of how these values can best be expressed. Parents universally subscribe to the idea that parental love is important to healthy child development. For some parents this means that only parents or close relatives and friends should be responsible for the care of the young child. For other parents, child care is a service to be distinguished from parental caring and should be delivered by professionals with the best possible training and resources.

Parents believe that the family is an important setting in which the child learns to trust and love in a protected environment. However, for some families, their belief in the family as a child care setting suggests that children should always be cared for in a family setting. These families believe that small children may well be intimidated by formal institutional settings. Furthermore, they feel that a contained and nurturing environment cannot be found outside the family setting. Families holding such beliefs may well seek out family day care. Other families, believing that children benefit from the stimulation of different kinds of settings, might well choose a more formal arrangement that offers different kinds of opportunities than does family life.

Not only do parents bring a number of complex concerns to the selection of child care, but husbands and wives both often have strong opinions on the kind and quality of care essential for their child. Both parents draw on their experiences with young children and their sometimes distinctive interpretations of the world in which they are preparing their children to live. Fathers' and mothers' different notions of the parental role and different family experiences and employment patterns express their individual concerns for their children in the selection of child care. For instance, one academic parent might be very concerned that the child participate in a program that fosters cognitive skills. Another parent who suffered from a lonely childhood might feel that the opportunity to play with other children is a first priority.

Through the selection of the child care they use, fathers and mothers express their concern about the social, cognitive, and emotional growth of their children and their sense of what environments will best enhance their child's development. They also express their concern about the physical safety of the child by examining child-care facilities. The selection of child care—in effect, a substitute for the parents—reflects fundamental parental values.

THE SELECTION OF GOODS AND SERVICES BY DUAL-EARNER FAMILIES

An analysis of how families think about child care illustrates three significant themes concerning the selection of goods and services by fathers and mothers in dual-career families. First, parents of young children in dual-earner families are buying services and goods that families produce for themselves in traditional homes. Second, because they are purchasing these services that "substitute" for the homemaker, parents evaluate the goods and services they purchase in terms of how well they reflect their values about home and family. Third, fathers and mothers in dual-earner families undertake considerable discussion and joint work in the selection of those goods and services that they see as most pivotal to the well-being of their family.

As mothers of young children enter the paid labor force, child care is only one of the goods and services that they are likely to purchase to replace the work that mothers contribute in a traditional family. Husbands and wives have little difficulty agreeing on the purchase of convenience foods, help in the household (if the family can afford the expense), and extra transportation. However, the selection of services that substitute for what parents feel are their traditional home responsibilities engages parents' scrutiny of the quality and type of service. If parenting will be provided in part by these services, the services must reflect those fundamental family values that are of greatest importance to them.

In dual-earner families, except for the most egalitarian of families, husbands and wives typically take on different chores, and these chores require different purchasing decisions. In part because the first major transfer of responsibility in families with young children is usually responsibility for children's care and entertainment during hours when they can socialize and play, both parents share concern about the selection of child-care services. Husbands and wives have strong opinions about what constitutes good child care. Their concern about child care and the selection of good child care reflects their joint caring as well as their vision of children as a primary responsibility around which their other responsibilities revolve.

Where the task is not the subject of much transfer of responsibility and where the chores themselves are not the focus of much attention either through their visibility or through the opportunity to socialize, husbands and wives may well not enter into detailed discussion about the selection of a service. The employed mother, however, is still apt to consider many of the goods and services that she purchases as substitutes for herself and for her own work in the home. She undertakes the measurement of goods and services against family values. She sees her selection of many services and goods as an important representation of her responsibility for the family's well-being.

Where fathers are actively involved in the selection of goods and services that support family life, the negotiations and discussions between husband and wife represent an important job in itself. Furthermore, fathers coming new to the task and joining their wives in homemaking, rather than undertaking the task alone, may bring distinctive perspectives to the task. What we have learned about the rewards and difficulties of communication between husband and wife in dual-earner families and the relative isolation of men in social networks raises a number of questions for further research and development.

APPROACHES TO THE DEVELOPMENT
OF PRODUCTS FOR DUAL-EARNER FAMILIES

The development of products aimed at the growing new market of dual-earner families has concentrated on convenience and efficiency. While these are certainly important values for two-earner families undertaking the combined tasks of homemaking, child rearing, and wage earning, other significant values emerge from interviews with dual-earner families. Perhaps most important, services and products need to help families to develop strategies for team-building among family members.

Time for enjoyable socializing is scarce. The allocation of pleasant time with children is often an issue of heated negotiation between husbands and wives. Parents in dual-earner families need not only to be able to cook nourishing, appetizing meals efficiently but also to develop strategies for working with each other and with their children in the preparation of meals. Parents need not only to clean their houses quickly; they need to involve all members of the family in a team effort to accomplish this homemaking task. Simply helping individual adults to undertake tasks more efficiently assists them in meeting family demands in the short run, but it does not aid in the creation of a different family environment in the long run.

Children, in particular, and even husbands, to some extent, are still often perceived as "putterers" and learners, rather than as potential full-fledged participants in the work of homemaking. The products developed to support homemaking activities do little to encourage all members of the family to work together. Products are designed for individuals rather than for teams and for teams that include novices.

Dual-earner families are under significant stress as they attempt to accomplish the daily round of activities. Women, still carrying the greatest amount of the homemaking burden, certainly feel the need for products that will enable them to carry out their responsibilities more efficiently. Even more important, however, they need products and services that will draw their husbands and children into the major activities of homemaking. And their husbands and children require reinforcement in a social environment that often does not offer them much reinforcement for undertaking homemaking activities. The development of products that encourage parents and children to operate as a team may well accomplish as much or more for families as products that simply assist individuals to operate more quickly and efficiently.

NOTE

1. The Working Family Project was comprised of a team of sociologists, anthropologists, and psychologists that worked with dual-worker families in the Boston area. It was funded by the National Institute of Education, Project No. 3-3094, and the National Institute of Mental Health, Project No. 24742. Staff included: Laura Lein, principal investigator; Janet Lennon, administrator; and Kevin Dougherty, Maureen Durham, Gail Howrigan, Michael Pratt, Michael Schudson, Ronald Thomas, and Heather Weiss, research collaborators.

8 A DYNAMIC MODEL OF ROLE ALLOCATION IN THE HOUSEHOLD
Marketing Management and Research Implications

Mary Lou Roberts and Lawrence H. Wortzel

By virtually any measure, there have been profound changes over the last few years in the composition of households and in the allocation of roles, and thus tasks, among household members. These changes have both complicated and made less certain the decisions made by consumer goods marketers with respect to targeting household purchase decisionmakers and designing and positioning product offerings.

Evidence of changing role allocations, such as husbands who shop for food, has appeared in a few publicly reported commercial studies (Benton & Bowles 1980; Cunningham & Walsh April 1980, October 1980; *Newsweek* 1979). Undoubtedly, many other studies exist in the files of commercial researchers and market research departments. The few studies that have been reported publicly focus solely on describing consumption-related outcomes (e.g., husbands frequently choose brands different from those that wives would have chosen). The factors that determine these outcomes, knowledge of which is critical for correct positioning, have not been investigated. In addition, these studies lack a conceptual framework. Thus, the marketer confronted with evidence of role change and its concomitant targeting and positioning problems has had to approach each situation individually and empirically.

Changing role relationships have been studied extensively by behavioral scientists and findings potentially useful to marketers have emerged. However, these findings are neither well-organized nor available in a form

129

that makes them easy to use in looking at product development and positioning or targeting alternatives directly. In their present form, these findings are also difficult to use as a conceptual foundation for conducting marketing research aimed at solving specific product development, targeting, or positioning problems.

A model that is solidly grounded in the empirical and conceptual literature of the behavioral sciences could strengthen the research approaches of both academics and practitioners. It also could help build a base of empirical knowledge that deals with the consumer behavior-related aspects of household task performance, consumption choices, and decision processes.

There has been at least one attempt to build a model that organizes a particular subarea of this field, role transferral from one spouse to the other (Roberts and Wortzel 1981), and there has been at least one attempt to build a model of household decisionmaking (Sheth 1974). However, both of these attempts fall short: the Roberts and Wortzel because it is too narrow and specific, and the Sheth because it is too broad and general.

This paper proposes a model that is both broad and specific: one that deals with both initial task assumptions and changes in task performance over time and that identifies the variables that affect role assumption and change. The proposed model will be applicable to both traditional (married couples) and nontraditional households. It will also provide a basis for identifying the marketing management implications of role assumption and change.

In accomplishing this task, we will first review the relevant literature and then propose the resultant conceptual model. Since our focus is household task allocation, not household decisionmaking, most of the literature on household decisionmaking, which is already quite familiar to marketers, bears no direct relationship to our subject. It should be noted, however, that the recent interest of marketing researchers and practitioners in the subject of household task allocations is predicated on the assumption that task performance directly influences marketplace behaviors. Some of the effects are readily apparent, as in the case of family members other than the wife who perform the grocery shopping task. Others are less easily observed and measured. For example, less well understood is the effect that husbands' increasing assumption of child care has on the purchases of products and services for children. Empirical tests of the propositions that we advance will result in the confirmation, or resolution, of the linkage between performance of household tasks and household consumption and decision-making behavior. Confirming the existence of this linkage should be an essential thrust of future research in household consumption behavior.

In literature on household task allocation we try to identify gaps in knowledge and also to point out the managerial implications of what is known. Principally, these are consumer behavior implications with indications for managerial action. In discussing the consumer behavior implications of the model, we make use of both propositions and research questions that suggest specific hypotheses or directions for needed empirical research. Propositions are used to describe the key parameters of the model. Research questions are used to describe information that has clear managerial, as well as theoretical, relevance. Thus, the propositions and related research questions should interest researchers and managers who have specific marketing problems to solve.

THE RELEVANT LITERATURE

Most of the literature on household task allocation is found in the behavioral sciences. Table 8-1 (end of chapter) summarizes this literature and organizes it by its major dimensions: demographic, sociological, and individual determinants.

Several things related to the general thrust of this literature quickly become apparent from an examination of the table. The first is that behavioral scientists have studied demographic and sociological determinants of household task allocation much more extensively than they have studied individual determinants. Individual determinants, however, make up most of the empirical research conducted by marketers.

More importantly, with the exception of Blood and Wolfe (1960), researchers have generally concentrated on studying the effect of a single variable rather than on the interactions among the large number of variables that have been shown to affect household task allocation. Even Blood and Wolfe did not conduct statistical analyses that would uncover interactions.

Another major gap in the empirical research conducted to date is the paucity of studies that deal with task allocations in nontraditional households (e.g., cohabiters and roommates). Nontraditional households comprise a significant and increasing proportion of total households, and demographic and economic trends suggest that they will continue to do so. This omission, therefore, is a serious one.

The most important limitation, however, is that all of the studies listed in Table 8-1 are cross-sectional, cutting into a process that most of the researchers recognize as ongoing. The absence of longitudinal studies means that the *process* by which a new household establishes its initial pattern of task performance and modifies that initial pattern over time has not been studied.

An understanding of the process of both initial allocation and change is critical to successful product positioning. The study of process provides important insights into the meaning of the tasks, reflecting the role, their performance dimensions, and their expected outcomes: all important inputs to positioning strategy.

The only model of household consumer behavior, Sheth's theory of Family Buying Decisions (1974), offers some useful insights into this topic, especially in the discussion of conflict resolution. However, it too is essentially a static model in that it makes little provision for changes in a household's decisionmaking processes over time.

THE PROPOSED MODEL

In attempting to bring order to the substantial but totally fragmented empirical findings that concern household task allocation, we have developed a structure that is suggested by and consistent with the existing literature. In order to make the model understandable, it is focused on the two-person, male-and-female household. With the two-person household as a base, it will be possible to add propositions to account for the presence of additional people. The model (Figure 8-1) is built around two organizing concepts. The first, task allocation stages, recognizes that the allocation of tasks is an ongoing process. There are three basic stages: the initial allocation of household tasks (represented by solid lines); evolutionary change in the initial allocations (dotted lines); and revolutionary change in allocations (jagged lines). Each of these stages is discussed in turn. However, it should be recognized that the inclusion of a concept of evolutionary change means that the stages are neither discrete nor clearly separable. Although difficult to show graphically, this seems the best representation of what actually takes place within the household.

The second major concept is that of expectations. Again, the importance of expectations has rarely been made explicit in the literature, but its importance can be made quite clear from an examination of some of the task allocation determinants listed in Table 8-1. Most, if not all, of the determinants will produce normative expectations on the part of one or both partners concerning the manner in which household tasks should be allocated.

It is easier to say that expectations are clearly important in this context than to find a precise definition of the concept. In searching for one, we settled upon the classic statement of sociologist W.I. Thomas, who said, "If men define situations as real, they are real in their consequences" (quoted by Merton 1957). Merton (1957: 421–22) goes on to point out that

> men respond not only to the objective features of a situation, but also, and at times primarily, to the meaning this situation has for them. And once they have

Figure 8–1. Model of the Two-Person, Male-and-Female Household.

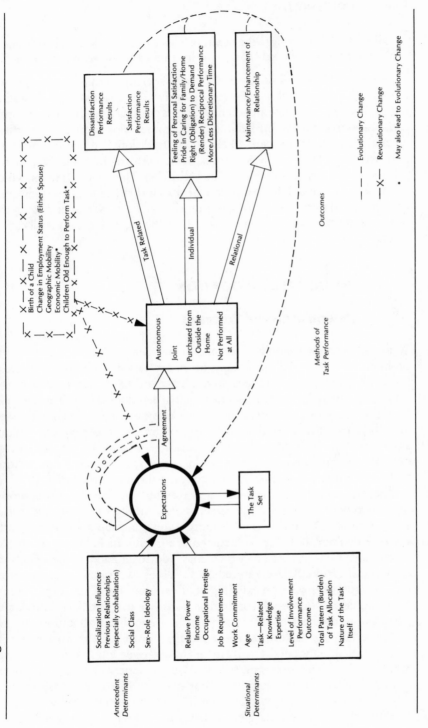

133

assigned some meaning to the situation, their consequent behavior and some of the consequences of that behavior are determined by the ascribed meaning...

Since household roles and tasks *do* have socially ascribed meanings (see Lopata 1971 and Oakley 1974 for extensive discussions), this quotation highlights the profound impact that expectations having strong normative connotations can have on behavioral outcomes. For most persons these normative expectations are likely to be traditional in nature: Women perform everyday household chores, men perform heavy tasks and the routine exterior chores (see also Tognoli 1979). These expectations, which are broad and general, form a powerful gestalt that perpetuates traditional gender-linked patterns of household task allocation. We next discuss the components of the model in more detail, beginning with the task-allocation stages.

INITIAL TASK ALLOCATION

Determinants and Processes

When any new household is formed, it must immediately deal with the problem of how to allocate many necessary tasks. It seems quite likely, however, that most households do not make ordinary household tasks the subject of a great deal of discussion or formal decisionmaking. The question of explicitness of the initial allocation decision has not been addressed directly by existing research, but the tone of the literature suggests that our assumption of little formal decisionmaking is valid. In the absence of extensive discussions or formal decisions, normative expectations modified by situational factors are likely to determine the initial allocation.

There are two types of variables in the realm of normative expectations: the antecedent variables that relate to (1) family of origin and social environment (Del Boca and Ashmore 1980), including social class and sex-role ideology, and (2) prior adult environments, including, for example, roommates or cohabitation, which may add to or modify the effects of early socialization. These antecedent variables cause individuals to enter into a relationship with an existing set of expectations. These expectations are often deeply (although sometimes unconsciously) held, enduring, and pervasive in their effects on patterns of household task allocation.

The situational factors are less enduring. Some, such as work commitment, undoubtedly persist with little change over long periods of time; others, such as relative power, may change dramatically and suddenly—for example, when a wife enters the labor market. Still others, such as task-related knowledge, may change gradually over a period of time.

While this set of determinants includes a broad range, the studies cited in

Table 8-1 make it clear that it is their level at any one time that affects the household's current allocation of tasks. We can therefore state our first proposition:

Proposition 1:   The expectations that partners hold relative to household task allocation determine the initial allocation of tasks.

Because our empirically based knowledge about initial task allocation is virtually nonexistent, several broad research questions must be raised. Which variables most strongly determine the initial allocation? What interaction effects are present? Are the determinant variables the same across a broad spectrum of tasks, or do they change from one task to another? Are the determinant variables consistent across population subgroups, or do they vary by age, ethnic, and social class groupings? What happens if the expectations of the partners differ substantially?

The last question leads to two corollaries to Proposition 1:

Corollary 1a: Two interacting sets of variables, antecedent and situational (see Figure 8-1 for a listing of specific variables that have been identified in extant research), determine household partners' expectations about the allocation of household tasks.

Corollary 1b: If the partners' expectations are not in substantial agreement, the extent to which they disagree is directly related to the degree of formal conflict resolution and decisionmaking with respect to initial task allocation.

This line of reasoning causes us to predict that the outcome of Corollary 1a will usually be a traditional, gender-determined task allocation. Specifically, most tasks, especially the indoor housekeeping tasks, will be performed autonomously by the female partner. This is, of course, a hypothesis that can and should be empirically tested.

Conflicts, as identified by Corollary 1b, can be resolved by any of the methods suggested by Sheth (1974). Little is known about these processes as they relate specifically to the allocation of household tasks. Scanzoni (1978) makes two important points relative to the general issue of negotiation in the household: (1) There are "virtually no non-negotiable issues among modern (younger) marriages," and (2) sex-role modern women bargain on the basis of individualistic interests, while sex-role traditional women bargain on the basis of family concerns (Scanzoni 1978: 187). He also suggests two other issues related to negotiation that need to be studied: how "tough" the bargaining is and whether it is reactive or goal-oriented. Throughout, Scanzoni makes a strong argument that changing sex roles have great impact on the nature of household conflict resolution.

This leads us to suggest two more research questions. What variables affect the type of conflict resolution process chosen by a particular household? What other variables, besides sex roles, affect the content of the conflict resolution process as far as household tasks are concerned?

We have already hypothesized that mutually consistent expectations are likely to result in autonomous, female-dominant patterns of household task performance. The literature also allows us to hypothesize with a reasonable degree of confidence that there will be more joint task performance when the female partner is sex-role modern, has a high degree of power relative to the male partner, and/or has a high absolute level of work commitment.

The marketing implications of these propositions are quite interesting. Where the primary determinant of task performance is one or more antecedent variables, it is likely that (1) the purchase decisions for the products used in the performance of each task are made by the persons performing the task and (2) the benefits sought in such purchases will be determined by prior experience or expectations. As situational factors become more important, it cannot be assumed that the purchase decision-maker and the task performer will be the same, at least at first.

If the role-acquisition process includes formal conflict resolution procedures, the likelihood is greater that tasks will be formally assigned. This may, in turn, increase the probability that the purchase decisionmaker and the task performer are different. For example, the male partner might clean the house, while the female partner might purchase the cleaning supplies because she does the household shopping. In this instance, the male might play an important influencing role that would not be easily picked up by traditional research questions dealing with who shops for what. Such a situation suggests that it is important for marketers to identify and then reach both influencer and purchaser.

There are important positioning implications that also stem from the expectations created by both antecedent and situational variables. These will be discussed as the next sets of variables in the conceptual model are presented.

The Task Set

Implicit in the proceeding discussion is the idea that, especially in the initial task allocation phase, the focus is on sets of tasks rather than just on a single task. There is, unfortunately, nothing in the literature that deals explicitly with the size and content of such a set. It seems that related tasks, such as meal preparation and grocery shopping, might be combined into a set and allocated to a single individual. This is really an empirical question, however, and such an assumption may be incorrect, at least for some households. Intuitively, however, it does seem clear that both background and present circumstances will influence the make-up of the set.

The large number of possible tasks creates a difficult research issue; however, the literature suggests that there are several ways of conceptualizing the set that may make the research problem more manageable. Pleck's (1981) and Nickols and Metzen's (1982) analysis of time budget data indicate that employed wives are spending less time on housework but that their husbands are not spending significantly more. Either employed women are performing the tasks more efficiently (by using labor-saving devices and easy-care products) or they (and their husbands) are simply not performing some tasks.* Both explanations seem plausible, although studies by Strober and Weinberg (1977, 1980) cast doubt on the hypothesis that working women make significantly more use of labor-saving devices than do nonworking women. Much support can be found in the popular literature for a nonperformance hypothesis (see Bird 1979 and Rivers and Lupo 1981, for example).

Task Expectations (and Meaning)

Roberts and Wortzel (1981) have described tasks as having both expressive and instrumental dimensions. The expressive component of a task focuses on its psychosocial meaning, while the instrumental component focuses only on the performance of the task. Vacuuming a rug, for example, can be viewed expressively as part of providing and maintaining a nest or instrumentally as simply picking up visibly unpleasant dust and clutter. Although little empirical work exists that would help to further refine this conceptualization, Levy's (1981) intriguing exposition on the structure of consumer mythology gives strong impetus to the importance of learning more about the meaning of routine household tasks to those who perform them.

The importance of task meaning is reinforced by much of the literature, which strongly suggests that many tasks are considered in the female domain while some others are in the male domain. Factor analysis of performance data on a relatively large set of routine tasks (Roberts, in

---

*An alternative hypothesis proposed by one of the authors of this paper is that men *are* performing more tasks but that they are simply more efficient than women.

progress) reveals that all eighteen tasks studied fall cleanly into two factors: one composed of traditionally female tasks and the other composed of traditionally male tasks. It can be expected that when the opposite sex takes on a task, its expressive and instrumental dimensions may be altered.

Since our empirical knowledge does not extend far beyond information concerning individual tasks, the research questions must be broad and general. Are there empirically and practically useful ways of grouping large numbers of household tasks into categories that can be more easily studied? Does the performance of at least some routine household tasks have a full and rich symbolic meaning? Are these meanings the same regardless of who performs the task? Alternatively, are most household tasks merely viewed as obligations that are devoid of expressive content and that should be dispensed with as quickly as possible? Do household tasks have a different meaning for females than for males? Does the significance of various household tasks differ among working and nonworking women? Among the husbands of working and nonworking women? Among different age, ethnic, and socioeconomic groups?

Defining sets properly has obvious implications for branding and targeting. To the extent that the coverage of family brands or of the use of individual products fits a task set, family branding can be used or multiple-use products can be targeted efficiently.

The concept of task meaning relates directly to positioning: first, by identifying whether positioning should be based primarily on expressive or instrumental considerations, and second, by helping to identify the specific positioning content within each domain. For example, a brand might be positioned simply as "getting the job done" for a task that was identified as primarily instrumental, such as cleaning the kitchen floor. However, if the task has a strong expressive component, the positioning must obviously address the expressive aspects of the task (expressing love for one's family by keeping the floor spotlessly clean). It might be thought that these aspects will be present most strongly in those traditionally female tasks when they are performed by nonworking females. The expressive dimensions would be the traditional wife and mother roles—nurturance and caring.

Working wives, on the other hand, might be expected to show a much lower proportion of expressive content in their household task performance; however, such a supposition could also be quite misleading. There is significant evidence that at least some working wives, especially those with children, evidence a degree of guilt that might indicate a hypersensitivity to the expressive component of at least certain tasks.

Similarly, when a traditionally female task is taken over by the male of the household, it might be supposed that the task then loses any expressive meaning, since men have traditionally not been concerned with caring or nurturing in the family. This supposition also might be quite incorrect for certain tasks. For example, many men have taken on an increasingly nurturing role in child care, and this is likely to be reflected in a high expressive component for child-related tasks. Moreover, husbands of working wives are expected to be supportive of their wives' efforts. Male performance of traditional female household tasks in working-wife families might therefore be much more than instrumental and might include an expressive component based on physical and emotional support for the female partner.

Methods of Task Performance

Categories of task performance go beyond determining which spouse performs the task. Two additional categories must be included: purchased services and nonperformance. In some households, the decision is broader than which spouse does the dusting and may include alternatives such as hiring a maid or simply dusting the furniture infrequently, if at all. The marketing literature has dealt with two modes of household decision-making that apply equally well to task performance: autonomous, in which either husband or wife alone makes the decision, or joint, in which both spouses share in the decisionmaking. There is sufficient evidence in the literature to allow us to develop propositions of a general nature concerning the manner in which tasks will be performed.

Proposition 2:   The more contemporary the antecedent and situational variables, the greater the likelihood of many household tasks being performed jointly.

Proposition 2 is well supported (see especially Hesselbart 1976), especially with regard to the effect of sex-role ideology. It should be emphasized, however, that the effect of sex-role contemporary ideology is only relative; in the majority of sex-role contemporary households, allocation of tasks still tends toward the traditional (see Haas 1980 for an interesting perspective on this issue).

The effect of women's sex-role ideology may be especially strong in determining household task allocations. The importance of wives' ideology alone in determining decisionmaking roles has been supported by Green and Cunningham (1975). Schaninger, Buss, and Grover (1982) found wives' ideologies more important than husbands' in explaining joint family financial decisionmaking. It seems apparent from the popular literature that the women's movement has made women much more sensitive on the subject of household tasks than are men, so it would seem likely that women's ideologies will be especially powerful in determining household task allocation.

Males' attitudes, and especially their experiences prior to formation of the household, do have potential impact on task allocation. Although supporting evidence is limited to a single study (Roberts and Wortzel 1980), one frequently hears comments such as, "I cooked for myself before I got married, and still do a lot." Sometimes one even hears a proud, "And besides, I'm a better cook than she is." Limited observational data such as this certainly lacks scientific validity, but with both males and females entering into first marriages at later ages, the effect of prior singlehood or cohabitation on household task allocation provides a worthwhile area for empirical study.

Proposition 3:   Employed women with contemporary sex-role attitudes are likely to engage in limited performance or non-performance of household tasks.

As mentioned earlier, working women spend less time performing household chores than do nonworking women, but their husbands do not spend much, if any, more time on these tasks than do husbands of nonworking women. What we do not know is how or if tasks are performed in the households of working women.

While data do not support expanded use of labor-saving products among working-wife households (Strober and Weinberg 1977, 1980), the available studies have considered only a limited range of products and services. Some of the products studied, such as washing machines, are viewed as necessities by virtually every household. An explanation still does not emerge when the intuitively reasonable hypothesis of purchase of household services is considered. The family economics literature (Angrist, Lave, and Mickelson 1976; Vickery 1979) contains studies that indicate that few working women have paid household help. The reasons appear to include difficulty and lack of experience in finding, managing, and retaining domestic help. Families with older children may rely a great deal on teenagers to perform at least those tasks that directly affect them, such as shopping for groceries and for clothing (General Mills, 1981).

Perhaps we will increase our understanding of this phenomenon if we expand the definition of household services to include labor-saving products such as food processors and dishwashers, products with a service component such as prepared foods of all types, and externally provided services such as shirt laundering.

Studying this subject in more detail may result in the discovery of opportunities to develop new labor- and time-saving products to aid in specific tasks or of more interest in purchasing services from institutions (e.g., a housecleaning or lawn-cutting service company) rather than from individuals. In short, the existing level of demand for services may be more a function of what is available and what households think they can manage well than of what might be purchased given a better set and easier availability of alternatives.

Beyond that, if women are spending less time on household tasks but men are not spending more, and if the purchase of services is not increasing, a non- or limited-performance hypothesis becomes tenable. Beyond impressionistic evidence, we know virtually nothing, however, about the nature and limits of either nonperformance or limited performance. Research questions are therefore in order.

Is there a particular set of tasks that is the most likely candidate for limited performance or nonperformance among a broad range of households? Or are the tasks chosen for limited performance or nonperformance quite idiosyncratic? What are the variables that determine these choices? What type of household is most likely to choose not to perform a large set of tasks? Is nonperformance a trend or merely a transient phenomenon?

The answers to these research questions once again have managerial as well as conceptual significance. To the extent that there is an emerging trend toward limited performance or nonperformance of certain tasks, primary demand for any task-related products will be affected. Beyond this effect, however, some additional marketing possibilities become extant, provided that the household's motivation for limited performance or nonperformance can be understood. Products designed and positioned for ease of use might be able to transform a nonperformed service into one that is performed at least occasionally. Products specifically designed and positioned to be effective when used only occasionally (a fabric softener that lasts through several washings for example) might have a competitive advantage for limited-use tasks and might even draw users from the ranks of regular task performance.

One possible motivation for limited performance or nonperformance of tasks, at least in households in which both partners work, is that the tasks simply are not required as often. When people spend less time in a home, it is not as likely to get as dirty, fewer rooms may be used, fewer dishes are dirtied, and so on. Another possibility is that both partners may simply care little about the results of performing some particular task. This leads us to Proposition 4.

Proposition 4:   When both partners have low standards relative to task performance and outcomes, they are likely to engage in limited performance or nonperformance of tasks.

While it seems reasonable that low standards are likely to lead to nonperformance, we know nothing specific about which households tend to have low standards and why. It might be reemphasized, however, that it is likely that the women's movement has resulted in a devaluation, among women at least, of both the perceived importance and the emotional and symbolic content of many household tasks. It could also be hypothesized that in the majority of traditional households in the past it has been high female standards, not the lower standards of males and children, that have driven consistent and meticulous household task performance. This hypothesis is based on the notion that the self-concept of the wife in a traditional household has been based on her performance as a wife and mother (Mason and Bumpass 1975).

Outcomes of Task Performance

The outcomes of task performance can be divided into two basic categories: task-related and psychosocial, which conform roughly to the two task dimensions, instrumental and expressive. Task-related outcome reflects either satisfaction or dissatisfaction with the direct results of task performance and focuses on the instrumental aspects of the task. There are two dimensions on which satisfaction and dissatisfaction can be felt: the way that the task was performed and the results of performing it. In other words, one can be dissatisfied or satisfied with the manner in which the vacuum cleaner was run over the rug as well as with the degree to which the rug is clean at the conclusion of the task (Roberts and Wortzel 1981). Research in the behavioral sciences has focused on who performs tasks; little research has been conducted on task related outcomes. Nevertheless, there are plausible propositions that can be established.

Proposition 5:   The existing pattern of task allocation is perpetuated when both partners are satisfied with both the manner of task performance and the outcomes of that performance.

Proposition 6:   As dissatisfaction with either the manner or outcomes of task performance increases, the likelihood of initiation of a formal process of conflict resolution increases.

Corollary 6a: The higher the standards of the nonperforming partner with respect to task outcomes, the more likely it becomes that dissatisfaction will lead to a change in task allocation.

Corollary 6b: If the initial allocation is consistent with traditional

sex-role expectations, dissatisfaction is not likely to lead
to a change in task allocation.

While there is no direct supportive evidence in the task allocation
literature for Propositions 5 and 6, their content is firmly grounded in the
literature of motivation and is clearly suggested by the literature on
consumer satisfaction and dissatisfaction (see especially Day 1977).
Dissatisfaction will cause some degree of tension within the individual that
is likely to spill over into other aspects of the relationship, while satisfaction
is unlikely to create tension. The tension induced by dissatisfaction will
motivate a desire to effect a change in the outcome. That having been said,
however, there is much more that we need to know.

How much dissatisfaction is required before conflict occurs? How much
conflict is required before a task is reallocated? Many women are socialized
to expect a higher rather than a lower level of outcome but at the same time
to minimize conflict with one's partner. This may present a dilemma when
some women are confronted with an outcome they consider unsatisfactory.
It may be that the least likely response is to confront the partner. A more
likely response may be to simply lower the level of expectation or to take
over all or part of the task. It seems reasonable to us that the most likely
response is to take over that part of the task or to redo that part of the task
causing the most dissatisfaction.

There may, of course, be reasons other than socialization that affect
satisfaction and dissatisfaction. Is, for example, the tolerable level of
dissatisfaction better explained by situational or personality variables?

Corollaries 6a and 6b are based on the contention that results are the
visible, tangible outcomes of task performance and that standards that
define acceptable results may be strongly held even though they may vary
greatly from one individual or one household to another. If the results are
not satisfactory, there will be pressure for change as described above. On the
other hand, dissatisfaction with performance is essentially internal, and it is
doubtful whether most individuals have clear standards regarding acceptable levels of dissatisfaction with performance. Women, especially, have
traditionally been socialized to believe that household tasks must be
performed for the welfare of the household, even though performing the
task may be onerous or even unnecessary.

Both of these subpropositions can and should be empirically tested. It is
tempting to speculate that there may in fact be a strong interactive effect—
again, especially among women—of lowered standards for results. This
may be coupled with an increasing unwillingness to accept dissatisfaction
with performance simply because the task represents a traditional female
role.

It might be thought that many household task outcomes will become increasingly devoid of psychosocial meaning; they simply will be performed by someone. However, tasks do seem to have some meaning, perhaps a different meaning than in the past, because of value changes. The psychosocial outcomes can likewise be divided into two categories: those that are individual in nature and those that are relational. Here, again, propositions can be established that reflect current values and mores even though they lack specific empirical support.

Proposition 7:   Individual outcomes are growing in perceived impor-
                  tance at the expense of relational outcomes.

Proposition 8:   Individual outcomes that are linked to individual prefer-
                  ences and desires are gaining in perceived importance at
                  the expense of outcomes that reflect pleasure in serving
                  the household or its individual members.

Proposition 7 stems from the complex of values that has often been summarized in the term "me generation." It effects appear in many current societal trends, such as the high divorce rate. Proposition 8 is an extension of that line of reasoning that divides the individual outcomes into those that are purely individual in nature and those that involve the individual's feelings about the household as an entity and about the other individuals who comprise it. Both the individual and the relational outcomes have an expressive component. The individual outcomes include, but may not be limited to, the rights, obligations, and feelings acquired as a result of task performance and the ability, or lack thereof, to use one's time in preferred ways. Working wives are likely to feel more strongly the right, perhaps even the obligation, not to perform certain tasks by virtue of their working status. Similarly, husbands of nonworking wives are likely to feel that their wives should perform most household tasks.

The other set of outcomes, which might be considered quasi-relational, reflects an orientation to serving the household and/or its individual members. These traditional quasi-relational outcomes, with their implicit emphasis on the service role, are devalued by the "me" complex of values.

Once again, these propositions are worthy of empirical investigation in the specific context of household task allocation and performance. Empirical testing might well uncover a broader range of outcomes, both individual and relational, than is evident from a survey of the existing literature.

To the extent that the foregoing propositions on outcomes are reasonable, the present positioning of many brands may become increasingly inappropriate. The indication is for more concern about task-related outcomes and less (and different) concern about psychosocial outcome dimensions. However, the situation does not have to be accepted as is.

Marketing can affect household members' perceptions of appropriate and worthwhile outcomes and by doing so can also affect the choice of brands they use in certain tasks. It is possible, for example, to reposition the meaning of a clean carpet from one of caring for the family to one of personal pride in a clean floor surface. In doing so, the marketer would also be reordering the salience of the benefits sought in a carpet-cleaning instrument and thus the desirability of alternative choices.

EVOLUTIONARY CHANGE

Relationships are inherently dynamic; some degree of change cannot be avoided over time. As an integral part of household relationships, task allocations, too, will change over time. The basic questions are, how much change and how rapidly? The propositions here must be speculative because of the lack of longitudinal research; but because relationships are dynamic, longitudinal propositions must be stated. Three propositions can be advanced in addition to those that deal with dissatisfaction with the initial allocation.

Proposition 9:   The more contemporary the sex-role attitudes of one or both partners, the more likely it becomes that task allocations will change rapidly and across a broad spectrum of tasks.

Proposition 10:   The more one or both partners are exposed to contemporary social values and sex-role orientations, via geographical or social mobility or the mass media, the more rapidly change will occur within the household.

Proposition 11:   The female partner is more likely than the male partner to be the proponent of change.

Proposition 9 is based in part on the earlier assumption that initial task allocation will not involve a great deal of formal decisionmaking and will therefore be largely traditional. Contemporary sex-role ideology should then create pressure for change, either through expressed dissatisfaction with task performance or simply through a broader desire to achieve what might be perceived as domestic justice.

Proposition 10 represents the common situation in which exposure to the changing social environment gradually creates pressure for change. The mass media is certainly one purveyor of changing values, although clearly not a creator of them. Even more powerful, however, is the personal exposure to different values and lifestyles that often results from either geographic or social mobility. Among women, the change may occur first in attitudes, specifically sex-role ideology, and gradually be manifested in a change in the pattern of task allocation. It could be felt directly in altered task allocation, but this seems less likely. Among men, the first change may be behavioral and forced, with attitude change following.

Finally, Proposition 11 once again stresses what we perceive to be the critical nature of the female partner's role in anything except a purely traditional pattern of task allocation. After all, according to the contemporary perspective, it is women who have most to gain from an alteration of the traditional pattern.

Our knowledge of the process and determinants of evolutionary change is so limited that the research questions must again be broad and general. What are the variables that are most likely to lead to evolutionary change? Is the process essentially a "first attitudes, then behavior" process, or does it frequently occur in some other manner? How much pressure for change must build up before change actually occurs? Which tasks are affected first? When change occurs, is the pattern of task allocation permanently altered, or is there eventual regression back toward the initial pattern? What circumstances or actions result in permanent change?

The impact of the type of change we are calling evolutionary is subtle precisely because it does occur over time. Yet as one observes the contemporary scene, especially attitudinal and behavioral changes engendered by the women's movement and changing social values, the overall impact of evolutionary change appears to be profound. Because it is gradual and therefore subtle, its impact is the least understood. However, if its overall impact is as great as we suspect, it is an area deserving of study by marketers.

REVOLUTIONARY CHANGE

Because the events that trigger revolutionary change are easily identifiable— entry of the female partner into the labor force, birth of a child, retirement, for example—and because their impact on the household is dramatic, this phenomenon has been studied extensively (see especially Blood and Wolfe 1960; Albrecht, Bahr, and Chadwick 1979; Pleck and Rustad 1980). In general, these events usually result in some lessening of household task performance by the female partner although, as we pointed out earlier, not necessarily in increasing task performance by other members of the household. That final statement leads to our first proposition about revolutionary change.

Proposition 12:   The effect of a critical life event is more frequently dealt with by altered methods of task performance (e.g., purchased services, limited performance, or nonperformance) than by altered patterns of task allocation.

It is clear from a careful examination of studies that analyze the effect of any one of these critical life changes that there is a tendency for patterns of task performance to change, but there is not a wholesale reversal of established patterns. When combined with the time budget studies that show that increased time expenditure by husbands in particular is small (in fact, it is measured in minutes per week, not hours), it appears that alternative coping strategies are being used by their female partners. Different methods, limited performance, or nonperformance seem most likely.

The research questions stimulated by this question could be numerous because they would appear to be quite task-specific. Their broad outlines seem to be: Which tasks are most likely to be affected by which events? Many tasks or only a few? Will the same strategy (whether performance shift or different method) be applied over a wide range of tasks, or will each task be dealt with in a unique manner? Do households seek information while attempting to cope with the change, or do they simply muddle through on their own?

The radical nature of the change caused by these events suggests another proposition:

Proposition 13:   The more radical the change in a household's life style caused by a critical life event, the more likely the household is to initiate formal decisionmaking processes to bring about altered patterns of task allocation.

This proposition is based more on the general tone of the literature in clinical psychology that deals with major life changes than on studies that present large amounts of empirical evidence about the effects of specific major events. The underlying theme is that these major life events are occasions when people tend to step back and take stock of their lives and that one result of this taking stock is that they make explicit decisions about many things they have previously taken for granted. Again, this proposition needs to be empirically tested in a marketing context. These critical life events are readily identifiable. They offer opportunities to better understand both task allocation and decisionmaking processes by investigating the processes of adjustment (for example, to the birth of a child or the retirement of a partner).

DISCUSSION AND CONCLUSION

The almost total lack of data dealing specifically with the consumer behavior-related aspects of household task performance coupled with current knowledge about changing household composition and sex roles make it clear that this is a field that warrants extensive study by marketers. The information needs are so great, as evidenced by the large number of research questions we have posed, that trying to propose broad research approaches is an overwhelming task. Nevertheless, there are several major issues that have emerged from our examination of the literature, from our conceptual model, and from the marketing implications.

One concern that recurs throughout our discussion is that the implicit meaning of household tasks may be changing, either as a result of or as a precursor to altered patterns of household task performance. This seems a valuable area for marketers of a wide variety of consumer goods to pursue. Marketers of specific products should gain a great deal of insight from qualitative research that can probe both the meanings and motivations that surround the performance of routine household tasks by both males and females. These insights may lead to the development of new products or the reformulation of existing products that enable users to expend both the amount and type of time that they perceive to be appropriate. Both product change and the development of alternative types of purchased services may be especially appropriate when the task is perceived to be devoid of expressive content or when its performance lacks symbolic meaning.

Another theme that has recurred is the increasing difficulty facing managers who need to know to whom they should target their products. If task performance is being altered in some consistent manner—for example, by men or teenagers who do more of the grocery shopping—at least the target is a stationary one. It may not be that simple. Limited performance, especially, may mean in practice that household members alternate performing the task on the basis of time available or when it absolutely cannot be avoided any longer. In that case, the target shifts. The redeeming feature of that type of situation, however, may be that if a task is interchangeable, both partners may approach it in similar ways. The result would be that the same positioning should work for both partners.

In fact, once other aspects of household task allocation begin to be sorted out, positioning may turn out to be less difficult than it appears at first glance. We have stated a number of times previously that task performance may not have become totally devoid of affective meaning. Instead, the meanings may have changed—from expressive to instrumental, from nuturance to supportive, from family-oriented to individual-oriented. What now seems to be the positioning dilemma may be headed toward resolution when we better understand how and why tasks are performed, who performs them, and the role that specific products play in the performance of specific tasks.

From this understanding, promotional strategies will emerge that echo the realities of the contemporary household without denigrating traditional meanings that still attach to the performance of some tasks or to the performer of the tasks, whether male or female. That is the challenge faced today in developing both products and promotion. Research based on a sound conceptualization of the problems that marketers face in dealing with changes in today's household will help managers meet that challenge. We hope our approach helps to stimulate just such research.

Table 8–1. Determinants of Household Task Performance.

Variable	Finding	Reference
Demographic		
Education and occupational status of wife	Higher-status wives have more power to compel husbands to share household tasks.	Blood and Wolfe (1960); Heer (1963); Scanzoni, (1970); Beckman and Hauser (1979); Ericksen, Yancey, and Ericksen (1979); Model (1981)
Employment of wife	Employed wives perform a smaller proportion of household tasks than do nonemployed wives.	Blood and Wolfe (1960); Walker (1969); Hedges and Barnett (1972); Meissner, Humphreys, Miles and Schen (1975); Robinson, Yerby, Feiweger, and Somerick (1976); Pleck (1979)
	Wives' employment does not substantially alter household division of labor.	Oakley (1974)
	Couples in which the wife has not worked continuously share tasks less equitably than couples in which the wife has worked continuously.	Weingarten (1978)

Table 8–1.   continued.

Variable	Finding	Reference
Demographic		
	Employed wives perform less household work, but husbands are not performing more.	Pleck (1979); Nickols and Metzen (1982); Fox and Nickols (1983)
	Professional women both share task performance with other family members and reduce task performance to lessen role strain.	Gray (1983)
Social class	More responsibility for household tasks is assumed by middle-class husbands than by lower-/or upper-class husbands.	Olsen (1960)
Number of children	As number of children increases more tasks are performed unilaterally by both husband and wife.	Blood and Wolfe (1960)
	Husband's housework, especially child care, increases when children are present.	Farkas (1976); Haas (1982)
	Smaller households are more likely to share household duties.	Harrell-Bond (1969)
Race/ethnicity	Black couples are more likely to share household tasks than are white couples. English couples are less likely to segregate marital roles than are Irish couples.	Ericksen, Yancey, and Ericksen (1979); Harrell-Bond (1969).

Table 8–1. continued.

Variable	Finding	Reference
Demographic		
Number and spacing of children	Amount of housework done by husband does not increase until four children present; amount of housework by husband increases when there is little spacing between children.	Campbell (1970)
Sex of children	Traditional gender-linked division of labor applies to children as well as to husband and wife.	Thrall (1978)
Amount of work time of husband	A recent study contradicts the popular belief that the more hours worked by the husband the less time he spends in housework and other family activities.	Clark, Van Nye, and Gecas (1978)
Age	Traditional, sex-typed division of housework prevails until retirement; more assumption of household tasks by males occurs after retirement.	Lipman (1961); Ballweg (1967); Albrecht, Bahr, and Chadwick (1979)
Sociology		
Support networks	Men lack social and kinship support networks to call on for assistance in child care and housework.	Lein (1979b)
Social pressure	Men may receive negative reinforcement	Lein (1979b); Pleck (1979)

Table 8–1.   continued..

Variable	Finding	Reference
Sociology		
	from their peers if they are known to assist in housework.	
Work scheduling	Inflexible work schedules lead to family stress, especially in the two-worker family. Alternative-shift arrangements for husband and wife can lead to greater involvement in home and family on the husband's part.	Hood and Golden (1979)
Early childhood socialization reinforced by adult learning	Boys are socialized to view their domain as being outside the home, while girls view the home as a focal point. Adults view the home as the sphere in which women dominate.	Tognoli (1979)
Definition of household tasks as being sex-segregated	Men care for the exterior of the home, while women care for the interior.	Blood and Wolfe (1960); Lopata (1971); and many others
Sex-role ideology	The traditional view is of men as breadwinners and women as nurturers.	For recent evidence of the strength of the effect of traditional ideology over modern attitudes, see Hesselbart (1976); Mason and Bumpass (1975); Perucci, Potter, and Rhoads (1978); Stafford, Backman and Dibona (1977); D. Cohen (1981)

Table 8–1.   continued.

Variable	Finding	Reference
Sociology		
Family life cycle	Perceived equity in performance of household roles is greater in later stages of the family life cycle.	Schafer and Keith (1981)
Individual Attitudes		
Work orientation	Salience of the work role versus the family role is an important determinant of involvement in family life and activities.	Safilios-Rothschild (1970a); Bailyn (1971); Rapoport Rapoport and Thiesseu (1974)
Favorable attitudes toward the activity	Liking household tasks is related to the time spent or the frequency of performance.	Hendrix (1980); Hendrix, Kinnear, and Taylor (1979); Roberts and Wortzel (1980)
Attitudes towards marital roles	Women who define themselves as having equal responsibility for providing for the family want husbands to share in household work more than women who do not have equal responsibility.	Scanzoni (1980)

9 MARITAL ROLES IN FAMILY FINANCIAL BEHAVIOR
A Theoretical Framework

JoAnne Stilley Hopper

Financial tasks and decisions are an increasingly important aspect of family decisionmaking behavior. Most families make decisions regarding budgeting, savings, investment, alternative financial services, bill payment, and credit usage.

The environmental and social changes of the last decade have changed family decisionmaking behavior. As the status of women has improved and their employment in the work force has increased, their roles within the family decisionmaking context have also altered. Gender-role norms that women hold for themselves and for their spouses have been modified by increasing educational levels, rising occupational status, and higher incomes among women (Scanzoni 1978). Thus, increased personal resources, decreased time flexibility, increased time pressures, and shifts in gender-role norms have opened many possibilities for a variety of alternative roles in family financial behavior.

Recent research efforts include investigations into how individual characteristics, family characteristics, and sex role orientations affect family financial behavior (Douglas and Wind 1978; Rigaux-Bricmont 1978; Hempel and Tucker 1980; Schaninger, Buss, and Grover 1982; Ferber and Chao-Lee 1974). Although researchers have examined the effect of these variables on financial behavior, they have made only moderate progress toward an intergrative theory of marital roles in family financial behavior. Hempel and Tucker (1979) have suggested that a broader framework is

155

needed that includes both family and individual spouses as decisionmaking units.

PREVIOUS RESEARCH

Two streams of research in support of the proposed theoretical framework merit special attention. The first concerns prior descriptive research on financial decisionmaking behavior. The other concerns research into family roles and power.

FINANCIAL BEHAVIOR

Marketing studies about how husbands and wives influence family decisionmaking first appeared in the late 1950s. One of the earliest studies that investigated responsibilities for family financial tasks was conducted by Sharp and Mott (1956), who posed questions about handling money, bill payment, and life insurance as well as nonfinancial family decisions and tasks. The study analyzed the roles that husbands and wives played in making economic decisions and the relative influence of the spouses in the decisions. The primary basis for role differences was urban households' income levels. The data was collected through responses by only one spouse within each family

Wolgast (1958) studied four decision areas: savings, household goods, automobiles, and money and bill payment. After examining the demographic independent variables, Wolgast concluded that children's ages, spouse's ages, and geographic location affected the amount of shared husband-and-wife decisionmaking. The study did not include psychographic or attitude variables and included only wives.

Early studies examining decisionmaking relied on responses from only one spouse. Davis (1970) concluded that both husbands' and wives' responses were needed since their perceptions often differed. Since Davis's study, most methodological studies of husband-and-wife decisionmaking have included the responses of both spouses. After Davis's initial work in the area of roles in decisionmaking, researchers began examining new decision areas, including home buying and family purchasing decision responsibility.

In a landmark study, Ferber and Lee (1974) studied the roles of husbands and wives in family financial responsibilities, including paying bills, accounting for expenditures in relation to budgets, and using money left over at the end of the pay period. The data was collected in two stages: in the first and second years of marriage. The result indicated a shift in the second year of marriage toward the assumption of more responsibilities by the wife. Moreover, husbands were more likely to save a higher percentage of the income in variable forms, such as real estate and securities, when they undertook the primary responsibilities. Ferber and Lee labeled the spouse that dominated these decisions as the family financial officer.

The role structure of family authority patterns was the major focus of a study conducted by Douglas and Wind (1978), which examined amount of money spent on food, amount of money set aside for savings and investment, choice of a bank, and amount of life insurance bought. The authors found the greatest variation in roles and authority patterns in the financial decision areas, where tasks were almost equally divided between husband-dominated and joint participation.

A recent study by Rigaux-Bricmont (1978) examined the effect of a large number of individual and family characteristics on economic behavior and indicated the importance of demographic variables in explaining family economic decisionmaking influence. The variable of time pressure was particularly important in explaining the role decisions of each spouse.

Current marketing studies of family decisionmaking have turned toward sex-role determinants and the effect of sex roles on family financial behavior. Schaninger, Buss, and Grover (1982) examined sex roles and family finance handling and decision influence and found that the wives' sex-role norms had the greatest effect on the roles played in family financial behavior. The results of the analysis also supported the hypothesis that traditional patterns of influence are changing.

Family Decisionmaking Theory

Although several studies have examined family financial behavior, the hypotheses tested in the research have lacked a theoretical base. Sociological theories exist, however, that may be useful in explaining and predicting family financial decisionmaking. The theories of social exchange and resource theory are particularly applicable.

Resource and Social Exchange Theory. Since the 1960s resource theory has been a primary theoretical base for explaining power and influence in the family. Resource theory suggests that the greater the resources of a spouse, the greater his or her influence will be in family decisionmaking. For example, the spouse with the highest income will have more influence than the spouse who brings less income into the family.

Scanzoni and Szinovacz (1980) stated that the resources possessed by each spouse are important in determining the amount of power or influence each spouse has in decisionmaking. Rather than concentrating on the resources of each spouse, however, Scanzoni proposed that more important is the degree of disparity between the resources each spouse possesses. The more disparity between the amount of resources, the more influence the spouse with the greater resources can exercise. Scanzoni suggested that two types of resources may be applicable to family decisionmaking behavior: tangible and intangible. Tangible resources are composed of the individual characteristics of education, income, occupational status, and previous experience in decisionmaking. Intangible resources are composed of self-esteem and a spouse's confidence in decisionmaking capability.

Social exchange theory has also been used to explain family decision-making behavior and the role of resource variables. This theory suggests that spouses will exchange love, respect, or other assets in return for power or influence in family decisionmaking. Safilios-Rothschild (1976) examined the amount of love each spouse possessed for his or her partner and how it affected family decisionmaking power. Her conceptualization of power included the degree of love shared by the spouses. The spouse that was the most loved possessed the most power in the family. That is, the exchange of power for love produced the dominance of one spouse in the decision-making. When both partners equally loved each other, an equality in power within the family was predicted.

Within a family system each spouse tries to maximize his or her gains and minimize his or her costs through an exchange of resources and influence. The relevant resources exchanged in a family situation may vary and may be derived from position within the family or from personality.

Heer (1963) also evaluated the effect of noneconomic resources on family decisionmaking behavior. Noneconomic resources such as personal attractiveness and performance in other family decisionmaking roles were cited as important resources in determining power in the family.

An alternative view of the importance of resources was suggested by Edwards (1969), who conceptualized resources as hierarchical; that is, resources may be ranked in an evaluation system. The position of the resources in the hierarchy are determined by evaluating members of the "exchange markets" of the family. He also stated that exchanges may not be equal. Because exchange equivalents may be unavailable, asymmetrical financial behavior transactions may occur.

In addition to the importance of the exchange of resources, an additional variable appears to apply to the process of family decisionmaking: the importance of the decision to each spouse. Blood and Wolfe (1960) suggested that the status of the husband's power was influenced more by his interest in the decision than his resources in decisionmaking situations.

A review of family decisionmaking resource and exchange theory has revealed several alternative views of the type and importance of resources and how they are exchanged. Although the theories vary, they stress the importance of the resources of the spouses and the influence of those resources in the process of exchange among family members. The resource variable and the concept of social exchange are an integral part of the proposed theoretical framework.

A FAMILY FINANCIAL BEHAVIOR FRAMEWORK

Framework Overview

Previous research suggests that individual characteristics, family characteristics, and situational factors may affect the role that each spouse assumes in family financial behavior. The gender-role norms of each spouse may also influence attitudes toward participation in financial behavior.

Although individual characteristics are important factors in determining roles in financial behavior, family characteristics and situational factors may be as important. Due to family circumstances, such as the presence of small children, a spouse may prefer to forgo financial responsibilities in exchange for the opportunity to use his or her talents in a parenting role. Situational factors such as illness, job changes, or economic circumstances may also influence the possibility of a role transferral or exchange. The theoretical framework presented here uses individual characteristics and sex-role constructs, situational factors, and spousal involvement in financial behavior as determinants of influence and roles in family financial behavior.

The model provides a framework for examining family financial behavior over a period of time rather than at one point in time. The framework also introduces the importance of the intervening variable of spousal involvement in financial behavior as an important factor in determining family financial roles. Financial behavior includes budgeting, savings, spending, asset acquisition, financing, and transferring payment responsibilities.

The role behavior of each spouse may result in several outcomes. Each spouse may participate in any of the family financial decisionmaking areas. Roles may be exchanged, transferred, or shared. Thus, the role of the family's financial manager may be dominated by one spouse, shared, or exchanged over the life span of the family. The following discussion includes justification for the use of each component of the model and the proposed relationships. A diagram of the framework appears in Figure 9-1, and a list of the components of the framework appears in Table 9-1.

Personal Characteristics

The personal characteristics of each spouse include two sets of variables: individual resources and sex role preferences. These are among the

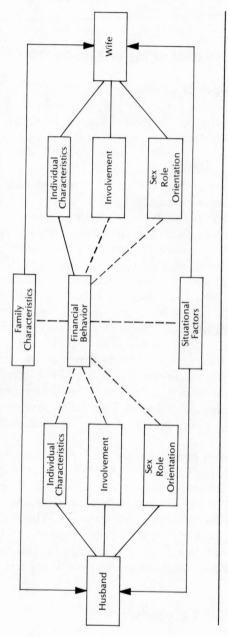

Figure 9–1. A Family Financial Behavior Framework.

Table 9–1. Determinants of Family Financial Behavior Roles.

Characteristics

  Income

  Occupation

  Education

  Uncommitted time

  Flexibility

  Expertise

  Sex-role orientation

Family characteristics

  State in the family life cycle
  Social class
  Length of marriage

Situational characteristics

  Economic factors
  Unplanned pregnancy
  Illness
  Career changes

Involvement

  Importance of participation
    in financial behaviors

personal characteristics that are hypothesized as determinants of spousal financial roles.

Individual Resources.   Individual resources include education, occupation, income, uncommitted time, flexibility, and financial expertise. According to the principles of resource theory, the greater the quantity and quality of the resources of each spouse, the greater the influence each spouse should have in decisionmaking and in the roles each spouse assumes or shares in family financial behavior.

  Scanzoni and Szinovacz (1980) concluded that income and education accounted for differences in women's sex roles. Rigaux-Bricmont (1978) examined marital influences in family economic decisionmaking and determined that spouses' income contributions and wife's occupation were significant factors in the family financial behavior roles. Thus, it appears that there is evidence of the importance of tangible individual resources as determinants of spousal roles in financial behavior.

In addition to the traditional resource variables of income, education, and occupation, the resource variables of uncommitted time, flexibility, and expertise in financial tasks may also be seen as correlates of family financial role behavior. Uncommitted time refers to the amount of time that each spouse has that is unobligated and available for performance of financial tasks or decisions. Flexibility refers to the ability to reschedule responsibilities in order to take part in financial behavior. Thus, flexibility and uncommitted time are determined by commitments to other family behavior and by each spouse's occupation. Schaninger, Buss, and Grover (1982) determined that time pressure was a significant factor in the role that the wife assumes in financial behavior. The variable of time pressure is similar to the suggested resources of uncommitted time and flexibility.

A related concept is the occupational expertise of each spouse in financial behavior. Due to occupational skills, spouses may be proficient in particular aspects of financial behavior. Prior experience in performing family financial duties may also contribute to the expertise of family members. Hempel and Tucker (1980) suggested the importance of experience in their paper on issues concerning family financial decisionmaking. Scanzoni and Szinovacz (1980) have also suggested the importance of previous experience as an important individual resource variable.

Sex Roles.   Current work in family decisionmaking has turned increasingly toward analyzing the effect of sex roles on family decisionmaking behavior. Major works have been undertaken by several researchers (Scanzoni 1978; Araji 1977; Green and Cunningham 1975; Burns and Granbois 1980; Schaninger, Buss, and Grover 1982). Previous work has concentrated on developing the assessing sex role scales and on analyzing the effects of sex roles on decisionmaking and task performance with the family context.

Although previous research in the sex-role area has shed light on aspects of household tasks and spending behavior, little effort has been devoted to the family financial behavior area. The only major work in the area was completed in 1982 by Schaninger, Buss, and Grover. The major contributions of the study included the development of a sex-role scale and an assessment of the impact of sex-role norms on family financial behavior. After factor analysis of twenty-four items, a four-construct scale was developed: (1) work and the family, (2) shared responsibility, (3) work with young children, and (4) importance of the wife's career. The alphas for all four constructs were above 0.90 and indicated good internal consistency among the items in each construct. The major findings of the study indicated that sex-role modern couples displayed more joint decisionmaking behavior for traditionally wife-dominated expenditures and that the sex-role attitude of the wife affected family financial behavior more than the sex-role attitudes of the husband did.

A review of the literature, and particularly the work of Schaninger, Buss, and Grover (1982), reveals the importance of the role of sex roles in family financial behavior. Thus, the sex-role attitude of each spouse is considered a second major individual aspect of the individual characteristics of family members. The sex-role scale developed by Schaninger, Buss, and Grover (1982) is recommended as a valid and reliable scale to use in measuring sex-role attitudes and their impact on family financial behavior.

Family Characteristics

In addition to the personal characteristics of each spouse, the characteristics of the family are possible determinants of role behavior in financial decisionmaking. The proposed framework examines stages in the family life cycle, length of marriage, and social class.

Numerous studies have documented how these characteristics affect family decisionmaking behavior. Ferber and Lee (1974) indicated the importance of the family life cycle in role behavior in financial decisionmaking. In a study of the division of family roles in households tasks, child care, and paid employment, Ericksen, Yancey, and Ericksen (1979) found that the presence of children under age 12 was a significant factor in determining the extent of role sharing among couples. Social class and duration of marriage were cited as determinants of marital influence in a study of family economic behavior conducted by Rigaux-Bricmont (1978). Thus, it appears that extensive evidence exists for the use of these variables in the proposed theoretical framework.

Situational Factors

Within the context of the family, situational factors may bring about a change in family financial roles. Job changes, unemployment, economic forces, unplanned pregnancies, illness, and additional job responsibilities are among unanticipated circumstances that could lead to changes in family decisionmaking and in the roles that each spouse performs within the context of the family's situation.

In a study of how a crisis affects the resulting role structure within the family, Bahr and Rollins (1971) simulated family-crisis situations. The results of the study indicated that the family leader tended to be replaced and that the leader's power decreased during the crisis. This suggests that situational factors may bring about changes in family decisionmaking behavior: An exchange or transferral of roles may take place due to situational factors that occur within or outside of the family. The conceptual role transferral model of Roberts and Wortzel (1981) provides an explanation of how the role transferral might take place. Scanzoni and Szinovacz (1980) indicated that dissatisfaction with role performance might also bring about role switching within the household.

The results of previous research have emphasized the relevance of situational factors on family behavior, and these factors are an important aspect of the proposed theoretical framework. The primary problem with using situational factors in the framework is the difficulty of measuring the effects of these factors on the family. The simulation of family-crisis situations in a laboratory through scenarios or through the use of a family-crisis game may be applicable to family financial behavior research. Both techniques have been used successfully. Bahr and Rollins (1971) used the SIMFAM game in their research on changes in the family leader, and Swasy (1979) used scenarios in his study of the bases of social power with the family.

Involvement

The degree to which each spouse is involved in the various types of financial behavior is a necessary component of the theoretical financial framework. Involvement may be defined as taking part in a decision. Several studies have examined the importance of involvement in family role behavior. Burns and Granbois (1977) examined the effect of involvement on several decision areas concerning durable goods and suggested that the degree of spousal involvement in a decision affects the decision outcomes. Their study also indicated that the highly involved spouse derives satisfaction from having his or her preferences manifested in the outcome of the decision. Burns and Granbois (1977) also established the importance of involvement in the resolution of conflict in family automobile purchases. Thus, the degree of involvement by each spouse in each type of financial behavior is an important factor in the role behavior of husbands and wives in family financial behavior.

Involvement is conceptualized as an intervening variable in the framework: That is, although one spouse may possess a greater quantity of resources and be liberal in sex-role orientation, his or her interest level in financial behavior may be less than the spouse's. Thus, a low level of involvement with financial behavior may bring about a smaller role in family financial behavior. Conversely, a high level of involvement may bring about a greater role in family financial behavior, although the resources of one spouse may be less than the resources of the partner.

A Typology of Family Financial Behavior

The typology of financial behavior includes budgeting, saving, spending, transferring payments, financing, and acquiring assets. Financial behavior roles include both decisionmaking and performing financial tasks. These roles may be shared by the spouses or undertaken by only one spouse. Budgeting includes allocating family funds. Saving behavior includes determining the amount of funds to save and the choices of savings options. Spending decisions are related to the timing and dollar amount of family and individual purchases. Transferring-payment responsibilities involve paying accounts, routine checking duties, and the like. Credit use and loan arrangements are among the tasks and decisions within financing role behavior. Asset-acquisition responsibilities include the purchase and control of insurance, stocks, bonds, and other financial assets. Real estate and other long-term assets would also be included within asset-acquisition role tasks and decisions. The components of the financial behavior typology appear in Figure 9–2.

IMPLICATIONS

The proposed framework can contribute to the work of both academicians and practitioners by providing a mechanism for the study of family financial behavior. An empirical test of the aforementioned variables will help us to

Figure 9–2.   A Family Financial Behavior Typology.

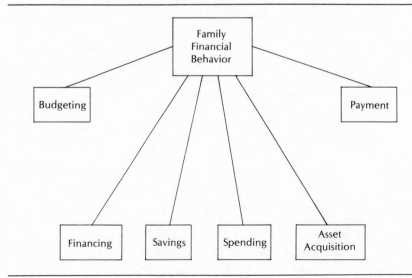

evaluate the effect of individual, family, and situational factors on the determination of family financial behavior roles. Marketing managers will learn more about the responsibilities and influence that each spouse has in family financial matters and thus will be better able to segment their markets and develop marketing strategies in accord with family financial behavior roles.

Although the framework provides a basis for the study of family financial behavior, much research is needed. Empirical research will reveal the direction and strengths of the relationships in the framework and will provide useful information for describing understanding, and predicting family financial behavior.

SUMMARY

The absence of a theoretical base for the study of family financial behavior has led to the development of the family financial behavior framework. The theoretical foundation for the framework is derived from resource and exchange theory, and major determinants of the roles performed in family financial behavior include individual characteristics, sex-role orientation, involvement of each spouse, family characteristics, and situational variables.

The framework suggests that the greater the quantity and quality of the resource variables of each spouse (personal characteristics), the greater will be a spouse's role in financial behavior. Sex-role modern families are more likely to manifest more active role participation by wives than traditional families.

Although sex-role orientation and individual variables are important, the family's situation at any point in time and the involvement of each spouse in financial decisionmaking may affect the financial behavior roles played by family members. Shifts in a spouse's career or health, economic changes, and other unplanned circumstances may lead to role transferral or exchange. The involvement of each spouse is particularly important in determining roles: The likelihood of a spouse exhibiting an active role in financial behavior is related to his or her interest in participating in financial behavior. Thus, involvement is conceptualized as an intervening variable in the framework.

Family financial behavior includes tasks and decisions such as budgeting, financing, transferring payments, acquiring assets, saving, and spending. Husbands and wives may exhibit several alternative financial role behaviors: One spouse may dominate some or all of the family financial decisions and tasks, the roles may be shared by both spouses, or the roles may be transferred or exchanged due to a change in individual or personal circumstances. Thus, the framework provides a basis for the analysis of family financial behavior throughout the life span of the family.

III HOUSEHOLD CONSUMPTION CHOICES

10 NONTRADITIONAL FAMILY FORMS, TIME ORIENTATION, AND HOUSEHOLD BEHAVIORS Perspectives and Research Directions for the Consumer Researcher

Chris T. Allen, Kathleen Debevec, and Kenneth K. Chan

The spectacular increase in the participation of women in the labor force in recent decades is having major consequences for U.S. society in a number of diverse areas (Huber and Spitze 1981). Intertwined with this labor market trend are, of course, shifts in sex-role norms (Scanzoni 1976, 1977) and the emergence of new, viable familial alternatives to the traditional nuclear family (Macklin 1980). Determining what we know and do not know about nontraditional family forms can be an overwhelming task: As noted by Macklin (1980: 905), "this is especially true if nontraditional is defined as all living patterns other than legal, lifelong, sexually-exclusive marriage between one man and one woman, with children, where the male is the primary provider and ultimate authority." Indeed, the varieties of "traditional" have become so numerous and multifaceted that they nearly defy categorization (Macklin 1980).

Fortunately, the delimiting perspective of the consumer researcher furnishes manageable insights concerning what we do and do not know about nontraditional family forms. The scope of this discussion is confined to household behaviors either directly or indirectly tied to consumption, with a primary focus on the two-paycheck, dual-earner family type that has been featured in much of the extant consumer-behavior literature. However, the consumption behaviors of a noteworthy nonfamily type—singles—are also explicitly considered. Additionally, given the common presumption that dual-earner families face substantial time pressures (e.g.,

169

Allen and Schaninger 1980; Huber and Spitz 1981; Redman 1980; Reilly 1982; Schaninger and Allen 1981; Strober and Weinberg 1977, 1980), the time issue will be considered in depth at various points. Finally, the question of communicating with nontraditional household forms via sex-role stereotyping in advertising will be examined, and some thoughts offered regarding what we need to know about the effectiveness of this positioning strategy for reaching nontraditional family types. The over-riding purpose throughout will be to suggest feasible research directions concerning the marketplace behaviors of the diverse family forms now prevalent in this culture.

DUAL-EARNER FAMILIES

Their Marketplace Behaviors

Much of the consumer research dealing with dual-earning families has derived from a common presumption: that "at all income levels and life-cycle stages, working wives (i.e., wives who have paid employment) appear to face greater time pressures than do nonworking wives" (Strober and Weinberg 1980: 338). As Reilly (1982) notes, this presumption has led a number of researchers to investigate the wife's work status and the family's level of convenience-oriented consumption. Much of the empirical evidence has not supported expected relationships (Douglas 1976a, 1976b; Redman 1980; Reynolds, Crask, and Wells 1977; Strober and Weinberg 1977, 1980). It appears that both conceptually and methodologi-cally, a dichotomous workwife-versus-nonworkwife family scheme is too crude to capture meaningful consumption differences.

A variety of forces can be identified that may alter the consumption patterns of dual-earner families (e.g., Bartos 1978a; Schaninger and Allen 1981), and research has demonstrated that categorization schemes that are slightly more sophisticated than the working/not working dichotomy can help capture hypothesized differences (Schaninger and Allen 1981). Schaninger and Allen (1981) used a three-way scheme to identify consumption differences among families. For example, they found that families where wives worked in low-status occupations (e.g., clerical or service jobs) were more likely to use convenience foods than families where wives worked in higher-status occupations (e.g., managerial or professional jobs). Related findings have been reported by Redman (1980) and Reilly (1982), who showed that amount of education (certainly a correlate of occupational status) is negatively related to the propensity of a workwife's family to use convenience food products. Schaninger and Allen (1981) also found important differences among their three family types in terms of deal proneness and television viewing habits. It is noteworthy that the consumption differences established between high- and low-status workwife families in the areas of convenience foods, deal proneness, and television viewing would have been totally obscured in a simple working or not-working typology.

Women's participation in the labor force is affected by factors other than the job's status level. One other dimension seems especially noteworthy when examining research that hypothesizes that dual-earner families face heavy time pressures. Maret-Havens (1977: 35) refers to this dimension as degree of labor force attachment: "many women work part time; others work forty hours a week or more. Some women work year round; others work only part of the year. Some women have worked continuously since leaving school; others enter, leave, and reenter the labor force at various times in the life-cycle." Categorization schemes that consider simply whether a woman is in or out of the labor force at the time of data collection ignore important information. Considering just the part-time or full-time employment issue makes this clear: Estimates are available that suggest that anywhere between 25 percent (Leon and Bednarzik 1978) and 50 percent (Aldous 1982) of employed females in dual-earner families are working part-time. The number of hours that a wife works per week and the continuity of her employment over time will, of course, have much to do with the time pressures felt by her family.

Most researchers have ignored the relationship between a workwife's degree of labor-force attachment and her household's consumption patterns. Some exceptions were found in practitioner-oriented studies. For example, full-time and part-time working women differ from housewives in a number of ways when it comes to their grocery shopping patterns (Dietrich 1977; Zbytniewski 1979). Part-time workers are much more deal prone than women who work full-time, and part-time workers are more likely to shop regularly at three or more grocery stores, compared to *both* full-time workers and housewives. It seems that part-time workers are willing to invest more of their time in grocery shopping than either housewives or women who work full-time. Such findings, of course, would be totally obscured in a research design that overlooked the labor-force attachment dimension.

What we can conclude with certainty about the consumption behaviors of dual-earner families seems quite limited, although one suspects that a great deal of proprietary information (e.g., Bartos 1978a) has been gathered for specific practitioner contexts that unfortunately cannot be tapped and integrated for public dissemination. While there are many directions for future research, an important one considered in the upcoming section involves increasing our sophistication in the area of family categorization schemes.

Research Directions

In their critique of consumer researchers' uses of demographic variables, Roscoe, LeClaire, and Schiffman (1977: 76) suggest that "considering the shifting nature of our socioeconomic environment . . . there is a real need to construct new demographic variables that will better reflect these changing conditions." Much can be done in the area of developing and testing household classification schemes that reflect recent changes in this culture, that are based on demographic variables, and that thus possess strong appeal from an applied standpoint. Moreover, such a stream of research need not simply be a matter of raw empiricism; indeed, the literature furnishes a number of specific directions for developing creative combinations of demographic variables to capture more of the diversity in American family types.

Certainly one family form that deserves further researcher attention is the dual-career couple. Based on their review of over a decade of research on this family type, the Rapoports (1980: 42) concluded that "the concept of the dual-career family is an imprecise one, and it covers a constellation of family types rather than representing a single homogeneous or uniform type. Nevertheless, as a concept it has had heuristic value both in social research and in social action." They pointed out that for researchers the value of the dual-career family is in providing a framework for analysis that extends beyond the individual. Schaninger and Allen (1981) clearly established the relevance of such a framework to consumption contexts. Although they used only the status level of the wife's job as an indicator of her career orientation, other demographic variables like age and education level might be used for further precision. Career orientation is an indicator of differences in family sex-role norms and thus will be particularly germane in consumption context linked to performance of traditional male and female roles (Schaninger and Allen 1981).

The sociological literature dealing with dual-earner families is a rich source of ideas about potentially meaningful variations in family types (e.g., Aldous 1982; Macklin 1980; Pepitone-Rockwell 1980). For example, in a recent piece Hunt and Hunt (1982) developed an intriguing hypothesis about dual-career couples; they essentially argue that to remain competitive in pursuing their careers, the partners in a dual-career couple recognize the importance of remaining child-free. Certainly the presence of children can produce severe role conflicts in dual-career couples (Holahan and Gilbert 1979), and Hunt and Hunt (1982) see the decision to have children in such families as a vivid statement of priorities. Indeed, their discussion of voluntarily childless, dual-career couples suggests comparisons to the "me generation," a label common in the consumer-behavior literature (Engel and Blackwell 1982). Unique consumption patterns would be expected from these voluntarily childless, career-oriented families.

Other devices that consumer researchers might consider in the family classification exercise are the indexes developed by Maret-Havens (1977) and others (Huber and Spitze 1981) to gauge degree of wife's labor-force attachment. The Maret-Havens index, for instance, considers whether the wife's employment is: (1) continuous or intermittent; (2) year-round or seasonal; and (3) full-time or part-time. Applying her index to females in the labor force in 1971, Maret-Havens (1977) categorized 14 percent as "career attached" and 42.8 percent as "casually or sporadically attached." Such a categorization scheme could prove potent for consumer applications, especially if it were used in conjunction with a system like that proposed by Schaninger and Allen (1981).

The above research directions are straightforward and can easily be framed in the context of concepts familiar to consumer behavioralists. Demographic variables like age, marital status, presence of children, occupational level, and educational status are common inputs in composites like family life cycle and social class. These composites, of course, are merely alternative family classification schemes. Labels like "upper-middle class" and "full nest one" are primarily used in thinking about types of families, not types of individuals. Perhaps the creative combinations of demographic variables being advocated here are most efficiently examined by combining variables like social class and family life cycle with status and degree of the wife's labor force attachment. The tradition in the consumer-behavior area is to treat social class, family life cycle, and wife's occupational status as separate topics: It may be more productive to treat them under one heading that more accurately reflects what they are—family classification schemes.

SINGLES

The last decade has seen a dramatic growth in the number of singles in U.S. society. Part of this growth can be attributed to the maturing of the baby boom generation; other contributing factors are the rise in the average age when first married and the increasing divorce rate (Barkas 1980; Francke, Abramson, Simons, Copeland, and Whitman 1978; Grossman 1979; Linden 1979a, 1979b, 1980; Sheils 1983; Stein 1976; Wortzel 1977a). Singles are an economically vital market segment because they tend to have substantial discretionary incomes, be less motivated to save, and not have the financial responsibilities of homeownership and child rearing. Indeed, recent estimates indicate that singles account for one out of every eight dollars of total consumer spending for goods and services (Linden 1979b). While marketing academics have not shown a great interest in singles as a focus for their research attention, there seems to be considerable evidence that the consumer behavior of singles differs from that of traditional American families. Some of the more notable differences are highlighted below.

Their Marketplace Behaviors

While food served at home makes up 16.4 percent of an average family's expenditures, it accounts for only 8.2 percent of a single individual's: Singles spend 41 percent of their food dollars on food away from home, 87 percent more than the average family (Linden 1979b). According to a recent study conducted by the National Restaurant Association, singles account for 24 cents of every restaurant dollar and for 20 percent of restaurant traffic (*Quick Frozen Foods* 1981). These findings also showed that the average per-person check size for singles if $3.06, compared to $2.43 for a member of the average household. The live-alone singles between ages 25 and 34 account for 29 percent of all eating out by singles.

Another major expenditure category—housing—dips heavily into singles' budgets. An average 22.8 percent of a single's budget is allocated to shelter, 38 percent more than the norm for U.S. households (Linden 1979b). Most singles occupy rented dwellings, and spend 19 percent of their budget on rent, pointing to a need for fewer home furnishings; singles' expenditures for furniture are below average (Linden 1979b). When purchases are made, practicality rather than status or prestige seems to be stressed. Mobility of furniture is important, with added emphasis on new designs and styles like modular arrangements (Loudon and Della Bitta 1979).

Consumer patterns are somewhat different for cohabiting households. Since there is often a significant increase in income in these households, housing costs claim a smaller budget share. Moreover, the added disposable income seems to be transferred in part to home furnishings; average home furnishing expenditures by cohabiting households in the age bracket of 25 to 34 are not only higher than for other singles' groups but also exceed the average for all households by a substantial percentage (Linden 1979b).

Outlays for clothing and health and personal care items by younger singles are below average. However, a significant rise in expenditures for such items is evidenced by those age 25 to 34 as well as by those in cohabiting households (Linden 1979b). This could reflect narcissism and self-enhancement (Loudon and Della Bitta 1979).

Singles are increasingly being targeted as a critical segment by automobile manufacturers: One-third of all car buyers are singles (Candler 1981). Young singles (under age 25) spend 28 percent of their income on transportation, compared with a household norm of just under 20 percent

(Linden 1979b). Such outlays decline considerably as one moves to an older age group or a cohabiting household. Candler suggests that young singles may be more involved than other population segments in conspicuous or symbolic consumption when purchasing automobiles.

Although the single lifestyle has many attractions, single individuals must cope with the problem of loneliness by seeking new ways to meet people. A booming part of the "singles industry" is the surge of health and sports clubs that cater to those not married (Barkas 1980; Sanoff 1983). Singles' spending for recreation is above average, and this is especially true of cohabiting householders: Their spending runs 27 percent above the average for all singles and also exceeds the average for all households by a significant margin (Linden 1979b). Barkas also suggests several other manifestations of singles' behaviors that may be related to their lack of opportunity for daily intimacy. He notes that singles smoke more, drink more, visit physicians more often, have more car accidents, have greater incidences of cancer of the digestive system, and have a higher number of admissions to psychiatric hospitals than a comparable married population (Barkas 1980).

Finally, singles also exhibit considerable uniqueness in their media habits. A recent Young and Rubicam study reported that singles do not read newspapers as much as other groups but are heavy magazine readers (Jervey 1982). That study also found that singles are not heavy prime-time television watchers but instead skew toward the late evening hours. However, older groups, particularly the divorced/separated/widowed segment, watch more television than younger never-marrieds. The study indicated that cable television is a logical choice by which to effectively reach yound singles: Because singles, and especially never-marrieds, have high discretionary income and are apt to live in central cities and suburbs, they are likely to subscribe to cable. Cable television is thus an attractive medium because its selective programming provides a means of showing specially tailored shows during those late hours when young singles are more likely to be viewing.

Research Directions

This brief review of singles' consumption patterns illustrates the importance of this household form for marketing. These patterns are certainly being recognized by marketing practitioners, who will continue to focus on singles. An important question is what research directions marketing academics should pursue to assist practitioners in their efforts to better understand singles' markets.

Clearly, the term "singles" encompasses and obscures as much diversity among individuals as does a term like "workwife" when labeling families.

Categorization schemes for the singles market need to be developed that partition important components of this diversity and facilitate comparisons with other major household forms. Recent efforts in redefining the family life cycle provide a meaningful step in this direction (Murphy and Staples 1979; Gilly and Enis 1982). Gilly and Enis (1982: 274) note that "simply collecting data and searching them for empirical relationships will not suffice. Empirical work should be guided by conceptual models, so that theory can be developed." While theory development is an admirable goal, efficiency in integrating findings would be improved if researchers would utilize common categorization schemes in conducting their studies.

One feature that many singles are likely to share with other nontraditional household units is pressures on their time. Increased understanding of the consumption patterns of the various emergent nontraditional household forms is likely to be furnished by a more careful consideration of how they think about, and choose to use, their time. This important avenue for future academic research is explored in the upcoming section.

TIME AND A HOUSEHOLD'S CONSUMPTION BEHAVIORS

The concept of time is receiving increased attention in consumer research because it is believed to be an important variable for understanding consumers' motivations and predicting their behaviors. It has been largely overlooked in past behavioral models but is gaining prominence as a variable with acknowledged cause-and-effect properties. For example, time is causal to the extent that an abundance or lack of it, as *perceived* by individuals, will elicit a variety of behaviors. The actual or perceived availability of time is also the result of personal, environmental, or situational variables, which indicates its effect-oriented character. Research has been directed toward conceptually understanding time and elaborating this dual role.

Historical Perspective

Early time research attempted to determine how individuals allocate their time to various activities (Sorokin and Berger 1938; Szalia 1966). It had a sociological flavor and was prompted by the desire to understand patterns of human behavior. Time diaries were the preferred method of data collection and remain in use today, although their validity and accuracy have been questioned (Hendrix and Qualls 1981; Szybillo, Binstok, and Buchanan 1979). In a marketing context, Lee and Ferber (1977) studied time budgets to determine if time usage was useful in explaining the acquisition of durable goods, credit cards, and insurance. Individuals' use of time was found to be a significant predictor of such ownership.

In an effort to understand how individuals come to allocate their time, researchers began questioning the concept of time itself. They attempted to define and characterize time. It was discussed initially from an economic perspective where it was thought to possess a value because of its scarcity (Becker 1965; C. Bell 1975; Berry 1979; Julkunen 1977; Nowotny 1975; Schary 1971) and considered to have properties of a commodity (i.e., it could be bought and sold) (Linder 1970; Hawes 1979). Time is viewed as having an opportunity cost (Becker 1965; Bell 1975; Menefee 1982; Schary 1971) and as a feasible substitute for goods (Becker 1965; Hendrix 1980; Menefee 1982) or money (Berry 1979; Jacoby, Szybillo, and Berning 1976). Time categorization schemes have also been developed; such schemes originally included work versus leisure (nonwork) time but have been expanded to account for discretionary and nondiscretionary uses of leisure time (Engel and Blackwell 1982).

This objective view of time continues but also has served as a foundation for a more recent subjective or perceptual view (Berry 1979; Feldman and Hornik 1981; Graham 1981; Hawes 1979; Hendrix 1980; Jacoby, Szybillo, and Berning 1976; Schary 1971). A purely objective conceptualization of time may be quite unrepresentative. For example, an individual's time orientation is, in part, a cultural phenomenon: Different cultures have diverse perceptions of time (Eickelman 1977; Graham 1981; Hall 1959; Julkunen 1977; Morey 1971; Nowotny 1975). Graham posits that present behavioral models are limited because they view time from a Western perspective (with a past, present, and future) and do not account for behavior in present-oriented societies. Individuals' perceptions of time have been related to gender (Cottle 1976), age (Markson 1973), income (Nowotny 1975), race (White 1977), and social class (LeShan 1952; Luscher 1974).

Feldman and Hornik (1981) suggest that the value and meaning one assigns to time will affect one's use of it, again reflecting the need for a subjective or perceptual view of time. They devised a model of time allocation showing the interrelationships among this subjective focus, personal characteristics, and situational constraints (e.g., environmental factors, resources).

The time concept has been featured in the family literature because of the presumption that nontraditional household forms experience substantial time pressures. The impact of working women in the household has been investigated relative to time use (Robinson 1977), division of labor (Huber and Spitze 1981; Nickols and Metzen 1982; Robinson 1977; Wales and Woodland 1977), and purchase of time-saving products (Douglas 1976a,

1976b; Reilly 1982; Schaninger and Allen 1981; Strober and Weinberg 1977, 1980). Robinson (1977) cites employment status and gender as being two of the most powerful predictors of time use. He also found that degree of education and the presence of children in the household influenced a limited number of activities, while age, marital status, and household technology had little effect on how time was spent by individuals.

Reilly (1982) has proposed a causal model linking wife's work status with convenience consumption that features a cognitive mediating variable—role overload. He contends that a wife's perception of her roles and their associated demands intervenes and affects the family's purchases of convenience items, and he has incorporated this construct into his model along with other variables (wife's education, wife's earnings, family income, and family social status). Consequently, an indirect relationship, operating through the cognitive mediating variable, is posited between wife's employment and convenience consumption.

Research Directions

Two major directions are proposed for future reserch. First, in order to understand the effect of time on consumption behavior, it is necessary to consider not only objective personal and situational variables but also the way in which these variables are interpreted and perceived by individuals. A cognitive mediation process appears to inevitably affect individuals' behaviors. A cognitively oriented time perception construct has its precedence in past research (in terms of subjective perceptions of time), but its significance as an intervening variable with antecedents and consequences is just beginning to be recognized. Reilly's (1982) proposed notion of role overload (which he operationalizes as perceived time pressures) may supply a first step toward understanding this intervening process. Such a cognitive construct, however, is likely to be multidimensional and may include a variety of dimensions (as illustrated in Table 10-1) beyond perceived time pressures.

One important perceptual dimension might be the value placed on time. Those who place great value on time may plan their activities or behavior more carefully than those who do not value it. Various household forms may value time differently. A household with children, for example, may value time more highly than childless households and therefore may use it differently. If both husband and wife are career-oriented, they may plan their free time more carefully and use it differently than would a dual-income couple that is not career-oriented.

Perceived availability of time may be another dimension of consumption behavior. Families without children may perceive a greater amount of

Table 10–1.   Household Forms, Time Perceptions, and Behaviors.

Antecedents	Cognitive Construct	Consequences
Household Forms	Time Perceptions	Behaviors
Singles	Time pressure	Convenience-oriented consumption
Presence or absence of children	Value of time	Meal preparation
Dual-career or dual-income families	Perceived availability	Shopping habits
High- or low-status working wife	Time perspective Assumptions about one's time	Media habits Decision-making strategies
		Use of leisure
		Use of services
		Retail patronage
		Innovativeness
		Energy allocation
		Allocation to activities
		Household task performance

leisure time than households with children. Singles may perceive themselves as having less committed time than those in multiple-member households; they may not feel pressure to perform household tasks and thus may allow themselves more leisure time than family households.

Another dimension of consumption behavior involves perspective of time. For example, dual-income couples or singles may tend to live for the present, while dual-career couples or couples with chidren may tend to plan for the future. Individuals' assumptions about time may underlie their perspective, such as its availability, divisibility (e.g., can it be divided into intervals), or whether it can be saved, traded, or invested. Different perspectives are then likely to yield diverse behavioral patterns. There of course may be other important dimensions to this proposed time perceptions construct: Its exact nature can be developed only via further research.

A second related research direction, then, might involve examining the consequences of individual time perceptions, especially in terms of the time-saving strategies they seem to effect. Figure 10–1 suggests many potential categories of behavior that may be affected by time perceptions. Prior research has examined workwife families and the time-saving strategies they employ (e.g., Strober and Weinberg 1980). It has been hypothesized that working wives will feel more time pressure and consequently engage in behaviors that will conserve time. For example, with regard to meal preparation, workwife families were expected to buy more convenience foods, to own more time-saving appliances, and to be more prone to eat out than nonworkwife families. Possible strategies overlooked, however, include using alternative cooking methods (e.g., wok cooking, crockpot cooking) or bringing prepared food into the home. It is possible that these latter two strategies might be used more by singles, dual-career families, and younger families.

In the domain of other household tasks, it has been hypothesized that working wives would own more labor-saving devices, reduce the quantity and quality of their household work, or decrease time allocated to leisure and sleep to relieve time pressures (Strober and Weinberg 1980). It has also been proposed that the husband would assume more household duties to relieve the wife's time pressure. While it has been found that employed wives spend fewer hours on housework, there is little evidence to suggest that husbands are spending more (Huber and Spitze 1981; Model 1982; Nickols and Metzen 1982; Pleck 1981; Robinson 1977; Wales and Woodland 1977). It has been inferred that many tasks may be postponed or never done (Bird 1979; Roberts and Wortzel 1982).

Other strategies for relieving time pressure might include hiring outside help (purchasing services), assigning responsibilities to children, or the wife's taking part-time work. There are a plethora of time-saving strategies available to families, and prior empirical studies indicate that different household forms use various types of strategies for saving time (Redman 1980; Reilly 1982; Schaninger and Allen 1981). Especially needed, then, is theoretical and empirical work that will uncover the potentially diverse time-saving strategies used by household units. Cognitive constructs—like the time-perception variable briefly described here—will help develop theory in this area.

COMMUNICATING WITH NONTRADITIONAL FAMILY FORMS: THE SEX-ROLE STEREOTYPING APPROACH

Changing familial arrangements are creating highly visible and lucrative market segments, many of which have obvious needs in areas such as time-saving or convenience-oriented products and services. The challenge to marketers is to develop products that supply the specific packages of benefits demanded by these segments and then to develop advertising strategies that communicate these benefits. One controversial approach used in this context is sex-role stereotyping; indeed, to appeal to the new, multidimensional American household, many seem to be recommending a search for more modern and representative sex-role stereotypes to replace the old, simplistic, worn-out ones (e.g., *Progressive Grocer* 1979; Scheibe 1979; *Wall Street Journal* 1982; Whipple and Courtney 1980). Unfortunately, while sex-role stereotyping has drawn considerable researcher attention, there is little available evidence concerning its effectiveness when used in a persuasive communication strategy.

Advertising Research on Sex-Role Stereotyping

A comprehensive review of the advertising literature dealing with sex-role stereotyping is well beyond the scope of this paper. It is important, however, to recognize the primary thrust of marketing research in this area. Numerous researchers have documented the presence and nature of sex-role stereotyping in ads (e.g., Courtney and Whipple 1974, 1980). These studies have featured content analysis and have focused principally on women's roles. The typical finding has been that advertisers' portrayals of women have been unflattering and nonrepresentative (e.g., Courtney and Whipple 1974, 1980), although some of the more recent studies suggest that the trend may be away from such unidimensional portrayals (Scheibe 1979; Schneider and Schneider 1979; Sharits and Lammers 1983). It should be noted that stereotyping is not oriented just toward women; Scheibe (1979), for instance, found that single men are rarely found in television ads, except in connection with romance and beauty products.

Advertisers seem interested in finding alternatives to the traditional sex-role stereotypes (*Wall Street Journal* 1982), but evidence on the effectiveness of more current and multidimensional role portrayals is very limited (Whipple and Courtney 1980). Whipple and Courtney (1980: 58) have addressed the issue of effectiveness: "we found progressive sex-role portrayals in television commercials to be at least equally preferred to, and in some cases more preferred than, traditional advertising approaches." Although the Whipple and Courtney study represents valid advertisement-effectiveness research in this area, what does it really tell us? Does a statement expressing preference for one advertisement over another reveal anything about the relative persuasiveness of the two ads?

There is, to be sure, no consensus that substituting one sex-role stereotype for another is the best approach for communicating to diverse target segments. One advertising researcher reports that "his studies show that women bristle at the stereotypical portrayal of a housewife in endless pursuit of dirt and the equally stereotypical picture of a chauffeur-driven working woman" (*Wall Street Journal* 1982). Roberts and Wortzel (1979) suggest that people are too multidimensional for any sex-role stereotype to facilitate communication, no matter how modern or progressive it may be. Bem's (1981) analysis implies that society's new attitudes about sex roles do not call for sex-role stereotypes to be more multifaceted or progressive but that sex-related stereotyping is becoming less acceptable. Advertising practitioners, in their efforts to develop messages that more effectively reach important new family segments, are adopting a tactic about which little is known. Consequently, one important research direction for academics would be to carefully consider the question of whether using multidimensional or progressive sex-role stereotyping enhances the persuasiveness of marketers' communications.

Research Directions

Developing a research program that addresses the effectiveness issue requires conceptual frameworks for analyzing the phenomenon of stereo-typing in advertisements, and identifying such frameworks requires careful consideration of what is expected to be gained by using stereotypes. Briefly, stereotyping may be used in two ways. First, the stereotyping approach may furnish a brand with a unique image that turns the brand into a communication symbol that then can be employed by individuals in self-concept enhancement (Sirgy 1982). Ads for Harvey's Bristol Cream sherry, Revlon's Charlie perfume, and Virginia Slims cigarettes are oriented toward such image-enhancement motives. A second approach is described by Scheibe (1979), who notes that advertisers need character roles that the viewer can easily identify with in order to facilitate communication of benefits to a specific target in the limited time span of ad exposure. For example, J.Walter Thompson's commercial for Aunt Jemima French Toast employs the "bungling father" role stereotype, presumably to help communicate the product's convenience attributes. Both these approaches imply that individuals give preferential treatment to imagery and information that they consciously or unconsciously deem self-relevant; this implicates the self as a key concept for analyzing advertising stereotyping effectiveness.

Self-concept has been part of the consumer-behavior literature for many years (Engel and Blackwell 1982; Sirgy 1982), and some researchers have specifically investigated sex-role self-concepts (e.g., Allison, Golden, Mullet, and Coogan 1980; Gentry, Doering, and O'Brien 1978). This research area, however, has been plagued by conceptual vagueness and serious operational problems and, for a variety of reasons, has not been one of intense activity (Peter 1980; Sirgy 1982). Indeed, if it were not for a resurgence of interest in the self in other disciplines (e.g., Greenwald 1980; Markus 1977; Rogers, Kuiper, and Kirker 1977; Wegner and Vallacher 1980), it is unlikely that a self-oriented conceptualization of consumer behavior would have been considered.

This discussion of relevant developments in the area of self must necessarily be brief, but it attempts to point out a meaningful direction for researchers, the foundation of which is furnished by Markus's (1977) self-schemata notion. She (1977: 64) defines self-schemata as "cognitive generalizations about the self, derived from past experience, that organize and guide the processing of self-related information contained in the individual's social experiences. Self-schemata take the form of trait-like dimensions that individuals use to think about themselves and thus come very close to a self-concept type of notion (see Markus, Crane, Berstein, and Siladi 1982). These variables seem to play a powerful role in guiding information processing and in the organization of memory, and unlike most self-concept operationalizations in the consumer-behavior literature, the construct validity of Markus's measurement procedures are reassuring (Cacioppo, Petty, and Sidera 1982; Markus 1977; Markus, Crane, Berstein, and Siladi 1982).

Two dimensions that people use in thinking about themselves are masculinity and femininity (Bem 1981; Markus, Crane, Berstein, and Siladi 1982), and the self-schemata model would predict, for example, that persons with feminine self-schematas will privilege feminine stimuli in information processing (Markus, Crane, Berstein, and Siladi 1982). The relevant question here, of course, is whether such a prediction would hold true if the information involved were an advertisement featuring sex-role stereotyping. This, however, becomes an empirical question, since individuals can be classified in terms of the gender schemata that are salient to them (Markus, Crane, Berstein, and Siladi 1982) and procedures are being developed to categorize advertisements in terms of the masculinity and femininity of the characters' sex-role portrayals (Kolbe 1983). One method for assessing the persuasive impact of an advertisement that emphasizes a specific gender orientation on individuals who think of themselves in a specific gender dimension is cognitive response analysis (Petty, Ostrom, and Brock 1981). Generally, the cognitive-response method has proved potent in diagnosing why persuasive communications do or do not seem to work. Moreover, research has shown that detecting whether a persuasive communication has activated a specific self-schemata dimension can be accomplished by examining individual cognitive responses (Cacioppo, Petty, and Sidera 1982).

The self-schemata model also proposes that the self plays an important role in whether or not information will be remembered. The work of Rogers, Kuiper, and Kirker (1977) demonstrates that if information stimuli are self-referenced (i.e., lead the individual to think about himself or herself in the processing of the information), then the stimuli will prove easier to recall. This has potentially important implications for advertising if stereotyping does lead the viewer to think about a product in self-referencing terms. It has been noted that advertisements featuring more progressive stereotypes prove easier to remember (Scheibe 1979): Perhaps this is because they are more likely to stimulate information processing that includes self-referencing.

The self-schemata framework offers some interesting research directions for exploring the effectiveness of advertisements that feature sex-role stereotyping. There are surely other directions that might be taken: For example, recent research regarding attitudes toward advertisement construct (Mitchell and Olson 1981; Shimp 1981) may be particularly germane for the stereotyping context, since stereotypes often are very effective (and usually negatively effective). The intent here is certainly not to advocate one specific research direction. However, since practitioners are likely to use more diverse stereotypes in ads in their efforts to communicate with different target segments, it is important for academic researchers to address further the questions of if and how such stereotyping affects the persuasion process.

SUMMARY

This discussion has considered several topic areas, all of which reflect change in the American household. A number of intriguing research directions have been revealed in the process. Added sophistication is needed in the way researchers categorize households of singles and families. The approach recommended here is to strive for conceptual schemata that maintain an operational emphasis on demographic (as opposed to, for example, attitudinal) variables. This emphasis on demographics, of course, will enhance the applied value of this research.

It also is suggested that a time-perception construct may help generate theories that eventually will furnish insights about behavioral patterns of diverse household forms. Such a construct should also help to clarify the complex relationships among household characteristics and the time-saving strategies.

Finally, communicating with diverse types of household units requires an examination of sex-role stereotyping strategy. As diversity in the American household leads advertisers to reject traditional stereotypes, there is likely to be a surge of interest in finding "better" ones. We need to know more about this communication strategy, how it works, and how it might perform compared to other strategy alternatives. The theoretical and experimental approach of the academic researcher in this area has much to offer the practitioner who wishes to better understand the effects of stereotyping in advertisements.

11 HOUSEHOLDS AND TECHNOLOGY
The Case of Home Computers—Some Conceptual and Theoretical Issues

Alladi Venkatesh and Nicholas Vitalari

Although the household is a major societal institution, marketing scholars and practitioners have been slow to accept it as a unit of analysis. Until recently, the major focus has been on the behavior of the single individual. Attention now seems to be shifting to both the household and the individual, presumably because of the fundamental changes occurring within the family or household setting, some of which are structural (e.g., the emergence of two-career families, single-parent families, and so on). Also contributing to this shifting emphasis is the growing interest among economists, cultural anthropologists, and family sociologists (Becker 1976; Berk and Berk 1979; Tittle 1981) who tend to regard the household as a significant social institution that plays a unique role in the consumption and production of a variety of goods and services. Much of the interest exhibited by marketers may be attributed to the recent work of Etgar (1978) and Roberts and Wortzel (1980, 1981).

In addition, changes in technology are likely to attract greater research effort on households. We have begun to hear expressions such as "the home of the future," "the electronic household," "household information services" (Tydeman 1982), which suggest that the household should be studied as a collective unit.

This paper attempts to understand the household, especially in its adoption and use of technology. It addresses two basic issues: the role of technology in the context of the household and, more specifically, the

187

problems and potential of home computer adoption and usage. The first part of the paper discusses how households adopt and interact with technology. The second part specifically addresses the issue of households and computer technology. Some empirical results from a recently conducted study of household adoption and use of home computers are presented to illustrate various issues developed in the conceptual part of the paper.

Technology and Households

Traditionally, the interaction between technology and society has been studied in the context of a technological revolution in industry: automated factories, massive business computers, and so forth. Households eventually enter a similar technological race. The technological revolution affects daily life within a household in time allocation patterns, in the choice of social functions, in the transmittal of cultural values, and in overall human behavior (Cowan 1976; Vanek 1978; Robinson 1980). When a given technology begins to affect the life of a household, it is a safe conclusion that the technology is being integrated into the social system and is accepted as a basis for future social behavior. For example, automobiles have totally transformed American value systems, creating what is generally known as the automobile culture. Other technologies popularized in the past two or three decades have introduced structural changes and new ideologies within the household: Washing machines and dishwashers, entertainment-oriented products such as radio, television, and stereo equipment, architectural changes in the design of kitchens, bathrooms, and other units of physical space—all give new meaning to child rearing, women's roles, family interactions, shopping behavior, and value systems.

Most technologies affect individuals at two levels: in the work environment and in the home environment (Ginzberg 1965). In many cases, a technology begins with an industrial application and is transferred to the household environment with some modifications. The effect of such a technological sweep can be major. According to available sociological literature, individual socialization occurs through interactions within dominant cultural institutions such as families, school, church, and work place (Duncan, Featherman, and Duncan 1972). The typology of institutions can be expanded to operational situations that we call social contexts. These include family roles (wife, husband, child), occupational roles (scientist, teacher, laborer, etc.), cultural experiences, travel and recreational patterns, work socialization, and so on. This study examines the household system. Although evidence shows that the structure of American family has changed in recent years, its influence on individual attitudes and behavior continues to be significant. Individual value systems and behavior are shaped, for the most part, within the context of the household. (See Moore and Moschis 1981 for an excellent development of the role of family communication in consumer learning.)

The Household as a System

Households may be regarded as human systems that adopt rational, economic (production-oriented), and social strategies to achieve their goals and to respond to the external environment (Stolte-Heiskanen 1975). The same strategies may be used to adapt to changes externally imposed by the environment or internally generated within the system. In adopting these different strategies, the household behaves as a rational system, or a social system. These descriptors are not necessarily mutually exclusive but from the point of view of a reasonable analysis can be considered conceptually distinct.

As a rational system, the household accepts or rejects new technologies based on measurable benefits that the technologies can confer on the household—for example, time and cost savings and improvement in material conditions. As an economic system, the household will be inclined to evaluate technologies in terms of their potential to produce goods and services that are appropriate to the functioning of the household. Households with better educated members can be considered to be better able to use a variety of household technologies, to organize their time more efficiently, and to minimize the routine, repetitive, and mundane aspects of life. Finally, as social systems, households adopt technologies because they may add power and prestige and improve their social status. Technologies may also develop better communications between members of the system and generate an interaction process in which each individual member plays a role.

Households and Social Change

Social change, as defined by Rogers, "is the process by which alteration occurs in the structure and function of a social system" (Rogers 1969). Such a change may originate inside the system, outside the system, or a combination of both. Zaltman, Kotler, and Kaufman (1970:2) identify two kinds of change: Planned social change "originates with a declared intention of objectives: it starts with a purpose of altering the free play of those social consequences that have ensued from demographic, physiographic, and technological change. Unplanned social change is a result of natural forces causing changes in society." Most social change phenomena are unplanned, and this is especially true of households that periodically come into contact with new technologies that originate from sources over which they have no control.

Because a household does not have control over the sources of technologies, it develops both defensive and adaptive mechanisms. Defensive mechanisms permit it to carefully evaluate technologies and determine how they affect the existing life patterns and what changes they would bring to the household's present approach to solving problems. New technologies mean new ambiguities, new complexities, new patterns of resource allocation, and new fears of the unknown. Parallelling defensive mechanisms are adaptive mechanisms, which facilitate change. Such mechanisms may include expectations about possible benefits, competitive and survival norms (e.g., computer literacy for children), and new experiences that would be entertaining and enlightening. Fears and expectations—the dangers posed by the unknown and the possibilities of better prospects—trigger social change.

Some Theoretical Perspectives on Technology and Technological Impact

The Notion of Technological Consciousness.   Technology, as defined by Ayres (1961), is the system of tool-using behavior. Technological consciousness develops through a process of socialization and cognitive development. Households receive a variety of technological cues and information and integrate a particular technology both consciously and unconsciously. To the extent that the integration is conscious, households react differently to various technologies mainly because of differing household characteristics. Both degree of socialization and level of cognitive development account for how households respond to the technological environment. Although technological consciousness may appear to be an individual construct, it can also be viewed as a household construct. The prevailing mode of thinking within a household and the systemic character of households suggest the characteristics and value systems that govern the attitudes and behaviors of individual members who comprise the household. Thus, we can speak of modern households, transition households, traditional households, and so on. Inkeles and Smith (1974) have shown that institutions mold individuals and that individuals internalize the values of the institutions and incorporate the salient features into their own behavior.

Technological Functionalism.   Technological functionalism is premised on the idea that technology is what technology does. As mentioned earlier, it is essentially a tool designed to meet a specific need of the user whether the user is an individual or an organized institution. Since our interest is in the behavior of households, we would like to view the household as a functioning social and economic system and a recipient of technology. The motivation of a household to adopt a particular technology can be discussed in terms of three theoretical dimensions: (1) instrumental/expressive, (2) passive/active, and (3) task-oriented/pleasure-oriented.

Instrumental/Expressive. The instrumental/expressive dimension is adapted from Parsons's classification of pattern variables (Parsons 1951): Technology is a tool that meets specific functional goals of the household. In order for a given technology to be employed successfully to realize instrumental goals, the user must have the knowledge of how technology can be utilized, have the ability to cope with the technological demands, and actually use it to meet specific functional needs. Instrumental goals are such objectives as need satisfaction, task performance, cost savings, and efficient use of time. For example, the telephone permits people to conduct business and establish instantaneous contact with others at great distances, allows two-way communication, and speeds up transactions. Such examples can be provided for other products, as well. The instrumental dimension of computers refers to their application in a variety of uses, such as management of home activities, word processing, family education, and maintaining various financial records. The expressive side of technology refers to the possibilities that technology creates for communicating emotions and affections and expressing family-related values through opinions and behavior. People engage in games and entertainment as a means of conveying their feelings toward others. Such activities have a high personal and psychological meaning in the context of the household. In much the same way that computers can be used for instrumental purposes, they can be used to satisfy expressive needs through entertainment, games, music, electronic mail, family contacts, and so on.

A hypothesis relevant to the expressive/instrumental dimension is that households consider both expressive and instrumental needs in the adoption and use of technology. Typically, technologies that are rich in their ability to satisfy both expressive and instrumental needs are likely to be more important in a household.

Passive/Active. The passive/active dimension of technology refers to the effort required by the user to achieve the desired results from the technology. Some technologies require greater effort from the users in active, direct, mental manipulation and involvement with the technology. Associated with this requirement is training and skill level. Watching television, for example, requires very little effort, but automobile driving is as full-involvement activity. It can be hypothesized that the skill level required to adopt or use a particular technology increases on the continuum as it moves from passive to active. Figure 11-1 shows how different technologies can be described as passive or active. Easton (1980) has argued that, other things remaining equal, passive technologies would find greater use in households. Automobiles obviously require active involvement, but the overriding need for transportation and its value as personal expression have made it a compelling technology. Home computers represent both active and passive dimensions: Computer games and computers as educational devices may attract different households because of their different passive/active dimensions.

Task-Oriented/Pleasure-Oriented. Although there is a relationship between the task-oriented/pleasure-oriented dimension of technologies and the passive/active dimension, they are not the same. Fried and Molnar (1975) have identified three variables that describe the task dimension: (1) serial characteristic variable, (2) operations-output relations variable, and (3) output form variable. The first variable states that sequential behavior pattern is measured on a temporal scale (i.e., turning the light switch versus wall papering). The second variable measures the degree to which operations that produce outputs are characterized by their separation. The last variable refers to the degree to which the operations are subject to routinization. Thus, the task-oriented nature of technology refers to the specific acts that the user has to perform before the technology can be put to its intended use. One example in an automobile would be starting the engine, looking through rear and side mirrors, and engaging the gear before making the automobile move. The tasks can be mechanical and routinized with minimal cognitive complexity, or they may involve some amount of training and learning. Easton (1980) argues that households adopt technologies that are not too task-oriented but instead are pleasure-oriented (television, stereo) and that they minimize the use of technologies that are high-task oriented (typewriters) unless they are high-need-oriented.

The Nature of Technological Impact.   The idea that technology can confer both benefits and losses to the user is not new. Stover (1962) observed that whether a particular technology is beneficial or not is often an empirical question about which it is difficult to theorize. DeCarlo (1964) commented that those who are affected by technology invariably have very little to say about whether a particular technology should be developed and, if developed, whether and how it should be distributed. Ogburn and Nimkoff (1955) proposed that technology has diminished the role of the household in the production sector and, consequently, its importance as a social unit. This has also led to a type of technological determinism that appears to shape the destiny of the household within a broader social context. More recently, Moses (1981) put forward the view that households act as free agents and choose the technologies that fit their specific needs. The

Figure 11–1. Passive and Active Dimensions of Household Technologies.

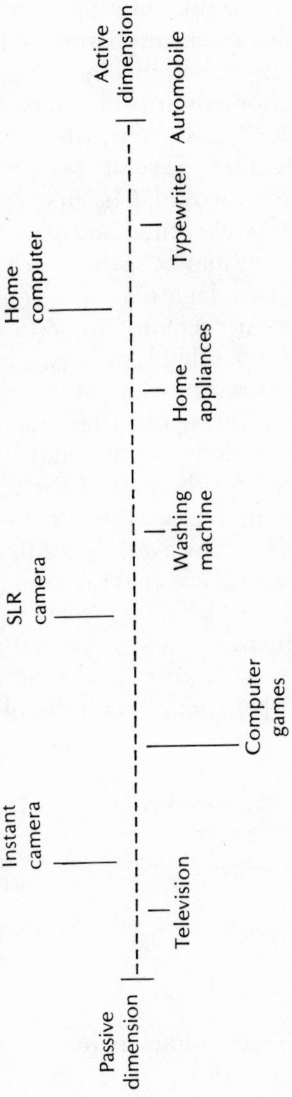

potential for such a choice and the fears and expectations surrounding it are a subject of household deliberation. Some authors have examined technology in terms of its effect on time allocation across various home-centered activities (Weiss 1969; Robinson 1977). For example, Robinson found that while the technology of the automobile makes possible a faster commute to work, the automobile also makes it possible to live further from work so that the total travel times of automobile owners and nonowners are the same. The same type of homeostatic trade-offs also appear to characterize the impact of television (Weiss 1969), which has taken time away from reading and radio listening. Several perspectives on the effects of technology have been put forward. The first view states that technology results in increased discretionary time, and makes it possible for the user to determine how the free time may be spent, which in turn permits additional control over one's life (see Figure 11-2). The second view states that technology reduces the effort required to perform task- and work-related activities and thus allows households to engage in many nontask activities. This eventually leads to an improvement in the quality of one's life (see Figure 11-3). The third view postulates that to derive benefits from technology (e.g., more efficient use of time) requires a certain level of competence or familiarity on the part of the user. Without appropriate skills and education, an individual will not find much use for a given technology. It is recognized, however, that different technologies require different levels of competence and that the level of difficulty will vary with each technology (see Figure 11-4).

A final, more comprehensive view suggests that the net benefits from a technology are not easy to capture. Given certain criteria by which to evaluate the consequent benefits of the technology, one can empirically

Figure 11-2.   Technology Increases Discretionary Time.

Technology ___(increases)___ > Discretionary time ___(control)___ > Decision over how time is spent

Figure 11-3.   Technology Increases Participation in Nonwork Activities.

Technology __(reduces effort)__ --> Increased participation in nonwork/nontask activities --→ Improvement in quality of life

Figure 11–4. Technology Requires User Competence.

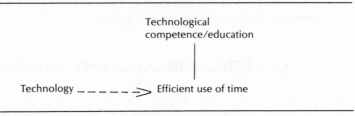

Figure 11–5. Effects of Adopting the New Technology.

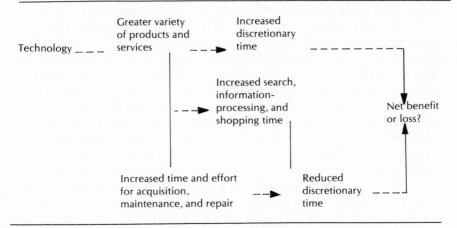

establish whether the technology resulted in improved conditions for the user. For example, new technology usually leads to a greater variety of products and services, a possibility that in many cases increases the discretionary time of the user. Similarly, more effort is required on the part of the households that adopt the technology in terms of search time, information processing time, and shopping time. The obvious effect on discretionary time is negative. Once the products have been acquired, more time must be available for product maintenance, repair, and augmentation. Consequently, the effect of adopting the new technology cannot be stated categorically (see Figure 11–5).

Thus far, the discussion has centered on the effects of technology without reference to any particular technology. Overall benefits can be identified as improved quality of life and material conditions, increased discretionary time, and increased efficiency in task performance. Despite some negative consequences of technological adoption, the overall net effect appears to be an empirical question. In the next part of the paper, attention is focused on the possible effects of computer technology. Computers are particularly significant because of the diversity of their use potential and the alleged revolutionary nature of their effect on users.

COMPUTER TECHNOLOGY AND HOUSEHOLDS

Recent advances in microcomputer technology have greatly decreased the cost and increased the power of computers. The result is that computers are now available to a large segment of the population for personal as well as industrial use.[1] The application of the technology has been so dramatic and rapid that popular magazines have dedicated lead stories to the potential impacts of the technology on the individual and society (*Advertising Age* 1982; *Business Week* 1981; *Time* 1983; *Scientific American* 1983). Of particular interest are predictions of widespread adoption of personal computers by households and the alleged arrival of the "home of the future," replete with new patterns of social and interpersonal behavior based on the emerging technology. Although computer technology is now available for adoption by households on an unprecedented scale, no serious research efforts have helped to understand the true nature of its impact. Because this technology is so new, it is likely that little systematic research has been accomplished. A recent report by Humes (1980) on electronic funds transfer systems was limited in its overall focus and briefly touched on some demographic and attitudinal characteristics of the relevant consumer segment. Specifically, in the realm of personal computers, a variety of problems appears to be emerging: For example, Heller (1981) refers to the complexity of the computer systems as a barrier to consumer acceptance; Wrege (1982) has suggested several hypotheses related to cyberphobia (fear of computers) and cyberphielia (compulsive passion for computers); and C. Cohen (1982) has discussed the pressures felt by families in helping their children to become computer literate. Some other examples suggest that the ultimate acceptance of computers may depend on the task-orientation of the user (Easton 1980). This study examines some of these issues.

The Social Impacts of Computer Technology

It has almost been a decade since Daniel Bell (1975), in his book, *The Coming of the Post-Industrial Society*, predicted the emergence of a new social order predicated on computer information systems and access to specialized knowledge. The capabilities of this technology were expected to create new opportunities for individuals and perhaps augment different patterns of social interaction, access to information, and allocation of time. At the same time some researchers argued that the mass adoption of this technology could lead to unanticipated, if somewhat dubious, consequences for society (Weizenbaum 1981; Kraemer and King 1977).

A considerable literature has developed in the last twenty years about the social effects of the computer in large organizations. Experience and empirical research suggest that computer technology can in certain circumstances alter task structures, roles, interpersonal relationships, and organizational structures. Broadly speaking, microcomputer technology can be evaluated in terms of its technological, economic, and social effects. Technological effects are such issues as increased power and mechanization of the task environment. Economic effects are increased productivity, labor savings, cost reduction, and other advantages or disadvantages that can be explained in economic terms. Both technological and economic impacts in the industrial and public sectors have been identified by several authors (Kraemer and King 1977; Kling 1980). Generally, adoption of information technology both in economic and technological terms has been felt to have contributed positively to the advancement of the industrial and organizations systems. Related to the technological and economic effects is the social effect of the microcomputer systems now becoming available to households and individuals. Some well-known scientists and sociologists (Simon 1977; Bell 1979; Weizenbaum 1981) have debated the social consequences of computer technology in both qualitative and quantitative terms. Missing from such a debate, however, is a reasonable assumption that the interaction between computer technology and the households can be viewed as a bi-directional process with the social impact of technology on the household occurring first, followed by changes in future technology occurring partially as a result of how households utilize it. Basic to this argument is a feedback from the household to the source of technology. A model capturing this bi-directional process will be presented in the last section of our paper after a short report on an empirical study.

An Empirical Investigation

We designed an exploratory study to examine the computer usage patterns and experiences of some of the early groups of buyers of home computers. About 300 households with home computers were contacted through membership lists of computer clubs in the Orange County area of Southern California. A self-administered questionnaire was handed to the principal user within the household. Of the total questionnaires returned, 282 were found usable.

The purpose of the study was (1) to determine the specific changes in time-allocation patterns across a variety of activities resulting from usage and application of computers in the home, (2) to identify specific ways in which computers are being used in the home and to identify general segments of usage, (3) to identify reasons and motivations for computer purchase, and (4) to determine sources of satisfaction for computer usage and to assess satisfaction levels for both. The detailed methodology and findings of the study are discussed elsewhere (Venkatesh, Vitalari, and Gronhaug 1983; Venkatesh and Vitalari 1983). Some of the highlights are presented here to illustrate the issues developed in the conceptual part.

The sample consisted primarily of males (95 percent) in professional/ managerial/technical occupations groups with higher education and higher income status. A large majority of the users (77 percent) had previous computer experience (i.e., prior to the purchase of the home computers). Although the sample does not represent the general population, it appears to be representative of early adopters of home computers. Because a majority of respondents had used computers before, the stage for household adoption of home computers already had been set, usually at the work place. We suggested earlier that for the technological cycle to be complete the flow usually begins from work situations. The prior exposure reported by our early adopters confirms this hypothesis for computer technology. This result cannot be used to predict that all future household adoption is contingent on prior exposure in work environment. In fact, nearly 27 percent of our sample has had no such exposure. It is more likely that as home computers become more popular this sample would represent the population of interest.

Our findings also suggest there are social contexts relevant to the adoption of computer technology. For example, because 95 percent of the users are predominantly male and in families with children, it appears that the computer is creating opportunities for the father to interact with his children. While this particular social context is not evidence of "computer widowhood," it points to an important development within the household in the initial stages of computer adoption—mothers are being left out. This is likely to be less of an issue as more women become involved with computers. This issue's effect on socialization within the household needs to be investigated further.

Households also behave as rational economic systems in their use of technology. An interesting finding in our study is the significant correlation between income and initial expenditures on hardware and software. This result is intuitively appealing and supports what could be an obvious hypothesis. However, an examination of additional expenditures on computer hardware and software after initial purchase reveals that correlation with income is less significant and that expenditures increase with the level of satisfaction with computer usage. This clearly suggests that here is a context in which the households make decisions as rational economic systems.

The level of technological consciousness within the household appears to make a difference in terms of how different households use the computers. Our results show that where the principal user has had previous experience, households have used computers for more complex applications, such as finance and home management, hobbies, and education; households without a user with previous experience have used computers more for games and word processing. Thus, the degree to which computer technology is exploited has to do with the cognitive development and cognitive competence of the household members.

An additional finding in our study refers to rankings assigned by the respondents to actual computer uses in the household and to uses they considered important. For example, the importance ranking for entertainment and games was low relative to other uses, while the ranking of actual use was rather high. The opposite was observed in the case of home and finance management. One can evaluate this result by invoking our earlier argument that households lean more toward pleasure-oriented technologies compared to task-oriented ones unless there is an overriding need for that particular use.

Another result in the study summarizes the effects of computers on home-centered activities. This research question hypothesizes that because the use of computers takes up time and because there are only a finite number of hours available per day, time is spent on computers at the expense of other activities. For the purpose of the study we identified four different types of activities: (1) activities that involve the user only (i.e., reading, hobbies, sleeping, etc.); (2) leisure time with family and friends; (3) outdoor activities; and (4) television viewing. We treated television viewing as a separate activity because of its dominant role in the American home. The respondent was asked to indicate if any increase or decrease had occurred in various activities because of and since the acquisition of the computer. Changes in these activities due to any other circumstances were not considered relevant.

Television viewing decreased dramatically, with 62 percent reporting decreases. Some computer users use television screens as display monitors, but only 16 percent of respondents used television sets for this purpose. Time spent alone increased by 34 percent, and time spent with family decreased by 18 percent. There seems to be a greater tendency for the user to spend time away from family and friends. The social consequences of this behavior should be interesting: The results already show more negative than positive effects on various activities.

Finally we investigated differences between groups of households based on how long they had owned their computers. It was assumed that initially there would be noticeable effects on home-centered activities but that once the households become familiar with computers and integrate them into their lives, the effects would be less pronounced. In order to investigate this hypothesis we performed a simple cross-tabulation analysis between length of ownership and reported changes in activities. The results were not significant, which intuitively appeared questionable. Because the sample included a large proportion of computer users who had previous experience (77 percent), it was decided to separate the sample into two groups—those with previous experience and those without. The results showed some dramatic differences. For example, during the first year of ownership, television watching decreased for 100 percent of the no-previous-experience group but only 67 percent of the experienced group. This differential was found in other categories, such as leisure time with family (40 percent and 11 percent, respectively), leisure time with friends (30 percent and 13 percent, respectively), and so on. Clearly then, the length of ownership begins to emerge as an important variable when previous experience is held constant. As more households adopt computers, they are more likely to resemble the no-previous-experience group of the sample and more likely to feel the effects of usage. In general, the findings demonstrate that adoption of home computers by households results in changes in time allocation across different activities.

A Causal Model of Technological Impacts on Households

Based on our study, we developed a causal model of technological impact (Figure 11-6). Fundamental to this model are two research questions:

1. Does the personal computer affect the structure and value systems of households over time? Do any of these effects persist—that is, do they produce new patterns and values that to some extent can be accounted for by the emerging technology? If so, what are the long-term implications?
2. How do household computer usage patterns influence the configuration of hardware and software of the personal computer as it evolves over time?

Both questions are important, although the main focus of our analysis is the first question with implications for the second.

Figure 11-6 is a conceptualization of interaction between the household social system and the technology system. The household system is comprised of four major components: user household, selection and choice of computer

Figure 11-6. A Causal Model of Technological Effects on Households.

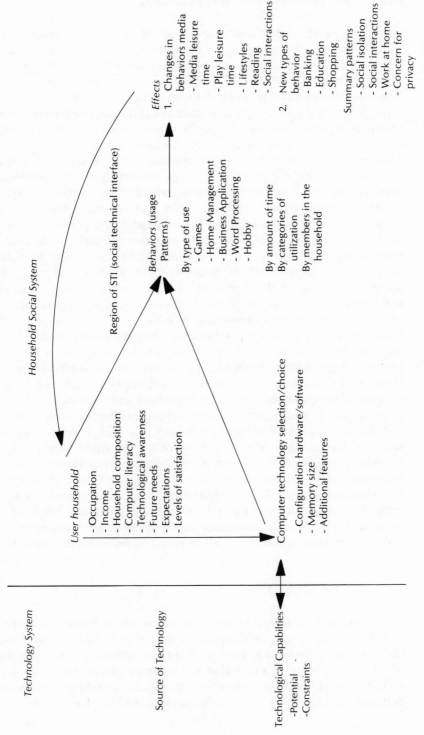

Technology System

Household Social System

Region of STI (social technical interface)

User household
- Occupation
- Income
- Household composition
- Computer literacy
- Technological awareness
- Future needs
- Expectations
- Levels of satisfaction

Source of Technology

Computer technology selection/choice
- Configuration hardware/software
- Memory size
- Additional features

Technological Capabilities
- Potential
- Constraints

Behaviors (usage Patterns)

By type of use
- Games
- Home Management
- Business Application
- Word Processing
- Hobby

By amount of time
By categories of utilization
By members in the household

Effects

1. Changes in behaviors media
- Media leisure time
- Play leisure time
- Lifestyles
- Reading
- Social interactions

2. New types of behavior
- Banking
- Education
- Shopping

Summary patterns
- Social isolation
- Social interactions
- Work at home
- Concern for privacy

201

technology, a set of behaviors, and a set of effects. Similarly, the two components in the technology system are comprised of the source of technology and technological availability and capabilities. Together, these six components determine the nature of interaction between the two systems. The exact relationships between and within the two systems are identified through a causal mechanism that links the different components of the system by directional arrows. Using the concept of sociotechnical interface (STI) from social systems and organizational literature (Hedberg and Mumford 1975; Danzinger 1979), we show that a set of household behaviors toward computer technology results from the interaction between the user household's characteristics and the selection of appropriate computer technology (i.e., hardware and software). The model also shows that the choice decision itself is influenced by the characteristics of the household subject to the availability and the capabilities of the existing technology, which are in turn determined by its source. The household behaviors are operationally described as usage patterns and are further decomposed by types of use, amount of time, members of the household, and categories of utilization. While behaviors are technology specific, the effects refer to changes in household activities and to lifestyles that result from the continued use of the technology. Thus, the effects are classified in terms of changes in behavior, new types of behavior, and some summary patterns of social effect. Embedded in the model is also feedback from the effects to the characteristics of the household, implying changes may occur in some of the characteristics of the household, such as computer literacy, technological awareness, and levels of satisfaction. Family income and size and the occupation head of the household are less likely to be affected. As a result of the changes occurring in some of the characteristics of the household (e.g., level of satisfaction with the computer system), the user household may now decide to alter its future selection of computer hardware and software. Emerging patterns of uses and experiences with the technology will force computer firms to respond to the needs of the household appropriately. In terms of our model, household choice processes and use patterns eventually will affect potential technological capabilities.

CONCLUSIONS

This paper has attempted to conceptualize issues in household adoption and use of technologies, with particular reference to home computers. It discussed some theoretical notions about the technology and household interface and presented a partial report on an empirical study.

The arena of households and computer technology falls into the general definition of what Kling (1980) calls the social analysis of computing. In his comprehensive survey article, Kling (1980:62) made some observations that are pertinent to this study.

> In coming to an understanding of computing technologies, particularly newer ones, it is important to understand which conceptions of social life are likely to aid in discerning critical social aspects. . . . [T]here are still not adequate theoretical accounts of computing in social life. The accounts of computing, whether developed by scholars or laymen, are strongly limited by the primitive state of social theory in general, and by the common myths that surround complex technologies in particular.

Given this compelling and provocative assessment, we believe that the effect of computing on households is a legitimate sphere of inquiry that should be seriously pursued.

NOTE

1. One recent estimate by the International Data Corp. (1983) indicates that the personal computer market will grow from $3.8 billion in 1982 to $14.2 billion in 1986. Assuming an average purchase cost of $5,000 for each personal computer, by 1986 close to ten million personal computers will be purchased by businesses while the other 40 percent will be purchased by households. Furthermore, the capability of the home computer is expected to expand while entry cost decreases, making the computer more useful to a broader subset of the population.

12 SHARING OF HOUSEHOLD MAINTENANCE TASKS IN MARRIED-COUPLE HOUSEHOLDS

Melody Douglas-Tate, Judy Peyton, and Elinor Bowen

This chapter examines the ways husbands and wives share chores and assesses how husbands' involvement in household tasks affects product and brand usage. The extent to which husbands are involved in household tasks is only recently coming to light, with important implications for marketing managers. Our studies show that significant segments of husbands take an active and decisive role in choosing and utilizing household products.

The information for this paper is drawn from the Leo Burnett Lifestyles '83 Project. Lifestyles research provides the opportunity to understand how consumers live and how products fit into their lives. The typical lifestyles data base has five major dimensions: (1) demographics, (2) attitudes, (3) recreational activities, (4) media consumption, and (5) product and brand usage. Information gained from lifestyles research is useful for marketing strategy and copy development. The Leo Burnett Company has conducted lifestyles research six times in the United States, beginning in 1967, and twenty-two times in twelve other countries.

This analysis is based on a subsample from the latest Leo Burnett lifestyles project, fielded in the winter of 1982. The project included a special emphasis on the division of labor in sample households for tasks ranging from food preparation to financial planning. The full data set consists of 2,787 households in which all persons over age 12 completed individual questionnaires. This study focuses on the information provided by 1,601 married-couple households for which both spouses returned questionnaires. The households are a subsample of those completing Nielsen Television Viewing Diaries in May 1982. Since we have recent information on many of the questions posed by other workshop participants, we attempt to share our data as much as is practical in this paper. The presentation has two parts; first, an examination of how husbands and wives share chores, and second, an assessment of how sharing chores affects product and brand usage.

DEGREE OF MALE PARTICIPATION IN HOUSEHOLD MAINTENANCE

In virtually all households with married couples, the wives retain major responsibility for running the households. A large proportion of married men occasionally perform a wide range of household tasks, but only a small number report sole responsibility for cleaning and food shopping and preparation. A substantial proportion of the men report that they never perform these tasks. The top eleven chores in which married men claim sole responsibility in less than 5 percent of households, are not listed. These chores included the preparation of lunch and dinner, setting and clearing the table, cleaning kitchens and bathrooms, dusting, laundering, ironing and sorting clothes (Table 12-1).

A Typology of Households Based on Male Participation in Chores

Husbands' participation in household tasks represents a continuum; tasks vary in the extent to which men are drawn into them (see Figure 12-1). Few husbands participate in activities that are uncommon for men, such as vacuuming, without also engaging in more common activities, such as taking out the trash or preparing breakfast.[1] There is no evidence for a predictable pattern of specialization, such as, for example, some men share in food preparation but do no laundry, while others do laundry but avoid the kitchen.

Cluster analyses were used to identify segments along the continuum. Cluster analysis shows four kinds of households, or segments, which differ in terms of the extent of male participation in household chores.[2] These household types are termed:

- Involved Sharers
- Uninvolved Sharers
- Typicals
- Traditionals

Table 12–1. Sharing of Household Maintenance Chores by Married Men (percentage).

	Married Men Doing Chores All the Time	Married Men Doing Chores Some of the Time	Married Men Never Doing Chores
Traditional Male Chores			
Yard work	50	37	13
Decide about investments	44	42	14
Take out the trash	36	51	13
Keep financial records	33	29	38
Pay bills	30	38	32
Traditional female chores			
Prepare breakfast	11	56	33
Main grocery shopping	11	42	47
Odds-and-ends shopping	10	72	18
Take clothes to dry cleaners	9	37	54
Clean windows	8	49	43
Vacuum	6	57	37

In all of the segments, men have at least some responsibility for deciding about investments, and for traditional male chores such as yard work and taking out the trash. But there is considerable variability among segments with respect to the other tasks. In what are termed Traditional Households, financial tasks and other traditional male tasks are the only things which a majority of husbands do. In Typical Households these chores are augmented by some responsibility for child care, pet care, and food preparation. In the remaining segments, a majority of men contribute to all the household tasks for which we have data, including grocery shopping, general cleaning and clothes care. The task-related behavior in these two kinds of households is similar. But, as will be illustrated later, husbands differ in terms of their attitudinal involvement in the tasks they share.

Demographic Correlates of Male Participation

There are a variety of familiar hypotheses about the demographic correlates of male participation in household responsibilities. Our information confirms that the strongest predictors are the wife's education level and her employment outside the home. We also found that the men who share tasks tend to be younger, have slightly higher household incomes, and live in

Figure 12–1. Household Task Participation.

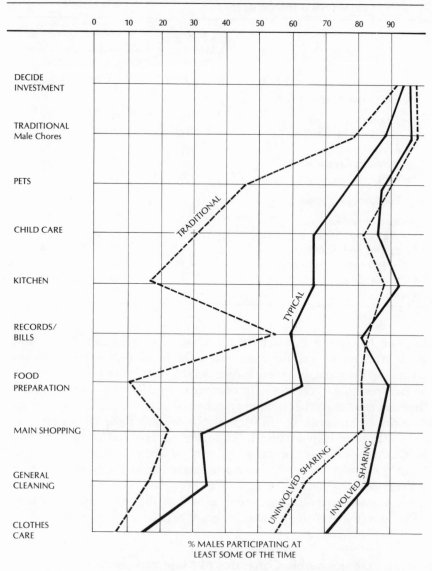

urban areas. But while these expected correlations are statistically significant, demographics do little to distinguish the households from each other
in terms compelling to marketers and advertisers. Reasonable numbers of
well-educated, working women and young, upscale, urban households occur

in all our clusters. Understanding male participation in household tasks requires examination of the attitudinal correlates.

Attitudinal Correlates of the Segments

Men who actively share responsibility for traditionally female chores may also share "homemaker" attitudes toward these chores. One segment of Male Sharers, in particular, shows interest in a variety of task-related behaviors that have long been used by consumer researchers to measure female identification with the homemaker role. We call this group the Involved Sharers, as opposed to the Uninvolved Sharers who do not exhibit this attitude (Table 12-2). The data does not permit a causal inference between attitude and behavior, but they do suggest that the male market for household products may be reached in much the same way as women in the market. In addition, both husbands and wives in the Sharing segments exhibit greater normative commitment to the sharing of tasks. (Table 12-3).

Product Usage and Brand Choice Among Household Segments

Examination of the lifestyle data shows that husbands may be significant targets for advertisers and marketers of household consumables. There are discernible differences among household clusters regarding product usage, husband and wife usage preferences, and brand choice. Our study included data on reported usage of a wide variety of household products such as cooked vegetables, potatoes, rice, gravy, and laundry products. Selected data are presented below to illustrate the general trends of the analysis.

Opportunity to Use Products

The lifestyles questionnaires asked respondents to report how often they had had any opportunity to use the above food and laundry products within the past year, if at all. The percentage of men who report any opportunity to use the food and laundry products varies in the expected direction across the four household segments. Figure 12-2 shows the results for frequency of preparing potatoes, and is representative of the trends in the data for the other product categories. Husbands' opportunities to use the food and laundry products increases as their involvement in household tasks increases, and can amount to a significant proportion of monthly product

Table 12–2. Husband's Psychological Involvement in Household Maintenance Tasks.

	Involved Sharers	Uninvolved Sharers	Typicals	Traditionals
I enjoy most forms of housework	3.2	2.2	2.1	1.7
I like grocery shopping	3.8	2.7	2.6	2.3
I love to cook	4.6	2.3	3.0	2.2
I try to plan most meals in advance	3.6	2.7	2.8	2.6
I am a careful comparative shopper	4.6	4.4	4.2	4.2
I am a gourmet	3.3	2.0	2.6	2.2
I look at labels for additives and preservatives	3.9	3.7	3.3	3.2
Before shopping I prepare a list	3.9	3.6	3.5	3.1
I enjoy participating in contests associated with products	3.1	2.8	2.7	2.5
When I see a new brand, I often try it just to see what it is like	3.0	2.6	2.8	2.7
It is hard to see the best buy at the supermarket	3.3	3.5	3.6	3.8
When I get a discount off coupon, I save it and use it when I can	4.6	4.1	3.9	3.7
I like to keep up on new products so I don't miss out on any improvements	3.5	3.2	3.3	3.1

Figures are means for responses to a six-point Likert scale. Strong agreement with an item was represented by a scale score of 6, and strong disagreement by a scale score of 1.

usages. Men's usage means are almost equivalent to women's for infrequent activities, such as preparing rice or gravy, and are at least half those of wives for the more frequently used products. Wives' product usage frequency varies less by segment. Thus, it seems that female prospects for the food and laundry products under consideration are equivalent across household

Table 12–3. Normative Commitment to Task Sharing.

		Involved Sharers	Uninvolved Sharers	Typicals	Traditionals
My spouse and I try to share household	Husbands	5.0	4.5	4.1	3.4
chores	Wives	4.6	4.2	3.8	3.2
A woman's place is in	Husbands	3.0	3.0	3.5	3.9
the home	Wives	2.8	3.0	3.0	3.4
Men should share work around the	Husbands	5.0	4.6	4.2	3.4
house	Wives	5.1	4.9	4.6	4.3

Figures are means for responses to a six-point Likert scale. Strong agreement with an item was represented by a scale score of 6, and strong disagreement by a scale score of 1.

segments, while more males with an opportunity to use products exist in the Sharing segments, especially the Involved Sharer group.

Husband and Wife Differences in Product Usage

Opportunity to use products, however, is not the only reason why husbands make significant prospects for advertisers and marketers. Independent choice of product forms and brands is also important. The data in this study suggest that enough husbands make product choices to warrant their consideration as independent prospects. We also find that husbands tend to simplify chores, either by using more prepared foods or by using fewer laundry products. These results suggest that the markets for certain products may be ready for some new approaches.

Study participants were asked to report on usage frequency for an exhaustive list of product forms. The percentage of total product usage constituted by each form was calculated for each respondent and matched against that of the spouse. If the percentages fell within 20 percent of each other, we concluded that spouses had a common tendency to use that product form. The results for cooked vegetables are displayed in Figure 12-3, by way of example. The figure shows that in about 40 percent of households, spouses tend to prepare cooked vegetables in the same way, and in 60 percent, they do not. While we do not encourage overinterpretation of

Figure 12–2. Frequency of Preparing Potatoes.

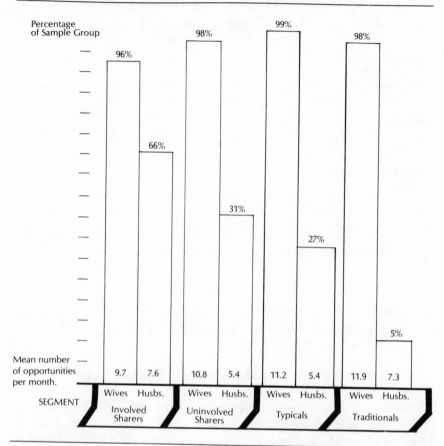

Note: Percentages shown are wives and husbands within their segments who reported having had an opportunity to use the product within the past year. Internal figures indicate mean number of opportunities per month, for those who prepare potatoes.

small percentage differences between husbands' and wives' tendencies, it does appear that there is a male bias toward use of canned vegetables.

For the food and laundry products we examined, several patterns were suggested. First, a significant proportion of men are making different choices in product form than their wives. Second, the proportion of households where men make a different choice tends to be greater for high incidence products than for low incidence products. Third, in four of the five product forms considered, the direction of male preference is toward simplification. Husbands avoid fresh produce in favor of canned or frozen forms, and prefer instant to long-cooking rice. Men also use a narrower

Figure 12–3. Husband-and-Wife Choice of Cooked Vegetable Product Forms.

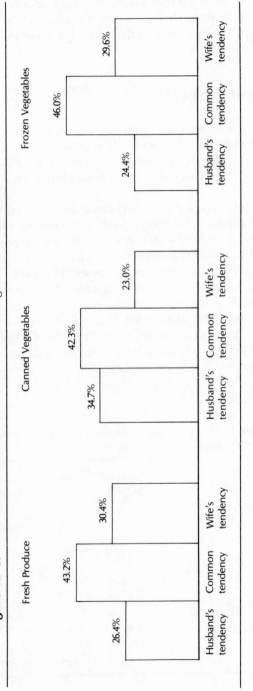

range of laundry products than their wives use. The only exception to these generalizations is that when men prepare gravy, an activity only infrequently undertaken by anyone in the study, they seem to do it from scratch rather than using prepared forms.

Brand Choice

Our final set of conclusions from the Leo Burnett study of household lifestyles has to do with husbands' influence on household brand choices. Once again, the sharing of homemaking tasks is associated with more involvement and influence in product consumption, this time reflected in brand choice.

Husbands were asked about brand-choice influence on eighty-four kinds of household products, beverages, foods, and personal care products. The figures shown in Table 12–4 are typical of the pattern across several kinds of products. They show that husbands' reported influence on brand choices increases with their involvement in household chores. The relationship holds, not just for personal products like razor blades or Scotch, but also for household supplies like paper towels.

The data also show that when husbands become more involved in sharing household responsibilities, the household's brand sets become somewhat larger and may include more store brands and generics. While the differences in the data are not large, the results are consistent.

Table 12–4. Husbands Claiming Influence on Brand Choice (percentage).

	Involved Sharers	Uninvolved Sharers	Typicals	Traditionals
Packaged cookies	63	55	43	37
Coffee	68	52	45	38
Paper towels	48	33	19	17
Razor blades	84	80	73	65
Scotch	90	87	81	73

SUMMARY AND CONCLUSIONS

Significant numbers of married men are sharing traditional homemaking chores with their wives, but their share is not an equal one, nor does this sharing seem to reduce the frequency of their wives' product-related behavior. Marketers and advertisers, we believe, will find the Involved-Sharing households numerous enough to warrant an appeal to the husbands, especially since these men are apparently making some independent product and brand choices.

Our data also suggest that husbands' participation in home chores occurs along a continuum of activity, and that there are no particular patterns of specialization involved. Future research might test the hypothesis suggested by these data: that men who begin to participate in an expanded number of household tasks will begin with the more common varieties, such as cooking breakfast, and undertake laundry or cleaning only after they have become cooks.

Demographics and attitude statements are helpful in describing the kinds of households in which husbands shoulder the responsibility to share in homemaking chores. Assuming, therefore, that women will continue to increase both their labor force participation and levels of education, the Sharing segments should increase as a proportion of all households over time. These households report a normative commitment to shared responsibilities and a degree of enjoyment or acceptance of these tasks on the part of the husbands. Normative commitment to egalitarian or roommate marriages is also likely to increase in American society as the education and employment of women increases. This trend provides further grounds for expecting that the proportion of Involved-Sharing households will increase over time.

Household attitudes on enjoyment of tasks are more difficult to interpret. Both husbands and wives in the Involved-Sharing segment register attitudes about homemaking chores in the mid-areas of our attitudinal scales, while in the other groups husbands show stronger dislikes and wives stronger enjoyment of the tasks. Our data do not enable us to predict cause and result in these attitudes and behaviors, but the information may be sufficient for preliminary use by marketers as it stands. The information suggests that (1) husbands and wives in the Involved-Sharer segment may be appealed to in the same ways, and (2) the male market for selected foods and laundry products may not, over time, be attitudinally different from the female market.

Finally, it must be remembered that the data in this paper represent but a first look at a small part of a large data base. Subsequent analyses will look at singles and single parents, as well as married couples, consider the importance of task sharing for a larger range of products and brands, and focus specifically on responsibility for shopping. In addition to a more comprehensive look at how households are run in America today, further studies will involve major analyses of eating patterns, the use of leisure time, and the consumer behavior and attitudes of American teenagers.

NOTES

1. A thirteen-item index of male participation in household chores (not shown here) was constructed and validated against normative commitment to task sharing and psychological involvement in tasks. The external validators were the items shown on Tables 12-2 and 12-3 of this paper.

2. The cluster analysis reported here was based on seven indices derived from factor analysis of husbands' responses to the questions about participation in chores. Tryon's method was used to identify "seed" groups that differed in terms of level of involvement. The cluster representing the most active task-sharers was subsequently reclustered on attitude variables and divided between "Involved Sharers" and "Uninvolved Sharers". The four clusters reported in this paper are approximately equal in size.

13 CONCEPTUALIZING FINANCIAL SERVICES DECISIONMAKING BY HOUSEHOLDS
Implications for Corporate Strategies

Kathryn Britney

Firms in the retail financial services industry have expanded the product line they offer households and individuals (C. Loomis 1981; J. Martin 1981). As a result of this corporate strategy, brokerage firms now offer life insurance and checking services, and banks offer brokerage services: The ultimate vision is for a household to be able to fill all its financial service needs with one vendor (i.e., one-stop shopping).

In this strategy the customer is considered the common thread. It is implicitly assumed that marketing many financial products to the same customer is more effective than the traditional one-service approach, but the exact nature of this synergy in marketing has not been defined and some doubt its existence (Osborn 1982; C. Loomis 1983).

Ansoff (1965: 106) warns that "sometimes the customer is erroneously identified as the common thread of a firm's business. In reality, a given type of customer will frequently have a range of unrelated product missions or needs. He would not necessarily satisfy them through the same purchasing channels, or use the same approach to buying." Is this the case in the retail financial services industry?

This paper illustrates the usefulness of analyzing consumers' current decisionmaking processes in determining if and how the customer is a strong common thread between the existing product line and the new ones that may be added to it. Although this study focuses on financial services, the methodology applies to any product or business that intends to add a new

217

product to an existing line in order to gain a competitive advantage through synergy in marketing to existing customers (e.g., decisions regarding the assortments to carry in retail stores, family branding decisions).

RELATIONSHIP OF PRODUCT MISSIONS OR NEEDS

A first step in discovering whether or not customers use the same buying approach for new products as for existing products is to determine the degree to which the products satisfy similar needs. One method of identifying the underlying needs served by a business (e.g., the financial services businesses) is to arbitrarily classify current products and services that appear to fill the same underlying need. This was done for a number of existing financial services as shown in Table 13-1. Based on this arbitrary classification procedure, the following six underlying financial needs of households and individuals were identified:

transfer of payments: the need to collect, store, and dispense funds;
savings: the need to store funds safely, protect the principal, increase value during periods of nonuse, and be able to easily and immediately obtain funds when needed (especially in case of emergencies);
investment: the need to invest current assets in order to increase asset-per-income return in the future;
financing: the need to borrow funds to finance the purchase of high-cost items, to invest, and to reduce short-term cash problems;
protection: the need to protect oneself and survivors against financial losses that cause major financial hardship; and
tax minimization and preparation: the need to consider tax-related issues in financial decisions and to prepare tax returns.

The degree to which existing products and proposed new ones serve related customer needs can now be assessed. For example, if a brokerage firm that has an existing product line of stocks, options, bonds, and commodities is considering adding life insurance, the preceding classification suggests that the proposed new product serves a different customer need than the existing ones (i.e., protection versus investment). Although the product missions of life insurance versus stocks and bonds are not totally unrelated since there is a small savings and investment component to life insurance, their primary missions for the customer are different.

If the needs served are different, what synergy exists in marketing these financial products through the same distribution system or firm? The answer to this question depends on the similarity of the approaches used by

Table 13–1.   Financial Needs and Services.

Needs	Examples of Existing Products and Services	
Transfer of payments	Checking account Automatic teller machine Credit card	Travellers checks NOW account Super NOW account Cash management account Money market fund
Savings	Savings account NOW account Super NOW account Money market fund Bond fund with check-writing privileges	

Investment	Equities
	Bonds
	Options
	Commodities
	Real estate
	Tangibles
	Mutual Funds
	Bonds funds
		Venture capital funds
		Annuities
		Money market funds
		Savings accounts
		IRA/Keogh
		Financial Planning
		Estate Planning
		Investment counseling
		Trustee and
		   fiduciary services
		Research and statistical
		   services

Financing	Mortgage Auto loan Education loan	Debt consolidation Personal loan Revolving credit Investor margin

Protection	Life Insurance
	Annuities
	Health and disability
	   insurance
	Credit insurance
		Homeowners (P/C)
		   insurance
		Title insurance
		Mortgage insurance
		Vehicle insurance

Tax minimization
   and preparation
	Accounting services
	Tax preparation services
	Capital gains/losses
	   statements
	IRA/Keogh
	Municipal bonds
		Tax shelters
		Tax planning
		Financial planning
		Estate planning

consumers who buy services that satisfy these different financial needs. The next task, therefore, is to compare consumers' decisionmaking processes for the existing and proposed new products.

THEORETICAL LINK BETWEEN DECISIONMAKING PROCESSES AND SYNERGY IN MARKETING

It would be expected that the more similar consumers' processes are for selecting financial vendors and products to fill their needs, the more similar the marketing strategies required to influence consumers' choices would be. To the extent that the requirements for successful marketing are the same for the different financial services, a firm might be able to achieve a competitive advantage by marketing them together. The competitive advantage could be achieved either by providing value added in the marketplace if the combination offers some synergy for the customer or by producing cost effectiveness in the firm if the combination offers more efficiency in marketing the products, or both.

The inverse of this theory implies that the more dissimilar consumers' decisionmaking processes are for financial services, the more dissimilar the marketing strategies required to influence consumers' service and product choices might be. In turn, the probability might be low that synergy in marketing exists that will allow the firm to be successful in both markets if it markets the products together (e.g., through the same distribution system or the same family brand).

To examine the potential competitive advantage (or lack of it) of marketing a new product with existing ones where their missions for the consumer differ, the above theory suggests the following analytical procedure:

1. Determine consumers' decisionmaking processes for selecting products and services that are currently used to satisfy the two different needs.
2. Based on consumers' decisionmaking processes infer the optimal marketing strategies needed to influence the choice of a company's product or service over the competition's.
3. Compare the optimal marketing strategies for commonalities that would serve as the basis for synergy in marketing if the new product was added to the existing line. Equally important, identify dissimilari-

ties or contradictions that might result in a competitive disadvantage for one or both products if marketed together.

RELATIONSHIP OF DECISIONMAKING PROCESSES

Consumer decisionmaking processes are complex and have been the subject of extensive in-depth research. What is proposed here is to use one of the consumer behavior models that have been developed as the organizing conceptual framework for comparing hypotheses and research findings about different aspects of consumers' current decisionmaking processes for the products or services being considered.

The five decision process stages suggested by the Engel, Blackwell, and Kollatt (1978) model are problem recognition, search, alternative evaluation, choice, and outcomes. If we use our example of adding life insurance to the product line of stockbrokers, we would want to compare what we know about consumers' current decisionmaking processes for choosing life insurance and stockbrokerage services.

A decision must be made about which customers to study and compare. This issue is discussed in a later section of this paper. The following example is based on the total market and the decisionmaking process of the average customer in these markets.

Problem Recognition

The problem-recognition stages for life insurance and stocks differ significantly in terms of both period in the household's life cycle when it occurs and frequency with which it occurs. Recognition of investing service needs (e.g., stocks and bonds) tends to occur later in the household life cycle when the household has funds available for investment (Dow Jones & Company, Inc. 1981: 3). In contrast, the initial purchase of life insurance is often associated with the life event of marriage, birth of a child, or a pay increase (SRI International 1979: vol. 2, 166).

SRI indicates that the decision to buy a life insurance policy occurs infrequently for households. More than 40 percent of all households had only one individual life policy, and for most of those with more than one policy, many years elapsed between purchases (SRI International 1979: vol. 2, 164-65). In contrast, for those households in the market for investment services, marketing efforts (e.g., changing yields, ideas) and changing economic conditions cause consumers to reevaluate their financial product choices relatively frequently. For example, active investors made an average of two brokerage trades a month in 1980 (Dow Jones & Company 1981: 20).

Search

Consumers are similar in their search behavior for meeting these different needs in that they do little or no comparison shopping (SRI International 1979: vol. 2, 64, 173). It appears, however, that consumers are more proactive in searching for a broker than for a life insurancce agent. SRI indicates that broker selection "is based overwhelmingly on friendship or on recommendations of family or friends, and not on a broker's approach to them" (SRI International 1979: vol. 2, 62). Life insurance agent prospecting appears to play a stronger role in establishing relationships that generate initial insurance purchases (SRI International 1979: vol. 2, 166).

Alternative Evaluation and Choice

Evaluation of alternatives and choice behavior is complicated in our example by the interaction of three choice decisions, namely, (1) the broker or agent; (2) the vendor or firm; and (3) the specific products and services. Research indicates that, on average, the choice of the broker or life insurance agent is a strong influence on the other two decisions. In life insurance "the agent affects amount purchased, company chosen, type of insurance bought, decisions to take a cash value loan or discontinue a previous policy" (SRI International 1979: vol. 2, 161). Similar influence is displayed by brokers; about 50 percent of active investors at full-service brokerage firms indicated that they would follow their broker if he or she moved to another firm (Dow Jones & Company, Inc. 1981:41).

In general, therefore, trust in the agent and service by the broker along with the reputation of the firm tend to determine consumers' choice decisions for these services. This aspect of consumer decisionmaking processes for life insurance and stocks are similar.

Outcomes

Customer satisfaction and postpurchase dissonance differ significantly for life insurance and stock purchases. For life insurance buyers, few review the decision unless stimulated by a triggering life event or approached by an agent to do so (SRI International 1979: vol 2, 168). In contrast, investors, especially active investors who account for 80 percent of the volume, are continuously reviewing their product decisions and their broker-and-vendor relationship decisions.

Summary

The consumers' decisionmaking process for life insurance appears to be dominated by the influence of the agent, not only in choosing the appropriate product but also in initiating the process. For most buyers, however, this choice process is activated only once or twice in an individual's lifetime. Similarly, the broker appears to be important in the decision-making process for stocks and bonds; however, the broker's role appears to be mainly one of providing service that attracts and keeps the repeat purchase business of active investors.

IMPLICATIONS FOR MARKETING AND SALES STRATEGIES

If these observations about the problem-recognition, search, and outcome stages for the two different financial services are correct, they suggest the need for extremely different marketing and sales strategies. An effective marketing strategy for a product or service for which problems recognition occurs infrequently or periodically during the household's life cycle (e.g., life insurance) is one that focuses resources on having the marketer in the right place at the right time. A push strategy (e.g., personal selling of life insurance) implies a sales strategy of 80 percent of the salesperson's time spent prospecting target market households and 20 percent doing repeat or replacement selling to existing customers. In contrast, an effective marketing strategy for stocks, for which problem recognition occurs frequently, should focus on continuing service that retains customer satisfaction and repeat business. In this case, a push strategy implies a sales strategy of 80 percent of the salesperson's time spent on servicing and repeat selling to existing customers and 20 percent on prospecting.

A second implication for marketing strategy is that the primary target markets for the two types of products are substantially different households in a given year. Need recognition for the initial life insurance purchase occurs with households in their early life cycle, while those needing investment services (especially the active investor) are house-holds in later stages of their life cycle.

Both buyer behavior processes are similar in that the role of the salesperson is extremely important in the selection of the firm and financial service. Therefore, personal selling is a key factor in providing a successful marketing strategy for both products.

IMPLICATIONS FOR SYNERGY IN MARKETING

At first glance it would appear that there is strong synergy in marketing these two product categories through the same distribution system since they both rely on personal selling as the key variable in optimal marketing strategies based on consumers' buying processes. However, the previous analysis indicates that this is the one similarity in the marketing strategies needed for dominant market share in these businesses. The strategies differ significantly in terms of:

the primary target markets and
the emphasis needed in sales-force selling effort (i.e., 80 percent prospecting and 20 percent repeat selling for life insurance versus 20 percent prospecting and 80 percent repeat servicing and selling for stocks).

A salesperson cannot implement these two contradictory strategies simultaneously. As a result, the salesperson will implicitly or explicitly choose to focus selling time in one direction (e.g., satisfying existing customer investment needs), thereby putting little or no selling time into the other financial need services (e.g., prospecting for customers who have a high probability of recognizing the need for new or more life insurance protection). If competitors in each of these different financial businesses are allocating their sales force resource in the most effective manner for the specific financial need, a firm which is compromising and trying to sell financial products that fill both these needs using a single sales force will be at a competitive disadvantage in at least one of these businesses.

It is concluded that there is little synergy in marketing these two financial services through the same distribution system. First, the customer is not a strong common thread. In a given year, the households that are in the problem recognition stage for these two financial services (i.e., life insurance versus stocks) tend to be completely different households. Second, different consumer buying processes for these two financial services call for extremely different marketing and sales strategies (except for the common important role of personal selling) to achieve volume sales in these two different products in a given year. One financial service requires a marketing strategy that focuses marketing resources (especially sales-force selling time) on new business activities, whereas the other focuses sales-force time on repeat purchase activities. Therefore, there is little common ground for synergy for the key variable in the marketing mix.

IMPLICATIONS FOR CORPORATE STRATEGY

It is important that the results of this analysis be put in perspective. We have established that:

1. The existing product line (e.g., stocks and bonds) and the proposed new product (e.g., life insurance) do not fill the same customer need;
2. Consumers' current decisionmaking processes for selecting products that fill these different needs (i.e., investment versus protection) differ significantly in ways that suggest the need for significantly different marketing and sales strategies to achieve high volume sales in these areas; and
3. A comparison of these optimal strategies shows lack of commonality on key dimensions, leading to the conclusion that there is little or no synergy in marketing them through the same distribution system.

A lack of synergy in marketing the products or financial services through the same distribution system probably will result in relatively low sales and market share for the new product that has been added. Obviously, if a firm is using a less than optimal marketing or sales strategy for the new product and there are competitors who are focusing resources on a marketing strategy that is more consistent with consumers' buying process for the product, it would be expected that the compromising firm will sell some of the product but that its relative market share will be low.

This hypothesis appears to be confirmed by life insurance and brokerage firm experience to date. Brokerage firms have not been particularly successful in gaining market share in financial planning or life insurance by trying to sell these products using their existing sales force (Sandler 1981). Similarly, life insurance firms have obtained relatively low sales and market share in mutual funds by asking their agents to sell these products (Osborn 1982: 53). Some have suggested that these failures are mainly due to the lack of the salespeople's ability to cross-sell the other products. However, this analysis indicates the result is expected given consumers' needs and decision processes for these products and the existence of competitors who tailor their marketing strategy to meet them.

The final decision, however, is one of profitability. Therefore, even if there is little synergy in marketing that results in a relatively small market share, there may be synergies on the supply side that would justify the decision to add the product. Finally, there is the possibility that the new distribution system will revolutionize and change consumers' buying processes and behavior for the new product.

WHICH CUSTOMERS?

In this paper the main determinant of optimal marketing strategies for the existing and new products is analysis of consumers' decisionmaking processes for satisfying the different needs. The analysis presented here is based on research about the average investor and life insurance buyer in the total markets. However, segments within these markets (such as, execution-only investors or direct-mail life insurance buyers) would probably differ significantly in some aspects of their decision processes (e.g., evaluation of alternatives and choice) although not in others (e.g., problem recognition) from the market average. As a result, the optimal marketing and sales strategies for specific consumer segments might provide more commonalities and potential for synergy in marketing than exist for the total markets. If a firm plans to target a particular segment (e.g., high-income households or dual-income households), the decisionmaking processes of these segments should be the basic unit of analysis.

CONCLUSION AND IMPLICATIONS FOR FURTHER RESEARCH

This paper has suggested an analytical approach for examining the potential synergy in marketing when adding a new product to an existing product line. The underlying assumption in this growth strategy is that the customer is a strong common thread, but this depends on the similarity of the needs and the customers' buying processes for the existing and new product or services.

One way to examine the potential synergy in marketing the new product with the existing product line, therefore, is to compare the degree to which the needs they fill are related and the customers' decisionmaking processes are similar. Based on the latter, one can determine the optimal marketing and sales strategies needed to compete for dominant market share in the two product or service markets and then answer the questions: Are the strategies needed similar? In what ways would there be synergy in marketing the products together? Is the customer in fact a strong common thread for these businesses?

Understanding whether or not products and services serve the same or related customer needs is an important first step in evaluating the potential synergy in marketing different products to the same customer. The approach illustrated in this paper was to arbitrarily group current products and services that appear to fill a similar need. Another approach is to group products and services using perceptual mapping, cluster analysis, or other numerical taxonomy methods that analyze data reflecting consumers' perceptions of which products and services fill similar financial needs.

The merits of the a priori classification method used in this study versus numerical taxonomy classification methods have been well documented in the marketing literature (Frank and Green 1968). In the financial services area, a study based on consumers' perceptions might answer many questions about the financial needs defined in Table 13-1, such as:

Do consumers perceive savings and investment as one need or as two separate needs?

Is protection perceived as one need or as two separate needs (i.e., protection of assets and protection of people)?

Do consumers classify all financing products and services together, or does mortgage financing group with other financial services related to buying a house (such as real estate brokerage) and define a housing need?

A major problem in doing research that examines the decisionmaking processes that consumers use to choose products and services for different needs is the expense of collecting the necessary data. This is particularly true in businesses such as financial services because of the low incidence and upscale profile of the key customers for many financial services. The financial service industry has partially solved this problem by pooling its resources in multisponsored, syndicated studies. However, because of the proprietary nature of these studies, it is difficult for the academicians who wish to do research in this area to obtain the necessary data. Given the importance and complexity of the strategic decisions being made, this might be an opportunity for joint industry and academic research that would benefit both parties.

IV DECISIONMAKING UNITS AND PROCESSES

14 HOUSEHOLD DECISIONMAKING
Units of Analysis and Decision Processes

E.H. Bonfield, Carol Kaufman, and Sigfredo Hernandez

The study of household decisionmaking leads to the study of a number of many interacting variables that affect the decisionmaking process and outcomes of decisionmaking. We begin with the problem of defining what is meant by the term "household." Since a taxonomy of households is possible, the role structure within the household will be a function of the household type. Decisionmaking processes that take place for households will, in turn, be dependent on household type and household role structure, as well as other internal and external forces. We will explore these perspectives in order to assess our present knowledge and to suggest some potential directions for future research.

THE UNIT OF ANALYSIS IN A CHANGING ENVIRONMENT

Consumer decision processes have been a focal point of the marketing and consumer-behavior literature for several decades. This perspective has evolved from the study of the single individual to include group-related behavior within the household. Indeed, researchers have recognized that all family members, rather than simply husband and wife, may share tasks through "the division of labor, mutual commitments, and the discharge of responsibilities, internal communications, and functional relations with the

231

environment" (Alderson 1957:175). However, all too often conceptual development has chosen the traditional family group (husband, wife, and sometimes children) as the building block for theoretical discussion and empirical verification. In his review of the household decisionmaking literature, Davis (1976) stressed the importance of studying the family as the appropriate unit of analysis and commented that "very little effort has been directed to the effects of different family structures" (1976: 256).

A natural result of focusing on the traditional U.S. family that over time parallels the family life cycle as described by Wells and Gubar (1966) has been research that emphasizes purchase outcomes rather than the complex interaction of multiperson variables across household forms. This exclusion of a broad spectrum of conjugal and cohabitative forms and of the dynamics of parent-and-child relationships has been noted in particular by family life cycle researchers. Murphy and Staples (1979: 20), concerned with integrating divorce and remarriage into life cycle theory, recommended more research into the "comparison between decisionmaking patterns of traditional and nontraditional (those headed by a divorced parent) households." Extending that work, Derrick and Lehfield (1980) criticized the family life cycle literature for the absence of several nontraditional household forms, such as the single adult (whether youthful, middle-aged, or elderly) and the single-parent family and maintained that much research information has been lost, since "the traditional American family of four now accounts for 14 percent of all households" (U.S. Bureau of the Census 1979c: 215).

Some investigations have found that nontraditional households have particular needs and wants that should be of interest to researchers. Wortzel (1977a) observed that the trend toward postponing marriage has established the young single adult stage as a potential household with longevity and purchasing characteristics rather than a negligible pre-marriage phase of the family life cycle. Cohabitation, a household form now socially acceptable, was similarly reported by Danziger and Greenwald (1977) to define a lifestyle deserving specialized market consideration, particularly with respect to credit, insurance, and other financial services. These observations are demonstrated empirically by the U.S. Census Bureau (1981a:1), which reported:

> Since 1970, the total number of households has increased by 30 percent: family households by 17 percent, and non-family households (maintained by persons living alone or with other unrelated persons) by 85 percent. Married-couple families with own children under 18 decreased by 2.4 percent between 1970 and 1981; in contrast, single-parent families with own children increased over 95 percent.

We expect three factors to interact to determine outcomes in household decisionmaking: (1) the appropriate unit of analysis, (2) the decision subject, and (3) the stage in the decisionmaking process.

Definitional Considerations

Unit of Analysis.   The U.S. trend away from traditional family household units suggests that it is no longer practical for marketers to treat the terms "family" and "household" as synonyms: A generalized conceptualization of the household is needed. It is important to adopt one definition of household, use it consistently, and avoid the "interchange of the terms household, family, nuclear family, conjugal family and extended family" (Heffring 1980: 492). The perspective we adopt is probably the most widespread; it is the definition of the U.S. Bureau of the Census (1979c: xivii):

> All persons occupying a single housing unit are classified as belonging to a household. A household includes the related family members and all the unrelated persons, if any, such as lodgers, foster children, or employees who share the housing unit. A person living alone or a group of unrelated individuals sharing the same housing unit as partners is also counted as a group.

We think it is necessary to establish a taxonomy of households because of the differences in wants and needs, as well as decisionmaking processes, in different types of households. The taxonomy shown in Figure 14–1 is based on the "redefined family life cycle" suggested by Gilly and Enis (1982). This classification appears to include approximately 97 percent of the U.S. population. The Gilly and Enis paradigm is based on chronological age and specified "critical points" in individuals' lives: marriage and divorce or death and the addition or departure of children. While Gilly and Enis refer to their paradigm as a "redefined family life cycle," we prefer to view it as categories of households.

To accommodate a viewpoint expressed by Gilly and Enis but not shown in their figure, we have used the term "grouping" in the key to category links to replace the term "marry." Two persons joining together to form a household, whether heterosexually or homosexually, in marriage, cohabitation, or as roommates, represent two-adult households in the Gilly and Enis paradigm.

The categories of household are complicated because each category may be entered from more than one direction, as well as exited in more than one direction. For example, a single parent may become a single parent because of the death of a spouse, because of a divorce, or because a child enters with no adult-household grouping taking place (the last case is recognized by Gilly and Enis but omitted from their figure for the sake of simplicity). In

Figure 14-1. The Household Life Cycle.

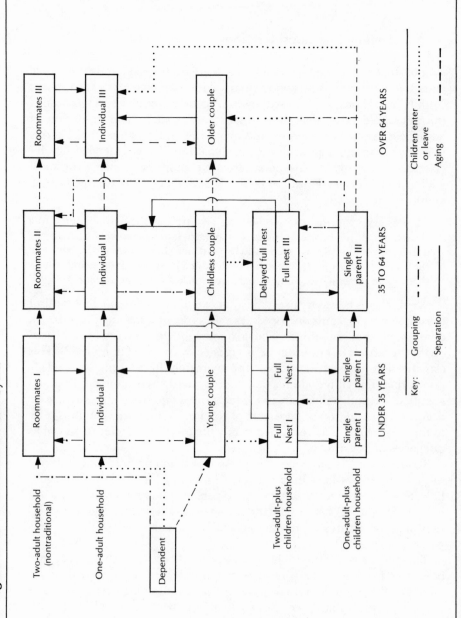

Source: Adapted from Gilly and Enis (1982)

this volume, Leigh and Martin discuss changes in roles and settings. These transitions can lead to changes in household category as well as in household decisionmaking.

There are further complications, of course, but they would be present under most systems for categorizing households (or families for that matter). Thus, such endogenous and exogenous characteristics as personality and culture respectively may influence decisionmaking. Our household taxonomy is used to categorize households, *not* to describe household role structure.

We have adapted Gilly and Enis's model to accommodate a household taxonomy rather than a family taxonomy. Other taxonomies are also possible. For a different potential taxonomy, see the paper by Bristor and Qualls in this volume.

A question that frequently arises in individual, but not household, decisionmaking research addresses the influence of others in decisionmaking. This suggests four questions to be addressed by household decisionmaking researchers:

1. Which members of the household participate in the decisionmaking process?
2. Who, if anyone, external to the household participates in the decisionmaking process?
3. Which members of the household influence decisions?
4. Who, if anyone, external to the household influences decisions?

The questions most frequently asked in household decisionmaking research have been who makes the decision and who performs the activity.

Decision Subject.   Although support is often given for accepting the household as the relevant unit of analysis in marketing and consumer behavior research, empirical studies have tended to specify the relevant decisionmaking unit "a priori by the research design rather than by the household" (Davis 1976:248). Of course, these designs specify the household as a family unit. While the family equals the husband and wife, as measured in the majority of household decisionmaking investigations, some work in at least some product categories attempts to include other household members. For example, Berey and Pollay (1968) interviewed mothers and children regarding breakfast cereal purchase. Their results supported a strong gatekeeper effect for mothers. Atkin (1978) observed interaction between children and one or both parents during cereal purchase decisionmaking in a supermarket. Atkin found children playing the dominant role.

Other research including children has also yielded varying results.

Jenkins (1979) used self-administered questionnaires to assess how husbands and wives perceived the role of children in decisions about furniture, automobiles, groceries, life insurance, savings, general family decisions, and vacations. Significant influence by children was found only for joint family activities, especially vacations. Similarly, Filiatrault and Ritchie (1980) compared family and couple decisionmaking units concerning vacation choices. Although children were found to have little influence, they were also found to be likely to form alliances with either parent to form a more powerful coalition. The variation found in the results is not surprising. Parents are expected to be more conscious of the role of their children in some decisions but not others. A family with young children considering a vacation would be expected to consider their children's preferences in making their selection. While other decisions may have more significant impact on children—life insurance purchases, for example—parents typically do not include them in their decisionmaking process.

Stage of Decisionmaking.   Changes in the relevant decisionmaking unit over the course of the decisionmaking process also produce variations in decision process participants. That is, the household members that are involved in any stage of the decisionmaking process are determined by the stage of the process. Household member involvement at any stage may reflect the importance and skill that an individual feels attached to his or her role at that stage. Szybillo and Sosanie (1977) tested this hypothesis in their study of role relationships over the stages of the decisionmaking process for family outings to fast-food restaurants and on one-day trips. They found children participating in all stages of decision processes concerning fast-food restaurants but that some stages in the decision processes for day trips included children while others included only adults. These findings extend the findings of specialization at stages of the decision process found by Ferber and Lee (1974), Davis and Rigaux (1974), and Bonfield (1978). In their chapter in this volume, Gutman, Reynolds, and Fiedler similarly show how changes in decisionmaking units affect means-and-ends chains in a value-structure map. Related to questions about who is involved at various stages of the decision process are questions about (1) how many stages should be considered and how these stages should be conceptualized and (2) whether the concept of stages in household decision processes is viable.

Determinants of Involvement in Decisions.   The evidence discussed thus far supports the position that the product category and decisionmaking stage influence which subset of household members makes up the relevant decisionmaking unit at each stage of the process. We now turn to an exploration of variables that determine relative involvement at each stage.

Davis (1976:250-52) suggested three concepts that help explain task allocation: (1) cultural role expectations, (2) comparative resources (e.g., education level and occupation), and (3) relative investment concerning costs and benefits. These concepts predict the degree of influence that a household member may have when participating in a specific decision.

These three hypotheses concern determinants of marital role allocation that are significantly broadened by shifting the unit of analysis to the more generalizable framework of the household. Both social and situational norms, which partially prescribe appropriate role behavior within the household, reflect a shift toward more egalitarian task sharing and away from the more traditional division of labor by sex-role norms. Thus, changing cultural role expectations may generate conflict and necessitate the use of complex decisionmaking to assign tasks.

Similar changes affect the concepts of comparative resources and relative investment. Women may derive increasing status and power from higher education, better salaries, and significant occupational responsibilities and may use these as leverage in trading off onerous for enjoyable tasks (Roberts and Wortzel 1980). Relative investment, indicating interest in a task, may provide further motivation for enacting negotiation strategies and may lead to adopting tasks that may lead to satisfaction for all household members.

This approach suggests that a decisionmaking unit—once formed—proceeds in its task, drawing solely on the roles, skills, and preferences of its members. It has been argued, however, that relevant others may also influence a decision (Wind 1976). Although models that deal with individual involvement in decisions are important, they are beyond the scope of this paper. The papers by Buss and Schaninger, Roberts and Wortzel, and Jaworski, MacInnis, and Sauer in this volume deal with this type of model.

Relevant Others.   Individuals and groups may indirectly influence the decisionmaking process and its outcomes because the preferences and norms of relevant others are perceived by those included in the decisionmaking process. The research in this area thus far has been concerned with preferences, intentions, and decisions by individuals rather than by households or other groups. For example, Wind's (1976) two approaches used conjoint measurement to quantify the relative importance of preferences of a spouse on the decisions of the individual decisionmaker. However, the Fishbein intentions model (cf. Ryan and Bonfield 1975, 1980) might be a more useful approach when an individual makes the final decision; its protocol requires determining all salient others and also leads to inferences about the relative influence of relevant others and about the effect of the individual's attitude on his or her decision.

Wind (1976, 1978) suggested that the household be viewed as a buying center, a concept adapted from the organizational buying-behavior literature (Wind 1978: 657):

> The concept calls for the identification, in each purchase situation, of the relevant individuals involved in the buying decision process (whether they are members of the same household or not) and using them (the members of the buying center) as the relevant unit of analysis.

In this context, Wind suggested that roles typically described for organizational buying centers might replace the typical household roles of husband, wife, and child. Thus, the roles of buyer, user, influencer, decider, and gatekeeper—each of which can be taken by more than one member of the household at any stage of the decision process—have become an accepted part of the consumer-behavior literature. Sternthal and Craig (1982: 226-29) discussed these roles as part of their consumer-behavior text. Assael (1981:340-43) described five analogous roles: information gatherer (gatekeeper), influencer (influencer), decisionmaker (decider), purchasing agent (buyer), and consumer (user). More than one person can take on each role at each stage of the decision process.

Tradeoffs in Decisionmaking

Decisions about a specific product or stage can be placed in the context of multiple decisions made within the household over time. These decisions may involve a balance among individually held and collective goals and preferences. Thus, influence may carry over or rotate from stage to stage or from decision to decision. A system of tradeoffs may develop within the household.

Coleman (1966:615) proposed that "individuals in social systems are faced with a sequence of social choices and can exchange their partial control over issues that interest them little for greater control over those that interest them more." Coleman, a sociologist complaining that sociologists had neglected development of a theory of collective decisions, based his proposal on the work done in political science and economics. He used as an example one legislator who exchanges a vote on one action with another legislator who will vote as the first legislator wishes on another issue: "Each loses his vote on an action where the outcome makes little difference to him but gains a vote on an action where the outcome matters more" (Coleman 1966:620). Thus, interdependency among household roles, leading to tradeoffs in decisions, can occur at different stages of the decision process and can involve different attributes of a product and different products. For example, a husband who prefers a high-performance car may yield (trade off) to his wife's preference for economy in order to influence the selection of black rather than light blue as the color of the car. Influence tradeoffs can only partially explain decision processes, since influence may flow to those household members who have the appropriate resources or meet the appropriate cultural role expectations, as would be suggested by Hempel's (1972) findings concerning relative husband-and-wife influence in home purchase decisions.

ROLE STRUCTURE AND HOUSEHOLD DECISIONMAKING: A BASIS IN TRADITIONAL FAMILY SOCIOLOGY

Marketing theorists have emphasized research designed to determine the relative influence of family members in specific product choice. Marketers' interest in studying household decisionmaking is a relatively new phenomenon. For other behavioral scientists, however, defining and understanding the roles played by husband and wife in family decisionmaking has been a topic of fundamental research for several decades. The marketer's focus on outcomes relies on these outcomes to infer interactions taking place during the decision process; it does little to address the underlying role structure that determines these results. More recently, marketers have attempted to eclectically incorporate family influence theories from other disciplines such as sociology, psychology, and family therapy (e.g., Davis 1976; Hempel 1972; Scanzoni 1977).

The integration of family role structure into family decisionmaking studies in marketing still presents difficulty for those who desire to build a general framework that includes less traditional household patterns. Jenkins (1980), for example, has suggested that the husband-and-wife dyad might not be appropriate for conceptualizing the household decision process. At a minimum, Jenkins suggested inclusion of children and in-law influences. While role taxonomies from group dynamics theory or organizational buying center theory—as we have already discussed—may be closer to reality, they may be improved if modified by marital roles. It is therefore useful to review family role-structure theory.

A number of tasks, or functions, are carried out by households. Some of these functions are carried out jointly—or by a group within the household—and some are carried out by individual household members. The stereotypical viewpoint has been that it is possible to classify these tasks as woman's work and man's work. Much of the evidence suggests that support for the stereotypical position is by no means universal.

Perspectives on Role Structure

In developing a theoretical framework for the study of family power, behavioral researchers have largely adopted the perspective of resource theory (Blood and Wolfe 1960). Within this context, responsibility for decisionmaking is assigned to either husband or wife based on the abilities or valued resources that each possesses. That is, greater resources imply greater power. Blood and Wolfe further suggested that wives tended to assume expressive roles, controlling decisions such as color and style of automobile purchases; while husbands tend to assume instrumental roles, such as durability and price. This basic hypothesis was tested by Blood and Wolfe and was supported in studies in the United States and other highly developed countries.

Later researchers have criticized and demonstrated conceptual gaps in the Blood and Wolfe theory. Reynolds and Myers (1966) have suggested an external/internal dimension that should be considered along with the instrumental/expressive dimension. Just as Blood and Wolfe associated instrumental and expressive decisions with husbands and wives respectively, Reynolds and Myers associated decisions about matters external to the household with husbands and decisions about internal matters with wives. While we tend to think that the blurring of sex roles is a recent phenomenon associated with the 1970s and 1980s, Reynolds and Myers (1966:59-60) noted a trend toward more joint decisionmaking not associated with sex differentiation on the internal/external or instrumental/expressive dimensions:

> Moreover, the steady trend seems to be toward *more* joint decision-making. There seems to be a general movement in husband-wife relationships toward more sharing of authority, less division of labor, and more companionship. Younger middle-class couples especially seem to show a high rate of joint involvement.

Myers and Reynolds (1967:246) also pointed out that Parsons had recognized at least as early as 1949 some ways that wives' roles were changing:

> Parsons [1949] contrasted the subservient traditional domestic wife, devoted to her home and children, with the career wife, who works outside the home and whose role is not clearly differentiated from her husband's. He suggested two other possible roles, a glamour-girl pattern in which courtship behavior is carried into marriage and a companion role in which the wife participates in community affairs, manages her home, and takes an active and equal part in family decision-making.

The impact of culture must also be considered. The interaction between cultural norms and individual resources operating within a cultural context appears to have impact on the relative power of each spouse, which, in turn, affects decisionmaking behavior (Rodman 1972). Rodman found that several resource theory predictions were not supported when considering lesser-developed countries. Rodman argued that the criteria for determining the comparative status of husbands and wives may be valued differently across cultures. This position, together with the delegation of power, its variation from decision to decision, and its change over time, provided a more complete foundation for understanding the power relationships in households. Further, delegation of decisionmaking power cannot be interpreted as a loss of power over a specific issue. Instead, it demonstrates the use of power to eliminate a distasteful or unimportant task (Safilios-Rothschild 1970b).

Relative educational level and comparative wage rates may also predict husband-and-wife behavior in decisionmaking. Farkas (1976) studied these factors as potential determinants of the division of labor for both within-home and marketplace tasks. Empirical support was found for both as clarifying the process of role allocation. These resources, however, may be assigned widely differing degrees of importance between spouses and across households. The valuation standards are particularly likely to vary between traditional and nontraditional role structures. Cohabitative and single-parent household groupings may be less likely to struggle for status achievement relative to other household members, while unequal power is the norm among more traditional households (Safilios-Rothschild 1976).

The roles of husbands and wives still appear to be greatly determined by tradition. Thus, income, leisure, training, and housework are often allocated with only partial attention to the family as the rational maximizing unit (Ferber and Birnbaum 1977). Housework still appears to belong to the wife, regardless of whether she is employed outside the home.

The household decisionmaking unit that emerges on a specific issue derives from the role structure that exists within the group. Husbands are not automatically dominant in a purchase decision because of their marital role. Instead, they may specialize in a particular decisionmaking area because of skills, interest, or delegation. There is some likelihood of interaction among these factors and the culturally determined role expectations of male household heads. Similarly, specialization in other decisions, or decision process stages, may be taken by wives, by a child, or by another household member, depending on the product class, stage in the decision process, or some other time-related constraint.

As societal norms and values change, more and different roles are available to household members. In his study of home purchasing decisions, Hempel (1972) found that marital roles differed according to the type of subdecision considered. In reviewing role changes from 1955 to 1973,

Cunningham and Green (1974) found increased specialization for some products and more joint decisionmaking for others. They suggested the merging of traditional sex roles helped explain these shifts, with income, age, and type of product affecting specific changes (Green and Cunningham 1975). These contextual variables, including background characteristics (such as ethnic origin and education), socioeconomic factors, and life cycle status, may causally lead to spouse choice and, hence, any household member's normative preference for a given family role (Cronkite 1977).

The potential for increased relative status for female household members has undergone considerable expansion as employment-related norms have responded to the women's liberation movement. Scanzoni (1977) maintained that as a result of changes in gender role norms, work may now be defined by women, as well as by men, as providing prestige, worth, and autonomy. Thus, the perspective on women's status has broadened to include housewives who are not employed outside the home, women engaged in jobs primarily to generate income, and women pursuing a career. Ericksen, Yancey, and Ericksen (1979) also noted the change from sex-related division of household tasks. They found evidence that role sharing is related to wife's education, husband's income, presence of children under age 12, and availability of a kinship support network. Acock and Edwards (1982) reanalyzed Scanzoni's (1979) data, which demonstrates the relevance of sex-role attitude for female status attainment. Utilizing a LISREL causal modeling approach (Bagozzi 1980), they found that sex-role attitudes were important in explaining both income and continuity in the labor market. Changes in sex-role attitudes include movement away from such viewpoints as maternal employment adversely affecting children. These changes in sex-role attitudes and viewpoints about the role of employment in women's lives affects family role structure and decisionmaking. For example, some study already has been made on husbands who prepare dinners for their families (Roberts and Wortzel 1980).

Female household members often may be co-providers. They may not fit the complementary status formerly accorded women. Instead, egalitarian agreements appear more evident as employment behavior and domestic tasks have become interchangeable between spouses and cohabiters.

Hempel and Tucker (1980) have suggested borrowing the notion of environmental uncertainty from contingency theory as a means of explaining variability in family role structures. Within their taxonomy, traditional marriage arrangements, similar to bureaucratic organizations in formalization of rules and lack of participation in decisionmaking, form an environment of high certainty. It is characterized by frequent consensus and lack of conflict. Hempel and Tucker thus hold that uncertainty in household decisionmaking has increased due to a shift toward egalitarian spouse and gender roles. Greater uncertainty increases the instances in which bargaining occurs due to conflict and, therefore, the likelihood of accommodative role structures.

Other researchers, in addition to Rodman, have had difficulties relating a resource framework to cross-cultural and ethnic perspectives. The assumption that males are instrumental specialists in the household has been disputed by Aronoff and Crano (Aronoff and Crano 1975; Crano and Aronoff 1978). Their work, which included data from many societies, found no support for the complementary hypothesis. They suggested that individuals in households will exhibit both instrumental and expressive behavior (Crano and Aronoff 1978) and that specialization by sex roles alone is a substantial oversimplification of actual interpersonal dynamics in the household.

Racial and ethnic stereotypes have been similarly challenged. Research has indicated that black households tend to be more egalitarian than white families; the naive assumption of black matriarchy has received little support (Willie and Greenblatt 1978). Cromwell and Cromwell (1978) dismissed the notion of Chicano patriarchy, as well as the notion of black matriarchy. They found that ethnicity was a poor indicator of decision-making and conflict resolution.

Changes in household living arrangements, away from the more traditional husband/wife/children households, have been found more frequently among blacks than whites. For both races, however, women are much more likely to head their own households than in the past (Bianchi and Farley 1980). Clarification of stereotypically held beliefs should aid in the more efficient development of a general framework for household decisionmaking research.

Suggestions for a More Complex Household Model

A more comprehensive treatment of household decisionmaking should unify sex-role structures into the decisionmaking process. This suggests that the potential for conflict must be addressed and negotiation styles included in the conceptualization. Likewise, the variance of the decision-making unit over the relevant process stages should reflect the preferences and tradeoffs that household members must make. Task allocation in household decisionmaking is clearly related to the role structure in the household. Role expectations and contingency rules are developed that affect the decisionmaking unit in any specific situation. For instance, Roberts and Wortzel (1980) have suggested that the intrinsic satisfaction in cooking might help explain the increasing assumption of the dinner-making task among male household heads. Because of the complexity of the interaction of sex roles and contextual factors in decision processes such as "who makes dinner," a unifying framework is necessary. Buss and Schaninger (1982) have provided a possible basis for such a framework for sex roles in their general model of family decisionmaking.

In the Buss and Schaninger (1982) approach, each household member is influenced by background conditions, such as demographics, parental attributes, and environmental characteristics. These tend to determine attitudes that individuals hold concerning both lifestyle norms and sex-role norms. Both sets of norms interact with specific situational factors at points in time to determine appropriate behavior for each person. When perceptions and expectations differ conflict arises, and the household employs conflict-management strategies. These conflict management strategies may employ either conflict-avoidance or conflict-resolution techniques and result in decision behavior, consumption behavior, and perhaps mutual satisfaction.

Conflict management includes bargaining. Scanzoni (1977: 186) has said that bargaining is necessary in order to organize the rights and duties of those participating in the decisionmaking process; in fact, Scanzoni equated bargaining with decisionmaking.

This framework, as presented by Buss and Schaninger (1982), has several adjustments to incorporate the changes taking place in household decisionmaking:

1. Individual antecedent characteristics replace traditional gender roles in affecting the attitudes each household member forms concerning relative responsibilities in the household.
2. Sex-role norms are treated as moderator variables in the conflict management process; appropriate conjugal behavior is defined by adherence to these norms.
3. Conflict may be an integral part of the decisionmaking process although not necessarily present in each problem-solving event.
4. These linkages in the decision role structure exist over time and, as such, are subject to feedback, tradeoff, and change as household members react to a dynamic environment.

A major problem with the Buss and Schaninger framework is that it is not linked to decisionmaking processes as typically considered.

DECISIONMAKING PROCESSES

Most studies of household decisionmaking have focused on the outcomes of decisionmaking—*who* makes the final decision—rather than on the process that has led to the outcomes (Davis 1976).

Some studies (e.g., Davis and Rigaux 1974; Bonfield 1978) have investigated how family member involvement and influence varies over stages within decision processes resulting in the purchase of a product or service. Most researchers have either made explicit assumptions about the number and type of stages in the decision process or made no statement about decision process stages. The most popular model includes three stages: problem recognition, external information search, and final decision (Granbois 1963; Sheth 1974; Davis and Rigaux 1974; Hempel 1972; Szybillo, Sosanie, and Tenenbein 1979; Bonfield 1978). Others have assumed four-stage models (Gredal 1966; Jaffe and Senft 1966) or six-stage models (Nelson 1978). Most researchers have based their decision model on Dewey's (1910) classic problem formulation model, but there is no consensus on how it should be adapted for household decisionmaking.

One limitation shared by the various formulations of decision processes is that they assume households actually go through these stages (Davis 1976). Given the present stage of development in household research, evidence is needed about what these stages actually are: The framework should not be established on an a priori basis. Providing a rationale for number and type of stages (Granbois 1963; Davis and Rigaux 1974; Wilkes 1975; Bonfield 1978) has been the exception rather than rule in research thus far. The problem of a priori decision-stage specification is also recognized as present in research on individual decision processes (Olshavsky and Granbois 1979).

One view of this problem is that the level of involvement associated with the purchase decision determines the type of decisionmaking process that will be followed. For high-involvement decisions, extended problem solving or decisionmaking processing is expected. In the case of low-involvement decisions, the decision process does not include problem solving. That is, no search for alternative is included (Engel and Blackwell 1982: 39). The concept of low involvement is controversial and has resulted in no agreement on what it is or its meaning for decisionmaking. Two relatively current views are found in consumer-behavior texts by Assael (1981) and Engel and Blackwell (1982).

While dealing with the involvement literature is beyond the scope of this paper, it is important to recognize that methodological innovations that facilitate improved understanding of household decisionmaking are needed. Even resorting to reconstruction of personal decisionmaking processes by individual household members may be preferable to a priori conceptualizations by researchers. At a minimum, observational studies and experiments should be developed to test the accuracy of a priori specification.

Our understanding of decisionmaking processes is further hampered by the fact that research has been limited to processes that culminate in an actual purchase. Three problems are associated with this limitation. First, household decision processes that culminate with a purchase tend to emphasize the consensual view of decisionmaking. Decision processes that do not result in a purchase may be more representative of decisionmaking marked by conflict or accommodation (Granbois 1971b).

Second, some sets of purchase decisions may be interdependent. For example, the decision to buy a car may affect decisions about taking a vacation (whether to take a vacation and the type of vacation that can be taken). These types of tradeoffs among products can be expected to be common, especially when the expenditure involved is large relative to household resources. The scarcer the resources the more tradeoffs and interdependence among household purchase decisions.

Third, the decision processes involved in money management, asset management, and saving behavior (R.Ferber 1973; Ferber and Lee 1974)— and their interdependence with other economic decisions—must also be considered. Work, career, and decisions about the number and spacing of children should also receive attention. These decisions have important social and economic consequences for the household. They help to determine the level of resources available for expenditure on products and the relative influence of household members on other decisions.

Research in household decisionmaking has also ignored the fact that several decision processes can be taking place simultaneously within a household. Although the tacit assumption is that decision processes occur in a sequential manner (i.e., one at a time), it is more likely that household members are performing tasks associated with different stages in several decision processes at the same time. A representation of this phenomena in diagram form would be similar to a series of PERT networks. Activities in a PERT network are analogous to stages in a decision process. Activities in a project and stages in a household decision process can be sequential or simultaneous. The problem faced by the household is one of allocating scarce resources (time, money, skills, etc.) to a large number of activities in various projects (decision processes). Given the reality of scarce resources, some projects are postponed or never completed. Decisions about project completion are also based on the tradeoffs made by household members and on each member's relative control of the available resources.

Consumer Information Processing Models

While information processing has received a great deal of attention from consumer researchers, little attention has been paid to the fact that more than one person is frequently involved in the purchase decision. Curry and Menasco (1979) examined different information processing strategies used by husbands and wives during their joint purchase of a high-cost durable good. Their model provides direct predictions concerning three stages in a couple's decision process: prechoice, negotiation, and postchoice. They concluded that disagreement about attribute weights between spouses could cause severe disagreement in product evaluation. Because they assumed different weighting characteristics would be relatively implicit, there was no reason to expect that any basis for resolution would be developed (Curry and Menasco 1979: 199). A basic research issue suggested by their study is whether compromise and capitulation are representative models of negotiation outcomes in joint decisions when disagreement about product evaluations occurs between spouses. The Curry and Menasco model can be useful in gaining understanding about the relationship between information-processing strategies of household members in joint decisions, conflict (i.e., major disagreement in product evaluations), and conflict-handling behaviors (compromise, capitulation, etc.). Curry and Menasco have developed a mathematical representation based on a number of assumptions found in the information-processing and multiattribute-model literature. The next step is to develop empirical evidence to test their model.

Park has provided landmark research in developing a method for obtaining decision nets (Park, Hughes, Thukral, and Friedman 1981) and utilizing the procedure in an attempt to understand husband-and-wife home-buying decisions (Park 1982). Park characterized the joint decision-making process as "muddling through." Husbands and wives were interviewed independently to determine individual decision nets on three occasions (where possible): before engaging in home search, after examining homes but before purchasing a home, and after either making an offer to purchase a home or purchasing a home. The results supported the muddling-through hypothesis: (1) Spouses appeared to have limited knowledge and awareness of their mates' decision strategies, and (2) they relied on "conflict-avoiding heuristics" (Park 1982: 152) in reaching a final choice. The three conflict-avoiding heuristics Park identified are (1) common preference levels on salient objective dimensions (i.e., attributes on which it was easy to identify each other's preference), (2) task specialization (i.e., one member specializes in decisions on the specific attribute), and (3) concessions based on preference differences (i.e., assuming that each knows the preference structure of the other and that the preferences are felt with different intensity, the spouse with the lower level of intensity concedes in the disagreement).

Park's findings are limited by the fact that only one product—one that can be characterized as a high-involvement product—is considered by only one household type. In addition, as with most decision net research thus far, the potential for demand characteristic contamination of the results is present. That is, as Park recognizes (1982: 154), the decision net plan may not exist until it is created through interaction between the individual and the interviewer. While these limitations are real, it is also recognized that Park's research is an important beginning built on already existing theory. It is important to follow this beginning with replication in different household types, with more household members, and across a range of products that vary at least along an involvement dimension.

Pattern Analysis

A potentially useful research protocol for the study of household decision-making has been developed by Yaverbaum (1982) to investigate decision-making by individuals in an organizational setting. The technique is derived from the March and Simon (1958) theory of subjectively rational choice. The technique resembles Bettman's (1979) work in information processing and appears to implement some of Bettman's suggestions for future research.

Pattern analysis is based on the hypothesis that information users follow discernible patterns in seeking that information—that is, an underlying structure of information gathering strategy is identifiable and measurable. The theory incorporates the premise that we exercise choice based on a limited, simplified model of reality. Because of this limitation, we organize our decisionmaking into programs or strategies suited to different situations (March and Simon 1958). Thus, our response to any given situation may range from routine to complex problem solving depending on the degree of search activity undertaken.

Yaverbaum (1982) postulated a four-stage model of human information processing utilizing the assumption that people may arrive at the same, or similar, conclusions in different manners. The four stages were:

1. *subjective decisionmaking:* characterized by limited internal and external search;
2. *subjective/analytical decisionmaking:* decisions based completely on others' opinions and experiences;
3. *analytical decisionmaking:* use of statistical analysis and modeling ranging from simple to complex; and
4. *analytical/subjective decisionmaking:* methods to evaluate alternatives are selected together with actual processing of cause and effect.

Yaverbaum expected problem solving to begin with the first or second stage followed by a shift to stages of higher complexity depending on the individual decisionmaker's style. The experimental protocol was constructed so that the choice of any specific source of management information implied one of the four stages in the subject's decisionmaking process. The pattern-analysis procedure revealed differences in the manner in which information was gathered and in the sequence of stage complexity used.

The notion of discernible stages in information-processing strategies can be traced at least to Howard (1963) and Engel, Blackwell, and Kollat (1978). More recently, Bettman (1979) has also noted that active information search may be internal initially followed by external search. Following Bettman, the direction (pieces of information sought) and the degree (quantity of information sought) of external search determine its character-istics: "Detailed patterns of external information search can be examined by measuring the sequence of information acquired from an information display" (Bettman 1979:135).

Within a marketing context, processing by brands and by attributes is relevant. Bettman argued for the development of measurement techniques for both internal and external search and for a method to assess the relationships between them. The "information monitoring approaches" (Bettman 1979:196) have used information displays that reflect simple product characteristic information and not the degrees of complexity that may occur in actual search. Yaverbaum's approach appears to provide a general framework for studying complexity as well as the characteristics of the specific context under consideration.

Yaverbaum was able to identify seven distinct patterns of decision-making by performing factor analysis on informational stimuli sorted by experimental subjects. Yaverbaum's results support the theory that groups of people go through the decisionmaking process in similar and identifiable ways.

Yaverbaum's approach may provide a methodology for the study of household decisionmaking (as well as individual consumer decision-making). Alternatives involving internal versus external search could be investigated, particularly the influence of other household members in the various degrees and directions of external search. Patterns of problem-solving behavior may be similarly identified and perhaps correlated to the other household variables discussed, such as relative investment, compara-tive resources, and cultural role expectations (Davis 1976).

Conflict

Davis (1976) has suggested that household decisionmaking and decision-making processes can be characterized as accommodative or consensual in terms of the presence or relative absence of conflict (Davis 1976: 252). Household decision processes have, for the most part, been characterized as consensual. First, a number of theorists have assumed traditional complementary roles in which little room is provided for major disagreements (Parsons and Bales 1955; Alderson 1957, 1965). Second, studies of decisionmaking processes have paid attention almost exclusively to processes culminating in a purchase—that is, these studies have concentrated on decisionmaking processes in which there is final agreement among those participating in the decisionmaking. Third, the possibility of an alternative evaluation stage has often been omitted in this research. It would appear that perhaps the greatest amount of conflict would occur at this stage, exceeded only by the point at which a decision was made to buy the product. It is hypothesized that more accommodative views of the decision process would be found in studying an alternative evaluation stage. Fourth, since self-report is the most common method of obtaining information from those participating in the decision process, it is possible that more socially acceptable (i.e., consensual) answers may be obtained. Fifth, purchase decisions have been typically studied as independent rather than interdependent decisions. The independent decision is basically a brand decision where the alternatives (brands) are typically similar, the degree of tradeoff among choices is relatively low, and the value systems of the household members tend to be more congruent, relative to the choices, than those involved in inter-dependent decisions.

The view of household decisionmaking processes is changing from a consensual to an accommodative view. Scanzoni (1977) maintains that changing sex roles in the last twenty years are transforming the traditional marital arrangement, which has been characterized by complementary roles and "spontaneous consensus." The new marital arrangement is characterized by more egalitarian roles and by continuous bargaining and negotiation in terms of each participant's rights and duties: "The give and take of bargaining processes is of course, a more concrete and substantive way to talk about the dynamics of decisionmaking" (Scanzoni 1979:186).

The recent application of consumer information-processing models to the area of joint decisionmaking recognizes that the decision process is not a smooth one and that major disagreements occur in the evaluation of products by household members. This perspective is inconsistent with the consensual view of decisionmaking.

Family sociologists have been instrumental in changing the view of families as consensual systems. Blood (1960) recognized conflict as a widespread and serious problem in contemporary U.S. families. Spreye (1969, 1971) assumes an even more radical position by criticizing family sociologists for conceptualizing the family as a consensus equilibrium system rather than a system in conflict. According to Spreye, since agreement in decisionmaking is the exception, the relevant question becomes, How do families manage to live with conflict? The concept of cooperation as an effective conflict-management strategy accompanied by a set of shared procedural rules has been developed. Household members agree to a contract where disagreements are allowed but where procedures for dealing with disagreements are also included.

Household researchers in marketing have discussed the nature of conflict, the types of conflict resolution behaviors adopted within households (Granbois 1971b; Sheth 1974; Davis 1976; Buss and Schaninger 1982), methods of conflict avoidance (Buss and Schaninger 1982), and moderator variables that may reduce the likelihood of conflict-resolving behavior (Burns and Granbois 1977). The evidence on household-conflict resolution strategies, however, is equivocal. Sheth and Cosmas (1975) found persuasion or bargaining to be used more often than problem solving, while Belch, Belch, and Sciglimpaglia (1980) found problem solving used more frequently. Both studies assumed that conflict resolution could be characterized as problem solving, persuasion, bargaining, or politics (Sheth 1974: 32–33).

Problem solving is characterized by seeking more information, additional deliberation on the information already held, seeking support from sources outside the household, and seeking additional alternatives. *Persuasion* is described by Sheth (1974:32) in part as occurring when "an attempt is made to test for consistency in the motive hierarchy of the members and to avoid any suboptimization that may be found." It is characterized by greater interaction among members of the decisionmaking unit with the possibility of an outsider being brought in to reconcile differences. No new information is sought about alternatives. *Bargaining*, although not specifically defined by Sheth, was said to be a specific recognition by the household that conflict exists. Sheth gave as an example the giving in on one issue in conflict in order for others to give in on some other issue in conflict. This notion appears to be the same as Sheth's later notion of *trading* (Sheth and Cosmas 1975). *Politics* was also not specifically defined by Sheth. One example of politics was the formation of coalitions and subgroups within the household in order to isolate individuals in the household with whom there is conflict.

Certain limitations are common to most studies of conflict in household decisionmaking: (1) Because researchers have defined the conflict concept differently, there is no single definition; (2) conflict is explicitly or implicitly viewed as dysfunctional—the emphasis on conflict avoidance and resolution supports this notion; (3) the number and dimensions of conflict-handling behaviors have been specified on an a priori basis; and (4) the relationship between conflict-handling modes and other factors, such as household type and lifestyle, have been largely ignored in seeking explanations for preferences for these modes.

The literature in organizational and industrial relations offers some insights into solving the problems caused by these limitations. First, conflict has been defined by Thomas (1976, 1978) as a condition rather than a form of behavior: "namely, the condition in which the concerns of two or more parties appear to be incompatible. This definition has the advantage of separating conflict from the behaviors that people use to deal with it, so that one can talk about the effectiveness of different 'conflict-handling behaviors'" (1978:56).

Second, the most basic change in conflict theory is reflected in the emergence of the term "conflict management," which is gradually replacing the older term "conflict resolution." Researchers have found that conflict has positive as well as negative aspects, and in many cases, it will be less beneficial to resolve or eliminate conflict and more beneficial to manage it effectively. Family sociologists agree that (Spreye 1969:700):

> There seems some agreement on the proposition that a certain degree of conflict may actually help reinforce [family] solidarity, aid in the maintenance of a functional division of labor, and generally alleviate the boredom of too much marital consensus. It should, however, lead to happy reconciliations and not be too severe in nature, otherwise it is seen to result in the dissolution of the family or other unfortunate consequences.

Third, conflict-handling behaviors have been classified by Thomas (1976: 900) as meaningful ways for people in conflict situations to relate to each other—that is, with assertiveness and cooperativeness. Assertiveness is defined as an attempt to satisfy one's own needs, while cooperativeness is the attempt to satisfy the other person's needs. While it is reasonable to hypothesize about these dimensions in organizational settings, it is even more logical to expect them in households where a mutually caring situation can be assumed. Thomas identified five conflict-handling behaviors relative to these two dimensions (see Figure 14-2): (1) competition (high in assertiveness and low in cooperativeness), (2) collaboration (high in both assertiveness and cooperativeness), (3) compromise (intermediate in both assertiveness and cooperativeness), (4) avoidance (low in both assertiveness and cooperativeness), and (5) accommodation (high in cooperativeness and low in assertiveness). In adapting this conceptualization to household research, it should be interesting to note whether the traits of assertiveness and cooperation are generalizable to individuals or whether they are situation-specific with respect to individuals. Thomas's model is concerned with dyadic situations, but conflict involving more than two people can involve coalition formation (Thomas 1976: 890).

Fourth, the relationship between personality types and preferred conflict-management behaviors has received some attention. Kilmann and Thomas (1975) found two dimensions of personality (thinking versus feeling and introversion versus extroversion) related to individuals' reported conflict-handling behaviors.

Figure 14–2. A Dyadic, Two-Dimensional Model of Conflict Behaviors.

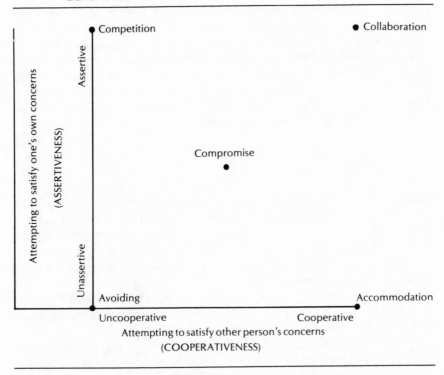

Source: Adapted from Thomas (1976).

In addition to personality, sex-role identity, sex of other, and affective relationship have been studied as possible determinants of conflict-handling behaviors. Baxter and Shepherd (1978) found no differences in conflict-handling behavior by sex of other. They found that conflicts with liked others were managed with less competition and with more accommodation, collaboration, and compromise. Subjects who viewed themselves as feminine were more likely to disapprove of competition. Masculine subjects appeared to be less likely to differentiate between liked and disliked others in their use of competitive behavior. For household research, lifestyle appears to be a more appropriate concept than personality when studying conflict-handling behaviors. Sex, sex-role identity (androgynous, feminine, masculine), sex of others in the decisionmaking unit, and affective relationship also appear to be relevant in the study of preferences for, and actual, conflict-handling behavior.

Finally, the efforts of organizational conflict researchers in the development of a contingency theory of conflict (Thomas 1978; Robbins 1978; Derr 1977; Filley 1978; Thomas, Jamieson, and Moore 1978) should be studied. A contingency theory of household conflict would attempt to explain which conflict-handling behaviors are more appropriate (i.e., functional) under different conditions. A major area of agreement in the organizational behavior literature is that collaboration or problem solving is not the most productive conflict-handling mode in all conflict situations (Thomas, Jamieson, and Moore 1978). We expect this finding to be supported in household research as well.

Power

The question of who decides is a question of power. The sociology and economics literature includes a number of theoretical perspectives for explaining power in the household. Among these conceptualizations are exchange theory (Heer 1963; Safilios-Rothschild 1970b, 1976), resource theory (Blood and Wolfe 1960), the theory of resources in cultural context (Rodman 1972), cultural role expectation theory (Parsons and Bales 1955; Burgess and Locke 1960), relative investment theory (Coleman 1966), and economic theory (Becker 1973, 1974). Some of these theories are discussed by Buss and Schaninger in their paper in this volume.

Davis (1976) has suggested that some of these conceptualizations are complementary rather than alternative explanations of household power. While the creation of an integrated theoretical framework is a possibility that must be considered, most theoretical perspectives are restricted to husband-and-wife relationships (marital power). Power theories should be explored that address relationships in households which go beyond the husband-and-wife dyad.

An alternative approach to the study of power has been suggested by Kipnis (1976), who presents a descriptive model of the power act from the point of view of the power holder. Kipnis's model is an adaptation of an earlier model developed by Cartwright (1965) and is shown in Table 14-1.

In a household decisionmaking framework, this descriptive model represents a theoretical map of the terrain of power as seen by each household member when their power motivation has been aroused. "Power motivations arise when an individual experiences an aroused need state that can only be satisfied by inducing appropriate behaviors in others" (Kipnis 1976:16). We can relate power motivations to the household decision process whenever a household member recognizes that his or her own need satisfaction depends on an ability to influence the behavior of one or more other household member.

Table 14–1. A Descriptive Model of the Power Act.

1. *Power Motivation*

   Aroused need state satisfied by appropriate behaviors in others

2. *Request for compliance*

3. *Resources*

4. *Region of inhibition*
   Physiological
   Values
   Costs
   Self-confidence
   Institutional norms
   Culture

5. *Means of influence*
   Persuasion
   Threats
   Promises
   Rewards
   Force
   Ecological change

Target's
motivations
and
resources

6. *Response of target*
   Compliance
   Private acceptance
   Self-esteem
   Esteem for powerholder

7. *Consequences for the powerholder*
   Changes in need state
   Self-perceptions
   Perception of target
   Changes in values

Source: Kipnis (1976: 17).

Most of the research using Kipnis's framework has concentrated on the means of influence or the power tactics used by the power holders. This topic has not received attention in the household decisionmaking literature. The question here is not who decides but how the one who decides in a particular situation gets his or her way. Kipnis's research protocol uses an inductive approach. The first step is to ask people to describe the actual tactics they use in a given decisionmaking setting. Next, these descriptions are used to construct questionnaires containing descriptions of influence tactics. Finally, factor analysis and other multidimensional techniques are applied to the questionnaire data to find the underlying dimensions of influence (Kipnis and Schmidt 1982). Previous studies found three dimensions of influence tending to emerge: (1) assertive tactics, (2) rational tactics, and (3) nondirective or manipulative tactics (Kipnis and Schmidt 1982). Kipnis and Schmidt (1982:5-6), however, isolated seven dimensions or influence strategies:

1. *Reason:* Use of facts and data to support development of a logical argument.
2. *Coalition:* Mobilization of other members of the [household].
3. *Ingratiation:* Use of impression management, flattery, and goodwill creation.
4. *Bargaining:* Negotiation through exchange of benefits or favors.
5. *Assertiveness:* Use of a direct or forceful approach (e.g., I demanded that he or she do what I requested).
6. *Higher Authority:* Gaining support of higher level members of the [household].
7. *Sanctions:* Use of [household] derived rewards and punishments (e.g., I threatened to send him to bed without dinner).

Falbo and Peplau (1980) attempted to uncover the dimensions underlying the power tactics used among different types of married couples. They also attempted to determine the impact of gender and egalitarianism on power strategies used in intimate relationships. Two major power-strategy dimensions were identified: (1) a direct/indirect dimension where positive and negative affect, hinting, and withdrawing are indirect power strategies while, asking, telling, and talking are direct power strategies; and (2) a bilateral/unilateral dimension where bilateral, or interactive, strategies include persuasion, bargaining, reasoning, and positive affect, while unilateral strategies—those in which one person takes independent action by simply doing what they want to—included laissez-faire, withdrawing, and telling. Falbo and Peplau used males and female engaged in intimate heterosexual and homosexual relationships as respondents. They found greater satisfaction among all couples who used direct strategies. Strong preference for independence was found among those using unilateral strategies. Among heterosexual couples, males were more likely to report using bilateral and direct strategies while females were more likely to report using unilateral and indirect strategies. Male heterosexuals used more functional strategies (i.e., strategies associated with more satisfaction) than female heterosexuals. Female homosexuals did not resemble male heterosexuals, nor did male homosexuals resemble female heterosexuals. Male and female homosexuals did not differ significantly in the types of strategies used. Egalitarianism was found to be related to the use of unilateral strategies.

Even though the external validity of the Falbo and Peplau study can be questioned because they used a nonprobability sample, their results suggest that gender and beliefs in egalitarianism have an impact on the power strategies used by couples and, therefore, by households. Thus, it can be hypothesized that some power strategies may be more functional than others as suggested by the association between marital satisfaction and the direct/indirect power strategy dimension.

Some researchers investigated the impact of personality variables and affective bonds on the choice of influence strategies. Falbo (1977) found positive peer ratings to be associated with the reported use of rational strategies (bargaining, reason, and compromise), while Machiavellianism as a power-relevant personality characteristic was found to be associated with the reported use of indirect (hinting and thought manipulation) and nonrational strategies (evasion, deceit, and emotional alteration).

Michener and Schwertfeger (1972) found that liking affected influencers' choice among alternative power strategies. Under conditions of liking, their subjects were more likely to favor value-change strategies (withdrawal and demand creation). Under conditions of disliking, their subjects were more likely to favor destructive strategies (outcome blockage and extension of the power network).

The studies by Kipnis and Schmidt (1982), Falbo and Peplau (1980), Falbo (1977), and Michener and Schwertfeger (1972) suggest that the use of specific power strategies is contingent on affective bonds and personality variables. These types of studies need to be replicated in household settings before valid generalizations can be made in the area of household decisionmaking. (Ian Wilkinson is exploring these research techniques among Australian households, but no empirical data are available as yet.)

Empirical research has been conducted on other sections of the Kipnis model, but little has been conducted in household settings. The consequences of the use of power for the power holder were studied by Kipnis, Castwell, Gergen, and Mauch (1976) in two field studies conducted in household settings. The first study was concerned with the consequences of the use of power on the power holder in the marital relationship, while the second study concentrated on the effects of power on housewife power holders in relationships with housemaid targets. They found that power holders who used strong means of influence (assertive power strategies) believed that they caused the behavior of the target persons (attribution of control). Moreover, power holders who believed that they caused targets' behaviors devalued the targets and acted to increase social distance from them. Since the studies were correlational, cause-and-effect relationships cannot be established. Nonetheless, it can be hypothesized that the continuous use of assertive power strategies can have dysfunctional effects on marital relationships, since the target spouse would be devalued by the power holder and the social distance between them would increase.

The Relationship between Power and Conflict

Are power and conflict two different concepts, or are they alternative or complementary views of the same behavior? We view them as complementary.

Family sociologists have taken the position that power and conflict are complementary concepts for understanding decisionmaking behavior. Staples (1971) suggested an index of conflict resolution as an indicator of marital dominance—that is, the best way of determining which spouse's decision will prevail is to study situations in which the interest of both are in conflict. Rollins and Bahr (1976: 620) took the position that marital power is a relevant concept only when conflict of goals exist among spouses. They defined marital power as "the relative potential of marriage partners to influence the behavior of each other when a conflict of goals exists between them." Scanzoni (1978) also recognized that conflict does not exist apart from power, although he felt that power can occur without the presence of conflict. He also stated that conflict persists because each spouse has enough power to pursue his or her own interests but not enough to stop the other's conflict-producing behavior (Scanzoni 1978: 98). Thus, we find a relationship between the balance of power and the persistence of conflict.

Finally, among some conflict theorists, power is considered as a method of conflict management when a condition of disagreement exists among interacting individuals (Filley 1978; Chesler, Crowfoot, and Bryant 1978; Derr 1977). Power is thus contained within the competition-handling behavior in Thomas's (1978) theory.

METHODOLOGICAL CONSIDERATIONS

The conceptual framework underlying household decisionmaking implicitly assumes that the household is prototypical of the small group. Group characteristics such as permanence, power, leadership, and specialization are apparent within household units (E.P. Cox 1975). The methodology used to analyze family consumer studies, however, has often emphasized correlating the individual's attitudes, intentions, and perceptions with family purchase decisions rather than studying the actual process within the group (Engel, Blackwell, and Kollat 1978). We consider in this context issues concerning the design, sampling procedure, and analysis and make suggestions for increasing content relevance to the household as the unit of analysis.

Self-Report versus Observation

The most frequently used method of determining family decision processes are interviews with one member of a family, independent interviews with various family members, and joint interviews with all relevant members (Runyon 1980: 180), all of which are self-report measures. For a time, the prevailing wisdom appeared to be that interviewing one spouse would provide adequate information for determining aggregate purchase influence—for example, what proportion of wives decides on the color of car purchased (Davis 1971). However, later research (Davis and Rigaux 1974; Bonfield 1978) has found considerable within-household disagreement when independent interviews were conducted.

The validity of individual and joint interviews has been questioned in family sociology as well. Reports by individuals have been criticized as indicating subjective rather than objective reality (Olson and Rabunsky 1972)—that is, perceptions rather than actualities may be what is being measured. In their study, Olson and Rabunsky found that individuals were unable to report who made decisions in their family and what decisions were made. They felt that their results indicated four specific problem areas: (1) Studies using recall to describe household power structure actually measure who is perceived as the authority rather than who actually possesses authority power; (2) cultural role prescriptions and expectations are likely to influence description of the perceived authority leading to socially acceptable answers; (3) self-report measures may ignore or diminish the existence of conflict in the decision process (this conflict may be assumed away by researchers or suppressed by respondents); and (4) recall may simply be inaccurate.

Interaction data has been suggested as more readily yielding information regarding both outcomes and processes in household decisionmaking. Observational techniques frequently are recommended.

Noncomparabilities between self-report and direct-observation techniques have presented a major difficulty for researchers who have tried to interpret results from similar studies that rely on one or the other procedure. The relationship between self-report and direct observation has been marked by lack of correlation (Olson 1969; Olson and Rabunsky 1972; Turk and Bell 1972). For example, Turk and Bell found that children exhibited decisionmaking power with respect to how "gift money" would be spent when an observational measure was used but that this power was not evident in questionnaires completed by the same households.

Self-report measures are obviously easier to obtain than observational measures. Some effort should be made to develop self-report measures that can be validated by observational methods. Obtaining valid self-report measures from individuals rather than from a number of members of the same household will enhance efficiency in gathering household decision-making information. Because of the cultural and other normative demand characteristics inherent in self-report operationalizations, an indirect technique would probably be best.

Two studies have attempted to assess self-report validity through the multitrait/multimethod approach suggested by Campbell and Fiske (1959). Rather than validating by observation, this technique allows testing for construct validity through the use of different measures—in these cases, self-report measures. Wilkes (1975) found relative influence varying across decisionmaking stages and across products—that is, global measures, such as who decided which car to buy, correlated poorly with activities at specific decision stages. Szybillo, Sosanie, and Tenenbein (1979) tested several scales of family-member influence. They found considerable convergent validity and were encouraged by the results for divergent validity. They suggested, as we have, that the scales that they found best still need further validation through observational techniques.

Anchoring

To insure that all respondents are answering the same question, operationalizations of decisionmaking stages and product categories should meet two criteria: (1) They should be the same across studies, and (2) they should mean the same thing to all respondents. While the first criterion is generally met, the second is not. This problem was recognized by Bonfield (1978) in replicating a study by Davis and Rigaux (1974). For example, Bonfield "anchored" respondents to "replacement or additional pots and pans for the kitchen" while Davis and Rigaux asked about "kitchenware." In addition to pots and pans, kitchenware includes kitchen furniture, refrigerators, ranges, knives, woks, steamers, and can openers. By anchoring to a specific frame of reference, the researcher controls what the respondent considers and thus reduces a source of error variance. While there are other potential explanations, concrete anchoring is one possible explanation for the higher levels of specialization found by Bonfield.

Sampling and Generalization

A number of studies on household decisionmaking have used convenience or quota samples (e.g., Berey and Pollay 1968; Davis and Rigaux 1974; Burns and Granbois 1977; Atkin 1978; Jenkins 1979). Some researchers have used probability-sampling techniques (e.g., Hempel 1972; Cunningham and Green 1974; Bonfield 1978; Ericksen, Yancey, and Ericksen 1979). Some researchers have been able to use ongoing data bases established specifically for the study of income dynamics and demographic changes of households over time (e.g., Safilios-Rothschild 1969; Farkas 1976; Cronkite 1977; Roberts and Wortzel 1980). These studies differ significantly in the degree to which the results found are generalizable. A convenience sample is useful primarily in developing research techniques and in exploratory research. Quota samples are somewhat more useful because groups can be sampled in exploratory research in which gross differences are expected. Small probability samples will either be subject to large confidence intervals or generalizable to a restricted population. Large data bases are most rewarding, but they are costly. Examining data gathered for other purposes for potential hypotheses can be useful when these bases are made available. Roberts and Wortzel (1980), for example, have made excellent use of Needham, Harper & Steers Life Style Study data. While we made the point earlier, we hasten to reiterate that the choice of respondent and the use of respondent perceptions of others' influence are also sampling problems.

Analysis

The purpose of statistical analysis is to test the hypotheses of the researcher, which may subsequently either be rejected or supported. Testing hypotheses requires appropriate translation of theoretical constructs into operational definitions, gathering the data, and selecting statistical techniques that closely match the descriptive, predictive, or causal import of the study. Research in household decisionmaking has incorporated several levels of complexity in its measures.

Relative influence or power within the household is frequently evaluated using the mean number of product subdecisions made by husband, wife, or both across one or several product categories (Hempel 1972; Green and Cunningham 1975; Burns 1976; Burns and Granbois 1977; Jenkins 1979; Filiatrault and Ritchie 1980). When evaluated together with each member's perception of his or her own and other household members' roles, some insight may be gained into the conflict and power structure in the household. It should be recognized that the set of decisions included in the research invariably has been selected by the researcher so that mean number of subdecisions hardly represents a valid measure of power or conflict.

Safilios-Rothschild (1970b) has suggested additional measures designed to determine the importance of decisions to each household member and also the frequency with which these decisions are made. This analytical modification adds explanatory value because, as Heer (1963) has observed, a household member having greater power in one decisionmaking area may not have similar power in others.

Insight into the question of relative power may come from the assignment of appropriate weights for separate areas of decisionmaking. Some direction may be found in considering intrahousehold patterns of information processing. Typical information-processing models consider the prechoice evaluation of multiattribute products in order to predict brand preference or choice. This framework may be extended to establish total utility ratings for each product in a series of products exhibiting interattribute tradeoffs (Curry and Menasco 1979). These weightings may provide a conceptual basis for assigning and predicting influence among household members.

Conjoint measurement is a statistical procedure that incorporates the notion of preference rankings over several related criteria. This technique, which is more commonly used in determining product-attribute perceptions, is based on the assumption that inferences can be made about individual value systems by considering conceptual choice rather than by self-report. In essence, it attempts to reflect the tradeoffs that individuals make in any judgment situation. For example, Wind (1976) adapted conjoint analysis to assess the effect that preferences of relevant others have on individual choice behavior and interpersonal decision weightings.

Because of its interactive nature, household information processing behavior clearly includes the possibility of conflict-management strategies (Buss and Schaninger 1982) that are a significant factor in household decision processes. Negotiation styles may also be determined. Indexes of conflict resolution could be utilized to assess household-member dominance in accommodative situations (Cromwell and Cromwell 1978). Thus, a multimeasure approach may be necessary to more adequately assess household decisionmaking processes.

SUGGESTIONS FOR FURTHER MODELING

The household decision process encompasses a complex interactional framework that integrates background and situational characteristics of the individual members with their role expectations and prescriptions. The potential for conflict exists within any decision context as tradeoffs are enacted over time within problem-solving categories.

This multidimensional nature supports several methodological procedures suggested by Safilios-Rothschild (1969:300): (1) Within a pretest, household groups should be surveyed to ascertain relevant decision-making issues, stages, and subdecisions. This exploratory phase may establish topics for study in which decision roles already exist. (2) Each respondent should be asked to rank the importance, frequency, and time consumed in carrying out each decision category by himself or herself, by the other members of the household, and by the household as a whole. Conjoint analysis may prove useful in this stage. (3) The researcher should analyze the results by testing hypotheses developed from the exploratory research.

Parallel self-report and observational measures should be implemented in order to ascertain the validity of the findings. Allowance should be made for measuring both conflictive and nonconflictive processes. Finally, consideration of the family as a unit, drawing on the dimensions of configuration (e.g., productive use of each individual's ideas) and coordination (harmony within households), may provide additional insights on a more aggregate level (Reiss, Costell, Berkman, and Jones 1980).

15 INFLUENCE, PARTICIPATION, AND INVESTMENT IN FAMILY DECISIONMAKING

Bernard J. Jaworski, Deborah J. MacInnis, and William J. Sauer

Interest in family decisionmaking has generated a wealth of research over the past decade (cf. Davis 1976; Sheth 1974: Chapter 2). A central concept within this literature is relative influence, which refers to the amount of influence one spouse has with respect to the other in affecting choice outcomes. For the most part, relative influence has been utilized as a proxy for the structure of marital roles in family decisionmaking (Baran 1978; Davis 1970; Davis and Rigaux 1974; Ferber and Lee 1974). Despite several reformulation attempts (Burns 1977; Davis 1970), it remains a central and popular concept in family decisionmaking research.[1]

At least four factors have contributed to its popularity. First, it is easy to measure and employ. It is typically operationalized by the following three-point Likert scale: "husband has more influence," "equal influence," "wife has more influence" (Baran 1978; Cunningham and Green 1974; Davis 1970; Davis and Rigaux 1974; Ferber and Lee 1974; Hempel 1974, 1975; Hendrix and Qualls 1978; Munsinger, Weber, and Hansen 1975; Sharp and Mott 1956; Shuptrine and Samuelson 1976; Wilkes 1975; Woodside 1975). Three- (or five-) point indices of this nature make data collection on influence relatively straightfoward. Second, information on relative influence has practical value for marketing managers. Once the dominant spouse has been identified, managers can design marketing campaigns directed toward the more influential partner. Third, widespread use of the concept in the family decisionmaking literature allows for comparison across research studies (Davis 1976). Finally, the generalizability of particular results can be assessed by consistent use and operationalization of relative influence.

Although a number of studies have examined influence within this framework, we believe it provides a limited, and perhaps rudimentary, account of family decisionmaking. First, the relative influence measure implicitly assumes that family decisionmaking occurs only within a dyadic framework (typically husband and wife). If our goal is to understand decisionmaking in a family context, however, it is important to develop a measure that extends to all family members. Children may be powerful sources of influence in some aspects of family decisions; however, within the relative-influence framework, their role has not been considered.[2] The following scenario highlights this point. After considerable search effort, a couple in the market for a stereo finally decides to purchase a certain brand of equipment. Meanwhile, their son returns from college and when told of his parents' decision informs them that the stereo they have selected is a low-quality product. Taking their son's advice, the parents then buy the stereo that their son recommends. What happens when the couple is presented with a questionnaire asking, "Based on the following three-point scale, who had more influence on the decision: husband had more influence, equal influence, wife had more influence?" Since the operationalization assumes that decisionmaking occurs only in a dyadic framework, and only among husbands and wives, any responses generated from the above question would be meaningless.

A second limitation is that previous operationalizations of the influence concept have been descriptive rather than process-oriented. Consequently, they have failed to capture the temporal aspects of family decisionmaking and therefore have limited our understanding of the interactive patterns of influence that guide family decisions. In contrast to those previous conceptualizations being grounded in the relative influence framework, we believe that influence is an ongoing process that is shaped and reshaped through intrafamilial contact.

Third, and related to the above two criticisms, even if relative influence enables a dominant partner to be identified for a given decision, it does not necessarily follow that other family members have no input or are not influential in the final decision. The significance of this argument can be illustrated by the following example. Typically, findings suggest that wives wield more influence than husbands in deciding on furniture style (Baran 1978; Davis 1970). However, even though the wife has more influence, it is unlikely that the husband *dislikes* the style of furniture. At a minimum he would have to be indifferent. In other words, the wife presumably is aware of the husband's preferences, and this knowledge may influence the ultimate decision. If this is the case, it may have implications for advertising strategy—namely, it may be premature to conclude that the mere position of family dominance should be a basis for any type of marketing effort. The extent to which other family members possess even slight influence is suggestive of their power in swaying decision outcomes.

Finally, the current use of relative influence lacks conceptual precision. Prior research has often used the term "influence" interchangeably with two other concepts—investment and involvement. It is argued in the following section that while these concepts are theoretically meaningful in family decisionmaking, each has a distinct meaning in a decision-making context.

DEFINING CONCEPTS

In this paper, "influence" is defined as the extent to which a family member directly or indirectly affects the process or outcome of a decision. A close examination of this definition indicates that influence may be viewed as a stage (process or outcome) by type (direct or indirect) matrix as shown in Table 15-1. The stage aspect of influence is consistent with some empirical data on influence in the family decisionmaking literature. Davis and Rigaux (1974), for example, have shown that influence varies depending on the stage (recognition, information search, or final outcome) of the decision process. In addition to stage, the nature of influence may vary by type of influence. According to Webster, the noun "influence" means "the act or power of producing an effect without apparent exertion of force or direct exercise of command" and the verb "to influence" means "to affect or alter by indirect or intangible means." According to this definition, influence is indirect or intangible since it does not imply any behavioral action on the part of the influencer. Family characteristics such as social class, role structure, and stage in the family life cycle constitute sources of indirect

Table 15–1. Influence by Stage and Type.

	Direct Type (Behavioral)	Indirect Type (Nonbehavioral)
Process stage	Problem recognition Redirect decision process	Family structure: Roles Family life cycle
Outcome stage	Outcome-oriented	Family structure: Roles Family life cycle

influence. These aspects of family structure represent nonbehavioral or unspoken boundaries that permeate each decision and extend across most family decisions. We call this concept indirect influence.

The second type of influence is situation-specific and includes behavioral actions that are directed at changing the process or outcome of a decision. Direct influence is a social phenomenon that requires a tangible display of action aimed at changing the behavior of another individual. Typically, consumer-behavior literature emphasizes this dimension of influence. For example, Ferber and Lee (1974) and Davis (1976) discuss how a husband or wife exerts influence. More recently, using a methodology other than relative influence, Filiatrault and Ritchie (1980) referred to an "influence structure." Their analysis also focuses on tangible measures of influence. While this paper recognizes the significance of direct influence in family decisionmaking, it also suggests that indirect sources are important as well.

It is interesting to note that influence has often been confused with a second concept, involvement. Indeed, it is not unusual to see in the published literature terms such as "relative influence/involvement." Part of the reason for the confusion lies in imprecise definitions. The term has been used in many ways and has undergone several definitional revisions. A consistent theme, however, running through the various definitions is the notion that involvement is a "motivational state of mind that is goal directed" (Zaltman and Wallendorf 1983:550). One indicator of involvement is actual participation in decision situations.[3] The participation component of involvement is the dimension most often referred to in the family literature. In keeping with this spirit, this paper limits the discussion of involvement to actual participation in the decision process.

By defining involvement in participatory terms, the distinction between influence and involvement (participation) becomes quite clear. Influence is a social phenomenon requiring more than one person. In addition, influence is change-oriented. Participation, by contrast, describes the composition of family members who partake in a given decision. There is no necessary definitional between participation and attempts at changing decision outcomes.

The third concept in a decisionmaking strategy is investment. Investment has previously been defined by Davis (1976) as the motivation that a family member has to exert influence. Generally, investment has been described in monetary terms; however, it is equally plausible that one could be highly invested in nonmonetary aspects of decisions (e.g., curfew of children, grades of children). Rather than speaking of investment in the narrow monetary sense, here it is more broadly defined as the perceived loss or gain of valued resources (e.g., economic, social, psychological) that may result from a given decision.

Additional insights into the nature of family decisionmaking may be gained by examining family decisions in a family rather than a dyadic context. Furthermore, we postulate the existence of three distinct concepts that may affect decision processes and outcomes. We have suggested that influence is comprised of two dimensions—direct and indirect. Participation is distinct from influence and refers to desire to partake in decisionmaking. Investment is defined in terms of perceived loss from decision outcomes and can be conceptualized in both monetary and nonmonetary terms. Direct influence, participation, and investment constitute decision-strategy variables. They are termed "strategy variables" since the degree to which they are employed varies with each decision outcome. The next section focuses on the interrelationships among these concepts.

INTERCONSTRUCT RELATIONS

A crucial step in the construction of a theoretical model is to specify how concepts may be related. This section suggests that influence, participation, and investment form a network of decisionmaking strategies for each family member. The next section extends the development to include several family members.

By definition, indirect influences are determined by family structure. In other words family structure can be viewed as a boundary that determines individual family members' decisionmaking strategies. Indirect influence may therefore place limits and constraints on the investment, level of participation, and direct influence attempts of a given family member. Central to this line of reasoning is the assumption that indirect influences are not decision specific but rather are exogenous to the system of variables called strategy variables. Figure 15–1 shows family structure affecting the strategy system.

The position of indirect influence as an exogenous variable suggests that it may have causal implications for the level of investment in a given decision. Two examples illustrate this point. First, consider a situation where a father has sole responsibility for lawn and garden care. Since he is performing this landscaping role, he has a high level of investment (monetary and nonmonetary) in any decision to buy lawn or garden equipment. Consider a second situation where the father is deciding to purchase a flute for his daughter. His role as income earner determines his level of investment (monetary) in the purchase decision. These two examples lead to the first proposition.

Proposition 1: Indirect influence determines the level ôf perceived investment in a given decision.

Figure 15-1. Network of Decisionmaking for a Single Family Member.

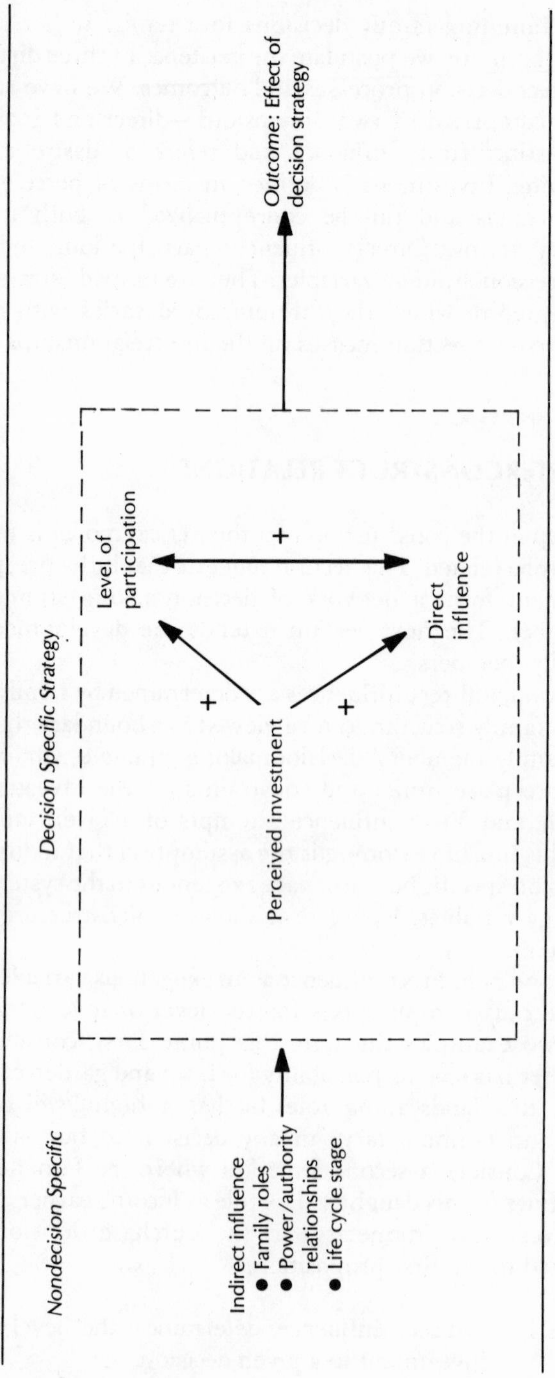

Indirect influence also affects decision participation. In a situation where the mother assumes the role (indirect influence) of family financial officer (Ferber and Lee 1974), it is hypothesized that any financial decision of major consequence will require her participation. In addition to familial role, social class may play an important part in participation. Sheth (1974) has suggested that middle-class families are more likely to plan, discuss, and participate in a decision than lower- or upper-class families because of differences in discretionary income.

Proposition 2:   Indirect influence determines the level of participation in a given decision.

Family roles and social class (indirect forms of influence) also affect individual family members' capacities to directly influence decisions. For example, one would expect general family characteristics such as father's or mother's role as income producer to relate to his or her capacity to alter a given decision.[4]

Proposition 3:   Indirect influence determines the likelihood of direct influence.

As previously discussed, direct influence, participation, and investment refer to situation-specific decision contexts. By defining the concepts in somewhat more precise terms than they have been previously, we are able to construct propositions that are easily testable. The interrelations between these concepts are discussed below.

First, the more a particular family member has to gain or lose from a decision the more likely it is that he or she will participate. For example, in a situation where a child would like to have a new bicycle (high nonmonetary investment), he or she may participate in family conversations, watch television advertisements, and collect information related to the desired product.

Proposition 4:   The greater the perceived investment in a decision, the higher the level of participation.

If an individual family member perceives an investment in the outcome of a decision, he or she may attempt to influence that outcome. To elaborate on the previous example, if a child would like to own a new bike (investment), he or she will probably try to influence the decision to purchase a bike.

Proposition 5:   The greater the perceived investment in a given decision, the greater the level of direct influence.

Typically, the more an individual participates in a decision the more he or she will attempt to influence the final decision. It is possible, however, to be highly involved in a decision yet have very little success with respect to influencing the final decision. Berey and Pollay (1968) found that the children who participated in the decision to buy certain cereals were no more likely to influence the outcome of the decision than those less assertive.

Proposition 6:   Participation is positively related to direct influence attempts.

This section developed a model of family decisionmaking that specifies the interrelationships of four constructs: indirect influence, direct influence, investment, and participation. Each component can be causally related to form a model of family decisionmaking. Note, however, that the discussion has focused only on the interconstruct relationships for a single family member (i.e., how the investment of family member A influences the participation of family member A). The next section extends the model to include the family as the relevant unit of analysis.

NETWORK OF DECISION PROCESSES

The remaining task is to examine the network of decisionmaking processes that exists both within and between family members. The primary goal is to explicate the interrelationships of decision strategies among family members. Hence, discussion centers on the three variables that comprise the decision-specific strategy.

Viewing family decisionmaking as a network of interrelated strategies has several advantages. First, it allows the researcher to test direct and indirect effects of investment, participation, and influence of one family member on the network of decisionmaking strategies of another family member. Thus, one can test the extent to which participation of one family member is related to (or predictive of) participation, investment, and involvement of other family members. Second, by viewing influence in the context of the entire family unit, we can overcome a major criticism of family decisionmaking by explicitly modeling the influence of children (Davis 1970, 1976; Sheth 1974). Third, modeling the decision process in this fashion encompasses a temporal view of family decisionmaking. Family decisionmaking is not static but is a process. A causal framework makes it possible to take a process-oriented perspective on decisionmaking, where several family members reciprocally affect one another over time.

When the model is extended to each family member and takes into account the relationships across family members (e.g., mother's participation predicting father's participation), the testable family network becomes increasingly complex. For example, in a situation where there is a mother and father with no children one would have seven constructs to model.[5] If we were modeling a family of four, thirteen constructs would be necessary. Further complexities arise because the network of decision processes varies depending on the type of family decision, the stage of the decision process (Davis and Rigaux 1974), and the typical styles of family decisionmaking across situations (autonomous versus joint). As a starting point we will decompose the model into its component parts. In the following discussion, various constructs for a given family member are elaborated in terms of their effects on the decision network of other family members.

Indirect Influence

While indirect influence reflects characteristics shared by all family members, it must be recognized that it (1) differentially affects various family members and (2) affects interrelationships between family members. First, indirect influence affects family members' participation in decisions. To illustrate, if it is typical for a single family member to make all decisions related to grocery purchases, it follows that his or her role as family shopper will have an impact on the participation of others within the family. Second, indirect influence of one family member should affect the degree of direct influence among other members. As an example, consider a traditional father who determines the curfew hours of his daughter. His role as authoritarian determines the lack-of-influence attempts by his daughter.

Direct Influence

It is hypothesized that direct influence within the family is a reciprocal process. For example, one family member influences a second family member not to buy product X. In turn, the second family member influences the first family member not to buy product Y. Together they decide to buy product Z. In this situation, influence can be viewed as a reciprocal interactive process between family members.

In addition, direct influence attempts necessarily affect the level of participation and perhaps perceived investment of other family members. Simply trying to overtly change someone's attitude or behavior necessitates their participation.

Perceived Investment

If one family member is highly invested in a decision outcome, he or she may increase the participation of other family members. Others' participation may take the form of a consultant role, as when a child asks a parent for help in buying a first car or for information about birth-control methods.

In addition, the perceived investment of a given family member may affect the investment, participation, and direct influence of other members. This is especially true where the product is to be consumed by the entire family. A child who wants a home computer system may try to involve both siblings and parents. The parents then become involved in the decision and while excited about the prospect of a home computer also are concerned about product cost and quality. At this point, all family members participate in the decision, all have some investment in the decision outcome, and all reciprocally influence one another, having an interactive effect on the ultimate decision outcome.

Participation

If a family member is participating in a given decision, it is hypothesized that he or she may try to involve other family members in the process. For example, a mother considering a new-car purchase may include other family members. If other family members do participate, it is possible that they may have some degree of direct influence.

It is also possible for participation of one family member to affect the direct influence of another family member. For example, a sixteen-year-old may want to purchase a used car. However, when the parent is consulted for help in paying for the vehicle, the parent immediately rejects the idea. In this respect, the parent's participation is minimal, but his or her influence in the final outcome is considerable.

Finally, the participation of a family member may affect the level of investment of other family members. In the home computer example, participation by the children may bring new issues to light, thereby changing investment of other members of the family. To summarize, family decisionmaking is a complex process that requires measuring several constructs that comprise decision strategy, participation, investment, and influence. Moreover, it is hypothesized that these constructs are interrelated both within and between family members.

METHODOLOGICAL CONSIDERATIONS

In order to model the type of family decision structure we propose, several methodological considerations must be addressed. First, it is important to recognize that accurate representations of constructs require that several indicators of constructs be implemented. In other words, it is inappropriate to use a single measure to assess any of the concepts. This is particularly true of the indirect-influence construct. Components of indirect influence (e.g., role structure, social structure, life cycle stage) require measures that accurately reflect family characteristics and social structural dimensions. In order to maintain a degree of construct validity, the use of multiple measures is necessary.

Second, family decisionmaking can best be understood from a process-oriented view and requires an analysis method that is capable of modeling reciprocal relationships. The most appropriate technique for analysis appears to be a structural equation methodology such as LISREL (Bagozzi 1980; Joreskog and Sorbom 1979). From a measurement perspective, LISREL allows one to theoretically build reliable and valid constructs to measure the relevant dimensions. It therefore establishes some degree of construct validity. Structurally, LISREL enables one to assess both direct and reciprocal relationships within and between family members.

Third, the proposed framework is most informative if data on all family members is available. More recent research concerning the reliability and validity of key informant data in organizations suggests that reliance on individual data at best provides mixed conclusions (John and Reve 1982) and at worst provides inaccurate results (Phillips 1981). Similar conclusions can be drawn in a family context. The analysis of group decision processes, either in an organizational or family environment, is most accurate if the interconstruct relations between all relevant members are considered.

Finally, as a starting point in this type of it research it is recommended that families of the same size be studied (e.g., family of four). The methodological problems associated with trying to model different-sized decisionmaking units has been addressed in another context (Bagozzi and Phillips 1982; Phillips 1981). Since we currently do not know how interrelationships between participation, investment, and influence exist between family members, it seems most appropriate to study families of a fixed size before attempting to assess the influence of smaller and larger family units.

IMPLICATIONS FOR MARKETING

The implications of this theory extend beyond family decisionmaking to both group decisionmaking and organizational buying behavior. Most past research has been outcome- rather than process-oriented. Furthermore, only direct effects have been tested. Possible indirect relationships bearing on decision processes and outcomes have been ignored. To use the ANOVA analogy, if second-order effects are found, then the focus should be on interaction terms. In a similar way, the key individuals who influence and participate in group decisions may not directly affect decision processes and outcomes. Influence, investment, and participation in an interactive framework may provide a more accurate description of decision processes and insights into the nature of decision outcomes.

To extend this argument to a specific example in family decisionmaking, we would hypothesize that advertising should not be directed only at the dominant individual, even in situations where one family member appears to be dominant (e.g., husband's influence on car purchase). To the extent that we have failed to model possible interaction effects, we have failed to specify the possible pathways of influence. In a situation where the dominant individual's influence is mediated entirely by other family members, it suggests that the marketing effort should be directed toward less dominant family members as well.

Extensions

Interestingly, work to date has not focused on how or whether relationships between family members change over time. For example, one may hypothesize that offspring influence increases proportionally with age. Thus, when offspring reach, say, age 20, the relationships between participation, investment, and influence between family members may be very different from what they were at age 15. Several factors may be responsible for these changes. One possibility is that social structural characteristics change over time. For example, as children grow older and move into their adult years it is likely that the power of family members changes. A second possibility is that the relationships between the four constructs themselves change over time.

Within the present framework, however, longitudinal assessments on interconstruct changes can be made. One may, for example, sample families at various stages of the life cycle and apply a multigroup option in LISREL (Joreskog and Sorbom 1978). In constructing such a model one could test whether the measured construct relationships change over time (i.e., participation relationship for an individual at age 13 is different for the participation relationship for the same individual at age 20). Furthermore, one could test whether the structural coefficients themselves change over time.

A second advantage of this type of model is that it helps to explain how influence may be related across a host of product decisions. Including different family decisions helps the researcher to begin to model the interrelationships between decisions. To what extent does participation in one type of family decision relate to participation in a second type of decision? Davis (1970) has offered some insight into this area, yet this proposed type of modeling would highlight connections between family members.

CONCLUSIONS

In sum, family decisionmaking is a complex phenomena that cannot be understood from a relative influence perspective. If the proposed theoretical model is correct, it follows that relative influence models have both misspecified and underestimated the total effect of influence taking place in family decisions. By beginning to specify the components of the family decisionmaking system we hope to stimulate research toward more developed models of family decisionmaking.

NOTES

1. Alternative frameworks have been offered to understand decisionmaking in the family (Filiatrault and Ritchie 1980; Park 1982).

2. In part, this exclusion may be related to the operationalization of the relative influence as a measure of influence between two individuals. To extend the analysis to more than two individuals requires comparisons between each possible combination of two family members (e.g., in a family of four there would be six comparisons). As the number of analyses increases, the findings become increasingly cumbersome to interpret. Therefore, one might hypothesize that the failure to develop adequate models for incorporating the influence of children may be related to an overreliance on the concept of relative influence.

3. Note that participation is only one aspect of involvement. Though an individual who participates in a decision is involved, it is not necessarily true that one who is psychologically involved participates. Children, for example, may be emotionally involved in the decision of a family vacation but lack the status for participating. Restricting involvement to participation is more precise.

4. To extend this argument one step further, it is likely that the relationship between indirect influence and direct influence is mediated by the father's investment in the decision. For example, if a father assumes a role of disciplinarian in raising the children (indirect influence), it is likely that he will have an investment in setting curfew hours. If the children ignore curfew hours, then he may exert influence.

5. Indirect influence pertains to all family members. The three variables that form decision-specific strategies for each family member would have to be measured independently.

16 THE VALUE STRUCTURE MAP
A New Analytic Framework For Family Decisionmaking

Jonathan Gutman, Thomas J. Reynolds, and John A. Fiedler

Although most research on consumer decisionmaking has ignored the family as a decisionmaking unit (Davis 1976), studies have been done that show male versus female influence for several types of economic decisions (Starch and staff 1958; Nowland & Company 1964, 1965; Haley, Overholser & Associates 1975). In addition research on family decisionmaking in the durable-goods category has been undertaken for several types of products (home buying by Davis and Rigaux 1974 and Hempel 1974; automobile and home furnishings purchasing by Green and Cunningham 1975 and Davis 1970). With few exceptions, even studies focusing on male versus female influence on family buying decisions have not investigated why some product category decisions are dominated by men whereas others are dominated by women (Davis 1976).

Consideration of this research question requires analyzing the role and influence of family members within the decisionmaking process. In this case, role structure refers to the behavior of family members at each stage of the decisionmaking process. Influence becomes the net result of the roles and is of fundamental importance to the marketing executive. Role structures, then, must be considered in the design and implementation of key marketing decisions such as the design and packaging of products, the selection of the types of retail outlets handling the product, media strategies, and creative strategies (Engel, Blackwell, and Kollat 1978: 151).

Various hypotheses have been put forth to explain the nature of family

279

role structures. One explanation of this process relies on cultural role expectations, another on comparative resources, and a third on relative investment. Davis (1976) makes two distinctions between the last two explanations: Resources define the potential to exert influence, while investment relates to a family member's motivation to exert influence. Additionally, relative investment relates to predictions about the involvement of family members with specific decisions rather than with the general authority structure of the family.

Thus, it is reasonable to expect that motivation to exert influence should be related to the impact of the consequences flowing from the decision. Given that the importance of consequences is related to their instrumentality in moving an individual toward or away from important values (Gutman 1982), a family decision's effect on personal values may be seen to create the key link of involvement with the decisionmaking process. Research that is directed at gaining an understanding of the relation of consequences and their subsequent relation to values with respect to family decisionmaking would appear to provide a framework for study in this area.

One of the underlying concepts relating consequences to instrumental values is that of knowledge structures in memory. Such structures encompass beliefs, attitudes, intentions, emotions, feelings, values, images, moods, representations of tastes and smells, and motor actions.

Of direct interest, then, is ascertaining what the contents of memory are in terms of how they might affect the decisionmaking process, particularly with respect to consequences and relevant values. In addition to contents of memory, aspects of structure or linkages between content elements are of concern—that is, we need to understand the basis for the linkages or associations between specific concepts (e.g., the types of associations that consumers make between a specific attribute of a product or service and the positive consequences or benefits implied by that attribute). This is of singular importance because any solitary attribute representation has no meaning. An attribute's meaning is defined only by the concepts with which it is associated—namely, the more personal associations including benefits. Thus, content of memory cannot be studied independently of structure of memory. Content may be seen to be revealed through structure and vice versa.

This paper discusses knowledge structures with particular emphasis on consequences and personal values. This approach is often referred to as means/end chain analysis (Gutman 1982). As a contribution to research in this area, the background of the means/end chain approach is discussed and an application bearing on family decisionmaking is presented.

MEANS/END CHAIN THEORY

The means/end orientation suggests that linkages between product attributes, consequences produced through consumption, and personal values of consumers underlie decisionmaking processes. The "means" can be thought of as products or services, and the "ends" as values important to consumers. The means/end chain theory seeks to explain how an individual's selection of a product or service enables him or her to achieve desired end states. Such a framework consists of elements that represent the major consumer processes that link values to behavior.

Two assumptions underlie the model: (1) All consumer actions have consequences, and (2) all consumers learn to associate particular consequences with particular actions. Consequences accrue to people from consuming products or services and may be desirable (benefits) or undesirable. They may occur directly from consuming the product or indirectly at a later point in time or from others' reactions to an individual's consumption behavior. The central aspect of the model is that consumers choose actions that produce desired consequences and minimize undesired consequences.

"Values" are held to provide consequences with their positive or negative valences. Values are important beliefs that people hold about their views of themselves and about their feelings concerning others' beliefs about them. Therefore, it is important that the research procedure determine relevant values and consequences and the relations between them. Of course, the attributes that products or services possess must be considered, since it is the attributes that produce the consequences. In addition, attribute/consequence relations play a role in decision behavior.

Overall, it is the attribute/consequence/value interrelations that are the focus of the model and subsequent research. Values provide the direction, consequences select specific behaviors in specific situations, and attributes are product characteristics that result in the consequences. As consumers have different values, they also will have different means/end chains headed by these different values. Knowledge of this structure permits us to examine the structure underlying consumer decision processes.

Identifying the Content and Organization of Cognitive Structure

The discussion now turns to procedures for ascertaining knowledge of consumers' "ways of thinking" or cognitive structures necessary for understanding their decision processes. Several such schemes have been developed (Young and Feigin 1975; Howard 1977; Gutman and Reynolds 1979; Gutman 1982; Olson and Reynolds 1983). The scheme developed here is based on the work of Gutman (1982) and Olson and Reynolds (1983). It includes the following levels for categorizing the contents of consumers' cognitive structures.

Level of Abstraction
Abstract   Terminal values
               Instrumental values
               Psychosocial consequences
               Functional consequences
               Abstract attributes
Concrete   Concrete attributes

Attributes have been divided into concrete and abstract levels because it is necessary to distinguish between aspects that are literally part of a product or service (salt in a food product) and those that are attributed to a product because of those attributes (strong flavor). At the consequence level, a distinction has been made between functional and psychosocial consequences to separate those consequences accruing directly to the consumer from having, for example, "styled hair" (i.e., romance, promotion, etc.). At the values level, instrumental values (i.e., self-confidence) have been distinguished from terminal values (i.e., security).

Procedures for Studying Cognitive Structure

The procedure for gathering data to reveal consumers' cognitive structures is to give respondents simple tasks involving the competitive product or service class. Subjects are required to verbalize the salient concepts or distinctions they use to differentiate among these types of products or service providers. However, it is not these elements by themselves that are of primary importance (for this would be similar to typical qualitative research). Rather, the linkages among these and other elements in consumers' cognitive structure lead to developing an understanding of the total perceptual framework.

To identify the full set of linkages connecting means to ends, consumers are given a laddering task (Gutman and Reynolds 1979; Reynolds 1982; Reynolds and Gutman, in press). Laddering consists of a series of directed probes based on mentioned distinctions that the individual has with respect to the competitive service class. The purpose of the laddering is to force the consumer up the "ladder of abstraction" in order to uncover the structural aspects of consumer knowledge as modeled by the means/end chain.

The first step in analyzing the large number of laddering responses is to conduct a thorough content analysis of all the elicited concepts. Then, each thought or response from each subject is assigned a category code. All laddering responses are now expressed in a set of standard concepts. This aggregate set represents the content component of the consumers' knowledge structures.

What remains is to identify the linkages between the concepts: the arcs of the network model. We begin by constructing a square matrix in which the rows and columns are denoted by the concept codes developed in the content analysis. The unit of analysis is an "adjacent" pair of concepts: a linked pair of responses from the laddering task. That is, whenever the row concept was the probe stimulus that elicited the column concept, an entry is made into that cell. Thus, the total entries in any cell of the matrix correspond to the number of times (across all subjects) that particular concept (row) directly elicited the other concept (column). It is from these data that the overall structure map of means/end relations relating to the product or service category usage is determined (Olson and Reynolds 1983). This completes the development of the aggregate value structure representation of consumers' knowledge structures. Each branch, then, represents a construct or perceptual point of view identifying a segment of the market.

ILLUSTRATIVE EXAMPLE

To illustrate these concepts and procedures, results of a research project done on the convenience restaurant category will be drawn on. The purpose of this research was to develop strategic advertising options for the convenience restaurant category following the framework of Olson and Reynolds (1983). To accomplish this required identification of the aggregate value-structure map and of consumer demographic groups of particular interest. Specifically, analysis by males, by females, and by families with and without children will demonstrate the applicability of this approach to the study of family decisionmaking.

Respondents in this study were first queried as to the situations in which they would be most likely to patronize fast-food restaurants. They then were asked to consider the similarities and differences among sets of three fast-food restaurants for these given situations. The analysis is based on thirty-nine respondents each providing three to five sets of hierarchically related perceptual constructs (ladders) that represent the ways these respondents think about fast-food restaurants. The aggregate analysis of these perceptual constructs, then, is based on 165 ladders representing over 400 "pairwise" connections or associations between attributes, consequences, and values. The total structure represents a perceptual framework referred to as a value-structure map, which corresponds to the salient points of view held by consumers.

Results

Figures 16-1 and 16-2 show the value-structure maps for men and women respectively. The maps have been constructed so that the elements at the bottom (the attribute level) lead to elements at the middle level (the benefit

Figure 16—1. Value Structure Map for Men.

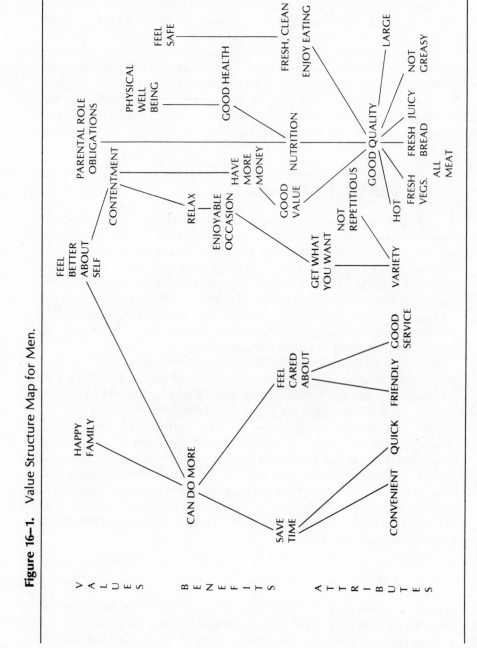

Figure 16–2. Value Structure Map for Women.

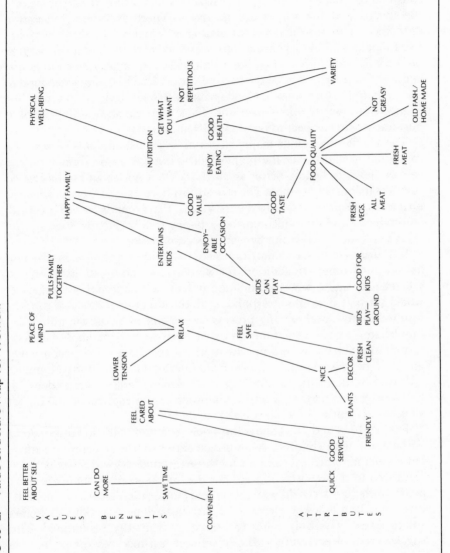

level). These benefits, in turn, lead to the elements at the top of the map (the values level).

Any pathway or linkage from bottom to top represents a hierarchical construct or ladder—in effect, a means/end chain, where the attributes are the means and the values are the ends. There are some interesting differences between the maps for males and females. The men's map has two fundamental blocks of relations connected at the values level. Service, on the left, leads to "can do more," which leads to values related to family and self. On the right, good quality and variety lead to contentment and to feeling better about the self. Good quality also leads to nutrition, which is connected to family role obligations. Thus, the men show a high level of nurturance with respect to fast-food restaurants.

The women have four major blocks of relations, only one of which is connected to another at the higher values level. "Can do more," for the women, leads to feeling better about the self but not about family-related values as it does for the men. The nice atmosphere leads to "relax," which in turn leads to self- and family-related values. Playgrounds lead to occupied, entertained children, which creates a happy family. Finally, food quality leads to physical well-being by way of good nutrition.

It is curious to note that nutrition leads to family role obligations for men but not for women. In addition, for women, "can do more" leads only to self-related values, whereas for men it leads to family-related values. It would seem as if women, responding to the situational mode of thought fostered by the interviewing process, are telling us about the utilitarian, immediate "problem solution" way they have of thinking about fast-food restaurants. Since many women are mothers, they have to keep themselves going: If they can maintain themselves, they can take care of their families.

It is also interesting to note that in both maps "enjoy eating" does not lead to higher values. This relation between eating enjoyment and higher values is evidently not as strong as it could be.

Figures 16–3 and 16–4 show the value-structure maps for respondents without and with children. As might be expected, the structural relations among elements are less complex for those respondents without children as compared to those with children. For the "no kids" map, there are three blocks of elements: can do more, relax, and food quality/taste. For the "kids" map, nutrition is a key element leading in various directions to higher values levels. The only route to "relax" is from the playground. This suggests that opportunities exist to connect fast-food restaurant features other than playground to "relax" and upward to higher levels.

Analysis

As mentioned previously, the branches of the value-structure map "trees" may be interpreted as perceptual points of view. Thus, each hierarchy can be

Figure 16-3. Value Structure Map for "No Kids."

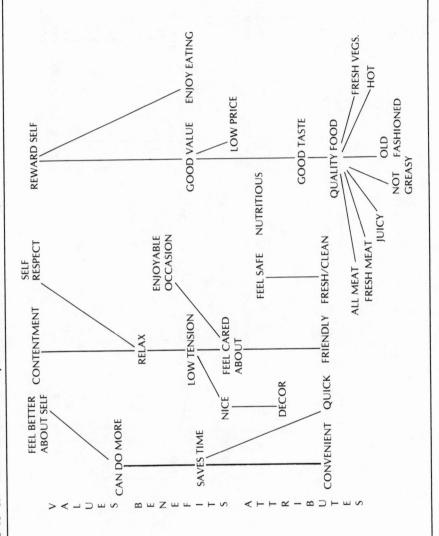

Figure 16–4. Value Structure Map for "Kids."

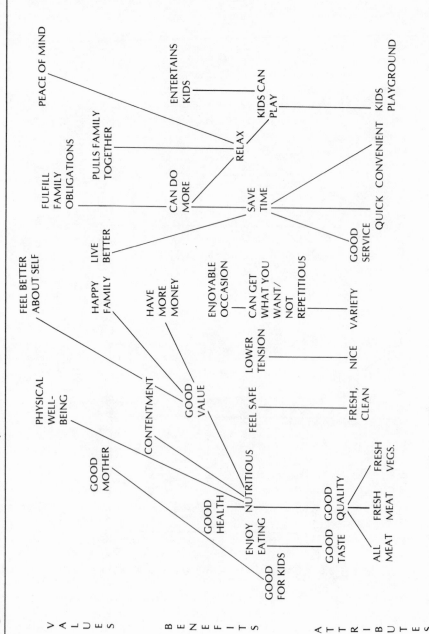

traced up the levels of abstraction to provide substantial understanding of the underlying motivations of a segment of consumers. Of course, the size of the segment is unknown but may be identified in subsequent quantitative field work.

Of primary importance in this analysis, then, are the perceptual segments that may be identified within these broad demographic breakdowns. Furthermore, following from the original interest of this research, advertising strategies can be developed that are targeted specifically to the motivations of a designated segment. This is of particular importance in this kind of product category where the alternatives are so highly interchangeable.

The development of strategies basically follows a three-step format. First, as demonstrated, the value-structure maps are drawn. Second, differences across levels are summarized for the key demographics. These differences serve as the basis for identifying strategic opportunities, particularly with reference to identifying gaps in terms of content or structure (linkages to a higher level). Finally, competitive advertising can be reviewed with respect to the constructs identified in the value-structure maps. The comparison of possible strategic options to those currently in place in the marketplace allows management a clear choice from among the remaining options.

Further, in this case as with many other decisions, the decision to patronize a fast-food restaurant is often a family decision. Analysis by males and females, and by those with and without children, provides a basis for developing a strategy that is sensitive to the dynamics of the family decisionmaking process. It also follows that such a strategy can address the individual as well as collective needs of the family members. There is evidence in this research to support the notion that the female head of household, when participating in the decision process to select a fast-food restaurant for family dining, feels that the family's happiness rests with her ability to select a fast-food restaurant that will promote family harmony. She is sensitive to the disharmonious effects that quarreling children have on her husband. She feels that she has a major responsibility in this area because of her role as the preparer of food at home. It seems that even though she may play a major role in the decision process, she is planning for overall family harmony rather than her own desires. The male is less apt to think consciously about social relations among family members and is more likely to focus on quality and nutrition considerations in his role as a father.

When eating with her children during the day, the woman's views are much more utilitarian. In this circumstance she is more apt to be concerned with giving herself more leisure time, and occupied children are instrumental in achieving this goal. However, males and females without children find being in an environment with children somewhat disconcerting. Any strategy development must take into account, therefore, not only the family members involved and the way they interact but also the time of day and other pertinent circumstances. This suggests the need for more research that takes these important aspects of family decisionmaking into account.

SUMMARY

In order to develop effective communications, it is essential for researchers to understand consumers and the basis of their decisionmaking strategies. Understanding the perceptual structures that serve as a framework for decisionmaking involves identifying the knowledge structures that consumers hold in memory. From a means/end chain perspective, this requires knowledge of how personal values interrelate with important consequences of behavior to provide the continuing motivational energy necessary to maintain goal-directed behavior over time.

This study of convenience restaurants shows substantial differences across the means/end chains for two important demographic subgroups: males and females (both with and without children). The differences noted here suggest that different knowledge structures are operating in this category and should be considered in the development of any potential strategy. Inherent to this position is the fact that persuasive communications involve more than mere product attributes, a point discussed by Reynolds (1982) in his definition of advertising as "image management."

17 ON BUILDING A TRANSITION-BASED PARADIGM FOR EXAMINING THE CHANGING HOUSEHOLD

James H. Leigh and Claude R. Martin, Jr.

A rich tradition of research centers on the family life cycle and concentrates on product needs and decisionmaking rather than stages of the cycle (e.g., Lansing and Morgan 1955; Wells and Gubar 1966; Wortzel 1977a; Wattenberg 1975). With increased knowledge about changes in family composition and lifestyle, new definitions have been offered (Murphy and Staples 1979). This paper does not continue along that path, nor does it examine behavior in any of the specific stages. Instead, it concentrates on the major transitions that occur over a life cycle, including the key dimensions of those transitions and their effect on decisionmaking and behavior. An alternative exploratory paradigm is presented that complements the existing concepts surrounding family life cycle. This paradigm is conveyed through a set of propositions that set the stage for further research.

CONCEPTUAL BASIS

Individuals carry out daily affairs in a number of different settings that are characterized as places with particular physical features where participants engage in particular activities for particular periods of time (Bronfenbrenner 1977: 514). The most important of these settings involve work and home life, and in each the individual performs explicitly or implicitly defined roles. By assuming the requisite roles and participating in the ongoing activities of these settings, individuals create a certain level of stability. Given that one fundamental goal of perception is the maintenance of environmental and internal stability (Hilgard 1951), familiar settings serve an important perceptual function. In fact, the family or household setting may be considered to be a major stable retreat from the uncertainties and inequities of the external world.

Humans must confront change. At the macro level, the world is constantly changing, and much of it is unknown and unrecognized by the individual. At a level more immediately relevant to the individual there is constant change as well, which can be debilitating without some counterbalancing measure of stability. Of particular importance are major changes that affect how an individual retreats from external threats and that tend to alter the character of the home and work life by inducing shifts in role expectations or setting or both. Bronfenbrenner (1977, 1979) labels these alterations of a person's position with respect to the environment "transitions."

Since families and households tend to operate as units, a transition experienced by one member tends to require at least a minimal concomitant transition by other members and, therefore, by the unit proper.[1] While the impetus for such changes may be exogenous to the family or household setting (e.g., an automobile accident that fatally injures a household member or a company-mandated move of a breadwinner to a position located in a different city), research interest focuses on the internal effects on the family or household.

An example of a change in role without a change in setting is a promotion to a new job position that does not require a change in the job or home setting. Such a change could provoke adaptive behavior, such as the purchase of a new car or new clothes that satisfy the status expectations accompanying the new job. Moreover, the new role may require psychological adaptation. An example of a setting change without a change in role is a family's move across town. Here the transition from one neighborhood to another could provoke a behavioral change (e.g., adapting to shopping for groceries in a new store) and a psychological change (e.g., adjusting to the absence of nearby friends). An example of a concurrent setting and role change transition is a divorce that alters a woman's position from sharing responsibility for raising a child to embracing a single-parent role in a new household setting. This transition requires major behavioral and psychological adaptation.

Most, if not all, of the research on the family life cycle has concentrated on role change and has virtually ignored setting changes. This focus allows for a much narrower designation of the cyclical stages for a family or household, but it ignores transitions that might have even greater relevance for consumer behavior. The concept of family life cycle has been used as a basis for identifying differences in product needs across the various stages and, to some extent, differences in decisionmaking. Including setting and role changes in the research models will help researchers to more clearly and fully understand the complex character of decisionmaking and behavioral adaptation that occurs within families and households over time. Moreover, it is our contention that concurrent changes in both role and setting result in the greatest effect on an individual's behavior and outlook and as a result on the households behavior.

While all three types of transitions are important, the concurrence of role and setting changes leads to our first proposition:

Proposition 1:   The change in role and setting must be viewed as interdependent, and research on the resultant transition must take into account this synergistic effect.[2]

We are essentially proposing that researchers of consumer behavior do not have the luxury of examining only those transitions induced by role changes and thus of ignoring setting changes when they occur. Instead, researchers must take a more complex approach that captures these interdependencies. An example of nonconsumer behavior research that supports this position is that of Hetherington, Cox, and Cox (1976, 1978). These researchers observed that a mother who is placed in the unaccustomed role of being a family head (i.e., as a result of divorce or death of the husband) and who faces a change in setting (i.e., a reduced financial situation requiring a move to smaller quarters) adapts by looking for a job or for a higher-paying job.

The research of Hetherington and her colleagues further identifies a vicious circle for the newly divorced or widowed woman. She must care for the house and children and create a new personal life for herself. In the absence of a father, the children demand more of her attention, but the mother has more tasks to which she must attend. In response, the children become more demanding. The data reveal that, in comparison with youngsters from intact families, the children of divorce are less likely to respond to a mother's requests. This phenomenon emphasizes our second proposition:

Proposition 2:   If one member of a family or household undergoes a transition, the other members also are likely to do so.

These second-order or indirect effects of primary transitions represent a relatively unexplored and scientifically promising terrain for research. It is insufficient to consider only aggregate changes in the family or household unit. Rather, the changes in roles and settings for *each* member must be considered. Ideally, this type of investigation would involve longitudinal study in which the transitions encountered by each participant are examined so that the effect of one member's transition on the other members may be explicitly explored.

Matters become more complex when more than one household or family unit is involved. For example, divorce and remarriage are likely to affect the participants of both the former and newly formed units. Moreover, indirect carryover effects from participants of one unit that involve the other should be isolated and controlled in order to make a clear assessment of the direct impact of the primary transition. Longitudinal study of both units is required. Further, an adequate cross-section of possible household scenarios is necessary, such as divorce and remarriage within one year versus a longer period, children versus no children, and so forth. The scope of such an investigation is well beyond present research knowledge, yet it should serve as a reminder of the direction in which research should progress and of the complexities involved in examining the changing household.

Whereas our first two propositions are general in scope and are relevant to research operationalization, the remaining propositions center on specific transition-related issues. They focus on transitions prompted by changes in role, setting, or in both role and setting, as well as on important individual difference factors.

A change from a familiar work or home setting to a new, unfamiliar one is likely to require major adaptation on the part of an individual. He or she must adjust to the new setting and at the same time adapt to the loss of stability that was provided by the previous setting. Furthermore, a change in the primary home setting is often accompanied by change in other settings as well, such as those involving shopping, recreation, and worship. This multiple-setting change can compound the problem of adjustment. Given that major setting transitions will, in all likelihood, require considerable adaptation and extend over a period of time, the question arises as to what factors will serve to reduce the extent of the adaptation necessary. Proposition 3 involves one such aspect:

Proposition 3:   Behavioral and psychological adaptation are enhanced if setting change is participated in by several members of the household or family rather than by an individual in isolation.

This proposition rests on the assumption that only the setting changes, not the roles. In the case of a family or household that moves to a new neighborhood and confronts a new grocery shopping setting, adaptation should be easier if a husband and wife normally share the shopping role. Transferral of familiar components from the prior to the new setting provides a degree of stability and commonality of purpose, even in the face of the adversity and doubt that accompany introduction to the new setting.

One way to ensure stability and enhance stability is for change to be jointly confronted by more than one member of a family or household. Another way is through role congruence across settings:

Proposition 4:   Behavioral and psychological adaptation are enhanced if the roles in the different settings remain the same.

Role transferral from one setting to another minimizes the amount of new learning that must occur in order to become adjusted to the new setting. Applying previously acquired role skills is stabilizing in itself, yet it also means that only a setting-orienting phase is necessary for successful adaptation. While new settings often imply new setting participants will be met that may not respond predictably (e.g., as encountered by a manager who moves laterally from one office environment to another), they do not necessarily require new role definitions. It is one thing to adapt an existing role to a new setting and quite another to acclimate to a new role structure for a new setting. In relation to propositions 3 and 4, therefore, it is the concurrent change in setting and role that requires the most extensive and lengthy behavioral and psychological adaptation.

While it is reasonable to conclude that role transferral between an old and a new setting enhances adaptation relative to concurrent role and setting change, it is also important to note that some roles should be easier to adapt to than others:

Proposition 5:   Other things being equal, behavioral and psychological adaptation are enhanced if a change in roles results in greater status and responsibility for an individual.

This proposition rests on the assumption that an individual will rise to meet the challenges that accompany a new role that provides greater status, including the acquisition of requisite new skills and perspectives. Because the greater social status afforded by the new role is personally rewarding, psychological and behavioral adaptation should be facilitated.

In addition, it may be proposed that an improvement in the quality of the new setting relative to the old one will enhance adaptation:

Proposition 6:   Behavioral and psychological adaptation are enhanced if the new setting is generally superior or superior in an important detail.

For example, a new shopper is likely to learn more about a store if upon initial comparison he or she determined that the new store excelled in certain attributes. If the positive setting change is accompanied by a positive role change, adaptation should be even more rapid and complete.

A final way that adaptation to a new setting is facilitated relates to the supply of information about aspects of the new setting that are important for the accomplishment of necessary tasks:

Proposition 7:   Behavioral and psychological adaptation to a major change in setting are enhanced to the extent that information is available and accessible prior to and after entering the new setting.

This proposition is particularly relevant to the major transitions that require adaptation to a number of new settings (e.g., when a family or household moves to a different city). Friendly neighbors, helpful fellow employees at work, a new-resident-oriented Chamber of Commerce, and local media are some of the more obvious sources for learning about a new city.

Individual and family or household difference factors, such as prior experience and intelligence, unquestionably moderate or influence the degree to which information about a setting will enhance adaptation. These difference factors also affect the ease of adaptation to a new setting and role structure apart from the moderating role served in information processing. While intelligence is seldom studied in consumer behavior research, experience is important to this discussion because of its major role in the transitions that are undergone in adapting to changes in roles and settings.

Operationalizing the concept of experience would involve specifying several complementary indicators by using individual and household streams of transitions as input. Aggregated and disaggregated measures of each individual and household unit would be formed to allow for consideration of both discrete and cumulative effects on individual and on household processes and results of adaptation. To accomplish this task, there is need to explicitly consider the nature of the transitions experienced in order to form measures that distinguish among transitions that directly correspond, those that are related, and those that are unrelated to subsequent transitions. In this way an understanding of the transfer of learned experiences within and across transition types (as well as individuals) may be obtained. The concept of experience transfer is derived from Hull (1943) on learning theory, by Mandler (1967) on cognitive structure, and by Engel, Blackwell, and Kollat (1978), Howard (1963), and Howard and Sheth (1969) on consumer behavior.

The proposition developed to encompass the range of relevant experience to adaptation follows:

Proposition 7:   Behavioral and psychological adaptation to a change in role or setting by an individual are enhanced:

(a) by the number of transitions previously undergone;

(b) by the extent of transferrable (i.e., related) experiences and by recent experience;

(c) if a directly related (i.e., stimulus as opposed to response transfer) transition has been experienced within a time period recent enough to be remembered and used; and

(d) by the number of transition experiences involving concurrent role and setting change.

While the greatest impact results if the adapting individual experiences the transitions directly, the possible communication of experience between household or family members cannot be assumed unimportant or nonexistent.

It is reasonable to assume that as experiences build in number and scope, the incremental benefit of an additional transition tends toward zero. Moreover, the slope of the respective learning curve is conditioned by the nature of the transitions encountered and by the composition of the experiencing unit (i.e., an individual, dyad, or entire family or household). Because of the importance and the idiosyncratic nature of such experience, transitions previously undergone both by household members and by the household unit should be essential ingredients in research into the effects of transitions on behavior.

DISCUSSION

These seven propositions form the core from which hypotheses relating to family or household behavior in specific contexts may be derived. The discussion has purposely been kept at a general level in order to be as encompassing as possible. While there is a risk of oversimplification in such an approach, we believe that sufficient substance is given from which research can be operationalized. Toward that end, two remaining topics must be addressed—the nature of adaptation and the aspects of consumer behavior that might be affected by an adapting, changing household—

before attention is directed to relating the ideas presented in this paper to the study of family and household change.

The distinction between behavioral and psychological adaptation is a functional one: Psychological adaptation refers to internal stabilizing adjustments made to improve perspective as a result of some destabilizing stimulus, such as a change in role or setting, whereas behavioral adaptation refers to adjustments made in external, overt responses. This distinction is important because psychological adaptation has an effect on the basic internal processes of an individual (i.e., perception, mental processing, deliberation, and storage), and as a result it affects behavior and behavioral adaptation as well. Behavioral adaptation, on the other hand, is more restricted in effect but is considered to be the type of adaptation that is of primary relevance to marketers. While marketers should be equally concerned about psychological adaptation to role and setting changes because of its possible effects on decisionmaking and behavior, it is assumed that behavioral adaptation will receive the greatest interest and attention.

In order to demonstrate that adaptation has in fact occurred, it is necessary to determine the point after a transition at which an individual's or household unit's responses become reasonably stabilized. The bases for comparison include (1) unadjusted, individual-specific pretransition levels; (2) individual-specific pretransition levels adjusted for differences in the nature of pretransition responses relative to posttransition responses; (3) general response patterns of others who confronted a similar transition; and (4) responses of individuals who are not newcomers to the new role or setting. Use of one or more of these bases for comparison in conjunction with multiple indicators of posttransition responses will allow for detection of initial destabilized responses resulting from the transition and the return to stability. If pretransition responses are available, the researcher may also assess the effect of the transition. From analyses based on these types of responses, it should be possible to assess differences in the ease and speed of adaptation between contexts and individuals.

While it is difficult to derive specific areas of consumer behavior for a family, household, or individual member that are susceptible to influence from a change in role or setting, several general categories must be identified. In the case of a change in setting, with or without a concurrent role change, the functional areas of information exposure, search, and utilization probably would be altered initially and subject to adaptation. Based on the propositions given, we might expect that a product available in the prior setting would benefit from an initial enhanced effect of information exposure and information cues, although experience with prior transitions could reduce this effect. Decisionmaking would also be affected by a change in setting, as would shopping behavior. A change in role, with or without a change in setting, is likely to affect the nature of individual and family or household demand for products and brands that are required for assumption of the new role or that are commensurate with or symbolic of the new status. Changes in information processing, decision-making, and shopping behavior could also occur, particularly if the new role is shopping-related. While these are only general areas of possible effect, they reinforce the idea that major changes in role or setting can affect virtually all aspects of consumer behavior.

The major weakness in using the transition-based paradigm is that there are literally hundreds of setting, role, and concurrent changes that can be identified and studied. For this reason research should be restricted to the major role and setting changes that are most likely to be confronted by a large cross-section of the population. Moreover, there is strong reason to believe that a minor role or setting change is unlikely to affect consumer behavior if no evidence of effects of major changes is found.

Development of a transition-based view of the changing household will complement progress already made in the examination of family life cycle. The work of Bronfenbrenner (1977, 1979) calls attention to some of the shortcomings of the family life cycle concept and supplements the family-role bias with the added concepts of other roles, of settings, and of transitions. These concepts certainly deserve consideration by researchers who are studying differences between stages of the family life cycle. While certain common life cycle stages are major and worth exploring, it is important to consider the experiences of the participants. Today's families and households typically differ from the traditional modal categories enumerated in the family life cycle concept. While the transition-based perspective will not account for all of these differences, it is preferable to treating disparate groups as similar. In order for marketers to meet the needs of separate families and households there must be a common basis for aggregation and generalization. The transition-based paradigm appears to provide a needed dimension to the family life cycle concept.

NOTES

1. This paper concentrates on the family or household as the participating unit. It should be noted that the comments are also applicable to collectives, a particularly rich area for exploration using the transition-based paradigm enumerated here. The interested reader may wish to consult Leigh and Martin (1982).
2. The propositions given here are derived largely from the work of Bronfenbrenner (1977, 1979).

BIBLIOGRAPHY

Acock, Alan C.; Deborah Barker; and Vern L. Bengston. 1982. "Mother's Employment and Parent-Youth Similarity." *Journal of Marriage and the Family* 44 (May): 441–55.

Acock, Alan C., and John N. Edwards. 1982. "Egalitarian Sex-Role Attitudes and Female Income." *Journal of Marriage and the Family* 44 (August): 581–89.

Advertising Age. 1982. "Videophiles Leading the Way." (June 2): 56.

Albrecht, Stan L.; Howard M. Bahr; and Bruce A. Chadwick. 1979. "Changing Family and Sex Roles: An Assessment of Age Differences." *Journal of Marriage and the Family* 41 (February): 41–50.

Alderson, Wroe. 1965. *Dynamic Marketing Behavior.* Homewood, Ill.: Irwin.

———. 1957. *Marketing Behavior and Executive Action.* Homewood, Ill.: Irwin.

Aldous, Joan. 1982. "From Dual-Earner to Dual-Career Families and Back Again." In *Two Paychecks: Life in Dual-Earner Families,* edited by J. Aldous, pp. 11–26. Beverly Hills, Calif.: Sage.

Allan, Carole B. 1981a. "Measuring Mature Markets." *American Demographics* 3 (March): 13–17.

———. 1981b. "Over 55: Growth Market of the '80s." *Nation's Business* 69 (April): 25–32.

Allen, Chris T., and Charles M. Schaninger. 1980. "Dual Career, Dual Income, and Non-Work Wife Families: Perspectives and Research Directions." In *1980 Educators' Conference Proceedings,* edited by R.P. Bagozzi, K.L. Bernhardt, P.S. Busch, D.W. Cravens, J.F. Hair, Jr., and C.A. Scott, pp. 93–96. Chicago: American Marketing Association.

Allison, Neil K.; Linda L. Golden; Gary M. Mullet; and Donna Coogan. 1980.

"Sex-Typed Product Images: The Effects of Sex, Sex-Role Self-Concept, and Measurement Implications." In *Advances in Consumer Research,* vol. 7, edited by Jerry L. Olson, pp. 604–09. Ann Arbor: Association for Consumer Research.

Angrist, Shirley S.; Judith R. Lave; and Richard Mickelson. 1976. "How Working Mothers Manage: Socioeconomic Differences in Work, Child Care, and Household Tasks." *Social Science Quarterly* 56 (March): 631–37.

Ansoff, H. Igor. 1965. *Corporate Strategy.* New York: McGraw-Hill.

Araji, Sharon. 1977. "Husbands' and Wives' Attitude-Behavior Congruence on Family Roles." *Journal of Marriage and the Family* 39 (May): 309–20.

Aronoff, Joel, and William D. Crano. 1975. "A Re-Examination of the Cross-Cultural Principles of Task Segregation and Sex Role Differentiation in the Family." *American Sociological Review* 40 (February): 12–20.

Assael, Henry. 1981. *Consumer Behavior and Marketing Action.* Boston: Kent.

Atkin, Charles K. 1978. "Observation of Parent-Child Interaction in Supermarket Decision-Making." *Journal of Marketing* 41 (October): 41–45.

Ayres, C.E. 1961. *Toward a Reasonable Society: The Values of Industrial Civilization.* Austin: University of Texas Press.

Bagarozzi, D., and J. Wodarski. 1977. " A Social Exchange Typology of Conjugal Relationships and Conflict Development." *Journal of Marriage and Family Counseling* (October): 53–60.

Bagozzi, Richard P. 1980. *Causal Models in Marketing.* New York: John Wiley and Sons.

Bagozzi, Richard P., and Lynn W. Phillips. 1982. "Representing and Testing Organizational Theories: A Holistic Construal." *Administrative Science Quarterly* 27 (September): 459–89.

Bahr, S.J., and B. Rollins. 1971. "Crisis and Conjugal Power." *Journal of Marriage and the Family* 33 (May): 360–67.

Bailyn, Lottie. 1971. "Career and Family Orientations of Husbands and Wives in Relation to Family Happiness." *Human Relations* 23 (April): 97–113.

Ballweg, J. 1967. "Resolution of Conjugal Role Adjustment after Retirement." *Journal of Marriage and the Family* 29 (May): 277–81.

Bane, Mary Jo. and Robert S. Weiss. 1980. "Alone Together." *American Demographics* 2 (May): 11–15.

Baran, Roger J. 1978. "Patterns of Decision-Making Influence for Selected Products and Services." In *Advances in Consumer Research,* vol: 5, edited by J. Keith Hunt, pp. 129–41. Ann Arbor: Association for Consumer Research.

Barkas, J.L. 1980. *Singles in America.* New York: Atheneum.

Bartos, Rena. 1982. *What Every Marketer Should Know about Women.* New York: Free Press.

———. 1979. "Exploring Mysterious Markets." *American Demographics* 1 (March): 9–17.

———. 1978a. "The Moving Target: The Impact of Women's Employment on Consumer Behavior." *Journal of Marketing* 42, no. 3 (July): 31–37.

———. 1978b. "What Every Marketer Should Know about Women." *Harvard Business Review* 56 (May/June): 73–85.

Baxter, Leslie A., and Tara L. Shepherd. 1978. "Sex-Role Identity, Sex of Other, and Affective Relationship as Determinants of Interpersonal Conflict-Management Styles." *Sex Roles* 4, no. 6 (December): 813–25.

Becker, Gary S. 1976. *The Economic Approach to Human Behavior.* Chicago: University of Chicago Press.

——. 1974. "A Theory of Marriage: Part II." *Journal of Political Economy* 82 (March/April): 911–26.

——. 1973. "A Theory of Marriage: Part I." *Journal of Political Economy* 81 (July/August): 813–46.

——. 1965. "A Theory of the Allocation of Time." *The Economic Journal* 75 (September): 493–517.

Becker, Gary S.; Elizabeth M. Landes; and Robert T. Michael. 1977. "An Economic Analysis of Marital Instability." *Journal of Political Economy* 85, no. 6 (December): 1141–52.

Becker, Gary S., and Robert T. Michael. 1973. "On the New Theory of Consumer Behavior." *Swedish Journal of Economics* 75: 378–95.

Beckman, Linda J., and Betsy Basak Hauser. 1979. "The More You Have, the More You Do: The Relationship between Wife's Employment, Sex-Role Attitudes and Household Behavior." *Psychology of Women Quarterly* 4 no. 2 (Winter): 160–74.

Belch, Michael A.; George E. Belch; and Donald Sciglimpaglia. 1980. "Conflict in Family Decision Making: An Exploratory Investigation." In *Advances in Consumer Research,* vol. 7, edited by Jerry C. Olson, pp. 475–79. Ann Arbor: Association for Consumer Research.

Bell, Carolyn Shaw. 1975. "The Value of Time." *Social Research* 42 (Autumn): 556–63.

Bell, Daniel. 1981. "The Social Framework of Information Society." In *The Computer Age: A Twenty Year Review,* edited by Michael L. and Joel Moses, pp. 163–211. Cambridge: MIT Press.

——. 1979. "Communications Technology—For Better or for Worse." *Harvard Business Review* 57 (May/June): 20–41.

——. 1975. *The Coming of the Post-Industrial Society.* New York: Basic Books.

Bem, Sandra L. 1981. "Gender Schema Theory: A Cognitive Account of Sex Typing." *Psychological Review* 88 (July): 354–64.

Benton & Bowles. 1980. "Men's Changing Role in the Family of the '80s." New York.

Berey, L.A., and R.W. Pollay. 1968. "The Influencing Role of Children in Family Decision Making." *Journal of Marketing Research* 5 (February): 70–72.

Berheide, C.; S. Berk; and R. Berk. 1976. "Household Work in the Suburbs: The Job and Its Participants." *Pacific Sociological Review* 19 (October): 491–517.

Berk, R.A., and S.F. Berk. 1979. *Labor and Leisure at Home.* Beverly Hills, Calif.: Sage.

——. 1978. "A Simultaneous Equation Model for the Division of Household Labor." *Sociological Methods and Research* 6 (May): 431–68.

Berk, S., and A. Shih. 1980. "Contributions to Household Labor: Comparing Wives' and Husbands' Reports." In *Women and Household Labor,* edited by Sarah F. Berk, pp. 191–227. Beverly Hills, Calif.: Sage.

Bernhardt, K.L. 1975. "Husband and Wife Influence in the Purchase Decision Processes for Houses." Ph.D. dissertation, University of Michigan.

Berry, Leonard L. 1979. "The Time-Buying Consumer." *Journal of Retailing* 55 (Winter): 58–69.

Bettman, James R. 1979. *An Information Processing Theory of Consumer Choice.*

Reading, Mass.: Addison-Wesley.

Bianchi, Suzanne M., and Reynolds Farley. 1980. "Racial Differences in Family Living Arrangements and Economic Well-Being: An Analysis of Recent Trends." *Journal of Marriage and the Family* 41 (August): 537–51.

Billings, Andrew, 1979. "Conflict Resolution in Distressed and Non-distressed Married Couples." *Journal of Consulting and Clinical Psychology* 47, no. 2 (March/April): 368–76.

Bird, Caroline. 1979. *The Two Paycheck Marriage.* New York: Pocket Books.

Blake, J. 1979. "Is Zero Preferred? American Attitudes toward Childlessness in the 1970s." *Journal of Marriage and the Family* 41 (May): 245–57.

———. 1976. "Can We Believe Recent Data on Birth Expectations in the United States?" *Demography* 11 (February): 25–44.

Blood, R.P. 1960. "Resolving Family Conflicts." *Journal of Conflict Resolution* 4, no. 2 (June): 209–19.

Blood, R.P., and D.M. Wolfe. 1960. *Husbands and Wives: The Dynamics of Married Living.* Glencoe, Ill.: Free Press.

Bomball, Mark R.; Walter J. Primeaux; and Donald E. Pursell. 1975. "Forecasting Stage 2 of the Family Life Cycle." *Journal of Business* 48 (January): 65–73.

Bonfield, E.H. 1978. "Perception of Marital Roles in Decision Processes: Application and Extension." In *Advances in Consumer Research,* vol. 5, edited by H. Keith Hunt, pp. 300–07. Ann Arbor: Association for Consumer Research.

Booth, Alan, and Susan Welch. 1978. "Spousal Consensus and Its Correlates: A Reassessment." *Journal of Marriage and the Family* 40 (February): 23–32.

Borland, Dolores C. 1982. "A Cohort Analysis Approach to the Empty-Nest Syndrome among Three Ethnic Groups of Women: A Theoretical Position." *Journal of Marriage and the Family* 44 (February): 117–29.

Brogan, Donna, and Nancy G. Kutner. 1976. Measuring Sex-Role Orientation: A Normative Approach." *Journal of Marriage and the Family* 38 (February): 31–40.

Bronfenbrenner, Urie. 1979. *The Ecology of Human Development: Experiments by Nature and Design.* Cambridge, Mass.: Harvard University Press.

———. 1977. "Toward an Experimental Ecology of Human Development." *American Psychologist* 32 (July): 513–31.

Brown, Prudence; Lorraine Perry; Ernest Harburg. 1977. "Sex Role Attitudes and Psychological Outcomes for Black and White Women Experiencing Marital Dissolution." *Journal of Marriage and the Family* 39 (August): 549–61.

Bumpass, Larry L., and James A. Sweet. 1972. "Differentials in Marital Instability: 1970." *American Sociological Review* 32 (December): 754–66.

Bureau of Advertising. 1972. *The Working Women.* (April).

Burgess, E.W., and H.J. Locke. 1960. *The Family: From Institution to Companionship.* 2d ed. New York: American Book.

Burns, Alvin C. 1977. "Husband and Wife Purchase-Decision Making Roles: Agreed, Presumed, Conceded, and Disputed." In *Advances in Consumer Research,* Vol. 4, edited by William D. Perreault, Jr., pp. 50–55. Atlanta: Association for Consumer Research.

———. 1976. "Spousal Involvement and Empathy in Jointly-Resolved and Authoritatively-Resolved Purchase Subdecisions." In *Advances in Consumer Research,* vol. 3, edited by Beverlee B. Anderson, pp. 199–206. Ann Arbor: Association for Consumer Research.

Burns, Alvin C., and Donald H. Granbois. 1980. "Advancing the Study of Family Purchase Decision Making." In *Advances in Consumer Research,* vol. 7, edited by Jerry Olson, pp. 221-26. Ann Arbor: Association for Consumer Research.

————. 1977. "Factors Moderating the Resolution of Preference Conflict in Family Automobile Purchasing." *Journal of Marketing Research* 14 (February): 77-86.

Burr, Wesley R. 1973. *Theory Construction and the Sociology of Family.* New York: John Wiley.

Burr, Wesley R.; Rueben Hill; Ivan Nye; and Ira L. Reiss, eds. 1979. *Contemporary Theories about the Family.* New York: Free Press.

Burr, Wesley R.; Geoffrey K. Leigh; Randall D. Day; and John Constantine. 1979. "Symbolic Interaction and the Family." In *Contemporary Theories about the Family,* edited by Wesley R. Burr, Reuben Hill, Ivan Nye, and Ira L. Reiss, pp. 42-111. New York: Free Press.

Business Week. 1981. "Computer Stores: Tantalizing Opportunity Selling Computers to Consumers." no. 2704 (September 28): 76-81.

Buss, W.C., and C. Schaninger. 1982. "The Influence of Sex Roles on Family Decision Processes and Outcomes." In *Advances in Consumer Research,* vol. 10, edited by Alice Tybout and Richard Bagozzi, pp. 439-44. Ann Arbor: Association for Consumer Research.

Cacioppo, John T.; Richard E. Petty; and Joseph A. Sidera. 1982. "The Effects of a Salient Self-Schema on the Evaluation of Pro-attitudinal Editorials: Top-Down versus Bottom-Up Message Processing." *Journal of Experimental Social Psychology* 18 (July): 324-38.

Cambell, F.L. 1970. "Family Growth and Variation in Family Role Structures." *Journal of Marriage and the Family* 32 (February): 45-52.

Campbell, Donald T., and Donald W. Fiske. 1959. "Convergent and Discriminant Validation by the Multitrait-Multimethod Matrix." *Psychological Bulletin* 56 (March): 81-105.

Candler, Julie. 1981. "A Drive for Recognition." *Advertising Age* 52 (June 22): S24-S26.

Carlson, Allan C. 1980. "The Nuclear Family Is Splitting." *Across the Board* 17 (June): 70-79.

Cartwright, Dorwin. 1965. "Influence, Leadership, Control." In *Handbook of Organizations,* edited by James G. March, pp. 1-47. Chicago: Rand-McNally.

Centers, Richard; Bertram H. Raven; and H. Rodrigues. 1971. "Conjugal Power Structure: A Re-Examination." *American Sociological Review* 36 (April): 264-78.

Chadwick, Bruce A.: Stan L. Albrecht; and Philip R. Kunz. 1976. "Marital and Family Role Satisfaction." *Journal of Marriage and the Family* 38 (August): 431-40.

Cherlin, Andrew. 1977. "The Effect of Children on Marital Dissolution." *Demography* 14, no. 3 (August): 265-72.

Cherlin, Andrew, and Frank F. Furstenberg, Jr. 1982. *The Shape of the American Family in the Year 2,000.* Washington, D.C.: American Council of Life Insurance.

Cherlin, Andrew, and Pamela B. Walters. 1981. "Trends in United States Men's and

Women's Sex-Role Attitudes: 1972–1978." *American Sociological Review* 46 (August): 453–60.

Chesler, Mark A.; James E. Crowfoot; and Bunyan I. Bryant. 1978. "Power Training: An Alternative Path to Conflict Management." *California Management Review* 21 (Winter): 84–90.

Clark, Robert A.; F.I. Van Nye; and Viktor Gecas. 1978. "Work Involvement and Marital Role Performance." *Journal of Marriage and the Family* 40 (February): 9–21.

Cohen, Carolyn B. 1982. "The Kid, The Apple and Me," *Popular Computing* vol. 6 no. 1: 78–80.

Cohen, Dorothy. 1981. *Consumer Behavior.* New York: Random House.

Coleman, James S. 1966. "Foundations for a Theory of Collective Decisions." *The American Journal of Sociology* 71 (May): 615–27.

Cooney, Rosemary S.; Lloyd H. Rogler; Rose Marie Hurrell; and Vilma Ortiz. 1982. "Decision Making in Intergenerational Puerto Rican Families." *Journal of Marriage and the Family* 44 (August): 621–31.

Cosenza, Robert M. 1982. "A General Paradigm of Dominance in Family Purchase Decision Making." Working paper, McLaren College of Business, University of San Francisco.

Cottle, Thomas J. 1976. *Perceiving Time: A Psychological Investigation with Men and Women.* New York: John Wiley and Sons.

Courtney, Alice E., and Thomas W. Whipple. 1980. "Sex Stereotyping in Advertising: An Annotated Bibliography." Cambridge, Mass.: Marketing Science Institute, Report No. 80–100.

———. 1974. "Women in TV Commercials." *Journal of Communication* 24 (Spring): 110–18.

Cowan, Ruth S. 1976. "The Industrial Revolution in the Home: Household Technology and Social Change in the 20th Century." *Technology and Culture* 17 (January): 1–23.

Cox III, Eli P. 1975. "Family Purchase Decision Making and the Process of Adjustment." *Journal of Marketing Research* 12 (May): 189–95.

Cox, William A. 1981. "Changing Consumption Patterns." *American Demographics* 3 (May): 18–19.

Craddock, Alan E. 1980. "Marital Problem-Solving as a Function of Couples' Marital Power Expectations and Marital Value Systems." *Journal of Marriage and the Family* 42 (February): 185–96.

Crano, William D., and Joel Aronoff. 1978. "A Cross-Cultural Study of Expressive and Instrumental Role Complementarity in the Family." *American Sociological Review* 43 (August): 463–71.

Cromwell, Vicky L., and Ronald E. Cromwell. 1978. "Perceived Dominance in Decision Making and Conflict Resolution among Anglo, Black and Chicano Couples." *Journal of Marriage and the Family* 40 (November): 749–59.

Cronkite, Ruth C. 1977. "The Determinants of Spouses' Normative Preferences for Family Roles." *Journal of Marriage and the Family* 39 (August): 575–85.

Cunningham, Isabella C.M., and Robert T. Green. 1974. "Purchasing Roles in the U.S. Family, 1955 and 1973." *Journal of Marketing* 38 (October): 61–64.

Cunningham & Walsh. 1980. (April, October).

Curry, David J., and Michael B. Menasco. 1979. "Some Effects of Differing

Information Processing Strategies on Husband-Wife Joint Decisions." *Journal of Consumer Research* 6 (September): 192–203.

Danziger, Carl, and Matthew Greenwald. 1977. "An Overview of Unmarried Heterosexual Cohabitation and Suggested Marketing Implications." In *Advances in Consumer Research,* vol. 4, edited by William D. Perrault, Jr., pp. 330–34. Atlanta: Association for Consumer Research.

Danziger, James N. 1979. "Technology and Productivity: A Contingency Analysis of Computers in Local Government." *Administration and Society* 11 (August): 144–71.

Davis, Harry L. 1976. "Decision Making within the Household." *Journal of Consumer Research* 2 (March): 241–60.

———. 1971. "Measurement of Husband-Wife Influence in Consumer Purchases." *Journal of Marketing Research* 8 (August): 305–12.

———. 1970. "Dimensions of Marital Roles in Consumer Decision Making." *Journal of Marketing Research* 7 (May): 168–77.

Davis, Harry L., and Benny Rigaux. 1974. "Perceptions of Marital Roles in Decision Processes." *Journal of Consumer Research* 1 (June): 51–62.

Day, Ralph L. 1977. "Extending the Concept of Consumer Satisfaction." In *Advances in Consumer Research,* vol. 4, edited by William D. Perrault, Jr., pp. 149–54. Atlanta: Association for Consumer Research.

DeCarlo, Charles R. 1964. "Perspectives on Technology." In *Technology and Social Change,* edited by Eli Ginzberg, pp. 8–43. New York: Columbia University Press.

Del Boca, Frances K., and Richard D. Ashmore. 1980. "Sex Stereotypes through the Life Cycle." In *Review of Personality and Social Psychology,* edited by Ladd Wheeler, pp. 183–194. Beverly Hills, Calif.: Sage.

Derr, C. Brooklyn. 1977. "Managing Organizational Conflict: Collaboration, Bargaining, and Power Approaches." *California Management Review* 21 (Winter): 76–83.

Derrick, Frederick W., and Alane K. Lehfeld. 1980. "The Family Life Cycle: An Alternative Approach." *Journal of Consumer Research* 7 (September): 214–17.

Dewey, John. 1910. *How We Think.* New York: D.C. Heath.

Dietrich, Robert. 1977. "Woo the Working Women—Or She'll Leave You." *Progressive Grocer* 56 (November): 63–74.

Dougherty, Kevin. 1981. "To Love and to Work: Interactions between Work and Family Life." Ph.D. dissertation, Manhattanville College.

Douglas, Susan P. 1976a. "Cross-National Comparisons and Consumer Stereotypes: A Case Study of Working and Non-Working Wives in the U.S. and France." *Journal of Consumer Research* 3 (June): 12–20.

———. 1976b. "Working Wife vs. Non-Working Wife Families: A Basis for Segmenting Grocery Markets?" In *Advances in Consumer Research,* vol. 3, edited by B.B. Anderson, pp. 191–98. Ann Arbor: Association for Consumer Research.

Douglas, Susan P., and Yoram Wind. 1978. "Examining Family Role and Authority Patterns: Two Methodological Issues." *Journal of Marriage and the Family* 40 (February): 35–47.

Dow Jones & Company. 1981. *Active Investors: A Survey Concerning Investments and Brokerage Firms.* New York: Dow Jones.

Duncan, Otis; Dudley Featherman; and Beverly Duncan. 1972. *Socioeconomic Background and Achievement.* New York: Seminar Press.

Duvall, Evelyn M. 1971. *Family Development.* Philadelphia: J.B. Lippincott.

Easterlin, Richard A.; Michael Z. Wachter; and Susan M. Wachter. 1979. "The Coming Upswing in Fertility." *American Demographics* 1 (February): 12–15.

Easton, Anthony T. 1980. "Viewdata—A Product in Search of a Market." *Telecommunications Policy* 4, no. 3 (September): 221–25.

Edwards, John N. 1969. "Familial Behavior as Social Exchange." *Journal of Marriage and the Family* 31 (August): 518–26.

Eickelman, Dale F. 1977. "Time in a Complex Society: A Moroccan Example." *Ethnology* 16 (January): 39–55.

Ellis, R. 1975. "Composite Population Descriptors: The Socio-Economic/Life Cycle Grid." In *Advances in Consumer Research,* vol. 2, edited by Mary J. Schlinger, pp. 489–92. Ann Arbor: Association for Consumer Research.

Engel, James F., and Roger D. Blackwell. 1982. *Consumer Behavior.* 4th ed. Hinsdale, Ill.: Dryden.

Engel, James F.; Roger D. Blackwell; and David T. Kollat. 1978. *Consumer Behavior.* 3d ed. Hinsdale, Ill.: Dryden.

Ericksen, Julia A.; William L. Yancey; and Eugene P. Ericksen. 1979. "The Division of Family Roles." *Journal of Marriage and the Family* 41 (May): 309–13.

Espenshade, Thomas J. 1981. "Demographics of Decline." *American Demographics* 3 (February): 22–23.

Espenshade, Thomas J., and Rachel Eisenberg Brown. 1982. "Life Course Analysis and Multistate Demography: An Application to Marriage, Divorce, and Remarriage." *Journal of Marriage and the Family* 44 (November): 1025–36.

Etgar, Michael. 1978. "The Household as a Production Unit." In *Research in Marketing,* vol. 1, edited by J.N. Sheth, pp. 79–98. Greenwich, Conn: JAI Press.

Evans, F. 1959. "Psychological and Objective Factors in the Prediction of Brand Choice: Ford vs. Chevrolet." *Journal of Business* 32 (October): 340–69.

Falbo, Toni. 1977. "Multidimensional Scaling of Power Strategies." *Journal of Personality and Social Psychology* 38 (August): 537–47.

Falbo, Toni, and Lititia Ann Pepleau. 1980. "Power Strategies in Intimate Relationships." *Journal of. Personality and Social Psychology.* 38 (April): 618–28.

Farkas, George. 1976. "Education, Wage Rates, and the Division of Labor between Husband and Wife." *Journal of Marriage and the Family* 38 (August): 473–83.

Feldman, Laurence P., and Jacob Hornik. 1981. "The Use of Time: An Integrated Conceptual Model." *Journal of Consumer Research* 7 (March). 407–19.

Ferber, Marianne A. 1982. "Labor Market Participation of Young Married Women: Causes and Effects." *Journal of Marriage and the Family* 44 (May): 457–68.

Ferber, Marianne A., and Bonnie G. Birnbaum. 1980. "One Job or Two Jobs: The Implications for Young Wives." *Journal of Consumer Research* 7 (December): 263–71.

————. 1977. "The 'New Home Economics': Retrospects and Prospects." *Journal of Consumer Research* 4 (June): 19–28.

Ferber, Robert. 1973. "Family Decision Making and Economic Behavior: A Review." In *Family Economic Behavior: Problems and Prospects,* edited by F.B. Sheldon, pp. 29–61. Philadelphia: J.P. Lippincott.

Ferber, Robert, and Lucy Chao Lee. 1974. "Husband-Wife Influence in Family Purchasing Behavior." *Journal of Consumer Research* 1 (June): 43–50.

Ferber, R., and F. Nicosia. 1972. "Newly Married Couples and Their Asset Accumulation Decisions." In *Human Behavior in Economic Affairs: Essays in Honor of George Katona,* edited by B. Strumpel, J.N. Morgan, and E. Zahn, pp. 161–87. San Francisco: Jossey-Bass.

Filiatrault, Pierre, and J.R. Brent Ritchie. 1980. "Joint Purchasing Decisions: A Comparison of Influence Structure in Family and Couple Decision-Making Units." *Journal of Consumer Research* 7 (September): 131–40.

Filley, A.C. 1978. "Some Normative Issues in Conflict Management." *California Management Review* 21 (Winter): 61–66.

Flavell, J.H. 1963. *The Developmental Psychology of Jean Piaget.* Princeton, N.J.: D. Van Nostrand.

Fox, Karen D., and Sharon Y. Nickols. 1983. "The Time Crunch—Wife's Employment and Family Work." *Journal of Family Issues* 4 (March): 612–82.

Francke, Linda Bird; Pamela Abramson; Pamela Ellis Simons; Jeff Copeland; and Lisa Whitman. 1978. "Going It Alone." *Newsweek* 92 (September 4): 76–78.

Frank, R.E., and P.E. Green. 1968. "Numerical Taxonomy in Marketing Analysis: A Review Article." *Journal of Marketing Research* 5 (February): 83–94.

Frank, R.; W. Massy; and Y. Wind. 1972. *Market Segmentation.* Englewood Cliffs, N.J.: Prentice-Hall.

French, Jr., John R.P., and Bertram H. Raven. 1959. "The Bases of Social Power." In *Studies in Social Power,* edited by Dorwin Cartwright, pp. 150–67. Ann Arbor: University of Michigan, Institute for Social Research.

Fried, J., and P. Molnar. 1975. "General Model for Culture and Technology." *Technological Forecasting and Social Change* 8, no. 2: 175–88.

Fritzsche, David J. 1981. "An Analysis of Energy Consumption Patterns by Stage of Family Life Cycle." *Journal of Marketing Research* 18 (May): 227–32.

General Mills 1981. *American Family Report: Families at Work.* Minneapolis, MI: General Mills, Inc.: pp. 59–75.

Gentry, James W.; Mildred Doering; and Terrence V. O'Brien. 1978. "Masculinity and Femininity Factors in Product Perception and Self-Image." In *Advances in Consumer Research,* vol. 5, edited by H. Hunt, pp. 326–32. Ann Arbor: Association for Consumer Research.

Gilly, Mary C., and Ben M. Enis. 1982. "Recycling the Family Life Cycle: A Proposal for Redefinition." In Advances in Consumer Research, vol. 9, edited by Andrew Mitchell, pp. 271–76. Ann Arbor: Association for Consumer Research.

Ginzberg, Eli. 1965. *Technology and Social Change.* New York: Columbia University Press.

Glick, Paul. 1978. "The Future of the American Family." Statement prepared for the House Select Committee on Population.

———. 1977. "Updating the Life Cycle of the Family." *Journal of Marriage and the Family* 39 (February): 5–13.

Glick, Paul, and Arthur J. Norton. 1977. "Marrying, Divorcing, and Living Together in the U.S. Today." *Population Bulletin* 32. Washington, DC.: Population Reference Bureau.

Glick, Paul, and Graham B. Spanier. 1980. "Married and Unmarried Cohabitation in the United States." *Journal of Marriage and the Family* 42 (February): 19–30.

Goode, W.J. 1960. "A Theory of Role Strain." *American Sociological Review* 25 (August): 483–96.

Gottman, John. 1979. "A Review of Marital Interaction." New York: Free Press.

Gottman, John; Howard Markman; and Cliff Notarius. 1977. "The Topography of Marital Conflict: A Sequential Analysis of Verbal and Nonverbal Behavior." *Journal of Marriage and the Family* 39 (August): 461–77.

Gottman, John; Cliff Notarius; Howard Markman; Steve Bank; Bruce Yoppi; and Mary Ellen Rubin. 1976. "Behavior Exchange Theory and Marital Decision Making." *Journal of Personality and Social Psychology* 34 (July): 14–23.

Graham, Robert J. 1981. "The Role of Perception of Time in Consumer Research." *Journal of Consumer Research* 7 (March): 335–42.

Granbois, Donald. 1971a, "Decision Processes for Major Durable Goods." In *New Essays in Marketing Theory*, edited by G. Risk, pp. 172–205. Boston: Allyn and Bacon.

———. 1971b. "A Multilevel Approach to Family Role Structure Research." In *Proceedings of the Second Conference of the Association for Consumer Research*, edited by M. Venkatesan, pp. 99–107. College Park, Md.: Association for Consumer Research.

———. 1963. "A Study of the Family Decision-Making Process in the Purchase of Major Durable Household Goods." Ph.D. dissertation, Indiana University.

Granbois, Donald, and R. Willet. 1970. "Equivalence of Family Role Measures Based on Husband and Wife Data." *Journal of Marriage and the Family* 32 (February): 68–72.

Gray, Janet Dreyfus. 1983. "The Married Professional Woman: An Examination of Her Role Conflicts and Coping Strategies." *Psychology of Women Quarterly* 7, no. 3 (Spring): 235–43.

Gray-Little, Bernadette. 1982. "Marital Quality and Power Processes among Black Couples." *Journal of Marriage and the Family* 44 (August): 633–46.

Gredal, K. 1966. "Purchasing Behavior in Households." In *Readings in Danish Theory of Marketing*, edited by M. Kjaer-Hansen, pp. 84–100. Amsterdam: North-Holland.

Green, Robert T., and Isabella C.M. Cunningham. 1975. "Feminine Role Perceptions and Family Purchasing Decisions." *Journal of Marketing Research* 12 (August): 325–32.

Greenwald, Anthony G. 1980. "The Totalitarian Ego: Fabrication and Revision of Personal History." *American Psychologist* 35 (July): 603–18.

Grossman, Allyson Sherman. 1979. "Labor Force Patterns of Single Women." *Monthly Labor Review* 102 (August): 46–49.

Gutman, J. 1982. "A Means-End Chain Model Based on Consumer Categorization Processes." *Journal of Marketing* 46 (Spring): 60–72.

Gutman, J., and T.J. Reynolds. 1979. "An Investigation of the Levels of Cognitive Abstraction Utilized by Consumers in Product Differentiation." In *Attitude Research under the Sun,* edited by J. Eighmey, pp. 128–50. Chicago: American Marketing Association.

Hall, Edward T. 1959. *The Silent Language.* Garden City, N.Y.: Doubleday.
Haas, Linda. 1982. "Parental Sharing of Childcare Tasks in Sweden." *Journal of Family Issues* 3 (September): 389–412.
———. 1981. "Domestic Role Sharing in Sweden." *Journal of Marriage and the Family* 43 (November): 957–67.
———. 1980. "Role-Sharing Couples: A Study of Egalitarian Marriage." *Family Relations* (July): 289–96.
Hadas, Edward S. 1982. "Cheap Chic: The Consumer Trades Down." Boston: The Babson Staff Letter.
Haire, Mason, 1950. "Projective Techniques in Marketing Research," *Journal of Marketing.* 14 (April): 649–56.
Haley, Overholser & Associates. 1975. *Purchase Influence: Measures of Husband /Wife Influence on Buying Decisions,* New York.
Harrell-Bond, Barbara E. 1969. "Conjugal Role Behavior." *Human Relations* 22 (February): 77–91.
Hawes, Douglass K. 1979. "Time and Theories of Consumer Behavior." Paper presented at AMA Special Conference on Marketing Theory, Phoenix, Arizona, October.
Hayghe, Howard. 1982. "Marital and Family Patterns of Workers: An Update." *Monthly Labor Review* 105, no. 1 (May): 53–56, table 4.
Hedberg, B., and E. Mumford. 1975. "The Design of Computer Systems." In *Human Choice and Computers,* edited by E. Mumford and H. Sackman, pp. 31–59. New York: American Elsevier.
Hedges, Janice, and Jeanne K. Barnett. 1972. "Working Women and the Division of Household Tasks." *Monthly Labor Review* 94, no. 1 (April): 9–13.
Heer, D.M. 1963. "The Measurement and Basis of Family Power: An Overview." *Marriage and Family Living* 25 (September): 1933–39.
Heffring, Michael P. 1980. "Measuring Family Decision Making: Problems and Prospects." In *Advances in Consumer Research,* vol. 7, edited by Jerry C. Olson, pp. 494–98. Ann Arbor: Association for Consumer Research.
Heller, Dorothy K. 1981. "User-Friendly Languages of the Future." *Interface Age* 6, no. 12 (December): 78–82.
Hempel, Donald J. 1977. "Family Decision Making: Emerging Issues and Future Opportunities." In *Contemporary Marketing Thought,* edited by Barnett A. Greenberg, pp. 428–31. Chicago: American Marketing Association.
———. 1975. "Family Role Structure and Housing Decisions." In *Advances in Consumer Research,* vol. 2, edited by Mary Jane Schlinger, pp. 71–80. Chicago: Association for Consumer Research.
———. 1974. "Family Buying Decisions: A Cross-Cultural Perspective." *Journal of Marketing Research* 11 (August): 295–307.
———. 1972. "A Cross-Cultural Analysis of Husband-Wife Roles in House Purchase Decisions." In *Proceedings of the Third Annual Conference of the*

Association for Consumer Research, edited by M. Venkatesan, pp. 816–29. College Park, Md.: Association for Consumer Research.

Hempel, Donald J., and Lewis R. Tucker. 1980. "Issues Concerning Family Decision Making and Financial Services." In *Advances in Consumer Research,* vol. 7, edited by Jerry C. Olson, pp. 216–20. Ann Arbor: Association for Consumer Research.

Hendrix, Philip E. 1980. "Subjective Elements in the Examination of Time Expenditures." In *Advances in Consumer Research,* vol. 7, edited by Jerry C. Olson, pp. 437–41.

Hendrix, Philip E.; Thomas C. Kinnear; and James R. Taylor. 1979. "The Allocation of Time by Consumers: A Proposed Model and Empirical Test." Working Paper No. 188, University of Michigan.

Hendrix, Philip E., and William J. Qualls. 1978. "Assessing the Validity of Subjective Measures of Household Task Responsibility with Time-Budget Data." In *Advances in Consumer Research,* vol. 5, edited by Keith J. Hunt, pp. 143–45. Ann Arbor: Association for Consumer Research.

Hesselbart, Susan. 1976. "Does Charity Begin at Home? Attitudes toward Women, Household Tasks, and Household Decision-Making." Paper presented at the annual meeting of the American Sociological Association.

Hetherington, E. Mavis; Martha Cox; and Roger Cox. 1978. "The Aftermath of Divorce." In *Mother-Child, Father-Child Relations,* edited by Joseph H. Stevens, Jr., and Marilyn Matthews, pp. 149–76. Washington, D.C.: National Association for the Education of Young Children.

———. 1976. "Divorced Fathers." *The Family Coordinator* 25 (October): 417–28.

Hicks, Mary W., and Marilyn Platt. 1970. "Marital Happiness and Stability: A Review of Research in the Sixties." *Journal of Marriage and the Family* 32 (November): 553–74.

Hilgard, Ernest R. 1951. "The Role of Learning in Perception." In *Perception: An Approach to Personality,* edited by Robert R. Blake and Glenn V. Ramsey, pp. 95–120. New York: Ronald.

Hiller, Dana V., and William W. Philliber. 1982. "Predicting Marital and Career Success among Dual-Worker Couples." *Journal of Marriage and the Family* 44 (February): 53–62.

Hisich, Robert D., and M.P. Peters. 1974. "Selecting the Superior Segment Correlate." *Journal of Marketing* 38 (July): 60–63.

Hoge, Dean R.; Gregory H. Petrillo; and Ella I. Smith. 1982. "Transmission of Religious and Social Values from Parents to Teenage Children." *Journal of Marriage and the Family* 44 (August): 569–80.

Holahan, Carole K., and Lucia A. Gilbert. 1979. "Conflict between Major Life Roles: Women and Men in Dual Career Couples." *Human Relations* 32 (June): 451–67.

Hood, Jane, and Susan Golden. 1979. "Beating Time/Making Time: The Impact of Work Scheduling on Men's Family Roles." *The Family Coordinator* 28 (October): 575–82.

Houseknecht, Sharon K., and Ann S. Macke. 1981. "Combining Marriage and Career: The Marital Adjustment of Professional Women." *Journal of Marriage and the Family* 43 (August): 651–61.

Howard, John A. 1977. *Consumer Behavior: Application and Theory.* New York: McGraw-Hill.

————. 1963. *Marketing Management: Analysis and Planning.* Rev. ed. Homewood, Ill.: Irwin.

Howard, John A., and Jagdish N. Sheth. 1969. *The Theory of Buyer Behavior.* New York: John Wiley.

Howrigan, Gail. 1977. "Child Care Arrangements in Dual-Worker Families." Qualifying paper, Harvard University Graduate School of Education.

Hu, Joseph. 1980. "Household Projections: An Alternative Approach." *American Demographics* 2 (October): 23–25.

Huber, Joan, and Glenna Spitze. 1981. "Wives' Employment, Household Behaviors, and Sex-Role Attitudes." *Social Forces* 60 (September): 150–69.

————. 1980. "Considering Divorce: An Expansion of Becker's Theory of Marital Instability." *American Journal of Sociology* 86, no. 1 (July): 75–89.

Hull, Clark L. 1943. *Principles of Behavior.* New York: Appleton-Century-Crofts.

Humes, Kathryn H. 1980. "EFT (Electronic Funds Transfer) and the Consumer." In *Computers and Banking,* ed. by Kent W. Colton and Kenneth Craemer, pp. 55-66. New York: Plenum Press.

Hunt, Jane G., and Larry L. Hunt. 1982. "Dual-Career Families: Vanguard of the Future or Residue of the Past?" In *Two Paychecks: Life in Dual-Earner Families,* edited by J. Aldous, pp. 41–59. Beverly Hills, Calif.: Sage.

Ingram, F.J., and O.S. Pugh. 1981. "Consumer Usage of Financial Services." *The Bankers Magazine* 131, no. 2 (July/August): 40–53.

Inkeles, A., and D.H. Smith. 1974. *Becoming Modern: Individual Change in Six Developing Countries.* Cambridge, Mass.: Harvard University Press.

International Data Corporation report, as cited in *USA Today,* (January 24, 1983): 16.

Jaco, D., and J. Shepard. 1975. "Demographic Homogeneity and Spousal Consensus: A Methodological Perspective." *Journal of Marriage and the Family* 37 (February): 161–69.

Jacoby, Jacob; George J. Szybillo; and Carol Kohn Berning. 1976. "Time and Consumer Behavior: An Interdisciplinary Overview." *Journal of Consumer Research* 2 (March): 320–39.

Jaffe, Laurence J., and Henry Senft. 1966. "The Roles of Husbands and Wives in Purchasing Decisions." In *Attitude Research at Sea,* edited by Lee Adler and Irving Crespi, pp. 95–110. Chicago: American Marketing Association.

Jenkins, Roger J. 1980. "Contributions of Theory to the Study of Family Decision-Making." In *Advances in Consumer Research,* vol. 7, edited by Jerry C. Olson, pp. 207–11. Ann Arbor: Association for Consumer Research.

————. 1979. "The Influence of Children in Family Decision-Making: Parents' Perceptions." In *Advances in Consumer Research,* vol. 6, edited by William L. Wilkie, pp. 413-18. Ann Arbor: Association for Consumer Research.

Jervey, Gay. 1982. "Y&R Study: New Life to Singles." *Advertising Age* 53 (October 4): 14.

John, George, and Torger Reve. 1982. "The Reliability and Validity of Key Informant Data from Dyadic Relationships in Marketing Channels." *Journal of Marketing Research* 19 (November): 517–24.

Johnson, Beverly L., and Howard Hayghe. 1977. "Labor Force Participation of Married Women." *Monthly Labor Review* 100, no. 1 (June): table 4.

Jones, Landon Y. 1981a. "The Baby-Boom Consumer." *American Demographics* 3 (February): 28-35.

————. 1981b. "The Emerging Superclass." *American Demographics* 3 (March): 30-35.

Jöreskog, Karl, and Dag Sörbom. 1979. *Advances in Factor Analysis and Structural Equation Models.* Cambridge, Mass.: Abt Books.

————. 1978. *LISREL IV: Analysis of Linear Structural Relationships by the Method of Maximum Likelihood.* Chicago: National Educational Resources.

Jorgensen, Stephen R. 1979. "Socioeconomic Rewards and Perceived Marital Quality: A Reexamination." *Journal of Marriage and the Family* 41 (November): 825-35.

Julkunen, Raija. 1977. "A Contribution to the Categories of Social Time and the Economy of Time." *ACTA Sociologica* 20, no. 1: 5-23.

Kassarjian, H. 1971. "Personality and Consumer Behavior: A Review." *Journal of Marketing Research* 8 (November): 409-18.

Kelly, Jeffrey A., and Judith Worrell. 1977. "New Formulations of Sex Roles and Androgyny: A Critical Review." *Journal of Consulting and Clinical Psychology* 45, no. 6 (November-December): 1101-15.

Kenkel, William. 1961. "Family Interaction in Decision Making on Spending." In *Household Decision Making,* edited by Nelson N. Foote, pp. 140-64. New York: New York University Press.

Kilmann, Ralph H., and Kenneth W. Thomas. 1975. "Interpersonal Conflict-Handling Behavior as a Reflection of Jungian Personality Dimensions." *Psychological Reports* 37: 971-80.

Kinkead, Gwen. 1980. "On the Fast Track to the Good Life." *Fortune* 101, no. 2 (April 7): 74-84.

Kipnis, David. 1976. *The Powerholders.* Chicago: University of Chicago Press.

Kipnis, David; Patricia J. Castwell; Mary Gergen; and Donna Mauch. 1976. "Metamorphic Effects of Power." *Journal of Applied Psychology* 61 (April): 127-35.

Kipnis, David, and Stuart M. Schmidt. 1982. "An Influence Perspective on Bargaining within Organizations." Paper presented at the Bargaining within Organizations Conference, Boston, October 15-17.

Kittson, Gay C., and Marion B. Sussman. 1982. "Marital Complaints, Demographic Characteristics, and Symptoms of Marital Stress in Divorce." *Journal of Marriage and the Family* 44 (February): 87-101.

Klein, Frederick C. 1982. "Stepfamilies, Growing Common, Pose a Host of Perils for Members." *The Wall Street Journal* CCI (December 23): 1, 10.

Kling, Rob. 1980. "Social Analyses of Computing: Theoretical Perspectives in Recent Empirical Research." *Computing Surveys* 12, no. 1 (March): 61-110.

Kobrin, Frances E. 1976. "The Primary Individual and the Family: Changes in Living Arrangements in the United States since 1940." *Journal of Marriage and the Family* 38 (May): 233-39.

Kohn, M.L. 1969. *Class and Conformity: A Study in Values.* Homewood, Ill.: Dorsey Press.

Kolb, Trudy M., and Murray A. Strauss. 1974. "Marital Power and Marital Happiness in Relation to Problem Solving Ability." *Journal of Marriage and the Family* 36 (August): 757–66.

Kolbe, Richard H. 1983. "Bem Sex-Role Inventory Analysis of Children's Television Commercials." In *1983 Educators' Conference Proceedings,* edited by R. Bagozzi, et al., pp. 264–68. Chicago: American Marketing Association.

Komarovsky, Mirra. 1961. "Class Differences in Family Decision-Making on Expenditures." In *Household Decision Making,* edited by Nelson N. Foote, pp. 255–64. New York: New York University Press.

Kourilsky, Marilyn, and Trudy Murray. 1981. "The Use of Economic Reasoning to Increase Satisfaction with Family Decision Making." *Journal of Consumer Research* 8 (September): 183–88.

Kraemer, Kenneth, and King, John L. 1977. *Computers and Local Government.* Vol. 2, *A Review of Research.* New York: Praeger.

Lansing, John B., and Leslie Kish. 1957. "Family Life Cycle as an Independent Variable." *American Sociological Review* 22 (October): 512–19.

Lansing, John B., and James Morgan. 1955. "Consumer Finances over the Life Cycle." In *Consumer Behavior,* vol. 2, edited by Lincoln H. Clark. pp. 36–51. New York: New York University Press.

Lee, Lucy Chao, and Robert Ferber. 1977. "Use of Time as a Determinant of Family Market Behavior." *Journal of Business Research* 5 (March): 75-91.

Leibowitz, Arleen. 1974. "Home Investments in Children." In *Economics of the Family,* edited by Theodore W. Schultz, pp. 432–52. Chicago: University of Chicago Press.

Leigh, James H., and Claude R. Martin, Jr. 1982. "Collective Behavior in Consumer Behavior." In *Marketing Theory: Philosophy of Science Perspectives,* edited by Ronald F. Bush and Shelby D. Hunt, pp. 228–32. Chicago: American Marketing Association.

Lein, Laura. 1984. *Families without Villains.* Lexington, Mass.: Lexington Books.

———. 1979a. "Parental Evaluation of Child Care Alternatives." *The Urban and Social Change Review* 12: 11–16.

———. 1979b. "Male Participation in Home Life, Impact of Social Supports and Breadwinner Responsibility on the Allocation of Tasks." *The Family Coordinator* 28 (October): 489–95.

Leon, Carol, and Robert W. Bednarzik. 1978. "A Profile of Women on Part-time Schedules." *Monthly Labor Review* 101 (October): 3–12.

LeShan, Lawrence L. 1952. "Time Orientation and Social Class." *Journal of Abnormal and Social Psychology* 47 (July): 589–92.

Levinger, George. 1966. "Sources of Marital Dissatisfaction among Applicants for Divorce." *American Journal of Orthopsychiatry* 36: 803–07.

———. 1965. "Marital Cohesiveness and Dissolution: An Integrative Review." *Journal of Marriage and the Family* 27 (February): 19–28.

Levy, Sidney J. 1981. "Interpreting Consumer Mythology: A Structural Approach to Consumer Behavior." *Journal of Marketing* 18 (Summer): 49–61.

Lewis, Robert A., and Graham B. Spanier. 1979. "Theorizing about the Quality and Stability of Marriage." *In Contemporary Theories about the Family,* vol. 1, edited by Wiley R. Burr, Reubin Hill, F. Ivan Nye, and Ira I. Reiss, pp. 268–94. New York: Free Press.

Linden, Fabian. 1979a. "Singular." *Across the Board* 16 (June): 25–27.

———. 1979b. "Singular Spending Patterns." *Across the Board* 16 (July): 31–34.

———. 1980. "The Nuclear Family Is Splitting (cont.)." *Across the Board* 17 (July): 52–55.

Linder, S.B. 1970. *The Harried Leisure Class*. New York: Columbia University Press.

Lindsey, Robert. 1980. "Experts Anticipating Bit of a Baby Boom This Year." *The New York Times* 68 (September 2): 1.

Lipman, A. 1961. "Role Conception and Morals of Couples in Retirement." *Journal of Gerontology* 16: 267–71.

Locke, Harvey J. 1951. *Predicting Marital Adjustment in Marriages: A Comparison of a Divorced and Happily Married Group*. New York: Henry Holt.

Locksley, Anne. 1982. "Social Class and Marital Attitudes and Behavior." *Journal of Marriage and the Family* 44 (May): 427–40.

Loomis, Carol. 1983. "The Fire in the Belly at American Express." *Fortune* 108, no. 2 (November 28): 86–104.

———. 1981. "The Fight for Financial Turf." *Fortune* 104, no. 2 (December 28): 58–65.

Loomis, Charles P. 1936. "The Study of the Life Cycle of Families." *Rural Sociology* 1 (June): 180–99.

Lopata, Helen Z. 1971. *Occupation: Housewife*. New York: Oxford University Press.

Lopata, Helen Z., and Joseph Pleck, eds. 1983. *Research in the Interweave of Social Roles: Families and Jobs*. Greenwich, Conn.: JAI Press.

Loudon, David L., and Albert J. Della Bitta. 1979. *Consumer Behavior: Concepts and Applications*. New York: McGraw-Hill.

Luech, Marjorie; Ann C. Orr; and Martin O'Connell. 1982. *Trends in Child Care Arrangements of Working Mothers*. Washington, D.C.: U.S. Department of Commerce. Current Population Reports, special studies p-23, #117.

Luscher, Kurt K. 1974. "Time: A Much Neglected Dimension in Social Theory and Research." *Sociological Analysis and Theory* 4 (October): 101–16.

MacDonald, Gerald W. 1980. "Family Power: The Assessment of a Decade of Theory and Research, 1970–1979." *Journal of Marriage and the Family* 42 (February): 841–54.

Macklin, Eleanor D. 1980. "Nontraditional Family Forms: A Decade of Research." *Journal of Marriage and the Family* 42 (November): 905–22.

Male vs. Female Influence in Buying and in Brand Selection. Vol. 2, 1950. New York: Fawcett.

———. Vol. 1. 1948. New York: Fawcett.

Mandler, George. 1967. "Organization and Memory." In *The Psychology of Learning and Motivation*, vol. 1, edited by Kenneth W. Spence and Janet Taylor Spence, pp. 327–72. New York: Academic Press.

March, James G., and Herbert A. Simon. 1958. *Organizations*. New York: John Wiley and Sons.

Maret-Havens, Elizabeth. 1977. "Developing an Index to Measure Female Labor Force Attachment." *Monthly Labor Review* 100 (May): 35–38.

Marks, S. 1977. "Multiple Roles and Role Strain: Some Notes on Human Energy, Time, and Commitment." *American Sociological Review* 42 (December): 921–36.

Markson, Elizabeth W. 1973. "Readjustment to Time in Old Age: A Life Cycle Approach." *Psychiatry* 36 (February): 37–48.

Markus, Hazel. 1977. "Self-Schemata and Processing Information about the Self." *Journal of Personality and Social Psychology* 35 (February): 63–78.

Markus, Hazel; Marie Crane; Stan Berstein; and Michael Siladi. 1982. "Self-Schemas and Gender." *Journal of Personality and Social Psychology* 42 (January): 38–50.

"Married Is Still the Favorite State." 1982. *Sales and Marketing Management* 124 (July 26): A–33.

Martin, James. 1981. *Design and Strategy for Distributed Data Processing.* Englewood Cliffs, N.J.: Prentice-Hall.

Martin, Peter. 1981. "Metamorphosis and Money." *The Economist* 280 (June 20): 63–66.

Mason, Karen O., and L.L. Bumpass. 1975. "U.S. Women's Sex Role Ideology, 1970." *American Journal of Sociology* 80 (March): 1212–19.

McAuley, William J., and Cheri Z. Nutty. 1982. "Residential Preferences and Moving Behavior: A Family Life-Cycle Analysis." *Journal of Marriage and the Family* 44 (May): 301–09.

McCall, Suzanne H. 1981. "Couples Satisfied with Earn-Alike Status." *Dallas Times* (4 May): 9.

———. 1978. "Husbands of Many Workwives See their Lifestyles Altered." *Marketing News* (21 April): 10.

———. 1977. "Meet the Workwife." *Journal of Marketing* 41, no. 3 (July): 55–65.

McFall, J. 1969. "Priority Patterns and Consumer Behavior." *Journal of Marketing* 33, no. 4 (October): 50–55.

Medling, James A., and Michael McCarry. 1971. "Marital Adjustment over Segments of the Life-Cycle: The Issue of Spouses' Value Similarity." *Journal of Marriage and the Family* 43 (February): 195–203.

Meissner, Martin; E.W. Humphreys, S.M. Miles; and W.J. Schen. 1975. "No Exit for Wives: Sexual Division of Labor and the Cumulation of Household Demands." *Canadian Review of Sociology and Anthropology* 12 (November): 424–39.

Melko, Matthew, and Leonard Cargan. 1981. "The Singles Boom." *American Demographics* 3 (November): 30–31.

Menefee, John A. 1982. "The Demand for Consumption Time: A Longitudinal Perspective." *Journal of Consumer Research* 8 (March): 391–97.

Merton, Robert K. 1957. *Social Theory and Social Structure* Glencoe, Ill.: Free Press.

Michman, Ronald D. 1980. "The Double Income Family: A New Market Target." *Business Horizons* 23, no. 4 (August): 31–37.

Michener, H. Andrew, and Margaret Schwertfeger. 1972. "Liking as a Determinant of Power Tactic Preference." *Sociometry* 35, no. 1 (March): 190–202.

Mitchell, Andrew A., and Jerry C. Olson. 1982. "Are Product Attribute Beliefs the Only Mediator of Advertising Effects on Brand Attitude?" *Journal of Marketing Research* 18 (August): 318–32.

Model, Suzanne. 1982. "Housework by Husbands: Determinants and Implications."

In *Two Paychecks: Life in Dual-Earner Families,* edited by J. Aldous, pp. 193-205. Beverly Hills, Calif.: Sage.

————. 1981. "Housework by Husbands, Determinants and Implications." *Journal of Family Issues* 2 (June): 225-37.

Moore, R.L., and G.P. Moschis. 1981. "The Role of Family Communication in Consumer Learning." *Journal of Communication* (Autumn): 42-51.

Morey, Robert V. 1971. "Guahibo Time-Reckoning." *Anthropological Quarterly* 44 (January): 22-36.

Moses, Joel. 1981. "The Computer in the Home." In *The Computer Age: A Twenty-Year Review,* edited by Michael Dertouzos and Joel Moses, pp. 3-20. Cambridge, Mass.: MIT Press.

Mott, Frank L., and Sylvia Moor. 1979. "The Causes of Marital Disruption among Young American Women: An Interdisciplinary Perspective." *Journal of Marriage and the Family* 41 (May): 355-65.

Munsinger, G.M.; Jean E. Weber; and Richard E. Hansen. 1975. "Joint Home Purchasing Decisions by Husbands and Wives." *Journal of Consumer Research* 1 (June): 60-66.

Murphy, Patrick E., and William S. Staples. 1979. "A Modernized Family Life Cycle." *Journal of Consumer Research* 6 (June): 12-22.

Myers, James H., and William H. Reynolds. 1967. *Consumer Behavior and Marketing Management.* New York: Houghton Mifflin.

Nelson, James E. 1978. "Children as Information Sources in the Family Decision to Eat Out." In *Advances in Consumer Research,* vol. 5, edited by H. Keith Hunt, pp. 419-23. Ann Arbor: Association for Consumer Research.

Newcomb, Paul R. 1979. "Cohabitation in America: An Assessment of Consequences." *Journal of Marriage and the Family* 41 (August): 597-603.

Newell, A., and H. Simon. 1972. *Human Problem Solving.* Englewood Cliffs, N.J.: Prentice-Hall.

Newsweek. 1979. "The Role Men Play in Brand Selection." Research Report.

Nickols, Sharon Y., and Edward J. Metzen. 1982. "Impact of Wife's Employment upon Husband's Housework." *Journal of Family Issues* (June): 199-216.

Nock, Steven L. 1979. "The Family Life Cycle: Empirical or Conceptual Tool?" *Journal of Marriage and the Family* 41 (February): 15-26.

Norton, Arthur H. 1980. "The Influence of Divorce on Traditional Life-Cycle Measures." *Journal of Marriage and the Family* 42 (February): 63-69.

Norton, Arthur J., and Paul C. Glick. 1979. "What's Happening to Households?" *American Demographics* 1 (March): 19-23.

Nowland and Company. 1965. *Family Participation and Influence in Shopping and Brand Selection: Phase II.* A report prepared for *Life* magazine, New York.

————. 1964. *Family Participation and Influence in Shopping and Brand Selection: Phase I.* A report prepared for *Life* magazine, New York.

Nowotny, H. 1975. "Time Structuring and Time Measurement: On the Interrelation between Timekeepers and Social Time." In *The Study of Time II,* edited by J.T. Fraser and N. Lawrence, pp. 325-42. New York: Springer-Verlag.

Nye, F. Ivan. 1979. "Choice, Exchange, and the Family." In *Contemporary Theories about the Family,* vol. 2, edited by Wesley R. Burr, Reuben Hill, F. Ivan Nye, and Ira L. Reiss, pp. 1-41. New York: Free Press.

Nye, F. Ivan; John Carlson; and Gerald Garrett. 1970. "Family Size, Interaction, Affect, and Stress." *Journal of Marriage and the Family* 32 (May): 216–26.

Nye, F., and V. Gecas. 1976. "The Role Concept: Review and Delineation." In *Role Structure and Analysis of the Family*, edited by F. Ivan Nye, Beverly Hills, Calif.: Sage.

Oakley, Ann. 1974. *The Sociology of Housework*. New York: Pantheon.

Oakley, Ann, and Maryon F. King. 1982. "A Distributed Processing Approach to Family Role Structure." Paper submitted to the *Journal of Marketing*.

Ogburn, W.F., and M.F. Nimkoff. 1955. *Technology and the Changing Family*. Cambridge, Mass.: MIT Press.

Olsen, Marvin E. 1960. "Distribution of Family Responsibilities and Social Stratification." *Marriage and Family Living* (February): 60–65.

Olshavsky, Richard W., and Donald H. Granbois. 1979. "Consumer Decision Making—Fact or Fiction?" *Journal of Consumer Research* 6 (September): 93–100.

Olshavsky, Richard W., and Maryon F. King. 1982. "A Distributed Processing Approach to Family Role Structure." Discussion paper no. 246, Graduate School of Business, Indiana University.

Olson, David H. 1969. "The Measurement of Family Power by Self-Report and Behavioral Methods." *Journal of Marriage and the Family* 31 (August): 545–50.

Olson, David H., and Carolyn Rabunsky. 1972. "Validity of Four Measures of Family Power." *Journal of Marriage and the Family* 34 (May): 224–33.

Olson, J., and T.J. Reynolds. 1983. "Understanding Consumers' Cognitive Structures: Implications for Advertising Strategy." In *Advertising and Consumer Psychology*, edited by L. Percy and A. Woodside, Lexington, Mass.: Lexington Books.

Orford, Jim; Edna Oppenheimer; Stella Egert; and Celia Hensman. 1977. "The Role of Excessive Drinking in Alcoholism Complicated Families: A Study of Stability and Change over a One-Year Period." *International Journal of the Addictions* 12, no. 4, 471–95.

Orthner, Dennis K. 1975. "Leisure Activity Patterns and Marital Satisfaction over the Marital Career." *Journal of Marriage and the Family* 37 (February): 91–101.

Osborn, Neil. 1982. "What Synergy?" *Institutional Investor* 16, no. 1 (May): 49–59.

Osmond, Marie Withers. 1977. "Marital Organization in Low-Income Families: "A Cross-Race Comparison."*International Sociology of the Family* 7: 143–50.

———. 1975. "Female Sex Role Attitudes." *Journal of Marriage and the Family*. 37 (November): 744-58.

Ostlund, L. 1973. "Role Theory and Group Dynamics." In *Consumer Behavior: Theoretical Sources*, edited by Thomas S. Robertson, pp. 230–75. Englewood Cliffs, N.J.: Prentice-Hall.

Park, C. Whan. 1982. "Joint Decisions in Home Purchasing: A Muddling-Through Process." *Journal of Consumer Research* 9 (September): 151–62.

Park, C. Whan; Robert W. Hughes; Vinod Thukral; and Robert Friedman. 1981. "Consumer's Decision Plans and Subsequent Choice Behavior." *Journal of Marketing* 45 (Spring): 33–47.

Parsons, Talcott. 1951. *Toward a General Theory of Action*. Cambridge, Mass.: Harvard University Press.

————. 1949. *Essays in Sociological Theory.* Glencoe, Ill.: Free Press.

Parsons, Talcott, and Robert N. Bales. 1955. *Family, Socialization, and Interaction Process.* Glencoe, Ill.: Free Press.

Pebley, Anne R., and David E. Bloom. 1982. "Childless Americans." *American Demographics* 4 (January): 18–21.

Pepitone-Rockwell, Fran. 1980. *Dual-Career Couples.* Beverly Hills, Calif: Sage.

Perrucci, Carolyn C; Harry R. Potter; and Deborah L. Rhoads. 1978. "Determinants of Male Family-Role Performance." *Psychology of Women Quarterly* 3 (Fall): 53–56.

Peter, J. Paul. 1980. "Some Observations on Self-Concept in Consumer Behavior Research." In *Advances in Consumer Research,* vol. 7, edited by J. Olson, pp. 615–16. Ann Arbor: Association for Consumer Research.

Peters, Marie. 1976. "A Study of Household Management and Child Rearing in Black Families with Working Mothers." Ph.D. dissertation, Harvard University.

Petty, Richard E.; Thomas M. Ostrom; and Timothy C. Brock. 1981. *Cognitive Responses in Persuasion.* Hillsdale, N.J.: Lawrence Erlbaum.

Phillips, Lynn W. 1981. "Assessing Measurement Error in Key Informant Reports: A Methodological Note on Organizational Analysis in Marketing." *Journal of Marketing Research* 18 (November): 395–415.

Pleck, Joseph. 1983. "Husbands' Paid Work and Family Roles: Current Research Issues." In *Research in the Interweave of Social Roles: Families and Jobs,* edited by Helena Lopata and Joseph Pleck, pp. 251–333. Greenwich, Conn.: JAI Press.

————. 1981. *The Myth of Masculinity.* Cambridge, Mass.: MIT Press.

————. 1979. "Men's 'Family Work' Role: Three Perspectives and Some New Data." *Family Coordinator* 28 (October): 481–488.

————. 1977. "The Work-Family Role System." *Social Problems* 24 (April): 417–27.

Pleck, Joseph, and Michael Rustad. 1980. "Husbands' and Wives' Time in Family Work and Paid Work in the 1975–76 Study of Time Use." Working paper no. 63, Center for Research on Women, Wellesley College.

Powell, Brian, and Lola C. Steelman. 1982. "Testing an Undertested Comparison: Maternal Effects on Sons' and Daughters' Attitudes toward Women in the Labor Force." *Journal of Marriage and the Family* 44 (May): 349–555.

Price-Bonham, Sharon, and Jack O. Balswick. 1980. "The Noninstitutions: Divorce, Desertion, and Remarriage." *Journal of Marriage and the Family* 42 (November): 959–72.

Progressive Grocer. 1979. "New Products, Marketing Ideas Will Fire Working Women." 58 (August): 104B.

Qualls, William J. 1982. "Changing Sex Roles: Its Impact upon Family Decision Making." In *Advances in Consumer Research,* vol. 9, edited by A. Mitchell, pp. 267–70. Ann Arbor: Association for Consumer Research.

Quick Frozen Foods. 1981. "Singles: Viable Segment of Restaurant Trade Even Though Inflation Has Taken Toll." 43 (June): 54–56.

Rank, Mark R. 1982. "Determinants of Conjugal Influence in Wives' Employment Decision Making." *Journal of Marriage and the Family* 44 (August): 591–604.

Rapoport, Rhona, and Robert N. Rapoport. 1980. "Three Generations of Dual-Career Family Research." In *Dual-Career Couples,* edited by F. Pepitone-Rockwell, pp. 23-48. Beverly Hills: Sage.

Rapoport, Robert; Rhona Rapoport; and V. Thiesseu. 1974. "Couple Symmetry and Enjoyment." *Journal of Marriage and the Family* 36 (August): 588-91.

Redman, Barbara J. 1980. "The Impact of Women's Time Allocation on Expenditure for Meals away from Home and Prepared Foods." *American Journal of Agricultural Economics* 62 (May): 234-37.

Reed, J.D. 1982. "The New Baby Bloom." *Time* 116, no. 1 (February 22): 52-58.

Reilly, M. 1982. "Working Wives and Convenience Consumption." *Journal of Consumer Research* 8 (March): 407-18.

Reiss, David; Ronald Costell; Helen Berkman; and Carole Jones. 1980. "How One Family Perceives Another: The Relationship between Social Constructions and Problem-Solving Competence." *Family Process* 19 (September): 230-56.

Renne, Karen S. 1970. "Correlates of Dissatisfaction in Marriage." *Journal of Marriage and the Family* 32 (February): 54-67.

Reynolds, F.D., and W.D. Wells. 1977. *Consumer Behavior.* New York: McGraw-Hill.

Reynolds, Fred D.; Melvin R. Crask; and William D. Wells. 1977. "The Modern Feminine Life Style." *Journal of Marketing* 41 (July): 38-45.

Reynolds, T.J. 1982. "Advertising Is Image Management." Keynote address at the meeting of the American Academy of Advertising, Lincoln, Nebraska.

Reynolds, T.J., and J. Gutman. 1984. "Advertising Is Image Management." *Journal of Advertising Research,* 24 (February/March) 27-38.

Reynolds, William H., and James H. Myers. 1966. "Marketing and the American Family." *Business Topics* 14 (Spring): 57-66.

Rhyne, Darla. 1981. "Bases of Marital Satisfaction among Men and Women." *Journal of Marriage and the Family* 43 (November): 941-55.

Rich, Stuart U., and Subhash C. Jain. 1968. "Social Class and Life Cycle as Predictors of Shopping Behavior." *Journal of Marketing Research* 5 (February): 41-49.

Rigaux-Bricmont, Benny, 1978. "Explaining the Marital Influences in the Family Economic Decision Making." In *American Marketing Association Educators' Proceedings.*

Rivers, Caryl, and Alan Lupo. 1981. *For Better, For Worse.* New York: Summit Books.

Robbins, Stephen. 1978. "'Conflict Management' and 'Conflict Resolution' Are Not Synonymous Terms." *California Management Review* 21 (Winter): 67-75.

Roberts, Mary Lou, *Family Life Styles.* In progress.

Roberts, Mary Lou, and Lawrence H. Wortzel. 1982. "A Dynamic Model of Role Allocation in the Household." Working paper series, School of Management, Boston University.

———. 1981. "Role Transferral in the Household: A Conceptual Model and Partial Test." In *Advances in Consumer Research,* vol. 9, edited by Andrew Mitchell, pp. 262-66. Ann Arbor: Association for Consumer Research.

———. 1980. "Husbands Who Make Dinner: A Test of Competing Theories of Marital Role Allocations." In *Advances in Consumer Research,* vol. 7, edited by Jerry C. Olson, pp. 669-71. Ann Arbor: Association for Consumer Research.

———. 1979. "New Life-Style Determinants of Women's Food Shopping

Behavior." *Journal of Marketing* 43 (Summer): 28–39.

Robey, Bryant. 1982. "A Guide to the Baby Boom." *American Demographics* 4 (September): 16–21.

———. 1981. "Age in America." *American Demographics* 3 (July/August): 14–19.

Robinson, John P. 1980. "Housework Technology and Household Work". In *Women and Household Labor,* edited by Sarah F. Berk, pp. 53–67. Beverly Hills: Sage.

———. 1977. *How Americans Use Time.* New York: Praeger.

Robinson, John P.; J. Yerby; M. Feiweger; and N. Somerick. 1976. "Time Use as an Indicator of Sex Role Territoriality." Department of Communications, Cleveland State University.

Rodgers, Roy H. 1967. *Family Interaction and Transaction: The Developmental Approach.* Englewood Cliffs, N.J.: Prentice-Hall.

Rodman, H. 1972. "Marital Power and the Theory of Resources in Cultural Context." *Journal of Comparative Family Studies* 3 (Spring): 50–59.

———. 1967. "Marital Power in France, Greece, Yugoslavia and U.S.: A Cross-National Discussion." *Journal of Marriage and the Family* 29 (May): 320–24.

Rogers, E. 1969. *Modernization among Peasants.* New York: Holt, Rinehart and Winston.

Rogers, T.B.; H.N. Kuiper; and W.S. Kirker. 1977. "Self-Reference and the Encoding of Personal Information." *Journal of Personality and Social Psychology* 35 (September): 677–88.

Rollins, Boyd C., and Stephen J. Bahr. 1976. "A Theory of Power Relationships in Marriage." *Journal of Marriage and the Family* 38 (November): 619–27.

Roscoe, A.M.; A. LeClaire; and L.G. Schiffman. 1977. "Theory and Management Applications of Demographics in Buyer Behavior." In *Consumer and Industrial Buying Behavior,* edited by A.G. Woodside, J.N. Sheth, and P.D. Bennett, pp. 67–76. New York: Elsevier North-Holland.

Rosenberg, Larry J., and Elizabeth C. Hirschman. 1980. "Retailing without Stores." *Harvard Business Review* 80, no. 4 (July/August): 103–12.

Ruble, Thomas L., and Kenneth W. Thomas. 1976. "Support for a Two-Dimensional Model of Conflict Behavior." *Organizational Behavior and Human Performance* 16 (June): 143–55.

Runyon, Kenneth E. 1980. *Consumer Behavior.* 2d ed. Columbus, Oh.: Merrill.

Russell, Cheryl. 1981. "Inside the Shrinking Household." *American Demographics* 3 (October): 28–83.

Ryan, Michael J., and E.H. Bonfield. 1980. "Fishbein's Extended Model: A Test of External and Pragmatic Validity." *Journal of Marketing* 44 (Spring): 82–95.

———. 1975. "The Fishbein Extended Model and Consumer Behavior." *Journal of Consumer Research* 2 (September): 118–36.

Safilios-Rothschild, Constantina. 1976. "A Macro- and Micro-Examination of Family Power and Love: An Exchange Model." *Journal of Marriage and the Family* 38 (May): 31–39.

———. 1970a. "The Influence of the Wife's Degree of Work Commitment upon Some Aspects of Family Organization and Dynamics." *Journal of Marriage and the Family* 32 (November): 681–91.

———. 1970b. "The Study of Family Power Structure: A Review, 1960–1969."

Journal of Marriage and the Family 32 (November): 681-91.

———. 1969. "Family Sociology or Wives' Family Sociology? A Cross-Cultural Examination of Decision-Making." *Journal of Marriage and the Family* 31 (May): 290-301.

Sandler, Linda. 1981. "The New Products Mutiny." *Institutional Investor* 15, no. 2 (October): 237-41.

Sanoff, Alvin P. 1983. "19 Million Singles, Their Joy and Frustrations." *U.S. News and World Report* 94, no. 1 (February 21): 53-56.

Scanzoni, John. 1980. "Contemporary Marriage Types." *Journal of Family Issues* 1, no. 1 (March): 125-140.

———. 1979. "Sex-Role Influences on Married Women's Status Attainments." *Journal of Marriage and the Family* 41 (November): 793-800.

———. 1978. *Sex Roles, Women's Work, and Marital Conflict: A Study of Family Change.* Lexington, Mass.: D.C. Heath/Lexington Books.

———. 1977. "Changing Sex Roles and Emerging Directions in Family Decision Making." *Journal of Consumer Research* 4 (December): 185-88.

———. 1976. "Sex Role Change and Influences on Birth Intentions." *Journal of Marriage and the Family* 38 (February): 43-60.

———. 1975. "Sex Roles, Economic Factors, and Marital Solidarity in Black and White Marriages." *Journal of Marriage and the Family* 37 (February): 130-44.

———. 1970. "Changing Sex Roles and Emerging Directions in Family Decision Making." *Journal of Consumer Research* 3 (March): 185-88.

Scanzoni, John, and G.L. Fox. 1980. "Sex Roles, Family and Society: The Seventies and Beyond." *Journal of Marriage and the Family* 42 (November): 743-56.

Scanzoni, John, and Karen Polonko. 1980. "A Conceptual Approach to Explicit Marital Negotiation." *Journal of Marriage and the Family* 42 (February): 31-44.

Scanzoni, John, and Maximiliane Szinovacz. 1980. *Family Decision-Making: A Developmental Sex Role Model.* Beverly Hills: Sage.

———. 1980. "Contemporary Marriage Types." *Journal of Family Issues* 1 (March): 125-40.

Scarpa, Ralph J. 1982. "Changing Demographics Bring Investment Opportunities." *American Demographics* 4 (January): 26-29.

Schafer, Robert B., and Patricia M. Keith. 1981. "Equity in Marital Roles across the Family Life Cycle." *Journal of Marriage and the Family* 43 (May): 359-67.

Schaninger, Charles M., and Chris T. Allen. 1981. "Wife's Occupational Status as a Consumer Behavior Construct." *Journal of Consumer Research* 8 (September): 189-96.

Schaninger, Charles M., and W. Christian Buss. 1982a. "Demographics as Predictors of Sex-Role Norms and Family Task-Allocation." Working paper, School of Business, State University of New York at Albany.

———. 1982b. "The Effect of Sex-Role Norms on Marital Task Allocation." Working paper, School of Business, State University of New York at Albany.

Schaninger, Charles M.; W. Christian Buss; and Rajiv Grover. 1983. "Intergenerational Transfer of Task Allocation within the Family." Working paper, School of Business, State University of New York at Albany.

———. 1982. "The Effect of Sex Roles on Family Economic Handling and Decision Influence." In *An Assessment of Marketing Thought and Practice,* edited by Bruce J. Walker, pp. 43-47. Chicago, IL: American Marketing Association.

Schary, Philip B. 1971. "Consumption and the Problem of Time." *Journal of Marketing* 35 (April): 50–55.

Scheibe, Cyndy. 1979. "Sex Roles in TV Commercials." *Journal of Advertising Research* 19 (February): 23–27.

Schlachter, John; Nabil Rozzouk; and Mark Mills. 1979. "The Family Life Cycle Revisited." In *Developments in Marketing Science*, vol. 2, edited by Howard Gitlow and Edward Wheatley, pp. 38–42.

Schneider, Kenneth C., and Sharon B. Schneider. 1979. "Trends in Sex Roles in Television Commercials." *Journal of Marketing* 43 (Summer): 79–84.

Schram, Rosalyn Weinman. 1979. "Marital Satisfaction over the Family Life Cycle: A Critique and Proposal." *Journal of Marriage and the Family* 41 (February): 1–12.

Schultz, Theodore W., ed. 1974. *Economics of the Family*. Chicago: University of Chicago Press.

Scientific American. 1982. Special issue on mechanization of work. 247 (September): 1–218.

Sharits, Dean, and H. Bruce Lammers. 1983. "Perceived Attributes of Models in Prime-Time and Daytime Television Commercials: A Person Perception Approach." *Journal of Marketing Research* 20 (February): 64–73.

Sharp, Harry, and Paul Mott. 1956. "Consumer Decisions in the Metropolitan Family." *Journal of Marketing* 21 (October): 149–56.

Sheils, Merrill. 1983. "A Portrait of America." *Newsweek* 101, no. 1 (January 17): 20–33.

Sheth, Jagdish N. 1974. "A Theory of Family Buying Decisions." In *Models of Buyer Behavior*, edited by J.N. Sheth, pp. 17–33. New York: Harper & Row.

Sheth, Jagdish N., and Stephen Cosmas. 1975. "Tactics of Conflict Resolution in Family Buying Behavior." Paper presented at the meeting of the American Psychological Association, Chicago, September.

Shimp, Terence A. 1981. "Attitude toward the Ad as a Mediator of Consumer Brand Choice." *Journal of Advertising* 10, no. 2: 9–15.

Shuptrine, F.K., and G. Samuelson. 1976. "Dimensions of Marital Roles in Consumer Decision-Making: Revisited." *Journal of Marketing Research* 13 (February): 87–91.

Simon, Herbert A. 1977. "What Computers Mean for Man and Society." *Science* 195 (March): 1186–91.

Simpson, Miles. 1980. "The Sociology of Cognitive Development." *Annual Review of Sociology* 6: 287–313.

Sirgy, M. Joseph. 1982. "Self-Concept in Consumer Behavior: A Critical Review." *Journal of Consumer Research* 9 (December): 287–300.

Snyder, Douglas K. 1979. "Multidimensional Assessment of Marital Satisfaction." *Journal of Marriage and the Family* 41 (November): 813–23.

Sorokin, Pitirim A., and Clarence Z. Berger. 1938. *Time Budgets of Human Behavior*. Cambridge, Mass.: Harvard University Press.

Spanier, Graham B. 1982. "Living Together in the Eighties." *American Demographics* 4 (November): 16–19, 42.

———. 1979. "Human Sexuality in a Changing Society." In *Human Sexuality in a*

Changing Society, edited by Graham B. Spanier, pp. 1–9. Minneapolis: Burgess.

———. 1976. "Measuring Dyadic Adjustment: New Scales for Assessing the Quality of Marriage and Similar Dyads." *Journal of Marriage and the Family* 38 (February): 15–28.

Spanier, Graham B., and Paul C. Glick. 1980a. "Paths to Remarriage." *Journal of Divorce* 3 (Spring): 283–98.

———. 1980b. "The Life Cycle of American Families: An Expanded Analysis." *Journal of Family History* 5 (Spring): 97–111.

Spanier, Graham B., and Robert A. Lewis. 1980. "Marital Quality: A Review of the Seventies." *Journal of Marriage and the Family* 42 (November): 825–39.

Spanier, Graham B., William Sauer, and William Larzellre. 1979. "An Empirical Evaluation of the Family Life Cycle." *Journal of Marriage and the Family* 41 (February): 27–38

Spitze, Glenna, and Joan Huber. 1982. "Accuracy of Wife's Perception of Husband's Attitude toward Her Employment." *Journal of Marriage and the Family* 44 (May): 477–81.

Spitze, Glenna, and Linda J. Waiter. 1981. "Wives' Employment: The Roles of Husbands' Perceived Attitudes." *Journal of Marriage and the Family* 43 (February): 117–24.

Sprenkle, Douglas H., and David H.L. Olsen. 1978. "Circumplex Model of Marital Systems: An Empirical Study of Clinic and Non-Clinic Couples." *Journal of Marriage and the Family* 40 (April): 59–74.

Spreye, Jetse. 1979. "The General Systems Approach to the Family." In *Contemporary Theories about the Family,* edited by Wesley R. Burr, Reuben Hill, F. Ivan Nye, and Ira L. Reiss, pp. 112–29. New York: Free Press.

———. 1971. "On the Management of Conflict in Families." *Journal of Marriage and the Family* 33 (November): 722–31.

———. 1969. "The Family as a System in Conflict." *Journal of Marriage and the Family* 31 (November): 699–706.

SRI International. 1979. *Consumer Financial Decisions.* Vol. 1, *Perspectives;* Vol. 2, *Analysis of Household Financial Services Relationships.* Palo Alto, Calif: SRI International.

Stafford, Frank, and Greg J. Duncan. 1979. "The Use of Time and Technology by Households in the United States." Working paper no. 8006, Institute for Social Research, University of Michigan.

Stafford, Rebecca; Elaine Backman; and Pamela Dibona. 1977. "The Division of Labor among Cohabiting and Married Couples." *Journal of Marriage and the Family* 39 (February): 43–57.

Stampfl, Ronald W. 1979. "Family Research: Consumer Education Needs in the Family Life Cycle." *Journal of Home Economics* 71 (Spring): 22–27.

———. 1978. "The Consumer Life Cycle." *Journal of Consumer Affairs.* 12 (Winter): 209–19.

Staples, Robert. 1971. "The Myth of the Black Matriarchy." in Robert Staples, ed, *The Black Family,* Belmont, Calif: Wadsworth, pp 149–159.

Starch, D., and staff. 1958. "Male vs. Female Influence on the Purchase of Selected Products." A report prepared for *True Magazine,* New York.

Stein, Peter J. 1976. *Single.* Englewood Cliffs, N.J.: Prentice-Hall.

Sternthal, Brian, and C. Samuel Craig. 1982. *Consumer Behavior: An Information Processing Perspective.* Englewood Cliffs, N.J.: Prentice-Hall.

Stolte-Heiskanen, Veronica. 1975. "Family Needs and Societal Institutions: Potential Empirical Linkage Mechanisms." *Journal of Marriage and the Family* 37 (November): 903–16.

Stover, Carl F. 1962. "Introduction." *Technology and Culture* 3 (Fall): 383.

Streib, Gordon F., and Rubye W. Beck. 1980. "Older Families: A Decade Review." *Journal of Marriage and the Family* 42 (November): 937–56.

Strober, Myra H., and Charles B. Weinberg. 1980. "Strategies Used by Nonworking Wives to Reduce Time Pressures." *Journal of Consumer Research* 6 (March): 338–48.

———. 1977. "Working Wives and Major Family Expenditures." *Journal of Consumer Research* 4 (December): 141–47.

Swasy, John L. 1979. "Measuring the Bases of Social Power." In *Advances in Consumer Research,* vol. 6, edited by William L. Wilkie, pp. 340–46. Ann Arbor: Association for Consumer Research.

Szalia, A. 1966. "The Multinational Comparative Time Budget Research Project: A Venture in International Research Co-operation." *American Behavioral Scientist* 10 (December): 1–12, 21–31.

Szinovacz, Maximiliane E. 1980. "Female Retirement: Effects of Spousal Roles and Marital Adjustment." *Journal of Family Issues* (September): 423–40.

Szybillo, George J.; Sharon Binstok; and Lauranne Buchanan. 1979. "Measure Validation of Leisure Time Activities: Time Budgets and Psychographics." *Journal of Marketing Research* 16 (February): 74–79.

Szybillo, George J., and Arlene Sosanie. 1977. "Family Decision Making: Husband, Wife and Children." In *Advances in Consumer Research,* vol. 4, edited by William D. Perreault, Jr., pp. 46-49. Atlanta Association for Consumer Research.

Szybillo, George J.; Arlene Sosanie; and Aaron Tenenbein. 1979. "Family Member Influence in Household Decision Making." *Journal of Consumer Research* 6 (December): 312–16.

Taeuber, Conrad. 1979. "A Changing America." *American Demographics* 1 (January): 9–15.

Teachman, Joy D. 1982. "Methodological Issues in the Analysis of Family Formation and Dissolution." *Journal of Marriage and the Family* 44 (November): 1037–53.

Thomas, Kenneth. 1978. "Introduction to Special Section on Conflict and the Collaborative Ethic." *California Management Review* 21 (Winter): 56–60.

———. 1976. "Conflict and Conflict Management." In *Handbook of Industrial and Organizational Psychology,* edited by Marvin D. Dunnette, pp. 889–935. Chicago: Rand-McNally.

Thomas, Kenneth; David W. Jamieson; and R. Kenneth Moore. 1978. "Conflict and Collaboration: Some Concluding Observations." *California Management Review* 21 (Winter): 91-95.

Thornton, Arland, and Deborah Freedman. 1979. "Changes in the Sex Role

Attitudes of Women, 1962–1977: Evidence from a Panel Study." *American Sociological Review* 44 (October): 831–42.

Thrall, Charles A. 1978. "Who Does What: Role Stereotypes, Children's Work, and Continuity between Generations in the Household Division of Labor." *Human Relations* 3 (March): 249–65.

Time. 1983. "Machine of the Year: Computers." 121, no. 1 (3 January): 14–39.

Tittle, Carol K. 1981. *Careers and Family.* Beverly Hills, Calif.: Sage.

Tognoli, Jerome. 1979. "The Flight from Domestic Space: Men's Roles in the Household." *The Family Coordinator* 28 (October): 599–607.

Tomeh, Aida K. 1978. "Sex-Role Orientation: An Analysis of Structural and Attitudinal Predictors." *Journal of Marriage and the Family* 41 (May): 341–53.

Turk, James L., and Normal W. Bell. 1972. "Measuring Power in Families." *Journal of Marriage and the Family* 34 (May): 215–23.

Tydeman, John. 1982. "Videotex: Ushering in the Electronic Household." *Futurist* 16, no. 1 (February): 54–61.

Underhill, Lois and Franchelli Cadwell. 1983. "What Age Do You Feel? Age Perception Study." *Journal of Consumer Marketing* (Summer): 18–27.

U.S. Bureau of the Census. 1983. *U.S.A. Statistics in Brief.* Washington, D.C.: U.S. Government Printing Office.

———. 1981a. "Households and Families, by Type: March 1981." *Current Population Reports,* p–20, #367. Washington, D.C.: U.S. Government Printing Office.

———. 1981b. "Household and Family Characteristics: March 1981." *Current Population Reports,* p–20, #371. Washington, D.C.: U.S. Government Printing Office.

———. 1981c. "Marital Status and Living Arrangements: March 1981." *Current Population Reports,* p–20, #372. Washington, D.C.: U.S. Government Printing Office.

———. 1980. "Population Profile of the U.S.: 1979." *Current Population Reports,* p–20, #350. Washington, D.C.: U.S. Government Printing Office.

———. 1979a. "Fertility of American Women: June 1978." *Current Population Reports,* p–20, #341. Washington, D.C.: U.S. Government Printing Office.

———. 1979b. "Projections of the Number of Households and Families: 1979 to 1995." *Population Estimates and Projections,* p–25, #805. Washington, D.C.: U.S. Government Printing Office.

———. 1979c. *State and Metropolitan Area Date Book 1979.* Washington, D.C.: U.S. Government Printing Office.

———. 1978. *A Statistical Portrait of Women in the United States: 1978.* Washington, D.C.: U.S. Government Office of Printing.

———. 1970. "Probabilities of Marriage, Divorce and Remarriage." *Current Population Reports,* p–23, #32. Washington, D.C.: U.S. Government Printing Office.

U.S. Department of Health and Human Services. 1982. *Women: A Developmental Perspective.* Washington, D.C.: U.S. Government Printing Office.

U.S. Department of Labor, Women's Bureau. 1975. *1975 Handbook on Women Workers.* Washington, D.C.: U.S. Government Printing Office.

U.S. National Center for Health Statistics. 1980. "Final Natality Statistics, 1978."
   Monthly Vital Statistics Report 29, no. 1.

Van Dusen, Roxann A., and Eleanor B. Sheldon. 1976. "The Changing Status of
   American Women: A Life Cycle Perspective." *American Psychologist* 31
   (February): 106–16.
Vanek, Joann. 1978. "Household Technology and Social Status: Rising Living
   Standards and Status and Residence Differences in Housework." *Technology
   and Culture* 19 (July): 361–75.
Venkatesh, Alladi, and Nicholas Vitalari. 1983. "Household Adoption of Home
   Computers—An Exploratory Study." Working paper, Graduate School of
   Management, University of California at Irvine.
Venkatesh, Alladi; Nicholas Vitalari; and Kjell Gronhaug. 1983. "Household
   Product Adoption and Changes in Allocation of Time: The Case of Home
   Computers." Working paper, Graduate School of Management, University of
   California at Irvine.
Vickery, Clair. 1979. "Women's Economic Contribution to the Family." In *The
   Subtle Revolution,* edited by Ralph E. Smith, pp. 159–200. Washington, D.C.:
   The Urban Institute.

Waite, Linda J. 1980. "Working Wives and the Family Life Cycle." *American
   Journal of Sociology* 86, no. 2 (September): 272–94.
Wales, T., and A. Woodland. 1977. "Estimation of the Allocation of Time for Work,
   Leisure and Housework." *Econometrica* 45 (January): 115–32.
Walker, Kathryn E. 1973. "Household Work Time: Its Implication for Family
   Decisions." *Journal of Home Economics* (October): 7–11.
———. 1969. "Homemaking Still Takes Time." *Journal of Home Economics* 61
   (October): 621–24.
Walker, Kathryn E., and M. Woods. 1976. *Time Use: A Measure of Household
   Production of Goods and Services.* Washington, D.C.: American Home
   Economics Association.
Wall Street Journal. 1982. "Advertising World's Portrayal of Women Is Starting to
   Shift." CCI (October 28): 33.
Walsh, Doris. 1982a. "About Those New Women." *American Demographics* 4
   (October): 26–29.
———. 1982b. "Why Insurance Companies Are Discovering Women." *American
   Demographics* 4 (April): 20–23.
Wattenberg, Ben J. 1975. "The Forming-Families: The Spark in the Tinder,
   1975–1985." In *1974 Combined Proceedings of the American Marketing
   Association,* edited by Ronald C. Curhan, pp. 51–62. Chicago: American
   Marketing Association.
Webster, Frederick E., and Frederick Von Pechman. 1970. "A Replication of the
   'Shopping List' Study" *Journal of Marketing* 34 (April): 61–63.
Weed, James A. 1982. "Divorce: American Style." *American Demographics* 4
   (March): 13–17.
Wegner, Daniel M., and Robin R. Vallacher. 1980. *The Self in Social Psychology.*
   New York: Oxford University Press.

Weingarten, Kathy. 1978. "The Employment Pattern of Professional Couples and Their Distribution of Involvement in the Family." *Psychology of Women Quarterly* 3, no. 1 (Fall): 43-51.

Weiss, Heather. 1977. "Adult Roles in Dual Worker Families." Final report to the National Institute of Mental Health, grant no. 24742.

Weiss, W. 1969. "Effects of the Mass Media on Communication." In *The Handbook of Social Psychology*, vol. 5, edited by G. Lindzey and E. Aronson, pp. 77-195. San Francisco: Chandler.

Weizenbaum, Joseph. 1981. "Once More: The Computer Revolution." In *The Computer Age: A Twenty Year Review*, edited by Michael Dertouzos and Joel Moses, pp. 439-458. Cambridge, Mass.: MIT Press.

Wells, William C., and George Gubar. 1966. "Life Cycle Concept in Marketing Research." *Journal of Marketing Research* 3 (November): 355-63.

Westoff, Charles F. 1979. "The Decline of Fertility." *American Demographics* 1 (February): 16-19.

Whipple, Thomas W., and Alice E. Courtney. 1980. "How to Portray Women in TV Commercials." *Journal of Advertising Research* 20 (April): 53-59.

White, David. 1977. "The Time in Your Life." *New Society* 24 (November): 400-02.

Wilkes, Robert E. 1975. "Husband-Wife Influence in Purchase Decisions—A Confirmation and Extension." *Journal of Marketing Research* 12 (May): 224-27.

Wilkie, Jane Riblett. 1981. "The Trend toward Delayed Parenthood." *Journal of Marriage and the Family* 43 (August): 583-91.

Willie, Charles V., and Susan L. Greenblatt. 1978. "Four 'Classic' Studies of Power Relationships in Black Families: A Review and Look to the Future." *Journal of Marriage and the Family* 40 (November): 691-94.

Wind, Yoram. 1978. "On the Interface between Organizational and Consumer Buying Behavior." In *Advances in Consumer Research*, vol. 5, edited by H. Keith Hunt, pp. 657-62. Ann Arbor: Association for Consumer Research.

————. 1976. "Preference of Relevant Others and Individual Choice Models." *Journal of Consumer Research* 3 (June): 50-57.

Wolgast, Elizabeth. 1958. "Do Husbands of Wives Make the Purchasing Decisions?" *Journal of Marketing* 23 (October): 151-58.

Woodside, Arch G. 1975. "Effects of Prior Decision Making, Demographics and Psychographics on Marital Roles for Purchasing Durables." In *Advances in Consumer Research*, vol. 2, edited by Mary Jane Schlinger, pp. 81-91. Ann Arbor, Michigan: Association for Consumer Research.

Wortzel, Lawrence H. 1980. "Marital Roles and Typologies as Predictors of Purchase Decision Making for Everyday Household Products: Suggestions for Research." In *Marketing in the 1980s*, edited by Richard P. Bagozzi, pp. 212-15. Chicago: American Marketing Association.

————. 1977a. "The Young Adult Consumer: An Introduction and Over-View." Report No. 77-118. Cambridge, Mass.: Marketing Science Institute.

————. 1977b. "Young Adults: Single People and Single Person Households." In *Advances in Consumer Research*, vol. 4, edited by William D. Perreault, Jr., pp. 324-29. Atlanta: Association for Consumer Research.

Wrege, Rachel. 1982. "High (Tech) Anxiety," *Popular Computing*, 6, no. 1: 46-52.

Yankelovich, Daniel. 1981. *New Rules*. New York: Random House.

Yaverbaum, Gayle J. 1982. "Requirement Analysis for Decision Support Systems: An Investigation of the Decision Process." Ph.D. dissertation, Temple University.

Ybarra, Lea. 1982. "When Wives Work: The Impact on the Chicano Family." *Journal of Marriage and the Family* 44 (February): 169-78.

Young, C.M. 1977. "Spacing of Children and Changing Patterns of Childbearing." *Journal of Biosocial Science* 9 (April): 201-26.

Young, S., and B. Feigin. 1975. "Using the Benefit Chain for Improved Strategy Formulation." *Journal of Marketing* 39 (July): 72-74.

Zaltman, Gerald; Philip Kotler; and Ira Kaufman. 1970. *Creating Social Change*. New York: Holt, Rinehart and Winston.

Zaltman, Gerald, and Melanie Wallendorf. 1983. *Consumer Behavior: Basic Findings and Management Implications*. 2nd edition New York: John Wiley and Sons.

Zbytniewski, Jo-Ann. 1979. "Working Women: Less Time, More Money." *Progressive Grocer* 58 (June): 56-66.

INDEX

ABOUT THE CONTRIBUTORS

Chris T. Allen is a Visiting Associate Professor with the Faculty of Marketing at the J.L. Kellogg Graduate School of Management, North-western University. He holds a Ph.D. from The Ohio State University and an MBA from Michigan State University. He currently is on professional leave from the University of Massachusetts where, over the past six years, he has taught a variety of marketing and consumer behavior courses. His work has been published in the *Journal of Marketing Research, Journal of Consumer Research, Journal of Advertising,* and *Journalism Quarterly.*

E.H. Bonfield recently joined the faculty of Rider College as Professor of Marketing after eight years at Temple University, most recently as Director of Temple's Doctoral Program in Business Administration. His Ph.D. was earned at the University of Illinois, following earlier study at the University of Alabama and marketing research experience with Market Facts, Inc. His primary area of research has been in the area of attitude theory and measurement, with his articles on this topic appearing in the *Journal of Marketing Research, Journal of Consumer Research* and the *Journal of Marketing.*

Elinor Bowen is Research Supervisor, Consumer Research Group, Leo Burnett USA. Her three year career at Leo Burnett has focussed on Lifestyles research. She was previously Assistant Professor of Political Science at the

University of Illinois, with research and publications in the area of public opinion, policy implementation, and research methodology. A graduate of Rutgers University, she holds an M.A. from Yale University and a Ph.D. from Case Western Reserve University.

Julia M. Bristor is currently a doctoral student in the Graduate School of Business Administration, University of Michigan. Her current research interests are in the areas of organizational buying behavior and qualitative methodology. Ms. Bristor received her M.B.A. and B.S. from The University of Michigan.

Kathryn Britney is Associate Professor of Marketing at Boston University. She was formerly Vice President and Manager of the Marketing Evaluation Department at Merrill Lynch, and Assistant/Associate Professor at Columbia Business School. She holds an M.S. from Purdue University and a Ph.D. from the University of Pennsylvania. Her publications have appeared in *Journal of Marketing Research, Journal of Consumer Research,* and *Marketing Science.*

W. Christian Buss is Assistant Professor and the Coordinator of the Field Project Program of the Marketing Department at the State University of New York at Albany. He received his Ph.D. in 1979 from the University of Pennsylvania. He is an active marketing consultant and has numerous publications in proceedings, journals and monographs.

Kenneth Chan is a doctoral candidate at the University of Massachusetts, Amherst. His research interests are in consumer behavior and advertising.

Kathleen Debevec is Assistant Professor of Marketing at the University of Massachusetts, Amherst. She received her Ph.D. from the University of Cincinnati. Her research interests include the effectiveness of sex-role stereotyping and imagery in advertising, and self-perception theory in information processing.

Melody Douglas-Tate is Group Research Director, Consumer Research Group, at Leo Burnett USA. Her sixteen year career in advertising research at Leo Burnett spans a broad range of the research areas which contribute to an understanding of how advertising works to affect consumer behavior. Lifestyles research, consumer buying styles, and value linkage systems have most recently been the focus of her attention. Ms. Douglas-Tate is a graduate of Lake Forest College.

John Fiedler is currently responsible for the media issues within the Polling and Planning Division of Reagan-Bush '84. Previously, he was Executive

Vice President, Director of Research Services for Ted Bates Advertising/New York. Mr. Fiedler's earlier employment included positions with Leo Burnett Advertising and Market Facts, Inc., both in Chicago. He holds a Master's Degree from the University of Chicago and a B.A. from the University of Wisconsin.

Jonathan Gutman is Associate Professor of Marketing in the Graduate School of Business, University of Southern California, where he has served as departmental chairman. He completed his education at Pomona College, receiving the B.A. in 1960, the M.S. from Purdue University in 1962, and the Ph.D. in psychology from the University of Southern California in 1967. His main research interest is in the development of the means-end chain model and his scholarly publications have appeared in journals such as the *Journal of Retailing, The Public Opinion Quarterly,* the *Journal of Personality and Social Psychology,* and the *Journal of Marketing.*

Dr. Philip Hendrix is Associate Professor of Marketing at Emory University, where he teaches consumer behavior, marketing research, and marketing strategy. He received his Ph.D. from the University of Michigan. His primary research interests include measurement of latent variables, time use, and energy consumption/conservation. He has published a number of articles on these and other topics. Forthcoming publications include "Operationalizing Household-Level Constructs" and "Antecedents and Consequences of Time Use."

Sigfredo A. Hernandez earned an M.A. Degree in Economics from Boston University in 1977 and is presently a Ph.D. candidate in Marketing at Temple University, and a faculty member at Rutgers University, Camden, New Jersey.

Dr. Jo Anne Stilley Hopper is currently an Assistant Professor of Marketing at Southeastern Louisiana University; and a former member of the Oklahoma State University faculty. She has published research in the *Advances in Consumer Research, Journal of the Academy of Marketing Science,* and *Southern Marketing Association Proceedings.* She received her Ph.D. from Louisiana State University in 1983. Her major research interests include husband-wife decision making and measure validation in consumer behavior research.

Bernard J. Jaworski is a doctoral student in marketing at the Graduate School of Business, University of Pittsburgh. His research interests involve marketing theory and sociological aspects of consumer behavior.

Carol J. Kaufman is a doctoral candidate at Temple University, and a marketing instructor in the Faculty of Business Studies of Rutgers

University. She holds a B.S. in Mathematics from Duquesne University, and an M.B.A. from Rensselaer Polytechnic Institute. Her research concerns lie in the area of alternative household forms and the patterns of task allocation and assortment establishment which they demonstrate.

Maryon Frederick King is a Doctoral Student and Lecturer in Marketing at Indiana University. She received her B.A. (in Zoology) and M.B.A. from the University of Maine at Orono. Her scholarly publications include the A.C.R. Health Care Conference and the A.P.A. Conference Proceedings. Her current interests include family decision making, information processing (especially with respect to referent-provided information) and services marketing.

James H. Leigh is Assistant Professor of Marketing at Texas A&M University, where he teaches consumer behavior and marketing research. Dr. Leigh is Co-Founder and Co-Editor (with Dr. Claude R. Martin, Jr.) of the annual journal, *Current Issues and Research in Advertising,* which is now in its seventh year of publication. His research has appeared in *Educational and Psychological Measurement, Journal of Advertising Research, Review of Marketing, 1981,* and in numerous conference proceedings.

Laura Lein, Director of the Wellesley College Center for Research on Women, received her Ph.D. in Social Anthropology from Harvard University in 1973. Her research has concentrated on the experiences of employed mothers and their families and has been supported by the National Institute of Education, the National Institute of Mental Health and the National Science Foundation. Recent publications include *Families Wihout Villains* (Lexington Press, 1984); *Children* with Lydia O'Donnell (Westminister Press, forthcoming); and the *The Ties That Bind: Men's and Women's Social Network,* edited with Marvin Sussman (Haworth Press, Winter 1983).

Deborah J. MacInnis is a doctoral student in marketing at the Graduate School of Business, University of Pittsburgh. Her research interests include advertising, strategic marketing, social cognition, and marketing theory.

Suzanne McCall is Professor of Marketing at East Texas State University. She holds degrees from the University of Miami and North Texas State University. She serves on the editorial review board of the *Journal of Marketing* and the *Journal of Marketing Science,* and has published articles in *Ladies Home Journal, Redbook, Working Women, Parents,* and the *Los Angeles Times.*

Claude R. Martin, Jr. is the Isadore and Leon Winkelman Professor of Retail Marketing at the Graduate School of Business Administration, University of Michigan. He has authored more than 60 articles appearing in national and international journals and written five books and monographs. Dr. Martin has been the Co-editor of *Current Issues and Research in Advertising*, an annual journal of research advancements in the field of advertising, since 1978. He currently serves as a consultant to the Board of Governors of the Federal Reserve System and several major corporations.

Patrick E. Murphy is Associate Professor of Marketing, College of Business Administration, University of Notre Dame. Previously he was Associate Professor and Chairman of the Marketing Department, Marquette University. During 1980–81 he served in the Office of Management Planning at the Federal Trade Commission. Professor Murphy has published articles in the *Journal of Marketing, Journal of Consumer Research,* and other marketing periodicals. He is currently Vice President elect of the Marketing Education Division, and is past President of the Milwaukee AMA Chapter. He holds a Ph.D. from University of Houston, an M.B.A. from Bradley University, and a B.B.A. from Notre Dame.

Richard W. Olshavsky is Professor of Marketing at the Graduate School of Business at the University of Indiana. He completed his education at Carnegie-Mellon University, where he received the B.S. in Mechanical Engineering, the M.S. and Ph.D. in Experimental Psychology. His scholarly publications have appeared in the *Journal of Consumer Research,* the *Journal of Marketing Research, Journal of Marketing,* and the *Journal of Experimental Psychology.*

Judy Peyton is Associate Research Director, Consumer Research Group, Leo Burnett USA. She has been contributing to advertising research at Leo Burnett for six years; previously she was employed by the University of Illinois Survey Research Laboratory. Lifestyles and futures are her major research areas. Ms. Peyton holds B.A. and M.A. degrees from the University of Illinois.

William J. Qualls is an Assistant Professor of Marketing in the Graduate School of Business Administration, University of Michigan. His current teaching interests are in the areas of buyer behavior, sales management, and marketing research. Dr. Qualls' research interest is in the area of studying family decisionmaking and organizational buyer behavior. Dr. Qualls received his D.B.A. from Indiana University with a specialization in marketing, social psychology, and statistics.

Thomas J. Reynolds is Associate Professor in the School of Management at the University of Texas at Dallas. He earned an A.B. degree in philosophy at Notre Dame University, and an M.A. and Ph.D. in mathematical psychology at the University of Southern California. His publications span several academic areas and are included in such journals as *Educational and Psychological Measurement, Multivariate Behavioral Research, Psychometrika,* and the *Journal of Marketing Research.* Dr. Reynolds currently serves as President of the Institute for Consumer Research, a research and consulting company specializing in the assessment of strategic positionings and the development of strategic options.

William J. Sauer is Associate Professor of Business Administration at the University of Pittsburgh. His research interests include consumer movements, elderly consumers, and the effects of group interaction on information processing of television commercials.

Charles M. Schaninger is Associate Professor and Chair of the Marketing Department at the State University of New York at Albany. He received his Ph.D. in 1975 from the University of Rochester. His prior work has appeared in the *Journal of Consumer Research,* the *Journal of Marketing Research,* and the *Journal of Marketing.*

Alladi Venkatesh is a member of the faculty at the Graduate School of Management, University of California at Irvine. His general research interests are household consumption behavior, marketing theory, and market segmentation. With Professor Vitalari, he is conducting research on the social impacts of computing in households, a project supported by a grant from the National Science Foundation.

Nicholas Vitalari is a faculty member at the Graduate School of Management, University of California, Irvine. His research interests include problem solving in systems analysis, decision support systems, and social impacts of computing. He is conducting research on the social impact of computing in households with Professor Venkatesh.

ABOUT THE EDITORS

Mary Lou Roberts is Associate Professor in the School of Management, Boston University. She holds a Ph.D. in Marketing from the University of Michigan. Her publications on various topics in marketing strategy and buyer behavior have appeared in the *Journal of Marketing, Journal of Marketing Research,* trade journals, and the proceedings of numerous professional conferences. She frequently consults with business and nonprofit organizations on a variety of strategic and research-related issues. She is a former president of the Boston Chapter of the American Marketing Association. Her personal research interests center on changing sex roles and their effects on individual and household consumption behavior.

Lawrence H. Wortzel, is Professor of Marketing, and Senior Research Associate, Center for Asian Development Studies at Boston University. Professor Wortzel received his M.B.A. and D.B.A. degrees from Harvard University. He has served as consultant to a variety of domestic and international organizations on problems of marketing research, strategic planning, new product development, and consumer behavior. He has been a consultant to The World Bank, and currently is a member of the Editorial Review Board of the Journal of Marketing and Faculty Associate of Management Analysis Center. His research reflects his interests in international marketing strategies, in the marketing of manufactured exports from developing countries, and in the consumer behavior of young adults and of families. His writing has appeared in the *Columbia Journal of World Business,* the *Journal of Applied Psychology,* the *Journal of Marketing,* the *Journal of Marketing Research* and the *Sloan Management Review,* among other publications.

349